Aspects of the Governing of the Finns

Studies in Modern European History

Frank J. Coppa
General Editor

Vol. 66

PETER LANG
New York • Washington, D.C./Baltimore • Bern
Frankfurt • Berlin • Brussels • Vienna • Oxford

George Maude

Aspects of the Governing of the Finns

PETER LANG
New York • Washington, D.C./Baltimore • Bern
Frankfurt • Berlin • Brussels • Vienna • Oxford

Library of Congress Cataloging-in-Publication Data

Maude, George.
Aspects of the governing of the Finns / George Maude.
p. cm. — (Studies in modern European history; v. 66)
Includes bibliographical references.
1. Finland—Politics and government—1917-1945. 2. Finland—Politics and government—1945-1981. 3. Finland—Politics and government—1981- I. Title.
JN7395.M385 320.94897—dc22 2009049016

Bibliographic information published by **Die Deutsche Nationalbibliothek**.
Die Deutsche Nationalbibliothek lists this publication in the "Deutsche Nationalbibliografie"; detailed bibliographic data is available on the Internet at http://dnb.d-nb.de/.

The paper in this book meets the guidelines for permanence and durability of the Committee on Production Guidelines for Book Longevity of the Council of Library Resources.

29 Broadway, 18th floor, New York, NY 10006
www.peterlang.com

Printed in Germany

TABLE OF CONTENTS

ACKNOWLEDGMENTS

Without the constant help of my family, this book would not have seen the light of day. It is therefore with great gratitude that I acknowledge my debt for advice and assistance to my daughter Ulrika Maude, her partner Shamus Smith, my daughter-in-law Susanne Erika Maude (née Laine) and to my son Andrei Maude. With thanks, too, for their charming little daughters, Ronja Irene, and Sofia Allegra. Above all, my thanks go out to my wife, Helena Maude (née Kalenius), who has patiently borne my frustrations in trying to write computer-English.

The librarians at the desk in the three university libraries of Turku and the city library have always done their level-best to help me.

At the New York office of Peter Lang my attempts to explain my problems have always been well received, both by Caitlin Lavelle, the Acquisitions Editor, and by the Production Coordinator, Nicole Grazioso.

The book that I have struggled to write is based, in large part, on the research of others. But the rough-and ready conclusions are of my own kind.

CHAPTER 1
A PRESENTMENT OF POWER. A SPRING PARADE

It was, apparently, a lovely spring day when a Finnish army began its march through Helsinki, now the capital of an independent state. The march was a ceremonial one. It was a victory parade, celebrating the vanquishing of an enemy within which had supposedly been infected by an enemy from without. The Finnish Whites, helped by the Germans, had won. The Finnish Reds, helped by the Russians, had lost. The Finnish civil war—or Finnish revolution—was over. Curiously, the war came to be known quite commonly by the victorious Whites as the War of Independence, though Finland had been in a state of independence *legally* from Russia for four and a half months already at the time of the parade. More curiously, independence had been granted by Lenin and the Bolsheviks, though the marchers undoubtedly regarded Russia as a main enemy, particularly in its Bolshevik form, whose tenets had corrupted, they believed, the Finnish losing side.[1]

The day of the White victory parade was 16 May 1918. The city had actually fallen to the Germans, helped by the Finnish Whites, quite a bit before. The Germans had had a victory parade of their own over a month previously on 14 April, but this time they were only discreetly present. A hundred or so German officers congregated by the university, while a German flyer looped the loop over the Finnish procession. It may well have been the case that the dominant role of the German army in liberating the city had prevented the massacre of the defeated Reds, for when the Finnish Whites had conquered the Red industrial city of Tampere they had massacred a lot of Reds, including nurses and hospital cases.[2] Outside Helsinki, in the rural areas, the Germans, too, had massacred prisoners.[3]

---

[1] The term "civil war," based to some extent on a geographical division, has later served as a more emotionally neutral term. Otto Wille Kuusinen, an important figure among the Finnish Reds, called it, from his exile in Russia, a "revolution." Without much of an explicit justification, the English historian, Anthony Upton (*The Finnish Revolution 1917–1918*, Minneapolis (Univ. of Minnesota Press), 1980, accepted this term. The present author believes he was right, but seeks for justification.

[2] Heikki Ylikangas, *Tie Tampereelle*, Helsinki (WSOY), 1993, esp. chap.IV.

[3] Aapo Roselius, *Amatöörien sota*, Helsinki (Valtioneuvoston kanslian julkaisusarja), 2006, p.88. Roselius, p.19 & 165 has now estimated that the number of combatants killed on the battlefield or executed summarily shortly after, was over 10,000: 3,000 Whites, over 6,000 Reds, and 1,000

By all accounts,[4] the Helsinki victory parade was a splendid sight. The differently-coloured uniforms of the various contingents that made up the White forces, along with the contrasting banners of the old flag of the Grand Duchy of Finland (the red and the gold emblazoned with a lion) and the new flag of a blue cross on a white background, all seemed to be complementing the beautiful day. Only once did a dark cloud lurk in the sky, but this could be interpreted as a salutary reminder of the fury the country had just gone through.

The parade was a heroes' parade. Every man jack of the army was a hero. Some were especially heroic, however. One of them led the parade. This was General Carl Gustaf Emil Mannerheim, a Swedish-speaking Finn, who had probably forgotten the little bit of Finnish he had ever known.[5] He had lately been in the service of the last Tsar of Russia, but left the Russian army when the Bolshevik revolution broke out. In coming home to Finland, he became, by accident of history, a Finnish patriot, *the* Finnish patriot in the eyes of many, even to this day.[6] Yet in the period when Finland had still been an autonomous part of the Russian Empire, whose autonomy was being whittled away by Tsarist bureaucrats, Mannerheim had not resigned his commission in protest.[7] But it is unfair to say, as a modern commentator has done, that Mannerheim was a kind of a turncoat.[8] In returning to serve Finland, he had not abandoned Imperial Russia—much to the chagrin of many of his Finnish contemporaries. By his bedside always remained, it is said, the portrait of the last Tsar of Russia.

But now he was leading the first ceremonial demonstration of the military might of Finland. Was this something of a comedown? It didn't appear to be. Rising up and down while astride his courser, glancing laughingly from left to

---

Russians or Germans. This figure does not include those Reds who were later executed in the camps or died of malnutrition or disease there, but includes those put down as missing.

[4] This text is taken mainly from the *Helsingin Sanomat* and *Hufvudstadsbladet* of 17.5.1918 and the *Turun Sanomat* of 24.5.1918. The author thanks the *Elokuvasäätiö* for the chance to see the film of the event.

[5] Ylikangas, op.cit., p.499, tells how Rector Kaarlo Tiililä, in congratulating Mannerheim after the fall of Tampere to the Whites, found that the general was unable to converse in Finnish. On the other hand, the *Turun Sanomat* of 24.5.1918 stated that Mannerheim spoke better Finnish than the chairman of the Helsinki City Council!

[6] In a TV national poll of the year 2004 to discover whom people thought to be the greatest Finn, Mannerheim topped the list.

[7] In the Mannerheim exhibition in Turku Castle (24.2–30.4.2006) a letter was on display to his sister Sophie explaining his reasons for not resigning. For a wider treatment, with, *inter alia*, reference to military obligations and ambitions, see also J.E.O. Screen, *Mannerheim*, Helsinki (Otava), 2001, pp.52–57.

[8] Risto Penttilä, *Historian roolipeli*, Helsinki (Otava), 2006, p.73.

right at the windows from which he was pelted with flowers, Mannerheim was in his element. Full of *amour-propre,* he was prickly by nature and was to show it over and over again in his rediscovered homeland. But his homeland was to do him well—far better than the country he had previously adopted. For in Russia, in spite of his valiant service in the Russo-Japanese War and in the First World War, and in-between in his role of spy as he travelled on a trip of "scientific exploration" through Chinese Turkestan, Mannerheim, though ending as a major-general, had not made the staff college. In Finland, he was to become a marshal (twice over) and commander-in-chief in three more wars.

Though Mannerheim was over fifty at the time of the 1918 parade, the newspapers delighted in referring to him as "youthful." That was the key word, for the whole army was constantly referred to as "young" (most armies are, mainly, "young," but charitably the term here might be interpreted as meaning something like "new army of a new state"). As far as the heroic leaders of the parade were concerned, there was one who could certainly outmatch Mannerheim in youthfulness. This was the hero of Karelia, Lieutenant-Colonel (before he was 29) Aarne Sihvo, the darling of the Finnish-speaking onlookers, the man who had defeated the Reds on the Karelian Isthmus. Sihvo was trained in Germany as a *jaeger* (light infantryman), one of the group of Finns who had gone there to undertake military training for the future liberation of their country. It had only been three years before! In spite of this rapid rise to power and glory, Sihvo, like Mannerheim, had a propensity to lose his temper and resign. But his reasons were not those of Mannerheim.

Among other striking features of the parade was a contingent described by the leading Swedish-language newspaper in Finland as "five hundred Teutons" (Germans or Swedes?) and then a remarkable figure, the painter Akseli Gallen—Kallela, then Mannerheim's secretary and with him at the battle-front, too. The painter had designed his own splendiferous uniform, which led the correspondent of the *Turun Sanomat* to say that had Gallen-Kallela been in politics he would have turned out to be a Finnish Theodore Roosevelt.

In the audience were a number of fine ladies and the wives of senior officers Paul Martin Wetzer and Wilhelm Alexander Thesleff (both had been in the Imperial Russian forces) presented Mannerheim with a golden-fringed white silk flag, on one side of which was Mannerheim's emblem (he was a nobleman) within a laurel wreath made up of the coats-of-arms of the different provinces of Finland. A Miss Alix Silen handed him lilacs and other young maidens strewed the ground with flowers. The city council and the university teachers had already done homage. It remained to go into the great white Lutheran cathedral, where choirs under two of Finland's leading composers, Heikki Klemetti and Oskari Merikanto, performed, one of the pieces being the patriotic poet V.A.Koskenniemi's "Song for the Fatherland" set to music by Klemetti. A *Te Deum* was also sung there: it had in it the line "Render unto us thy mercy." This was precisely the very quality that the victorious Whites intended to forget, for everyone but themselves. University, church, White army, White womanhood, most of them tended to forget it. The nearest explanation for this of any adequacy is that a traditional hierarchical society was suffering from an emotional shock compounded of the ambivalent and downright hostile feelings by now engendered in the bulk of the Finnish ruling classes by Russia and its alleged minions.

Terror

There thus existed a White terror, which, according to the received wisdom of the victors, was a response to a Red terror. This was partly true.[9] But once the revolution officially began, Jaakko Paavolainen has recorded, too, incidents where individual Reds were shot in the localities in the earliest days.[10] And, as is usually the case, the Whites went on longer with their response, which was also far more multi-dimensional. On the day before the White victory parade, the *Helsingin Sanomat* published a little drawing of a "reipas tyttö" ("a spry girl"), one of the auxiliaries in Mannerheim's army, called Lottas after the heroine of Johan Ludvig Runeberg's poem. She was in a sort of uniform, but with a skirt not trousers. Women in the Finnish Red army, captured in uniform, *who wore trousers and not a skirt* were liable to be shot. For among these women were not merely auxiliaries but fighters. The killing of these "Russian brides," as they were called (with reference to the Whites' own feeling that the Finnish Reds were a local variant of Russian Bolshevism—and Bolsheviks had women soldiers), was an extreme manifestation of the shock experienced by the Whites at the changes occurring before their eyes in Finnish society.[11] Historically, belonging to "Russia" had been alright for most

---

[9] Ylikangas, op.cit., p.36 has recorded 43 killings by the Reds before the revolution occurred, in addition to which drunken Russian sailors were responsible for one of the most notorious incidents, the murder of the industrialist Alfred Kordelin, his friend, and an 8-year old boy at Mommila on 7 November 1917. The future president Risto Ryti and his wife narrowly escaped death on this same occasion.

[10] Jaakko Paavolainen, *Poliittiset väkivaltaisuudet Suomessa 1918. II, "Valkoinen terrori,"* Helsinki (Tammi), 1967, p.40 et seq. But in the Reds' surrender at Varkaus on 21 February, after which scores were killed arbitrarily or by drumhead court martial, Paavolainen noted the connection with the Reds' hostage-taking (and killing) and confusion over a partial cease-fire, ibid, pp.71–72.

[11] Mirja Turunen, *Veripellot,* Jyväskylä (Atena), 2005, pp.180–185, on the fate of Elli Kokko, a farmworker and committed Socialist, who became head of a women's unit. She was shot more than two weeks after Mannerheim had said that these executions without a proper trial should cease. Seppo Rustanius, *Punaiset esiliinat* (documentary film shown on Finnish TV, 26.2.1997).

Finns when the empire had been a distant guardian of order, but not obtrusively so as far as Finland was concerned. Now that the Russian Empire was breaking up, and yet had by the late summer of 1917 100,000 troops in Finland—many of whom were gripped by revolutionary fervour, Russia and its people had become synonymous with disorder and with changes that the average Finn could not accept. The Russian word for "freedom," *svoboda,* took on a negative connotation in Finland. Thus the Finnish revolutionaries *in their fervour* became identified with a Bolshevism that did in practice supply them in any case with some arms and some soldiers. Volunteers in the Finnish White army in the province of Ostrobothnia felt that they had enlisted to fight the Russians.[12]

From its side, the self-proclaimed Red government forbade its supporters to engage in killing, torture, or hooliganism. Because of the partially spontaneous nature of the uprising (it was therefore a *revolution* in Marxist and, at a stretch, even in Kautskyist terms),[13] the leadership of the revolutionary Social Democrats had difficulty in controlling events in the field. The revolution started when that section of the party that favoured it lighted a red lamp on the tower of its Helsinki headquarters on the night of 26 January 1918.[14] Only a few days later the revolutionaries engaged in killing. In one case, at Suinila, on 31 January, this was due to a difference of opinion between the leadership of two Red detachments when a White unit was already surrendering: in another case, in eastern Finland, an engineer, Gustaf Stråhlman, was done to death.[15] And there were other examples very early on in the revolution, one of the most cruelly ironic being the murder of the lawyer and Young Finn M.P. Antti Mikkola on 1 February.[16]

However, it is safe to assume that the mere act of armed rebellion was sufficient to provoke the White government, which had then fled to Vasa, to declare that captured revolutionaries be considered as having committed high

---

Pekka Elomaa & Jouni T.Kemppainen "Paha Maisema," *Helsingin Sanomien kuukausiliite,* March 2002, for the fate of the 36 members of the Valkeakoski women's unit, shot in a lonely field after digging their own graves. The youngest was 15 years old.

[12] Ylikangas, op.cit, p.24 believes that the White leadership intentionally developed this explanation. The Ostrothnians shot any Russians once they got into Tampere. But in the fighting against the Finnish Reds there showed little quarter either: ibid., pp.436 & 441.

[13] Karl Kautsky (1854–1938), who felt he was the heir to Marxist orthodoxy, had a considerable influence on the Finnish Social Democratic Party. His attitude to the Finnish revolution was, however, ambivalent.

[14] Jussi T.Lappalainen, *Punakaartin sota,* I,Helsinki, (Valtionpainatus keskus), 1981, p.45.

[15] Ylikangas, op.cit., pp.35–37 & Turunen, op.cit., pp.63–66.

[16] Jaakko Paavolainen, *Poliittiset väkivaltaisuudet Suomessa 1918, I. Punainen terrori,* Helsinki (Tammi), 1966 pp.128–129. As a lawyer, Mikkola had once advertised his services in Socialist newspapers.

treason. Their declaration of 1 February was interpreted by Mannerheim as implying the death penalty.[17] How far in practice Mannerheim thought it necessary to go is a matter of dispute among historians, particularly with reference to what has become known as his "Shoot on the Spot"–order of 25 February. This required instant execution of those involved, for example, in the destruction of roads, bridges, and telephone communications.[18]

As time went on, the White and Red terror increased. The most notorious example of the former was the massacre of Red prisoners after the Red industrial city of Tampere fell to the Whites by 5 April 1918.[19] Elsewhere, the Reds had also gone in for blood-letting. On the night of 19–20 April, three church dignitaries had been taken to Kouvola and killed. It was said later that on the breast of one of them, the Reverend Uno Renvall, was found the New Testament open at St.Luke 22, the betrayal of Christ.[20] In the last week of April, Gösta Björkenheim, the managing director of the great Kymi factory complex in Kymmenlaakso, was shot on the railway bridge over the Kymi river.

Björkenheim, though broken in spirit before his execution, had been a man of courage nonetheless. A scion of the Swedish-speaking upper class in Finland, he had not fled on the Red seizure of power in the valley but had felt the possibility of a *modus vivendi* with them. A tough negotiator in previous years, he had yet been philanthropically disposed towards the workers' interest and in 1917 had donated the sum of 400,000 marks for improvements in the medical care and housing conditions of the workers. So he had been the strict but kindly master, who had represented *holhous,* the benevolent guardianship by the knowledgeable class. But the workers had not had the feel of power and this they wanted.

Before his execution, Björkenheim, or Gösta, as he was familiarly known, had run foul of the local worker's leader, Walter Vihriä, who endeavoured to compete in running the factories. Vihriä was captured by the Whites. In his captivity, he wrote his life-story in four pages, blaming Socialism for misleading him. He had been promised an amnesty, but on completing his text, he was then shot along with many more, who were marched through the streets to their execution. The press thought he was a nasty fellow.[21]

As a matter of fact, in 1912 there had been a great strike in these factories, the settlement of which was largely due to Oskari Tokoi, then head of the

---

[17] Screen, op.cit., pp.157–158. Paavolainen, op.cit., esp. chaps. II–VI, took a more negative view of the whole of the Finnish White command, including Mannerheim and Sihvo.

[18] Turunen, op.cit., p.108.

[19] Ylikangas, op.cit., p.502–514.

[20] Turunen, op.cit., pp.126–129. *Turun Sanomat,* 19.5.1918.

[21] *Turun Sanomat,* 18.5.1918. Turunen, op.cit., p.73.

national organization of trade unions, the SAJ. Tokoi admitted afterwards that he was closer to Gösta in outlook than to the local paperworkers' union leader, Eero Haapalainen.[22] Then, in 1918, both Tokoi and Haapalainen were together running the revolution.

Less than twenty years before the revolution, in 1900, when the then managing director of the firm, Ernst Dahlström, retired, he had been presented with an address, featuring the factories of the industrial complex and designed by one of Finland's leading artists, Hugo Simberg. Every worker in the factories had signed the address or made his mark Happier days?[23]

At least, they had been happier days for those, too, who were now in the dreadful internment camps as a result of the White victory, where executions and death by starvation and disease occurred throughout the summer and autumn. In poignant humiliation, those condemned to be shot woke up sometimes to ask whether the executioners had forgotten the time, and why the delay.[24]

Few were the influential members of the traditionalist, triumphant society whose unease drove them to protest at this sort of victory. The teenager Martti Haavio (later a distinguished poet), who had fought as a schoolboy on the White side, debated with himself on whether or not the defeated Reds deserved pity.[25] But on 28 May, a letter had appeared in the leading Swedish-language paper in Finland, the *Hufvudstadsbladet*. It was written by Baron Hjalmar Linder and was entitled "Enough Bloodbath," Linder pointing out that Mannerheim himself had forbidden summary executions (incidentally, the temperamental Mannerheim was not intending at the moment to stay in his newly-discovered homeland having finally resigned in some dudgeon on 27 May).[26] But like Mannerheim, in taking his own side to task, Linder showed plenty of courage, objecting not merely to the executions, but also to the unsanitary conditions in the camps and to the distress of the families whose breadwinner was imprisoned. He had a suggestion: the sending of the prisoners to Germany to work as forced labourers for a period and with the prospect of being able to bank their earnings. This proposal was ignored, naturally enough, by the revolutionaries' leader, Otto Wille Kuusinen, now safely in exile in Russia, though Kuusinen grudgingly acknowledged "Baron

22 Oskari Tokoi, *Maanpakolaisen muistelmia*, Helsinki (Tammi) 1959, pp.155–156.

23 The address was on show in an exhibition of Simberg's work held in Turku in January-February 2001.

24 Väinö Salmi, *Olin punikki*, Helsinki (Akateeminen kustannusliike), 1967, p.188. Salmi described the main Hennala guardhouse as "the ante-chamber of hell": p.164.

25 *Enteitä ja uhmaa*, ed. Raija Majamaa, Helsinki (SKS), 1987, p.26.

26 Screen, op.cit., pp.180–181.

Linder's" concern.[27] Nothing came of Linder's proposal, anyway. But in his letter to the *Hufvudstadlsbladet*, Linder had brought forth two important political points: the resentment that would arise in the defeated Red population coupled with a *tu quoque* admonition to the White leadership, whom, Linder argued, blamed the Reds for making a *coup d'état,* while subsequently making their own *coup d'état* by expelling the largest party from Parliament, who were, of course the Social Democrats, with 48%, according to Linder, of the seats there. It is worth remembering that most of the Social Democrat M.P.s had not supported the revolution.

Linder was immediately answered by the editorial board of the *Hufvudstadsbladet.* The answer was to the effect that there should be no indulgence for the Red bandits and that the purging had to be thorough to be effective. If the families of the Reds suffered want, it could not be helped; everyone was suffering from shortages. In any case, when the Reds were in control, they had plundered the countryside. As for the *coup d' état* argument, the newspaper reversed it by saying that the Social Democratic Party had put itself out of parliamentary representation by engineering a *coup d'état* of its own.

One or two others dared to write or speak. An internationally-known professor of medicine, Robert Tigerstedt, wrote a critical report on the camp conditions. Characteristically, as late as 1934, this service to humanity was not mentioned in the insertion dealing with his life in the leading Finnish biographical publication, *Kansallinen elämäkerrasto.* Another kind soul, the young natural scientist Uunio Saalas, though a non-Socialist, was active in trying to identify the slain Reds for the sake of their families and also did social work helping the Red prisoners, as best he could, on the island of Suomenlinna off Helsinki. In June 1918 he was bold enough to address a White civil guard midsummer celebration in Karjalohja on the need to heal the class confrontation and build up an understanding of why the dreadful events had occurred. He got short shrift.[28] In Parliament, Arthur Lagerlöf, a prominent businessman,asked the government to make a greater use of its prerogative of pardon for the rank-and-file of the Red prisoners.[29]

But the most significant of all was an expert in administrative law called Kaarlo Juho Ståhlberg. A member of Parliament in the liberal-minded Young Finn interest, Ståhlberg, a former Senator, had been for many years Professor

---

[27] O.W. Kuusinen, *The Finnish Revolution: A Self-Criticism*, London (The Workers' Socialist Federation), 1919, p. 28.

[28] Uunio Saalas, *Muistelmia lapsuuteen ja nuoruuteeen*, Helsinki (Werner Söderström), 1963, pp.386–393.

[29] *Valtiopäivät 1918. Pöytäkirjat, 5 &6 .7. 1918, pp1515 & 1538.*

of Administrative Law in the University of Helsinki. True to his vocation, he was a dispassionate man, who had counselled his nephew against joining the jaegers being trained in Germany in 1915–1916 for the liberation of their country from the Russian yoke (the nephew did join the jaegers nonetheless and was killed in battle). During the Red revolution, K.J. Ståhlberg found refuge in the Meilahti hospital in Helsinki, a place in which he was able to dwell on the future of his country, once people like his nephew had helped to down the Reds.

With the columns of the *Helsingin Sanomat* open to him,[30] Ståhlberg, in abhorring revolution, nevertheless pleaded for reconciliation with the supporters of the defeated cause. But those guilty of crimes in connection with the revolution should suffer punishment according to the law—and he did mean revolution and not counter-revolution.[31] Ståhlberg therefore blamed the Reds for the trouble and exculpated, by omission, the Whites. Since he was wanting the nation to be *whole (eheä)* once more, this was distinctly one-sided. His assumption was that the revolutionary Reds (and he constantly used the word "revolution") had started it by rejecting the avenues for reform available in the Finnish constitutional system. Instead, they had modelled themselves on the Russian revolutionary forces: this meant that they were under the pernicious influence of hooligans, anarchists, and Bolsheviks. His view was that of the classic Roman lawyer. *Nulla poena sine crimine. Nullum crimen sine lege. (No penalty without crime. No crime without law).*[32] In short, sentencing must not be arbitrary nor unnecessarily severe, but the Whites were not to blame.

Ståhlberg's interpretation of the history of his time was, however, in need of amendment. And the first thing to note is that the penetration of Russia into the thought-processes of the Finns was a far more extensive—and even deeper—phenomenon than Ståhlberg had assumed it to be. He, too, had not remained untouched.

---

[30] Yrjö Blomstedt in *K.J.Ståhlberg.Valtiomieselämäkerta*, Helsinki (Otava),1969, pp. 352–354, has worked from the original statement made by Ståhlberg and dated 6.4.1918. The above analysis is based on the articles in the *Helsingin Sanomat* of 7.5 & 8.5. 1918 and on the statement made by Ståhlberg and his ilk in the issue of 29.5.1918.

[31] Ståhlberg's greatest lacuna was that he, as a man of law, did not protest against the composition of the tribunals that judged the Reds after their surrender. On these field courts, see Turunen, op.cit., chap. entitled "Valkoisen terrorin kasvot": a lawyer was not a necessary member of these courts- p.250. In any case, lawyer or not, the guiding body of law in them was actually *Russian* military law, ibid., p.253. Turunen is somewhat amazed at this. But to the present author this is yet again evidence of imperial Russian influence on the Finnish military command.

[32] K.J.Ståhlberg, *Puheita 1883–1918.*,Helsinki (Otava), 1951, pp.192–193. His statement was made on 29.5.1918 The author is grateful to Professor Kauko Wikström for a discussion of this aspect of Ståhlberg's views.

The Russian Connection

In the early weeks of 1917, many Finns must have shared the viewpoint of the young Uunio Saalas that the restoration of Finnish rights, largely suspended in 1915 by the Imperial authorities, was hardly going to occur.[33] Though Finland was prosperous as a result of orders from Russia for a war in which the Finns themselves did not on the whole take part,[34] both Finnish-speakers and Swedish-speakers shared a gloom about the political future of their country. The time had long gone by in Finland when a Swedish-speaking Finnish bureaucrat, Lars von Haartman, could honestly say that he was happy that Finland belonged to Russia.[35] This had been a paternalistic view of the aristocracy, a last scion of which was Mannerheim.

Since the turn of the century, both Finland and Russia had been struggling with a process of modernization. But its shape was not the same. In Russia, the key question was seen by those who ran the state as essentially deriving from the need to intensify the diplomatic, military and naval security of the land, particularly in the light of the rise of a united and militarily powerful German Empire. This security concern of the imperial Russian government was the one that impinged on the Finnish-Russian relationship. Very swiftly, it had required the abolition of the separate Finnish army and an increasing use of Russian in the administration. The Finns easily dubbed it "russification" and were, many of them, unwilling to see the tightening up even of communications (for example, the pilot service) that Russia required.[36] A constitutional crisis had ensued, which for the Finns, was the core of their hostility to "russification." The latter was a smaller phenomenon within the larger framework of a unification process in key fields such as defence.

For years the constitutionalists in Finland had argued that the bond between Finland and Russia was in essence monarchical and that Finland had a government of its own in the Senate, which was in a relationship to the unicameral legislature, established in 1906 and meeting for the first time in 1907. Unfortunately for this contention, the Senate was also in a relationship to the Tsar. The Senators were his servants and only by indirect influence, for example, by using the Finnish Minister State-Secretary in St. Petersburg, could the Tsar's wishes and, more importantly, *those of his advisers* be modified. In an

---

[33] Saalas, op.cit., p.385.

[34] Until the autumn of 1917 as noted by Pertti Haapala, *Kun yhteikunta hajosi*, Helsinki (Kleio), 1995, esp. 162–164.

[35] Kristiina Kalleinen, *Isäänmaani onni on kuulua Venäjälle*, Helsinki (Suomen Kirjallisuuden Seura), 2001.

[36] George Maude, "Finland and Britain. 1854–1914," unpublished Ph.D thesis, Univ. of London, 1970, pp. 297–301.

article in the *Helsingin Sanomat* of 9 August 1917, Ståhlberg himself argued that the Finnish institutional system under the Tsar had allowed for a Finnish "use of law," but that the ultimate say in legislation and taxation and several other matters had rested with the Tsar. Legislation was of course passed in Finland, but its acceptance required not merely the approval of the Senate but also of the imperial monarchy, and from 1910 the consent of an Imperial Duma and Imperial Council, shunned by the Finns. The development of Russian constitutionalism had become a threat to Finnish constitutionalism.

In the first decade of the twentieth century, there had been broadly three schools of thought among the Finnish bourgeois leaders as to how to react to Russian pressures: the constitutionalists tried to pursue a policy of passive resistance until their claims were recognized either in Russia or in Europe; an offshoot from this movement, the Activists, were, in frustration, prepared to use violence instead. A third group the Compliants, tried to pursue a line of concession, the minimal possible so as to avert a greater wrath. By 1914 all three groups had become disenchanted.

But now, in March 1917, the Imperial monarchy had collapsed. The cause of the collapse was the First World War and the crass inability of the Tsarist military leadership to cope with German might. International conflagration, in the form of the First World War, thus created a *causa ultima* for Finnish independence. On the other hand, the *causae proximae* for the country's independence had not yet arisen. It took many months for the German forces to strike up the Baltic. But the nearer the German forces came to the Russian capital, the more important might Russian control of Finland appear. For the March revolutionaries in Russia had insisted on continuing the war, but the Finns kept up their claim that they h ad the right to be out of it because of the deal they had made pre-war over the "Neva millions."[37]

Under these desperate circumstances, nevertheless, control over Finland from the Russian capital appeared to be increasingly shaky. Even though military government was imposed in 1915, the Finns were not going to fight for Russia and the country's defence rested on Russian troops. Indeed, the whole edifice of Finland-with-Russia had become obscure. No one knew what

---

[37] Owing to the refusal of many young Finns to submit to call-up in the Russian army, the Finns, after their own revolution of 1905–1906, managed to strike an uneasy set of delaying actions by which they were taxed for the building of the Neva bridge (into Finland, but built in Russia). The Finns were kept out of Russian compulsory military service. Russians came over the bridge to defend the country. There was a strong symbolism in this. Pertti Luntinen, *Sotilasmiljoonat*, Helsinki (SHS), 1984, p. 179, does not seem to think that Finland paid all that much. Nonetheless when J.K. Paasikivi, the head of the Finnish treasury, paid the money, his enraged fellow-countrymen deprived him of his post: Pertti Luntinen, *F.A.Seyn*, Helsinki (SHS), 1985, p.144. Paasikivi was later to become president of Finland.

was going to happen, when suddenly, in March 1917, a palace revolution stabbed the air.

A very basic question then faced the Finns Had the provisional government, set up after the Tsar's abdication, inherited the Tsar's powers? Attempts were made in Finland to regulate matters or, at least, to produce models for that task through discussions with Russian experts A committee led by the Old Finn politician Antti Tulenheimo, but with members of other parties including the Social Democrats, produced a draft in June 1917, which somewhat reduced the imperial powers. But the two Social Democratic members, Otto Wille Kuusinen and Yrjö Mäkelin, would have nothing of it, for it left the summoning and dissolution of the Finnish Parliament in the hands of the supreme governmental power. Kuusinen and Mäkelin wanted Parliament to summon and dissolve itself. In vain did Ståhlberg then protest that this matter had been solved in the existing Finnish constitution. The matter, he maintained, was one for the "supreme governmental power."[38] And it is clear that Ståhlberg's aim was to get as much of this power as possible transferred to the purely Finnish executive, at that moment, the Senate. In short, the matter really had not been solved in the existing Finnish constitution, the pattern for which was changing as the prospect of independence haunted the opinions of those who were bold enough to think about it. The Finns saw independence as a constitutional question, while for the Russians, still fighting a hopeless war, Finnish independence might mean a loss of control that would let the Germans in.

The Enabling Act

In early July, the Finnish Social Democrats succeeded in convincing the Russian Mensheviks and Social Revolutionaries to accept the right of the Finnish Parliament to summon and dissolve itself, though with the *caveat* that the ultimate solution to Finnish-Russian relations was to be in the hands of an All-Russian Constituent Assembly.[39] However, undoubtedly the key supposition was the Finnish Social Democrats' erroneous belief that the Bolsheviks were about to seize power in Petrograd in July 1917. This they failed to do, but the Finnish Social Democrats, some Agrarians, and several

---

[38] Blomstedt, op.cit., p.324. *Helsingin Sanomat*, 10.8.1917 & 11.8.1917.

[39] Carl Enckell, *Poliittiset muistelmani*, I, Helsinki (Werner Söderström),1956, pp.84–85. The Assembly met for only one day on 18 January 1918, when the Bolsheviks destroyed it. But on 31 December 1917 the Bolsheviks had already recognized the complete independence of Finland. Alan Moorehead, *The Russian Revolution*, London (Collins). 1958,chap.15.

Independence men,[40] still passed the Enabling Act, granting *internal* sovereignty to the Finnish Parliament.

Thus, in spite of the fact that the Social Democrats had themselves joined the Senate on 24 March 1917 where they worked, contrary to their Kautskyist principles,[41] along with the bourgeois Senators, their view of constitutionalism was different. They were parliamentarians, who had already won, in the election of 1916, 103 seats in a Parliament of 200, though that Parliament was never called till the March 1917 revolution.

At this point, these heady politicians ran up against ran up against Finland's leading constitutionalist, K.J. Ståhlberg. He opposed the promulgation of the law. For the Enabling Act had not even been put before the Finnish Senate for its approval: the Senate was simply *informed* that it had been passed by the Finnish Parliament. Ståhlberg was aghast.[42] His biographer has seen that, as a constitutional lawyer, Ståhlberg could not abandon his belief in the tripartite constitutional form of Montesquieu: a legislative organ, a judicial organ distinct from it, and an executive organ equally distinct.[43]

In any case, in opposing the Enabling Act, Ståhlberg, albeit temporarily, was saving the day for the Russian connection. At the same time, he blamed those who backed the Enabling Act for presenting its themes in that form to the Russians.[44] For, apart from the alarming constitutionalist ideas proclaimed in it (which Ståhlberg said were to be found nowhere else in the world–he had forgotten or did not know the very close relationship between the Swiss electorate–admittedly only male–and the less powerful executive), the Enabling Act was also, in effect, a declaration of independence in all but foreign policy, defence policy, and the rights of Russians in Finland. It was too much for the cautious Ståhlberg, who, very unfairly, blamed the sponsors of the Act for demanding "*complete* independence." This they had not done. They were also blamed by Ståhlberg for "irritating government circles and public opinion" in Russia.[45] On the other hand, the principal figure among the bourgeois "Independence men," the Procurator-General Pehr Evind

---

[40] These included men of some distinction who hoped to negotiate with Russia a recognition of Finnish sovereignty.

[41] Kautsky was opposed in principle–till 1926–to Socialists going into government coalitions with the bourgeois parties. Hence in 1917 the Finnish Social Democrats went into the Finnish Senate (government) as individuals and not as party members. Upton, op.cit., p.29.Even the latter tactic was a doubtful one to Kautsky. Hannu Soikkanen, *Kohti Kansanvaltaa*, Helsiinki (Suomen Sosialidemokraattinen puolue), 1975, p.123.

[42] *Helsingin Sanomat*, 10.8.1917.

[43] Blomstedt, op.cit., p.326.

[44] K.J.Ståhlberg, *Puheita 1883–1918*, Helsinki (Otava), 1951, pp.170–171.

[45] *Helsingin Sanomat*, 10 & 11.8.1917.

Svinhufvud, the chief law officer, blamed the supporters of the Enabling Act because "it was only half way to independence."[46]

This is a very broad claim, and there was a certain truth behind it, though it was not the truth that Ståhlberg himself wanted to dwell on in his polemic against those who supported the Enabling Act.

What united both Ståhlhberg and Svinhufvud, however, was their insistence upon a strong executive.

Back in Russia, one of the leading Social Revolutionaries in Russia, Alexander Feodorovich Kerensky, had become minister of justice and minister of war in the government of Prince Lvov and then was rapidly to succeed Lvov as prime minister. What he did not like about the Finns was their lack of support for continuing the war with Germany, their unwillingness to do anything for the Russian war effort, and the lurking threat of a complete Finnish independence, which might have been exploited by the Germans. As noted above, both the Mensheviks and Social Revolutionaries had accepted the Finnish Parliament's right to summon and dissolve itself, and to have control over taxation. It would hardly therefore seem that Ståhlberg's concern for the upholding of a Finnish executive was the point that would worry Kerenskiy since he was backed by the Mensheviks and he was a Social Revolutionary himself. These questions could anyway be put off till the All-Russian Constituent Assembly met. And, indeed, for the moment, the Enabling Act had exempted the questions of foreign and defence policy and the question of the rights of Russians in Finland from being under the sole purview of the Finns, in Parliament or otherwise.

As an administrative lawyer and a constitutionalist, Ståhlberg wanted to do things in a different way, however. He liked to negotiate over the table, essentially on a position-paper prepared by himself, and with fellow-lawyers, on the other side like Freiherr Boris Nolde. As late as 15 October 1917, Nolde was in Helsinki, where he negotiated with the traditionalist Finnish leadership, including Ståhlberg. In these negotiations, Ståhlberg argued that the supreme governmental power *over* Finland should now be transferred *to* Finland. But there would be exceptions: foreign affairs, defence, and the rights of Russians in Finland.[47] These were the very themes of the Enabling Act! Yet there was a difference. When Ståhlberg was negotiating the transfer of the supreme governmental power to Finland, he meant to keep it in the hands of a Finnish *executive* (apart from the above-mentioned exceptions) and not a Finnish Parliament.

---

[46] Einar Juva, *P.E.Svinhuvfud*, II, Helsinki-Porvoo (Werner Söderström),1961, p.41.

[47] Blomstedt, op.cit., p.331.

Nonetheless, his negotiating stance in the middle of October raised another question. For two months earlier, in his letters to the *Helsingin Sanomat* on his refusal to endorse the Enabling Act, he had argued for an *independence* that would have had the *cachet* for an international recognition *because recognized by the Russian governmental authorities.* Yet now he was prepared to reserve powers to Russia, including the important external relations! Two months previously, he had added, that "independence" should not rest upon "the wobbly basis of temporary statements" or upon the feeling that "revolution was still continuing in Russia."[48] But revolution *was* continuing and it was the extreme revolutionary party in Russia, the Bolsheviks, who were prepared unconditionally to grant Finland independence.[49] Since Ståhlberg did not favour revolution, had he found another way to produce independence for his country, by negotiating over the table for it? Or had Ståhlberg backtracked on what he had said in the columns of the *Helsingin Sanomat?* It was left to other members of the Finnish delegation, Rabbe Wrede and J.R Danielson-Kalmari, to point out that what had been presented to Nolde was a minimal Finnish programme and that in the country there was a strong feeling for *complete* independence.[50]

The rub lay in the question that Ståhlberg had almost dismissed in his July letters to the *Helsingin Sanomat*: this was the *potentiality* of revolution in Russia. It could hardly be denied that there was a connection between the Enabling Act, passed by the Finnish Parliament on 18 July and Russian Bolshevism, since the Finnish Social Democrat leader Oskari Tokoi had mistakenly proclaimed in his country's Parliament that the Bolsheviks had seized power in Petrograd ("the July days"). They had only tried to do so and failed. Some would argue that they had not even tried. Upton makes the point that Lenin had been on holiday, while the main trouble might have been that troops in Petrograd had rebelled against being sent to fight the Germans.[51] But the Bolsheviks were to try again and succeed this time. In contrast to what Ståhlberg had implied, the revolution in Russia *was* going on. And it was the success of the Bolsheviks that brought Finland its immediate formal independence. Whatever the dreams the Bolshevik leaders harboured of taking the country back once the time was ripe, it was *their* revolution that gave Finland immediate and full independence when the Bolsheviks, once in control in Petrograd, accorded independence on 31 December 1917.[52]

---

[48] *Helsingin Sanomat*, 11.8.1917.
[49] Enckell, op.cit, I, p.85.
[50] Blomstedt, op.cit., p.332.
[51] Upton, op. cit., p.85. These arguments do not exclude, however, a Bolshevik exploitation of the situation at a grass-roots level.
[52] ibid., p.43–44.

Ståhlberg could hardly be expected to have known the tortuous ins-and-outs of revolutionary politics in Russia. But he might have appreciated the force of revolution and character of revolution more strongly, particularly in relation to his own country. Revolution in Russia, in the course of a world war, had done what years of attempted negotiation could not do for the Finnish cause. Neither passive nor active resistance from the Finnish side had brought improvement; nor had the policy of conceding to Imperial demands either. It was the bourgeois Russian revolution of March 1917 that had brought the abolition of the restrictions on Finnish rights embodied in the February Manifesto of 1899. Constitutionally, since those March days of 1917, things had, however, seemed to be slipping again, and the constitutionalists nominally in power in Russia from March 1917 onwards could neither control their own country, nor even let Finland drop away. They, like Ståhlberg, preferred to sit round a table, where they haggled over a power they did not necessarily have.

On the other hand, if the Finns had truly looked abroad, history—not Ståhlberg's strong point—would have provided several examples of constitutional revolution in which the representative organ took over. Failing this sort of revolution, there was another sort, in which the revolutionaries roamed the streets and countryside in their desire for power at any price. The *argumentum ad hominem,* in this case, further runs as follows: Ståhlberg's obsession to do a deal with some kind of constitutionalism in Russia distracted him from seeing what was going on under his nose in Finland, too. The Social Democratic Party, which sponsored the Enabling Act in Parliament, was the party most bound of all to the power of the unicameral legislature, which they had accepted in 1906 and which brought them finally a simple majority of seats—103 out of 200—in the parliamentary election of 1916. Having for years tried to get reform measures through this Parliament in the final period of autonomy only to find that these were blocked off by Finnish officials serving an unsympathetic authority in the Russian capital, the Social Democrats understandably *and with the support of some bourgeois politicians and Agrarians*[53] strove to drive the Act through Parliament. Then they were opposed by Ståhlberg, who wanted instead a noble statement from Russian jurists and gentleman-politicians about Finnish independence and where the supreme governmental power should reside in the new state. *Carpe*

[53] The followers of the Agrarian Union, led by Santeri Alkio, a former member of the Social Democratic Party, believed that the latter party could not fully comprehend the problems of Finnish country folk. But they were prepared to consider cooperation with the Social Democrats and in this period did not consider the Agrarian Union to be a bourgeois party, though they loved their property. See note 128.

diem? Ståhlberg's role was an apt illustration of the truth of what the unorthodox Russian Marxist G.V. Plekhanov wrote about the role of the individual in history: "in the given social conditions" the individual's role can be a significant contribution to disaster.[54]

But there was someone else, too, in this unfortunate political farrago over the Enabling Act, who exemplified the truth of Plekhanov's dictum even more, and who was ready to play the politics of "saving the day for the Russians" and, in part, with the very same reasoning that was in Ståhlberg's mind, namely to defend the independence of the Finnish executive. And this man was very much a Russified Finn, which Ståhlberg was not.

Carl Johan Enckell was the last Finnish Minister State-Secretary in the Russian capital. There he had been born in 1878, the son of a Swedish-speaking Finnish general in the Russian service and of a mother of Polish origin, having thus a truly imperial background. A dapper man, the English historian Anthony Upton has regarded him as a tough specimen in defeating the politics of the Enabling Act.[55] But perhaps he was only frightened. His friend, Ernst Nevanlinna, an Old Finn,[56] had telephoned him to say that, on the strength of the Enabling Act, the Social Democrats intended to form a new Senate (government) in Helsinki (which would be the tool of a Socialist-dominated Parliament).Like other conservatives[57] who disliked the Enabling Act, the argument that many Agrarians and Activists and Independence men had also supported the Social Democrats in promoting the Act cut no ice, for the underlying conviction of those who opposed the Act was that its bourgeois supporters were being duped by the Social Democrats. There was, however, another way of looking at this matter. What was behind the promotion of the Enabling Act was a potential coalition, between Socialists and non-Socialists. The tough men of the Activist cause had always wanted cooperation with the workers,[58] while the Agrarian leader Alkio found the bourgeois opposition to Parliament hypocritical and a cover for their fear of economic revolution.[59]

---

[54] G.V. Plekhanov, *The Role of the Individual in History*, London (Lawrence and Wishart), 1950 ed., pp. 38–40.

[55] Upton, op.cit., p.88 "resolute" & p.95 "a strong and determined man."

[56] The Old Finns had a background in "compliance" being willing to work with Russia to avoid "the greater evil," losing all.

[57] Ari Rasilainen, in his doctoral thesis, *Oikeudellinen argumentointi politiikassa*, Helsinki (Suomalainen lakimiesyhdistys), 2004, p.235 & pp.238–239,has pointed out that in this period Enckell was close to E.N. Setälä, Ståhlberg, and Svinhufvud, all of whom were then Young Finns, who considered themselves to be liberals. But both Setälä and Svinhufvud were moving Rightwards and joined the newly-founded National Coalition Party in 1918. It is the contention here that Ståhlbeg, too, had a strong conservative edge.

[58] On this movement, see p.8.The Social Democrat leader, Yrjö Mäkelin's son, was a member of this movement and there were other young Socialists in it In 1917 Kai Donner, one of the

Enckell had got wind of the proposed Enabling Act in early July and had got Prince Lvov to send a delegation of Mensheviks and Social Revolutionaries to Helsinki, with the message that this could not be a unilateral decision, but had to be negotiated with the forthcoming All-Russian Constituent Assembly (ultimately, a paper tiger, as noted). The Russian delegation was anyway unsuccessful.[60] What then did Enckell do next? He waited. For one thing, the political context in which he worked in Petrograd changed. If there had been an initial attempt of the Bolsheviks to take power there, it had failed, but, in any case, the street action did result in a change of government. Prince Lvov resigned as prime minister and was succeeded by Alexander Feodorovich Kerensky. This change was meant as a token of the need for a shift to the Left in Russia. Kerensky was a member of the Social Revolutionary Party. On the other hand, he was not a Bolshevik so that his elevation was also intended to convey a certain stabilizing of the situation once the apparent Bolshevik *coup* had failed. But, unfortunately, Kerensky was in favour of the hopeless prosecution of the war against Germany.

He had come to power on 21 July, three days after the Finnish Parliament had passed its Enabling Act. On 24 July, Enckell paid Kerensky a courtesy visit, in the course of which—according to Enckell—the new Russian prime minister assumed a Napoleonic pose and taunted the Minister State-Secretary of Finland about the Finnish Parliament's "declaration of independence" indicating, too, the possibility that Russia might use force against Finland. Though the ultimate fear did not on this occasion s expressly surface, an independent Finland, so near the Russian capital, might turn out to be a Finland dominated by the Germans.

In the meantime, the Russian Governor-General in Finland, Stakhovich arrived in Petrograd to find out what was going o there. He failed to see Kerensky and had to come down from Finland another day. In Helsinki, the Social Democrats, realising that the Bolsheviks had not triumphed, got the Finnish Parliament to write a conciliatory address to the new Petrograd government, mentioning, however, with respect the Petrograd Soviet of Workers and Soldiers where Kerensky's own party, the Social Revolutionaries, had much support.

On Stakhovich's second visit to Petrograd, Enckell got to work and helped him to produce a manifesto dissolving the Finnish Parliament, though with an extra piece about Finland's getting increasing self-determination. At

---

leaders of the Jaeger movement, was encouraging Socialists to join. See Matti Lackman, *Heikki Repo- Punainen Jääkäri*, Oulu (Scripta historica XI) offprint 1987, p.212.

59 Enckell, op.cit, I., p.91.

60 ibid.,p. 85.

the Petrograd railway station, on his way south to the front in south-western Russia, Kerensky signed the draft. He was by now less bellicose about Finland and, according to what Enckell was told by Stakhovich, signed unwillingly and told the Governor-General to use the document and the parliamentary dissolution contained in it "only in the direst of emergencies." In its final form, the manifesto was signed by all members of the new Russian provisional government on 31 July. It was applied by Governor-General Stakhovich, forgetting the caution enjoined on him by Kerensky and threatening the Social Democrat leaders Oskari Tokoi and Kullervo Manner with the occupation of Finland by Russian troops if it were not obeyed.[61]

It was certainly true that the number of Russian troops in southern Finland had been increased and some of them were Cossacks, a group not sympathetic to those suspected of links with the Bolsheviks. The reality of the situation, however, was that Russia was so stretched in its battlelines already that there would have been insufficient troops to make or hold a conquest of Finland.[62] The dissolution was fatal for the stability within Finland. The Enabling Act should not have disturbed Kerensky, for by its statutes foreign affairs, defence, and the rights of Russians in Finland were safeguarded: these were concessions to Russia in the eyes of the drafters of the Act, but if Russia collapsed . . .

Rasilainen has argued that Enckell's own fear of the use of *force majeure* against Finland, in the person of Stakhovich (actually a person of a wavering nature), was a concoction that hid Enckell's real aims. These related to the internal politics of Finland rather than to a Russian threat. The problem of how to select the executive organ was not, indeed, solved at this time. The existing Senate had been appointed by the Russian provisional government, after a coalition was got together with some difficulty between the Social Democrats and the non-Socialist parties. It has become known as the Tokoi Senate after the surname of the chairman of the Finnish Social Democratic Party. The March Manifesto that gave it birth, though published in the name of the Russian provisional government, was, in fact, largely drafted by none other than Ståhlberg![63]

After the dissolution of the Finnish Parliament, the Social Democrats retired a few weeks later from the Senate. In a rump Parliament, they tried to meet and were dispersed by Russian troops. In the October election, they lost their majority and fell to 92 (instead of 103 seats). In any case, Parliament did

[61] Enckell, op.cit., pp.92–93. Rasilainen, op.cit., p240 argue that Enckell at the time did not believe this threat nor did the two Social Democrats.

[62] Hannu Soikkanen, p. 271.

[63] Blomstedt, op.cit. p313.

not sit till November. For three months therefore, the country was without its Parliament, while the Senate contained only non-Socialist members for the Social Democrats left the Senate. To many of the Social Democrats, a dictatorship of the proletariat began to appear to be ever more alluring. Yet Social Democracy had been built upon the attainment of power by parliamentary means. Instead of a constituent assembly in 1905–1906, the Social Democrats had accepted a unicameral legislature. If they were to live in a constitutionalist state, and many had been prepared for this, then the key aspect of constitutionalism for them was not the executive but a Parliament which the democracy would elect. The Social Democrats were not learned in the law like Ståhlberg. What they wanted was change, one way or the other.

As to Carl Enckell, he had behaved like a servant of the Tsar, encouraging the provisional government, the inheritors of the Tsar's authority, and the Governor-General to dissolve the Finnish Parliament when they did not like what it was doing. This was to employ the same tactics used in the first decade of the century and it put paid, albeit temporarily, once again to social reform.[64] For what went down in the Parliament of the Enabling Act were the laws on the eight-hour day and the reform of the municipal franchise (based hitherto on the principle of no representation without taxation, a system by which a rich man might accrue twenty-four votes). Amendments to these injustices, the Social Democrats had been trying to put on the statute book for many a year. Tsardom had previously frustrated them; now the Finnish conservative forces and a Russianized Finnish official in Petrograd did the job. Ståhlberg himself had earlier been well aware of a certain tension between the defence of Finnish constitutional rights and the need to adopt social legislation.[65] Now it looked as if this tension was still there. What this meant was the deferment of the laws on the 8-hour day and on municipal franchise reform rather than have the sovereignty of Parliament declared. In this connection, a curious twist of fate was to occur, however. Upton has pointed out that the Russian Governor-General Stakhovich then dreamed up a "solution" by which the Provisional Government in Petrograd would take on the responsibility bringing in both a reformed municipal government law for Finland and an 8-hour day act likewise. But the Finnish Social Democrats refused.[66] In this they were patriotic Finns. But their attitude also spoke of their desire for power, and power in their homeland. Enckell, Ståhlberg, and Svinhufvud, different though they were from each other, had all equally

---

[64] E.g., in 1909 when Governor-General Vladimir Alexandrovitch Boeckman sacked Parliament over social reform measures.

[65] Blomstedt, op.cit., p.171.

[66] Upton, op.cit., p.97.

underestimated the reality that the Social Democrats of Finland were also committed to bring about change by revolutionary force where necessary.[67] The Red Guard organizations sprang up spontaneously in many parts in the autumn of 1917 to be faced in other areas by White Civil Guards. Inadvertently, the risk of revolution through the Red Guard organization grew, as economic conditions worsened during the succeeding autumn.

In the debates on the Enabling Act in July 1917, the constitutionalist leader Pehr Evind Svinhufvud, recently returned from his Siberian exile, had not known how to vote,[68] though he has traditionally been regarded as some kind of rock-like embodiment of human decisiveness.[69] He was muddled and avoided Parliament and even the Senate wherever possible.[70] The *coup*, skilfully engineered by Enckell with his old-time methods, brought back unity to the bourgeois forces in Finland. That same *coup* also helped to provoke an even greater shock to Finnish society, the name of which was revolution. Ironically, the dissolution of Parliament had been meant to prevent revolution. In fact, Enckell's intrigues and Ståhlberg's ponderous and dilatory exercises in constitutionalism helped to provoke it. The revolution was a cleavage between a Finnish Right and a Finnish extreme Left. The tragedy was that at one time it looked as if these two Finnish forces might unite to wrest their country from its traditional Russian connection.[71]

Ståhlberg, as noted, had argued that the passing of the Enabling Act would irritate Russian opinion. But the Russians had plenty of other things to think about beside Finland. Over and again, it must be emphasized that Kerensky reluctantly signed the order for dissolving the Finnish Parliament which Enckell had written for Governor-General Stakhovich to present to him in a hurried moment at the railway station when Kerenskiy was leaving for

---

[67] As was Karl Kautsky: Hannu Soikkanen, op.cit., p.383. In the present author's opinion, Kautsky's reluctance to accept a constitutional government with bourgeois parties exacerbated the revolutionary tendency.

[68] Einar Juva tells how Svinhufvud was muddled and confused over the Enabling Act; *P.E. Svinhufvud,*. II, Helsinki (Söderström), 1961, pp. 45–46.

[69] In Eino Jutikkala's pen-portait, A *History of Finland,* London (Thames and Hudson) 1962, pp.244–245, a somewhat simplified picture of Svinhufvud is given. He could be both cunning and indecisive.

[70] Juva, op.cit.,pp.36–37.

[71] Note Tokoi's praise in Parliament on 20.4. 1917 of the young men who left Finland to join the jaeger movement in Germany to receive military training for the liberation of Finland. *Valtiopäivät, I, Pöytäkirjat,* 2.4.1917. The jaegers later became a significant factor in the White cause in Finland. In spite of this, at the time, the Young Finn M.P. Rudolf Holsti did not like Tokoi's reference to violence, preferring presumably resort to negotiation for Finland's freedom. See Juhani Paasivirta, *Suomen itsenäisyyskysymys,* I, Porvoo-Helsinki, (Söderström) 1947, pp.117–118. Nor did Holsti like the German connection, preferring the cause of the Western allies.

Mogilev. It was Enckell, above all, who was the one irritated by the Enabling Act; more, he was maddened by the actions of those Finns whose policies were different from his own. He and his confrères were fond of quoting the misrule of Parliament in eighteenth-century Sweden (of which Finland was then an integral part), forgetting that the parliamentarians in that case were largely officials, which Enckell, in 1917, was, too. The desire of a Parliament to elect its own ministers (a Senate) was of the very essence of parliamentary constitutionalism. The Parliament that passed the Enabling Act had only 103 Social Democrat members. Would this small majority have excluded the non-Socialists as ministers, many of whom, had voted for the Enabling Act? Hardly, for this was not a British parliamentary system, and the Social Democrats themselves were well aware of the fact that the *modus vivendi* of Parliament as seen in the fact that the Enabling Act won the support even of non-Socialist members was an alternative to the desecrations of revolution. Sadly, Enckell, Ståhlberg, Nevanlinna, and others preferred the road to St. Petersburg and the power of officialdom it still managed to exert.

Revolution Approaches

It is perfectly true that revolution has economic causes. These may emerge after an improvement in the living standard is suddenly checked.[72] The Finnish revolution fits such a pattern. Because of the constitutional quarrels between Finland and Russia, the separate Finnish army no longer existed. The Finns were paying the Russians to defend their country.[73] Once the war with Germany had begun, Finland was filled with Russian troops and sailors to defend Petrograd by defending Finland. This brought a paying population into Finland, which rose to 100,000 men by the summer of 1917. The trade in horses flourished by the sale of mounts to the Russian armed forces.[74] By 1915, work on the Finnish fortifications was employing 30,000 Finns. The engineering industry also expanded, thanks to Russian war orders: it grew over 50% from 1913 to 1916, and even flourished until the early months of 1917.[75] The trade westward in sawn timber practically ceased, but paper exports eastward boomed: as the German armies advanced into the

[72] The author acknowledges with gratitude the discussions he had on this theory with Professor T.S. Ashton at the London School of Economics in 1949.

[73] "The Neva millions" see note 37.

[74] Information given to the author by his grandfather-in -law, Kalle Johansson, who engaged in the trade.

[75] Pentti Virrankoski, *Suomen taloushistoria*, Helsinki (Otava), 1975, pp.187–188. Pertti Haapala, *Kun yhteisikunta hajosi*, Helsinki (Kleio), 1995 pp.156–158,believes that, broadly speaking, Finland did not do too badly out of the First World War till the summer of 1917.

borderlands of Russia, occupying areas in which Russian paper had been produced. Finnish paper exports to Russia took over the market and supplied 85% of the paper used there.[76] At the same time within Finland prices began to rise steeply and foodstuffs became dearer, exacerbating not merely the tension between town and countryside, but also within the countryside aggravating the gulf between the landed and the landless and in some cases the crofters. Finland had gone off the gold standard in 1915 and the exchange rate between the Russian ruble (in which the Russian troops were paid) and the Finnish mark was deleterious to the mark and prices escalated.[77] But by the summer of 1917, as Russia fell into collapse, a serious side-effect was felt in Finland. By 1918, the decline in the consumption of foodstuffs was 40% from what it had been in 1913, the last year of peace, while industrial production, if measured at 100 in 1913 had already dropped in value to 68 by 1917.[78] Work on the fortifications ceased by the autumn of 1917.

After the 1917 March revolution in Russia, voluntary workers' units began to form in the localities in Finland. The historian of this movement in Finland, Marja-Leena Salkola, seems to accept in large part the analysis of the Communist Tuure Lehén that the aim of these organizations was originally to safeguard the collective actions of the workers rather than to change society. She also works from the earlier research of Aimo Klemettilä according to which some of the units were formed for the purpose of keeping order, while others were revolutionary in intent. This was a repetition of the situation in Finland in 1905–1906 when such units, voluntarily formed, began to press the bourgeoisie either for a constituent assembly or, as was the solution, a unicameral legislature. And, as in 1905–1906, these formations produced counter-formations of civil guards to protect the interests of the bourgeoisie and property-owners in the countryside.[79]

The workers' leadership was, by May 1917, becoming worried. In that month, at Kaisaniemi in Helsinki, a workers' meeting urged the creation of a revolutionary fighting force, which the leadership forbade the Social Democratic Party members to join! Increasingly, whatever the workers' units

---

[76] Virrankoski, op.cit., p.188 & Enckell, op.cit., pp.48–49.

[77] Pekka Kosonen et al.,*Suomalainen kapitalismi*, Helsinki (Love), 1979, p.27. Virrankoski, op.cit., p.189.

[78] Riitta Hjerppe, *Suomen talous 1860–1985*, Helsinki (Suomen pankki) 1988, p. 103. Virrankoski, op.cit., p.189.

[79] Marja-Leena Salkola, *Työväen kaartien synty ja kehitys punakaartiksi*,I, Helsinki (Valtion painatuskeskus), 1985, pp. 97, 208–209(though Salkola faults Klemettilä for not distinguishing the category into which each organization fell).

had been formed for, they began to radicalize and demand the passing of legislation for the 8-hour day and for the reform of the municipal franchise.[80]

As previously, in 1905–1906, workers' demonstrations were held to pressure Parliament, which passed both acts.[81] Then Enckell got Parliament dissolved. The acts then lacked the approval of the Senate and thus could not become law. The Senate soon lost its Social Democratic members by resignation and the country drifted into a tense stalemate, with the increasingly aggressive workers' organizations now lacking a constitutional point at which to pressurize. Darkly, after the dissolution of Parliament, one of the most patriotic of the workers' leaders, Yrjö Mäkelin, hinted that the workers might have stronger weapons than the ballot paper,[82] while in its address of 20 October the umbrella organization of the trade union movement, the SAJ, encouraged the formation of more workers' local organizations in an atmosphere of growing militancy.[83] The food situation had deteriorated. For months, workers' organizations and especially the SAJ had asked for an equitable distribution policy for foodstuffs, run by society, which Salkola has called a demand for socialization.[84] Unfortunately, the failure to get through the bill on municipal franchise reform considerably worsened the establishment of an equitable system of food distribution, and workers felt justified in making their own forays into the Finnish countryside for the appropriation of foodstuffs.[85]

As in the autumn of 1917 the Red Guard grew in strength, the leadership of the Social Democratic Party realized only too well that they had created a force they could not easily control. The November (from 14th to 20th) general strike of the trade union movement (SAJ) was backed by the Red Guards and neither organization wanted to end it.[86] The political leadership of the party *did* want to end it. They had become afraid of their own followers almost as much as the bourgeoisie distrusted the masses (in Finnish *rahvas*, a negative connotation).[87] Here was the rub, for this, if ever, was the time for revolution, before the military men of the Right had got *their own* cause organized. What

---

[80]Salkola,pp., I,106–109 & 155–156.
[81] Salkola, op.cit., I, pp., 45–47,178–182 & 198.
[82] Salkola, op.cit., II, p.39
[83] ibid., II, p.94., 126, & 131. There had been 37 previously and now 72 new organizations sprang up.
[84] Salkola, op.cit. II, pp.19–20.
[85] Salkola, op.cit., II, p.27. Upton, op.cit., p.179.
[86] Upton, op.cit., p.157, 167–168.
[87] The Social Democrat leader Eetu Salin—by mid-November 1917—felt that the Red Guards were bent on defying the decisions of the Social Democratic Party Conference:. But he seemed afraid to challenge the Guards: Salkola, op.cit., II, pp.245–246.

the leadership seemed to favour—in the best manner of the later Kautsky[88]—was outside pressure on the constitutional system. However, in the autumn parliamentary elections Social Democratic representation had fallen from 103 to 92 and that Parliament had not met till early November.

Having lost their simple majority, it was possible to fault the SDP on further grounds. For having fallen in the second parliamentary election, they continued to sit in the new Parliament (once it finally met), while yet proclaiming that the *true* Parliament was still the old one that had passed the Enabling Act and in which the Social Democrats had had their slight majority.[89]

Yet, potentially, in autumn they still had allies within the existing system. Paasivirta argued that the October election result alienated the Activists from cooperation with the Social Democrats, but Upton has shown that in the Independence Club at any rate as late as the middle of November *some* support among the Activists for cooperation with the Social Democrats was still there.[90] The same went for the Agrarians. Indeed, the latter were prepared to support the Enabling Act, on which they had previously been divided. At this point the Agrarian Union was stumbling towards its most powerful role in Finnish political life, that of balancing between the two extremes of Left and Right, and being committed ideologically to neither.

But the slide into revolution was nevertheless beginning. The Social Democratic leadership was, by hook or crook, now bound, in whatever way it turned, to the set of specific measures of the sort demanded in the proclamation *Me vaadimme* ("We demand") with the aid of which, through the general strike, it hoped to put pressure on Parliament. Failing this, there was also the option of revolution, which the Petrograd Bolsheviks, especially Lenin and Stalin, were urging on the Finns.

The strident nature of the demands put forward by the Social Democrats in *Me vaadimme* drove the Agrarians to suggest a compromise around the revival of the Enabling Act, in its basic sense of proclaiming the sovereignty of Parliament. Alas, members of the other non-Socialist parties played at this point a trick reminiscent of the summer machinations of Nevanlinna and Enckell when they had engineered the fall of the Enabling Act. The conservative forces now embarked on a plan of strategic voting to get their way. It was in the shape of the plan known as "the Condorcet winner."

---

[88] Kautsky, *Yhteiskunnallinen vallankumous*, Pori (Osuuskunta kehitys, 1906, p.105.This was translated by Väinö Tanner. He did not join the revolution in 1918.

[89] Rasilainen, op.cit.,p.259 & 281, quotes the critique launched against them precisely on these grounds by the *Uusi Päivä* (later the *Helsingin Sanomat*), 27.9.1917 & 13.1.1917.

[90] Paasivirta,*Suomen itsenäisyys kysysmys 1917, II, p.166.* Upton, op.cit., p.154.

The Speaker of Parliament, Johannes Lundson, determined the order. of voting. There were three resolutions. The *Me vaadimme* (covering also the Enabling Act) of the Social Democrats, the simple Enabling Act acceptance of the Agrarians, and the conservatives' proposal for a regency. Lundson first put the Enabling Act against *Me vaadimme.* The Social Democrats, now more extreme than ever, preferred the specifics of *Me vaadimme* but including the Enabling Act. The trick lay in the fact that the conservative members of Parliament also voted for *Me vaadimme!* This knocked out the compromise of the Agrarians in suggesting the Enabling Act alone: the vote was 135 to 58. Thereafter a Lundson set up another vote between the conservative proposal for a regency and the victorious proposal of the first vote, *Me vaadimme.* Since the latter demands were too extreme for most Agrarians (particularly the 8-hour day, which they feared would spread to the countryside, and the clamour to free the crofters from labour services), the Agrarians felt compelled to vote for the proposed three-man regency. This was intended to be an executive of a conservative, an Agrarian and a Social Democrat. It sounded reasonable. The Social Democrats, however, would not accept this position of permanent inferiority to the non-Socialist parties and because the Social Democrat would not accept it, the Agrarians would not join the troika. The conservative forces thus won and Svihufvud became head of state by 106 to 90 votes. The Left were outclassed by ingenious mathematics. The Social Democrats talked, as revolutionaries, of a constituent assembly, but they stayed in Parliament, though the hope of political cooperation between the Agrarians and the Social Democrats was had been temporarily dished.[91] Yet even Kautsky had made an allowance for an independent peasantry![92]

It was a mistake of the Social Democrats to place a *Me vaadimme* proclamation before the Enabling Act, but in times of dearth demands radicalise. And Social Democracy had to treat with respect its own coalition with the Red Guards. As the Bolsheviks had seized power in Petrograd, the Social Democrats were now able to listen to them with greater hope, but the talk of revolution produced nothing concrete as yet.[93]

The Social Democrats, recalling undoubtedly the all-or-nothing line of their mentor Kautsky and disenchanted by their previous experience of sharing

---

[91] Upton, op.cit., p.143. Also p.153 where Upton gives an extended explanation of these parliamentary antics, according to which the Agrarians had proposed a milder variant of the Enabling Act as a temporary measure before the installation of a regency and that this was passed but could not satisfy the extreme forces of the Left. See also Hannu Soikkanen, op.cit., p.243.

[92] ibid.,p.101.

[93] Tuomo Polvinen, *Venäjän vallankumous ja Suomi*I, I, Porvoo-Helsinki (Söderström), 1967, pp. 120–123.

power with the bourgeoisie in the Senate, gradually became locked in a violence Kautsky himself had little sympathy with. Ideas may blind and he showed no understanding of Finland in this fateful year. What he had done was to argue in such a way as to hinder the possibility of any kind of coalition. What was left was his favoured method of seizure of power by general strike. But he seems to have sent no messages in this fateful month of November 1918. Writers on him ignore Finland,[94] though it is one of the most poignant examples of revolution there is. Ordinary people, like the young girls whose fate is recounted in note 11 of this text, were swayed by the onset of revolution. Kautsky, in the meantime, contented himself with assertions about revolution coming before democracy, that democracy could not arise out of itself.[95] History gave him many examples, but Finland was a complicated case where its bruised democracy was losing trust; by 10 November even Salin was arguing for revolution.[96] However, by 14 November a general strike was taking place in Finland. Was this a strike *à la Kautsky* to press Parliament? When the trade unions struck, they won the 8-hour day and local government reform But they did not get bread and did not get socio-economic change.[97] The SDP ended the strike on 20 November, while the SAJ umbrella trade union organization wanted it to continue to a seizure of power. In the localities there was also much support for a continuation of the strike. And the workers were told throughout the country that that the "truce" might be a short one. But if you were going to have a revolution, this was the time. It has been estimated that in the middle of November there were 30,000 Red Guards and only 20,000 civil guards on the White side.[98] Yet, for the moment, the Social Democratic Party chose to stick with Parliament.

The Agrarians, once the strike had started, then tried another approach to the SDP, offering acceptance of the Enabling Act and subsequently the chance of a government coalition with them. They were then told to refer their offer to another organ, the Revolutionary Council! In disdain, the Agrarians turned

---

[94] E.g., Gary P. Steenson, *Karl Kautsky. Marxism in the Classical Years 1854–1938*, Pittsburgh (Univ. of Pittsburgh Press), 1978 & 1991.

[95] Kautsky.,*Köyhälistön vallankumous ja sen ohjelma,* Helsinki (Kustannusosakeyhtiö kansanvalta), 1925, p.27. The edition bears the marks of the 1918 edition.

[96] Upton, op.cit., p.144.

[97] A point hammered home by subsequent Soviet historians, e.g., Viktor Holodkovski, *Työväen vallankumous 1918*,Moskova (Kustannusliike edistys), 1978, pp.66 & 68.

[98] Salkola, "Työväenkaartit ja suojeluskunnat" in *Itsenäisen Suomen historia*,I, ed. Osmo Apunen, Jyväskylä (Weilin & Göös), 1991, pp.204–205. Salkola has admitted that some of the Red Guards were hardly military units

to the side of the bourgeois parties, while in the meantime the SDP restructured the Revolutionary Council into impotence.[99]

Pehr Evind Svinhufvud became Holder of the Supreme Power, a single-handed executive–until, with the increasing disorders of the Left, the Right organized over the next few weeks its military forces and plans, and the "Russian" Finnish military commanders, Mannerheim, Ignatius, Wetzer and Thesleff (whose ladies had presented the flowers on 16 May), helped further to batter the country into peace.[100] As one of Finland's leading novelists, Frans Eemil Sillanpää, was shortly to tell it, this was for many "the peace of the grave."[101]

It is worth recalling that in the struggle before and around the creation of a unicameral legislature in 1905–1907 the ranks of the Right had been deeply suspicious of the grant of power to the masses. Even the liberal Ståhlberg had initially argued for the creation, out of the old Diet of Four Estates, of a bicameral Parliament with "the quality" in an upper house, composed of nobility and priesthood.[102] Now, just about a decade later, that fear of the *demos* had re-emerged, this time also among the Left. The masses were to go into revolution as a means of controlling them. Comfortable in victory, the Whites must have immensely enjoyed their *Schadenfreude*, for they had always believed that the masses were a dangerous lot. Fortunately for their cause, however, they had discovered the masses of another kind, those who formed the bulk of Mannerheim's army, the loyal and trusting peasantry, particularly those from Ostrobothnia. Mannerheim addressed his army as a "peasant army."[103] Many of them thought they were called to fight the Russians,[104] but the Russians (Lenin and co.) were withdrawing from Finland, were taking their troops out,[105] and had granted to Svinhufvud the independence of his country on 31 December 1918. The preoccupation of the Bolsheviks was rather making peace with Germany than backing the revolution in Finland.

---

[99] Upton, op.cit.,pp.154–157,

[100]Hannes Ignatius was declaredly in spirit anti- Russian, but his military traditions were those of the imperial ex-officer class.

[101] Frans Eemil Sillanpää, *Hurskas kurjuus,* Helsinki (Otava), 1955 ed., originally published in 1919.

[102] Blomstedt, op.cit., p.210.

[103] The first reference of Mannerheim to "the Finnish farmers' army" seems to have been in his proclamation of 30.1.1918 to *Russian* troops stating that his Finnish army was not fighting them! Marvin Rintala, *Four Finns,* Berkeley & LA (Univ. of California Press), 1969, p.30. But see below, notes 104 & 105. Stig Jägerskiöld believes that a "quiet unperturbability" in Mannerheim won the respect of his Ostrobothnian peasant soldiers: *Mannerheim.Rauhan vuosina,* Helsinki (Otava), 1973, p.60.

[104] Ylikangas, op.cit., pp.21 & 24.

[105] Some Russians still fought alongside the Finnish Reds.

As to that revolution, the Bolsheviks had had difficulty in calling up sufficient troops from Petrograd to start it even when they were giving advice to do so in the tense days of the November strike on account of the critical situation in Petrograd itself.[106] In truth, the Finnish Whites got much more out of the old, doomed White Russia than the Russian revolutionaries of the extreme Left could give their potential kindred in Finland. Enckell and his coterie derailed the constitutionalism of the Left in Finland, while ex-Tsarist officers destroyed the revolution of the Left there. Interestingly enough, at the time of the Enabling Act, Kautsky gave one of his rare pieces of advice to the Finns. This somewhat out-of-touch figure had blamed the Finnish Social Democrats for not throwing in their hand with a total *Russian* revolution.[107] as if the great collapse of European capitalism was imminent, a collapse in which the breaking-free of the nationalities had little significance for him.[108] In broad terms, the demiurge of the revolutionary forces in Finland might have agreed that Russian Tsarist oppression and the Finnish upper class had been in practical collaboration against the workers even when these two sides were quarrelling over constitutional details of how Finland should relate to the Russian authorities. The cause of the workers in Finland was nevertheless Finland and Finnish social change. In 1909. devotees of traditional Finnish constitutionalism like C.F.A Langhoff, the minister state secretary in St. Petersburg might call to see the British ambassador to plead for "Finland" and the great parliamentarian, Leo Mechelin wrote a letter to the *Times* about the same cause,[109] but three years later, in 1912, the Social Democrat, O.W. Kuusinen was boiling over in the Finnish Parliament about the sins of the *Finnish* officials in the department of industry who were neglecting the truths about the abnormally long hours worked in the factories of southern Finland.[110] Yes, you might pass laws (as the 8-hour day was passed on 16 November 1917), but what kind of officials would enforce them? This was the question and it was a question of the keen edge of revolution, of the need felt for power rather than compromise.

This example, however, is a key pointer to another problem of the 1918 revolution, which is the importance of locality. Ylikangas has mentioned that the Ostrobothnian peasants who joined the Whites did not, on the whole, have to endure the same set of circumstances as the crofters of southern Finland, let alone the factory workers there. Large industrial complexes were

---

106 Upton, op.cit. p.142

107 Hannu Soikkanen, op.c it., pp.215 This was at the time of the Enabling Act

108 He regarded it as "separatism": ibid, p.216.

109 Maude, unpublished Ph.D. thesis (Univ. of London),1970, pp. 340 & 267.

110 Under the protection of parliamentary privilege, Kuusinen named these officials as Tigerstedt, Solitander, and Paloheimo. *Valtiopäivät. Pöytäkirjat*, II,1912, pp.791–796.

rare in Ostrobothnia and so, too, were big estates.[111] Additionally, most of northern Finland at that time was not involved in the conflict. But the 45% of the total Finnish population that Ylikangass finds were *represented* by the Reds was an area that also contained many Whites. Class was the determining factor in the localities, some areas were more uniform than others, partly depending on where you draw the lines. At the time of the November strike, Tokoi—almost in admonition—told the trade union congress that they represented 170,000 organized workers.[112] But as a force this was still a minority of the population. It may be argued that revolutions are made by minorities,[113] a piece of knowledge contained in that old Marxist phrase about the "dictatorship of the proletariat." In any case, geographically speaking, the situation in Finland had a rough and ready resemblance to the variegated situation in Europe as a whole. Most European workers had gone to war in 1914 and when revolutions broke out in various places, towards the end of the war or after, they had a haphazard character with little common geography, either internally or externally. There *were* internationals. There were several of them! But the *institutional life* of the individual states, cherishing the older traditions, developed its own strength, sometimes demonically

A Constitutional Solution?

The parliamentary combination that passed the two key laws on the 8-hour working day and the municipal franchise reform was very close to that which had passed the Enabling Act in July. In embryo, therefore, the possibility could have been envisaged of a Social Democrat- Agrarian Union government which would have included members of the progressive wing of the Young Finn party. Some such has been suggested by an English historian with the historian's hindsight.[114] Objectively speaking, this might have been possible. Subjectively speaking, the long hiatus in parliamentary rule from July to November soured the Social Democrats. The coterie who sacked the

[111] Ylikangas, op.cit.,pp.21–24.

[112] Upton, op.cit., p.147.

[113] Angrily, Moorehead, op.cit. p.284, points out that the Russian Constituent Assembly in January 1918 consisted of "only Left-wing political parties" and was then suppressed by a Left-wing party representing a minority, the Bolshevik Party.

[114] Upton, op.cit. p 169, but without the Agrarians. He torpedoed this suggestion in the same paragraph he recommended it.

Parliament over the Enabling Act in July 1917, led principally by Enckell, bear their own share of blame in this matter.[115]

On 28 January 1918, a Red revolutionary government was set up, all members of which had to belong to the Finnish Social Democratic Party. The revolution had started on the previous day.[116] Attempting to explain—even to himself—a few months later as to why this "unnecessary" revolution had occurred, the Agrarian leader, Santeri Alkio, could only suggest that the revolution had been caused by the pernicious influence of the "hypnotism" of Russian soldiery and their revolutionary fervour.[117] In contrasting the two nations, the Russians and the Finns, the Agrarian leader touched on a theme that had fascinated Lenin several years earlier. Even as late as 1913, Lenin argued that, in spite of recent Tsarist oppression, the Finns retained their "culture, educational level, freedom, literacy, educated womanhood, and so on" while the Finnish struggle against Tsarism might help to arouse the Russians from their slavery.[118] This was not a piece of racism, but a consciousness of the historical difference in the moulding of the two nations in which the arch-enemy was not so much capitalism as an *antiquated* form of Russian despotism called Tsarism

In the this light, it is hardly surprising that having a called a revolution the Finnish Social Democratic leaders (but primarily O.W. Kuusinen) began work on a new constitution for an independent Finland. Optimistically, the revolutionary leaders also drafted a constitution for a parliamentary democracy, the structure of which indicated that what was envisaged as a permanent solution was not a one-party state. Osmo Rinta-Tassi has maintained that the optimism behind this constitutional draft rested upon the fact that in the 1916 election the Social Democrats had received almost half the votes[119] (and, in fact, 103 out of 200 seats). The constitution was only a proposal and was never in force, owing to the fact that the revolution was, throughout its brief *existence*, battling for survival.

---

[115] Eino Ketola, *Kansalliseen Kansanvaltaan*, Helsinki (Tammi), pp. 230–233 lays much stress on Enckell's responsibility for the deterioration of the political situation in Finland after the July dissolution of Parliament.

[116] Osmo Rinta-Tassi, *Kansanvaltuuskunta punaisen Suomen hallituksena*, Helsinki (Valtion painatuskeskus) 1986, p.104 & Jussi T.Lappalainen, *Punakaartiensota* I, Helsinki (Valtion painatuskeskus), 1981, p.49.

[117] Aulis J. Alanen, *Santeri Alkio*, Helsinki (Werner Söderström), 1976, p. 495.

[118] V.I. Lenin, *Lenin Suomesta*, Moskova (Kustannusliike Progress), 1983, p.44.The volume is a collection of Lenin's references to Fnland in his speeches and writings.

[119] Rinta-Tassi, op.cit., p.110.

It is, however, worth noting what was then devised.[120] The Finnish state was to be a republic (article 1).[121] The nature of this republic went straight back to the Enabling Act of July 1917 (article 2), for "the supreme governmental power" was to be exercised by the national Parliament of Finland. It is true that there was also going to be "a highest executive state organ" (articles 58 & 59), but headed only by a "chairman" (*esimies*), the whole organ being under the supervision of Parliament. The members of this executive, "the People's Delegation" (*kansanvaltuuskunta)* were to be elected for a three-year period by Parliament and from Parliament. They could participate in the debates of Parliament, including the debates of its committees, and could make proposals, but they could not vote when the final decisions were to be made in Parliament (article 60). When the "People's Delegation" made its own decisions, they could not do so without the presence of members of the parliamentary supervisory board (article 62).

The difference between the role of Parliament and Delegation could even be explained in Ståhlbergian terms (he undoubtedly wanted no truck with it). But, in any case, Parliament was to make the law and the Delegation was to use the law (*lainkäyttö*). And that was all. The Delegation was subject to Parliament's will to be given a caution if it did not follow that will. Should the Delegation persist in its interpretation, it needed *the confirmation of Parliament* for it and when Parliament was not in session a consultation could occur between the Delegation, the parliamentary supervisory board, and the finance committee of Parliament—or Parliament could be recalled (article 65). There was, in short, a mood of politics in all this and that mood was in favour of a powerful, vigilant Parliament. It was noteworthy that in the constitutional draft there was no mention of a presidential power: the chairman of the Delegation was chosen for three years and could not immediately have a second term (article 59).

If the constitution embodied a stand against any extremes of executive power, it also strengthened the role of the citizenry vis-à-vis Parliament itself. The constitution contained the right of initiative for a law proposal of at least 10,000 of the citizens (article 45). Where Parliament did not accord this in a particular case, then one-third of the members of Parliament or at least a number of citizens equivalent to one-twentieth of the votes cast in the previous

---

[120] The Red Constitution will be found in a collection of texts published by the Whites in 1918. It is entitled *Kapinan aikana painetut Suomen Asetuskokoelman Numerot 10–33.*Helsinki (Suomen Senaatin kirjapaino), 1918.

[121] Svinhufvud's regency ("Holder of the Supreme Power") was, in contrast, a derivation from the law of 1772, when Finland was a part of Sweden, which declared that on the extinction of the ruling house a regency should be appointed, i.e., as a preservation of monarchical powers and power.

election could require a referendum upon it. The influence of the Swiss constitution, often a favourite with the revolutionaries, is apparent.[122] It may be suggested that the use of the referendum would be a substitute for street action outside Parliament. Should all these safeguards fail, then the right of the citizens to rebel by force against the tyranny of a Parliament whose *majority* denied the constitution was writ clear (article 43). The Swiss constitution did not grant its citizens that final right, but John Locke did.[123]

The liberal nature of the draft constitution is evident and was matched by articles on freedom of religion (still restricted in Finland—Jews could not marry there, for example) and on the freedom of the word and freedom of association (articles 6, 7, and 8). The sole socio-economic right mentioned was the right to strike (article 10). But a number of laws and decrees in addition to the constitution laid down the rights of women to apply for posts in central and local government, and abolished the decree of 1865 which had made the one-year contract for agricultural work unbreakable.

What more? It has been noted already that much of the leadership of the Social Democratic revolutionary movement did not believe that a fundamental restructuring of society was possible at the moment. This was the view of Oskari Tokoi, Matti Turkia, and Kuusinen.[124] The view was challenged by Eero Haapalainen, who believed in the possibility of going from a take-over of political power into a social revolution.[125] In the draft constitution, an innocuous sounding article 9 was all that there was about the economic transformation required for fundamental social change; this read as follows: "the state and other public bodies have the right to acquire property and start or participate in economic enterprises." The reality of the situation was that the revolutionaries quite early decided to take over many enterprises, though with very mixed success It is worth remembering that State enterprise as such, or state investment in private firms, was not unknown in Finland, when large amounts of capital were needed.

[122] Markku Suksi, *Bringing in the People. A Comparison of Constitutional Forms and Practices of the Referendum*, Dordrecht (Martinus Nijhoff:Kluwer), 1993, esp.pp.220–226. Apart from the 1931 referendum repealing prohibition, the referendum as a powerful political instrument *in an advisory capacity* was not used till the referendum on Finland's entry into the EU in 1994.

[123] John Locke, *An Essay Concerning the True Original, Extent and End of Civil Government* (1690) in *Social Contract. Essays by Locke, Hume and Rouseau, with an Introduction by Sir Ernest Barker*, London & New York (OUP), p.197:"He, therefore, who may resist, must be allowed to strike." From Locke's gloss on George Berkeley (Barclay).

[124] Upton, op.cit., pp.148, 255. The latter admitted his mistake a year later. Kuusinen, op. cit., pp. 7–9, in his condemnation of Social Democracy.

[125] ibid., p.148 & 168.

For the sake of getting industrial production going, a directive from the revolutionary government on 11 February 1918 allowed production to start either at the expense of the state or owner. Rinta-Tassi has found that 163 factories were appropriated in consequence and some farms. The unpleasant and in the end brutal case of the workers' control of the Kymi factories under Valter Vihriä has already been mentioned. Baron Hjalmar Linder's property, whether industrial or agricultural, was also taken over, and the works of H.G. Stenius.[126] Kuusinen, in his *mea culpa,* suggested in 1919 that socialization would have been relatively easy in 1918 because "of the simple nature of the conditions of production," the centralization of the paper industry (ten firms would have been sufficient to appropriate), the hatred of the peasantry for the owners of the sawmills, and the fact that the state owned two-thirds of the forest land.[127] This juxtaposition of advantages, the first of which was somewhat surprising in a Marxist narration, would have needed for its utilization, again according to Kuusinen, the strength and determination of "the dictatorship of the armed proletariat."[128] This was said later by Kuusinen when recanting on the constitutional model he had worked on in February 1918.The Agrarian leader, Santeri Alkio, who had struggled so hard to come to terms with the Social Democrats in the summer and autumn of 1917, may not have heard of this Socialist constitutionalism of February 1918. In any case, once the revolution got under way, the Finnish Reds had behaved like Bolsheviks in Alkio's opinion, "seizing property (the dread of all Agrarians, G.M.) and shedding blood."[129]

This chapter has nevertheless to end with Kautsky and to pay tribute this time to a certain revision in Kautsky' own thinking. Reference has been made here to an institutional strength in aspects of Finnish political and administrative life (by those capable of manipulating it). But one institution had to be built up through revolution and counter-revolution. In the end, both Whites and Reds had to try to create their armies by conscription. The winners were the professionals, the Finnish officers from the Tsarist army and the Finnish Jaegers trained in Germany (even given the status of a Prussian battalion!)[130] as well as the German forces who came over in April 1918. Various shades of Whites were to create the Finnish army, the institution of last resort in Finnish life.

---

[126] Rinta-Tassi, op.cit., pp.372–376. See also note 21 and pages 5–6 of this text.
[127] Kuusinen, op.cit., p.15.
[128] ibid., p.8.
[129] Alanen, op.cit., p. 495.
[130] On this, see Matti Lauerma, *Kuninkaallinen Preussin Jääkäripatalijoona 27:Vaihheet ja vaikutukset,*Porvoo-Helsinki, 1966.

In a previously–mentioned later text of Kautsky's, he stressed that while France and Germany were constitutionalist states they were also military states and once the military road had been chosen, it could not be reversed through the ballot-box.[131] These remarks have sometimes been appropriate to Finland, though Kautsky scorned the place.

They were appropriate to Finland in January 1918. The Senatorial government had scuttled out of Helsinki for Vasa several days before the Red revolution broke out. The Whites' military committee made its decision to move to Vasa on 17 January.[132] Vasa, a town on the west coast of Ostrobothnia, was a White outpost. Thereto this government awaited the success of Mannerheim's army and the German army (which arrived on the Finnish mainland in April). Many of the foot-soldiers in the German army were undoubtedly Social Democrats. But it made no difference, certainly not to Mannerheim, whose reluctance to accept the aid of the German military had no reference to its privates' opinions. The German army at that moment of history was, in any case, still well-disciplined. Apart from Mannerheim's egocentricity, "he could manage himself," the principal element in his opposition to the Germans was his belief that Finland should take the West rather than Germany into account. In the history of independent Finland, this problem was to become the crux of a festering sore. Even in 1918, when Mannerheim travelled to the West, only Winston Churchill showed immediate enthusiasm for Mannerheim's plan to attack Petrograd.[133]

But within and without Finland there was another festering sore of even greater moment than the indifference of the West to quashing Bolshevism at its source. And this festering sore was spawned in Finland. The revolutionaries in Finland had taken Kautsky as seriously as they could. It was commonplace in Finland to look for inspiration in the German-speaking world: the Finnish educated class went to study there. Finland itself, however, did not have the political theory to cope with the emergence of a factory-based working class. Its own class structure was based, politically, on the ancient concept of "estates" till the reform of 1906. Searching for truth in the works of Kautsky (and an enormous part of his production was translated into Finnish) was not easy, for he was obsessed by the great industrial countries and by what he felt was *der Todenkampf des Kleinbetriebe* ("the death struggle of the small firm") and he was unaware of the fact that the nationalist movements of eastern, central and

---

131 Kautsky, *Köyhälistön vallankumous*,p.27.

132 Screen, op.cit., p.150.

133 Churchill was Secretary for War, but the Prime Minister, David Lloyd George was by now opposed to the commitment of further British troops on Russian soil: John Roderick Bullen, "The Royal Navy in the Baltic.1918–1920," London Univ. Ph. D thesis, 1983, pp.3 4–36.

northern Europe were prepared to go to great lengths to cherish the agrarian proletariat,[134] once they gained control of the state. In Finland, the attempt to provide land for the peasantry was to produce confusion (to say the least) among the Right.[135] Alternatively, the attempt meant an extension of private enterprise among some of the previous dispossessed. Finland was struggling to develop its politics, but it already had a deep legal culture, which fed these politics. The core of this culture was *pacta sunt servanda* ("contracts are to be honoured "). The application of this legal saw was not a straightforward matter, as the Right pointed out. But it was easier to accept than the Social Democrat Edvard Gylling's proposal to nationalize the land and then rent it out.

Gylling's solution to the whole agrarian problem, whether of the crofters with their labour services, or for the landless, rested on land nationalization. It was lambasted in Parliament as a Marxist exercise to draw rural labour into urban employment, thus strengthening the industrial proletariat. A member of the liberal Young Finn party, Rudolf Holsti, ridiculed it as part of the false promise of a future based on necessitarian terms—one which ignored the complexity of the European agrarian economy.[136] Another Social Democrat, Oskari Tokoi, was even fiercer and defended the larger land unit as against peasant agriculture.[137]

The Left, with all its manifold solutions, thus fell apart in the success of the counter revolution Santeri Alkio, the Agrarian leader, who had been so close to cooperation with the Social Democrats, had rapidly grown hostile to the Bolshevik influence on the Finnish Social Democrats. Yet, after Lundson's trickery in Parliament, Alkio was willing to listen to Gylling's suggestion for cooperation between the Social Democrats and Agrarians. In the light of Gylling's basic beliefs about agriculture, this could only have been a *political* deal, even though against Kautskyist principles.

---

[134] Karl Kautsky,*Der Erfurter Programm in seinem grundsätzlichen Theil*, Stuttgart (J.H.Dietz), 1899 ed., pp.14–30. The copy used by the author of this text (from the library of the Univ. of Turku) was once owned by the Finnish historian J.K. Danielson-Kalmari. He was not a revolutionary. Kautsky's comments on the development of the revolutionary situation in Finland, published in Olavi Puro's journal "Kuluttajan Lehti" on 28.2.1918 (Hannu Soikkanen, op.cit., pp.315 & 644) came too late in the day and in any case
seem to have contained the usual denigration of the agrarian proletariat characteristic of Kautsky.

[135] See chapter II.

[136] Statements of Edvard Gylling and Rudolf Holsti in the Finnish Parliament. *Valtiopäivät.:* Pöytäkirjat, 17.3.1914, pp.376–398.

[137] Oskari Tokoi, *Piirteitä maatalouskysymyksestämme*, Pori (Osuuskunta kehitys), Pori, 1911, pp.86–87.

The heart of Alkio's hostility was due to the violence and land appropriation of the Bolsheviks.[138] Armed Finnish Red Guards, whom Alkio undoubtedly regarded as under Bolshevik influence, broke open his discussion with Gylling, and proved Alkio's point.[139]

But the shattered population[140] of revolutionary Finland harboured truths, in however distorted a form, whether economic or political. As to the latter, whether they had fled to Russia, or stayed—cowed—in the Finnish homeland, they were constantly aware of a nexus between Finland and Russia. So was Mannerheim. He had wanted to solve the relationship with Russia by reconstituting Russia through a conquest of Petrograd. The Finnish Communists wanted to solve the relationship with Russia by reconstituting Finland in a quasi-Soviet image. There was a middle way out of this either-or, but it was not to be apparent for many a year.

---

[138] See this chapter, note 129.

[139] Arvo Ylärakkola, *Edvard Gylling*, Helsinki (Otava), 1976, p.54.

[140] In Jämsä and its surrounds, where there had not been a previous Red terror, the Whites killed over 30 members of the Left. Thereafter, the area became for years one of the strongest Communist areas in the country: *Helsingin Sanomat, 19.2 & 16.3. 1995.*

CHAPTER 2
POWER AND RETREAT OF POWER. ANOTHER SPRING PARADE

Nine years have passed. There is to be another parade, as there now is every year, for it is 16 May 1927. But General Mannerheim did not attend, having become a *persona non grata* to many of the political forces and personalities of the newly-independent state. So low had he fallen in his own self-esteem that two years earlier, he had even thought of a job in the French Foreign Legion.[1]

Twenty-eight different sections of the armed forces plus five aeroplanes took part in or above the parade. There were four tanks rumbling along, but most troops were marching or on horseback. Key words in the newspaper reports were *reipas* (perhaps better translated this time as "brisk") and *ryhdikäs* ("straight-backed"). In connection with the parade, however, the motorized battalion had its flag blessed by a chaplain of the forces holding the rank of dean. He gave a homily on the subject of fear. He started with Isaiah (41.10), moved rapidly on to St. Paul, mentioning in passing that even an eye-surgeon might tremble with fear in his innards before embarking on an operation, but, in the case of the motorized battalion, the flag he was blessing might inspire them to sacrifice for their nation and land. The examples were mixed, but the point was made. Estonians, officers and cadets, were observing it all, while on the steps of the university stood the female sellers of white flowers.

The President, Lauri Kristian Relander, an Agrarian, should have addressed the parade, but he was ill and in his place the prime minister, Väinö Tanner, a Social Democrat, gave the word. It was amazing. Less than ten years before, his party had led a revolution (though he had not gone with them). His very brief message was that permanent peace had not been attained in the world, so armies were needed. He then sped away in a car. Cartoons later appeared in the press, showing the White civil guards, who took up the end of the parade, smiling to themselves.[2] They had reason to smile, for in 1919 the Social Democrats, in their minimal programme, had demanded the suppression of the civil guards. And, in April 1920, Tanner himself had been

---

[1] Screen, op.cit., pp.240–243.

[2] One such cartoon is reproduced in Hannu Soikkanen, *Kohti Kansanvaltaa, I,* Helsinki (Suomen Sosialidemokraattinen puolue), 1975, p.453.

roughed up in a Satakunta village by *a group of civil guards* led by a local "man of law," Sheriff Wahlroos, a former lieutenant in the Tsar's army.[3]

As to the May parade, the leading paper of the Social Democratic Party, *Suomen Sosiaalidemokraatti,* was not pleased at Tanner's presence. It reminded its readers of the White Terror and called the march "a celebration of bloody memories." In commenting on this, the *Helsingin Sanomat* felt that—in the interests of making the nation whole again—the day of this annual celebration (named, in fact, "the parade of honouring the flag") could possibly be changed. But the general line of Socialist opposition to such a parade, the *Helsingin Sanomat* rejected with the rhetorical question: what would have been the fate of the working class if the Finnish rebels and their Russian allies had won? It was a telling point. The conservative organ *Uusi Suomi* had a couple of other telling points. It noted the absence of the rest of the Social Democratic minority government (without mentioning the absence of General Mannerheim), while its pen-name Olli, with reference to the split in the Social Democratic Party over Tanner's presence, said that he might be able to pay a fine to get back into his own party, as White workers had to pay a fine to get a job in a Red-unionized workplace.[4]

Prime minister Tanner, a graduate in law of the University of Helsinki, had not participated in the 1918 revolution. He had been a Senator along with the bourgeois members in the spring and summer of 1917 and had, with reluctance resigned, one of the last to do so. He had refused, once the revolution broke out, to take the position of head of finances in the revolutionary government. He was an old-style constitutionalist, for whom the constitution was greater than the party. Since a section of the SDP was nominally constitutionalist—and Tanner genuinely so—his party was able to participate in the general election of March 1919. They polled 80 seats: a remarkable achievement, only 12 seats less than in September 1917. This was all the *more* remarkable since many of the potential SDP voters were over the border in Soviet Russia, while in Finland 38,000 were still denied their civil rights for serving the revolution.[5] It was, Väinö Tanner, the leader now of this broken party, who was to illustrate best of all the wider import of Ståhlberg's proposals for the relations of the parties.

[3] Väinö Tanner, *Kahden maailmansodan välissä,* Helsinki (Tammi), 1966, pp.11–13.
[4] *Helsingin Sanomat,* 17.5 & 18.5.1927 & *Uusi Suomi,* 17.5.1927.
[5] Hannu Soikkanen, op.cit., p.356.

Ståhlberg, the Pragmatic Theoretician

In July 1919 Ståhlberg had become president of Finland. In party-political terms, the core of Ståhlberg's policy of reconciliation,[6] was his acceptance of the Finnish Social Democratic Party as a constitutionalist party. But for this to occur, he had to ensure that the structure of the Finnish state could comprehend this latter Party, and could comprehend even his own kind of party, the liberal-minded Progressives,[7] who might form a shield for the constitutionalism of the surviving Social Democratic Party, while the environment of the new state had still to be one in which the reaction could also be soothed. So Finland needed the republic, which it had originally thought of as its state form.

The White government, under Pehr Evind Svinhufvud, having got the country's independence from Lenin, backtracked on the republic in the days of the counter-revolution.[8] Instead, they plumped for a monarchy as a kind of complement after calling the German forces in. Thus, they called in, too, a German prince, initially hoping for a son of the German Kaiser. But the Kaiser's cousin would do. He started, still in his homeland, taking Finnish lessons. The collapse of imperial Germany, including General Erich von Ludendorff's Eastern policy, put paid to the Prince of Hesse's ambitions to be a king. He decided not to come.[9]

From the summer of 1918, Ståhlberg had been in the forefront of the fight against him or any other possible monarchical candidate. His view was that this was tantamount to inviting reaction in. He feared the sequence of reaction, another revolution, and a further bout of reaction.[10] Ståhlberg's main argumentation for the republic therefore concerned the making of Finnish society a whole again. But, as matter of fact, that was the monarchists' point, too. *What was at issue was that fundamental question of political endeavour, the characterization of the state.* Was this to be obtained by an over-arching structure or by a structure of component parts?

---

[6] See chapter I, p. 8.

[7] In December 1918, the two former parties, the Young Finns and Old Finns, reformed as Progressives and National Coalition Party, the more conservative members of the Young Finns Party joining the National Coalition Party.

[8] The Agrarian leader, Kyösti Kallio, recalled how even after the suppression of the Reds, the White government had still planned for only a temporary president. Kari Hokkanen, *Kyösti Kallio 1873–1929*, I, Helsinki-Porvoo, (Söderström), 1986, p.304.

[9] His final letter of withdrawal did not arrive till 20 December 1918. Göran von Bonsdorff & Frank Jernström, *Från Självständighet till Lappo. Svenska folkpartiet, II*, Ekenäs (Svenska folkpartiet), 1984, p.25.

[10] Blomstedt, op. cit., p.353. Ståhlberg's article in the *Helsingin Sanomat*, 7.5.1918.

In his speech to Parliament of 12 June 1918, Ståhlberg negatively portrayed a monarch as being "above and beyond the influence of the parties."[11] It was, of course, precisely for this reason that the monarchists wanted a monarch! In their baggage, too, was rejection of the reforms of 1905–1906 that had brought in a unicameral legislature. This time Ståhlberg, whatever he had once believed about the efficacy of a bicameral legislature,[12] and whatever he had said about the failure of the Enabling Act to preserve the executive, now came out as a defender of the party system in Parliament, the constitutionalist Left realising that he would not betray the unicameral legislature on which the party system would be based.

Ståhlberg spoke for his liberalism. And in doing so, he spoke for his Party. To speak in the vernacular of Finnish society he had his own cow in the ditch ("oma lehmänsä ojassa"). The Young Finns in becoming the Progressive Party did not turn themselves from a minority into a majority. In the parliamentary election of 1916 the Young Finns had fallen from 29 to 23 seats in a Parliament of 200 members: in the 1919 election the Progressive Party, their successors, were to come back only to 26 seats. The Social Democrats in 1916 had, indeed, won 103 seats and in 1919 were to fall to 80, but this was remarkable in the background of a failed revolution that tainted their party. The Agrarians, who had won only 19 seats in 1916, were to triumph in 1919 with 42 seats. The upshot of this was that if the Progressive Party had to have any clout in the Finnish political system, they had to have it through a presidency and/or a *coalition* government. Was the presidency only a monarchy by other means, simply without the hereditary element? The presidency was sold to the monarchist Right as a strong executive that made a monarch unnecessary. But the core of the Ståhlbergian solution was this: *that government by coalition was the cement of the party system once the party system was to be the cement that would hold society together.* There is an irony in this. For a rapprochement between the SDP and the Agrararians might have helped to forestall revolution in the tense period of late 1918. Now coalition was to be used to make parliamentary government weaker than ever along the lines imposed on the first unicameral legislature in 1906 by the old constitutionalists; that is to say, the use of *qualified* majorities for all longer-term legislation, which a fractious coalition party can prevent by a few votes (under proportional representation).

The poet has found in another context in another country that "the centre does not hold." But Ståhlberg found, very tentatively, a way of making this happen. It is true that the conservative forces went into a party of their own,

---

[11] Ståhlberg, op.cit., p.181.

[12] See note 92, p.22.

which they called "the coalition party" (nowadays, "the National Coalition Party"). The word has held a fascination of its own. But such a coalition- party was never to give the conservatives any kind of majority. Nor has this occurred when, on several occasions, the conservative forces have also assumed that their party is a party of ability ("kykypuolue"). To use these talents, they have had to be in a coalition *with other parties*. The Progressives were also a party of the educated classes, but of those of a more liberal persuasion. As it turned out, they, too, had always to work with other parties.

Most difficult was it for the Social Democratic Party to come round to the working of a coalition government—and this, in spite of the fact, that they were the true heirs of Ståhlberg's thinking. The latter built the necessity for coalitions upon the two control elements introduced by the Grand Old Man of Finnish constitutionalism, Leo Mechelin, in accepting the unicameral legislature in 1906: namely that permanent legislation should require a two-thirds qualified majority vote in such a Parliament, while constitutional change should require a five-sixth majority vote.[13] But in 1916, on a low poll, the Social Democrats gained 103 seats out of a possible 200; in short, a simple majority. After the March revolution in Russia in 1917, the Finnish bourgeois leaders were prepared to grant the SDP all the seats in the Senate (government in Finland). Timorously, the SDP leaders refused and went in a coalition Senate as *individuals* along with bourgeois colleagues. But when in July the Enabling Act was passed, bourgeois figures like Enckell and Nevanlinna awoke to the danger that the Social Democrats would want to pack the Senate with their members; in other words, present Finland with revolution by constitution—just as Kautsky always envisaged might be possible.

Ståhlberg's assumption, after the failed revolution in Finland, was that this ought never to be possible again. The counter-revolution worked for him by shattering for the time being the SDP. Instead, the SDP was expected to be conciliated by entering coalition governments with sympathetic parties having *a controlling significance* over such governments.[14] On the other hand, support might flow from parties not even in the coalition but satisfied on specific issues. Whatever the complexity of alignments, Ståhlberg had found a way through based on a respect for minorities that might lead to the creation of

---

[13] On the Mechelin influence in Ståhlberg's thinking, see Antero Jyränki, *Lakien laki*,Helsinki (Lakimiesliiton kustannus), 1989, p.486 et seq.

[14] Commentators sympathetic to coalition governments seem to have difficulty in classifying the Finnish governmental coalitions: Abram de Swaan, *Coalition Theories and Cabinet Formation*. Amsterdam (Elsevier), 1973, pp.252–253. They do not fit Riker's "minimal winning coalitions" either: correspondingly, his concept of an "oversized coalition" does not fit Finnish politics necessarily. See William Riker, *The Theory of Coalition Politics*, New Haven (Yale Univ.Press), 1967, p.66.

diverse types of majority coalition governments. It was a pleasing concoction, but whether it would work or not remained to be seen. At any rate, Ståhlberg had been able to lay down some factors of trust for government, he believed.

But the Social Democrats themselves were slow to buy into this. Among other things, they were still mesmerised by Kautsky, who did not like coalitions till 1926! The lure of gaining a majority once more had not disappeared.[15] That went even for a majority in opposition.

Ståhlberg now knew what he was doing. In spring 1919, Ståhlberg refused to be sidetracked by Mannerheim into becoming prime minister and wrote to him to say that. Even Mannerheim agreed that Ståhlberg's work in drafting a constitution (with its *qualified* majoritarian inhibitions) was of immediate importance, emphasizing the possibility that a *simple majority* of Social Democrats and Agrarians might be in formation and give Mannerheim himself trouble.[16]

The Kingly Mannerheim

It would be wrong to think that the republic was set up again simply because of the persuasive power of Ståhlberg. The republic rose once more because of the fall of a great Power, the fall of imperial Germany. This was a question of the widest import: even some republicans had wanted a German alliance without a German monarch.[17] Nor did monarchism die because the Prince of Hesse pulled out. It reeled, however. Even Mannerheim agreed to be a candidate in the July 1919 *presidential* election. In pleading for the republic, and in opposing Mannerheim, the alternative candidate in the election, Ståhlberg, laid down an important corollary to the republican standpoint. Since the monarch would have been a foreigner, he would have looked for support abroad "and would have been a direct danger for the independence of Finland."[18] Ståhlberg did not accuse Mannerheim of wanting to be the monarch. Mannerheim, who had been appointed regent of the Finnish state on 12 December 1918, had nevertheless that much of the monarch about him that he considered a *coup d'état* of his own in 1919, provided the National Coalition Party would back him.[19] It remains to be said that the projected

[15] In the columns of the *Suomen Sosialidemokraatti* Hannes Ryömä pleaded for cooperation with the bourgeois Centre (e.g. with the Progressives), but the secretary of the SDP, Taavi Tainio, was reluctant: Hannu Soikkanen, op.cit.,pp.323–324 & 321–322.

[16] Blomstedt, op,cit., p.374.

[17] Kallio's republicanism took in a German alliance, though it has to be said that in the early autumn of 1918 Kallio's own republicanism wavered a bit. Hokkanen, op.cit., pp. 302–305.

[18] Ståhlberg, op.cit., p.180.

[19] Screen, op.cit., pp.201–202.

coup, inspired by the Activists, was stimulated by the correct appraisal that Mannerheim was not going to win the July presidential election. If this were the case, it would dash the hopes of attacking Petrograd and finishing off the Bolsheviks once and for all. Making a king out of Mannerheim does not seem to have been a concretely expressed goal in this plan.

But there always remained something of the kingly about him: Rudolf Walden and Hannes Ignatius are said to have considered him for king even in 1918, before the *coup d'etat* project of the summer of 1919, and Ignatius, at any rate, continued in December 1919 to urge Mannerheim to take power by force. The first reason Ignatius gave in justification was his fear of Left (constitutionalist Social Democrats) and Centre cooperation;[20] in short he tried to utilize the very fears Ståhlberg had played on with Mannerheim but this time to stiffen the general's military courage. But control by force of Finland's internal politics was only to be a prelude to the military expansion of the Finnish state for Ignatius–and this is just what Mannerheim's opponents in Finland were becoming afraid of in contemplating Mannerheim's own vast ambitions. In mid-June, supported by a group of Activists, Mannerheim had dreamed more concretely of using the Finnish armed forces to help restore the Russian Whites to Petrograd.[21] In consequence, for many Finns who were becoming antagonistic to him, *he* had now become "the foreigner," monarch or not, who would plunge Finland into danger.[22] But there was something in it for Finland, too, namely the annexation of East Karelia (Russian Karelia) to the Finnish state. It had never been in the old Grand Duchy of Finland, but the language spoken there was closely related to Finnish, that is, the Karelian language (this was then spoken in some older parishes of the old Grand Duchy, for example, Suojärvi). It was this matter, possession of East Karelia, that excited Mannerheim's Finnish supporters much more than the conquest

---

[20] Matti Lappalainen, *Hannes Ignatius. Mannerheimin harmaaa eminenssi*, Helsinki (Werner Söderström) 2005, pp.332 & 346. The sub-title refers to Ignatius as "Mannerheim's grey eminence." Additional support for the suspicion of the kingly ambitions surrounding the figure of Mannerheim may be found in the negative views of Santeri Alkio, on which Alanen, op.cit., p.544, where Alkio states the danger that Mannerheim might become "a dictator of the monarchists" even if he failed to bring a monarch to Finland.

[21] It is for this reason that Penttilä's analysis of Mannerheim as a "turncoat" is wrong. See note 8, page 2. In answer to the present author's question on 24.10.01 to J.E.O Screen, the English biographer of Mannerheim, Screen stated that in 1919 Russia was Mannerheim's overriding concern.

[22] The fears of Alkio, the Agrarian leader, that Mannerheim as regent or president would pursue "foreign ambitions" were contained in his phrase that the regent was too "kinglike": "should be a Finnish man." Blomstedt, op.cit, p.377.

of Petrograd.[23] It has to be admitted that possession of East Karelia was a goal adopted at one time by nearly all politically-minded Finns, whether of the Left, Right, or Centre.[24] But by the summer and autumn of 1919, the achievement of this end seemed to be a policy hovering on adventurism.

The scheme suggested to Mannerheim by the Activists in mid-June was, first of all, to use the royal powers of the 1772 Swedish constitution when Finland had been an integral part of Sweden.[25] His appointment as regent in December 1918 could be interpreted as a stand-in for a monarch.[26] The royal powers of the Swedish constitution granted the right to dissolve Parliament and declare war. A group of Activists, fearing that Mannerheim would not win the forthcoming presidential election against Ståhlberg, wanted Mannerheim to defer confirming the new constitution drafted by his opponent Ståhlberg, briefly dissolve Parliament, then confirm the constitution, and declare war in the temporary absence of an obstreperous Parliament. Mannerheim went along with this on one condition: the National Coalition Party should back him. But they would not do this. Their leader, Lauri Ingman, pointed out that once the constitution was confirmed, the right of making war would be transferred from president to Parliament.[27] In the end, therefore, a constitutionalism triumphed.

Mannerheim had risen to power in Finland in 1918 on the success of the counter-revolution, whose forces he led. He resigned almost immediately after victory, angered at the White government's plans to have a reorganization of the Finnish armed forces by the Germans. Mannerheim had not wanted the Germans in and the calling-in of German military help had been the work of the civilian government over the head of Mannerheim himself, who had agreed to command the White forces on condition that no foreign troops were used. Later, he found that German troops were necessary, but his crony Hannes Ignatius had to work hard to convince him. The German commander, Rüdiger von der Goltz, found Mannerheim Entente-minded.[28]

---

[23] Matti Lappalainen, op.cit.,pp.348 & 352. Screen, op.cit., p.199. Mannerheim had nevertheless promised on 23 February 1917 that he would "not sheath his sword" till East Karelia was liberated. Hannu Soikkanen, op.cit., p.289.

[24] Many among the Reds were equally keen on possession of this area: ibid, p.289. On the Agrarian leader Alkio's *völkisch* approach to this question, see Alanen, op.cit., pp.554–558; he was less interested in the possession of Petrograd. Even Ståhlberg joined the East Karelian Committee founded by the Rightist J.K. Paasikivi in June 1918. Alanen, p.566.

[25] When Finland had been conquered by Russia from Sweden in the war of 1808–1809, it had been allowed to keep its Lutheran religion and Swedish fundamental laws.

[26] The Finnish term *valtionhoitaja* would be more accurately rendered by the phrase protector of the realm.

[27] Screen, op.cit., pp.201–202.

[28] Matti Lappalainen op.cit, pp.298–300.

But it was this very fact that enabled Mannerheim to rise again since the failing German connection had constituted an obstacle to the recognition in Western Europe of Finland as an independent state. Even before becoming regent in December 1918, Mannerheim had been in Britain and France to secure this recognition, which succeeded, however, only when, as regent, he agreed to the formation of a new government after the March 1919 parliamentary elections in Finland.[29] In broad terms, this brought in Centrist governments hardly to Mannerheim's liking. And while the Western Powers had determined that the Finnish parliamentary democracy would have its showing, they were far less decisive in the matters that concerned Mannerheim most.

In his six months as regent, he dreamed his dreams again. In the First World War, as a Russian major-general, he had fought on the side of the British-Franco-Russian alliance. In a sense, his scheming in the spring and early summer of 1919 was for the reconstitution of this alliance for the conquest, primarily, of Petrograd so as to knock Bolshevism out once and for all. But the conjunctures, national and international, were far beyond his manipulative skills. The White Russians' leader, Admiral Alexander Vassilievich Kolchak, was reluctant even to give a guarantee of Finnish independence, while General Sir Hubert Gough, when he came over in May 1919 from Britain, required the Finns to win Kolchak's consent for the cession of East Karelia and for a joint Finnish-Russian onslaught on Petrograd,[30] both of which seemed to be doubtful of attainment, since Sergei Dmitrievich Sazonov, the White Russian foreign minister in exile, had anyway imposed restrictive conditions on the recognition of Finnish independence.[31] The French were more enthusiastic, but neither the British nor the French could promise meaningful aid. Russia had collapsed, but with war-weariness in the West, the victorious Powers of the First World War were beginning to feel that Russia should be left to slip away into untouchability. Mannerheim and his ambitions were too great for Finland—and too great for the West Herein lay the twists of fate that bedevilled his career. Having served the Russian Empire well (yet never having made the staff college), he was pitchforked by the Russian revolution back to Finland where he was ultimately to rise far higher than he would ever have risen in Russia, in spite of the fact that he had become a Finnish patriot by accident of history. He was an archaic figure, for whom Russia had been too big, Finland too small, and the West too far away. Yet he embodied something that the later Kautsky had come to fear,

[29] Screen, op.cit., p.192.
[30] ibid., p.200.
[31] ibid., p.215.

something Marx himself had, however, dismissed with too much contempt. This was the dominance of the military *persona*.[32]

Meanwhile, however, he was out of power. This was partly his fault. He had reluctantly accepted a presidential system and had been a candidate for presidency. But while the new constitution brought in an electoral college for the presidential election, this first presidential election was to be undertaken by Parliament for fear of disturbing once more the political passions of the populace. Parliament voted 50 for Mannerheim and 143 for Ståhlberg. The new president was the very man who had drafted the constitution! He would much have preferred to stay on as head of the Supreme Administrative Court, but he sacrificed his peace of mind for the peace of his country. Ståhlberg next offered the dejected Mannerheim the post of head of the armed forces, but the stringency of Mannerheim's conditions upset his chances. He slunk off abroad, still bombarding governments and even Ståhlberg with proposals for intervention in Russia.[33]

It would be quite wrong, however, to assume that Mannerheim's function had been—and was—restricted to the restoration of White power in Petrograd, and thereafter the rest of Russia. Mannerheim was himself the tool of powerful political and economic forces in Finland. As to the politics of these forces, they were mainly Right-wing but also included some Centrists. The group therefore cut across parliamentary alignments. As to economics, the group was mainly, though not entirely, to be identified with the paper, pulp, and timber interests of the Finnish economy and with the need to re-establish some form of the old linkage with Russia.

Among these men were General Rudolf Walden, a potentate of the paper industry, previously involved in the Russian trade, a minister of defence in the government of Lauri Ingman (November 1918–April 1919) and a close friend of Mannerheim; Leo Ehrnrooth, briefly foreign minister in the succeeding government of Kaarlo Castren, and chairman of the central association of the country's woodworking industry; Kaarlo Castren himself, a Progressive, who was prime minister from April–August 1919, and was head of the KOP bank; Carl Enckell, former minister state-secretary of Finland in the Russian capital, the despoiler of the Enabling Act, head of the great Finnish engineering firm of Kone Ltd, and foreign minister in both the Ingman and, briefly, Castren governments; and August Ramsay, head of the other powerful Finnish

---

[32] This important revision in Kautsky' s theorizing is to be found in his *Köyhälistön diktatuuri* (1918) and repeated in his *Köyhälistän vallankumous* (1925).

[33] Screen, op.cit., p.213 This was done by means of a letter to Lauri Ingman, the former prime minister of the National Coalition Party government. Screen tells that the letter was then published in the press on 2.11.1919.

commercial bank, SYP, and minister of finance in the Castren government. Ehrnrooth, for example, had talked with the White general, Nikolai Nikolaievich Yudenich, whose pathetically-clad army had tried to strike for Petrograd as late as October 1919. Ehrnrooth had also had discussions with Russian imperial business circles, while Enckell sought to exploit his own Russian contacts to drum up support among Western diplomats for Mannerheim's plan to attack Petrograd from the Karelian Isthmus.[34]

Though Mannerheim did not abandon his master-plan, he could not, after July 1919, gather the forces to fulfil his policy. He lost his power in Finland through the formation of Centrist governments he could hardly accept. Neither the British nor the French could supply him with troops. The British kept a naval station on the Karelian Isthmus, from which they occasionally launched attacks on Soviet vessels in Kronstadt. They bottled the Soviet fleet up, but made no attempt to conquer Petrograd.[35] The French were more concerned with pressure by way of the Black Sea.[36]

Within Finland, politicians who had previously been favourable to intervention over the border began to limit their interest in this question Already in early May 1919, when Mannerheim was still regent, Santeri Alkio put it to his diary that he did not want to see, as a consequence of the conquest of Petrograd, an English wardship over his country. But if Finland could take Aunus (the Russian region called Olonets) or Estonia this would be quite in order.[37] Actually, at the time when Alkio was writing these comments, a Finnish attempt to seize Aunus was occurring. It was a real mess. Though aiming to support a breakaway movement among the inhabitants there, the Finnish detachments were partly composed of schoolboy volunteers under fanatical officers.[38] Mannerheim supported it.[39] There were several irregular forays of this kind (even as late as 1922) over into the vast region of East Karelia.[40] But by this time Mannerheim was long gone into withdrawal.

---

[34] Markku Kuisma, *Metsäteollisuuden maa*, Helsinki, (SHS),1993, pp.553–554.

[35] Winston Churchill was the principal exception to this limited British policy. He feared a German connection with Russian Bolshevism. John Charmley, *Churchill. The End of Glory*, London, Hodder & Stoughton, 1993, p.156.

[36] Louis Clerc, in his university doctorate, *La Finlande dans la diplomatie française*, I, Strasbourg 3, 1907, points out that from the end-part of the First World War, French military and naval policy was more concerned with the Ukraine, South Russia and Siberia, until the fixation with Poland began; pp.89–90, 118, 166, & 171, the French becoming prepared to leave the Baltic to the British.

[37] Alanen, op.cit., p. 558.

[38] *Itä-Karjala*, Helsinki (Akateeminen Karjala-Seura), 1934, pp.71–72.

[39] Screen, op.cit., p.192.

[40] Marvin Rintala, *Three Generations: The Extreme Right-Wing in Finnish Politics*, Bloomington (Indian Univ. Press), 1962, p.102.

Nevertheless, in the speeches he had made in December 1918, on receiving the regency, he had laid down a sort of political creed for his country. It was a simple creed as is often the case when military men talk politics. It went like this: unanimity to defend the country and its freedom, with a nation pulling together in support of a government working for all classes of society.[41] And this was enunciated in the same year as the massacre of the Red prisoners when Tampere fell! It was a military creed—"all should serve"—and the easiest role for its realization was war, but by the autumn of 1919 the number of those in Finland who wanted to go into that route was falling.

As to Santeri Alkio, the Agrarian leader, he had joined Paasikivi's East Karelian Committee in June 1918, but his views of Mannerheim were hardly consistent and even in the spring of 1918 he distrusted Mannerheim's "Russian-Swedish" lead,[42] while still keeping the East Karelia option open. Mannerheim's hope that he might find a base in an Agrarian-Conservative political rapprochement was groundless.[43] His was a creed that certainly underplayed the essential conflictual element of democratic politics in favour of conflict abroad, though it might also be called "defence." But it was a creed, too, that recognized, that independent Finland's position was not secure, because the environment in which Finland lived was not secure. Ståhlberg was uninterested in an active foreign policy, and never made an official visit abroad in his six years of presidency. But if his outlook on foreign relations were to be characterized, the favourite term of one of his political predecessors, Sakari Yrjö-Koskinen, would be the most appropriate summing-up: *une politique d' effacement.*[44] Effacement, so as to live one's own life in peace.

Effacement

For effacement could also be imposed on a state; even when not so apparent, it might be adopted for fear of giving offence to the powerful. In March 1918 the White Vasa government made a peace treaty with Germany (since Russia had been at war with Germany when Finland had been a part of the Russian Empire). J.K. Paasikivi, was a supporter of that peace. With that peace, however, went treaties of a different kind, commercial and navigational in

[41] Screen, op.cit., p 189.

[42] Blomstedt, p.377.

[43] ibid., p.202.

[44] As quoted by President Urho Kekkonen in 1972 as a foreign policy outlook it was high time to get over! *Ulko-poliittisia lausuntoja ja asiakirjoja 1972*, Helsinki 1973. p.55

nature, which deprived Finland of much of its freedom in these latter questions.[45] Finland began to be subordinated to Ludendorff's *Ost-Politik*. But all that passed—for the moment—with German defeat.

By 1920, therefore, Paasikivi had come to follow much of Ståhlberg's line of thinking, particularly when peace with the other great Power, Russia, was concerned. Paasikivi was more cautious now—as Ståhlberg was. Primarily, this meant that Paasikivi, an old Compliant,[46] wanted as genuinely as Ståhlberg, to end the state of war with Russia rather than expect vast territorial gains. He was the principal negotiator of the three main negotiators (the other two were Rudolf Holsti, a Progressive, and Väinö Tanner of the constitutionalist Social Democrats). This was ultimately signed in October 1920 at Tartu in the now independent state of Estonia. But the *expectations* among certain circles in Finland were not restricted merely to the making of peace. There was a strong feeling, especially in Rightist circles, that lands that had not been gained by war might be gained by the peace.

Two slices of geography were uppermost as far as the apparently land-hungry Finns were concerned. The first was the vast region of Petsamo in the north and the second was East Karelia. As it turned out, only the first was gained.

The Petsamo area had actually been awarded to Finland as far back as 1864 in exchange for a strip of land on the Karelian Isthmus upon which the Sestroretsk arms factory was built.[47] No one then seemed to be bothered in Finland to claim the *quid pro quo*, even though a movement started in the 1880s for a Finnish foothold on the Varanger Fjord.[48] Soviet Russia now had an ice-free port at Murmansk at the end of a rickety railway and so could presumably do without any further development up north. It would be too glib to say that Finland had a felt need for an ice-free port on the northern seas. Having got the area and its entry into the northern seas, the Finns did little to develop a significant port area up there and communications with the

[45] E.g., exports of the timber, paper, and pulp industry were to be under German control: Juhani Paasivirta, *Suomi vuonna 1918*, Porvoo-Helsinki, 1957 pp. 113–117. Tuomo Polvinen, *J.K. Paasivkivi*, I, Porvoo-Helsinki (Werner Söderström), 1989, pp. 414–416. Hannu Rautkallio, *Kaupanteko Suomen Itsenäisyydellä*, Helsinki (Werner Söderström), 1977, has shown the enormous extent of the German plans for controlling the Finnish economy.

[46] The Compliants were mainly Old Finns who before the First World War tried to make sufficient concessions to the Imperial Russian standpoint so as to preserve the greater part of Finnish autonomy.

[47] Maude. "Petsamo," *Historical Dictionary of Finland*, Lanham & London (Scarecrow Press), 1995, pp. 190–191.

[48] Paul Knaplund, *Britsh Views on Norwegian-Swedish Problems 1880–1895*,Oslo (Norsk historisk kjeldeskrift institutt), 1952, pp.15 & 129. *Valvoja*, 1884, pp. 471–475. Maude, unpublished Ph.D thesis, pp. 108–117.

rest of Finland were difficult for years. Only in the tense period between the Winter War and the Continuation War was the ice-free port and the route southwards of greater value. On the other hand, the Petsamo region ran between Norway and Soviet Russia and it possession by Finland was a factor that in 1941 lured the Germans to cross it in their attempts to strike to the Soviet port of Murmansk.

But by this time there was another lure for the Germans. In 1924 the Finnish Geological Commission found nickel deposits, but these were not leased out for exploitation to International Nickel until 1934 and production had still not quite begun when the Winter War broke out in 1939. Strategically, the whole area was conquered by the Russians in the Winter War and then handed back, not being finally taken into the Soviet Union till 1944. It could hardly be regarded as a part of the geographical defence line of the Finnish state. And its natural resources, apart from water-power, were under-exploited in the period 1920–1939.[49]

The real prize the Finnish negotiators were after was East Karelia or, more specifically, at least the two border parishes of Repola and Porajärvi, and what was growing there, namely timber. These two parishes had been occupied by Finnish irregulars in the confusion of 1917 and thus by the time of the Tartu deliberations had been for over two years administered by the Finns.[50] Among the delegation members from the Finnish side at Tartu was none other than General Rudolf Walden, Mannerheim's crony, an important figure in his country's paper industry. High hopes were placed upon him to influence Paasikivi to obtain cessions of territory in East Karelia. But the members of the Soviet delegation would not budge. Paasikivi could do nothing but take the blame. In truth, there was someone else who would not budge. That was President Ståhlberg back in Helsinki.

It is clear that the Russians wanted some of the Finnish islands close to the frontier on the *Karelian Isthmus*. Ståhlberg also made it clear to his own delegates that he would give up neither islands nor any other territory that had been within the borders of the old Grand Duchy of Finland.[51] Paasikivi seemed to regret this and his premonitions about what the Russians might do later to secure their own strategic needs were to prove correct. The frontier on the Isthmus and some Finnish islands were too near Leningrad.[52] But *Staatsraison* was not President Ståhlberg's strong point. If there were to have

---

[49] Hans-Peter Krosby, *Finland, Germany and the Soviet Union 1940–1941. The Petsamo Dispute*, Madison & London (Univ. of Wisconsin Press), 1966, pp. 4–6.

[50] Rintala,*Three Generations*,p.102.

[51] Blomstedt, op.cit., pp.410–411.

[52] Blomstedt, op.cit., p.409.

been such an idea in his mind, it might have been based on the fact that the Karelian Isthmus contained a large number of peasant-farmers. They were Agrarians who had supported the republic, and would hardly have wanted to lose their farmland for the sake of East Karelia, let alone for the matter of improving the security of Petrograd!

But the Soviet delegates at Tartu had, with respect to East Karelia, yet another reason for their unwillingness to trade. In February 1920, Lenin had written to Edvard Gylling, the former delegate of finances in the 1918 Red government of Finland, who had escaped to Sweden after the fall of Viipuri at the end of April 1918, and had travelled from Helsinki to Stockholm disguised as "the bridegroom" of a young high-school graduate who accompanied him as his "bride."[53] In April 1920 he arrived in Soviet Russia to answer Lenin's call, which was to help to run the East Karelian Independent Labour-Commune as it was called—"independent" in the Russian sense of "autonomous."[54] The idea was that this should be a refuge for Finnish Communists who had fled to Russia after the failure of the 1918 Finnish revolution as well as serving the existing Karelian-speaking population. It was also meant to be an answer to the Finnish negotiators at Tartu who claimed that the East Karelians needed self-determination. The matter was disputed at Tartu to no avail.

It was an issue that Gylling was familiar with. As a member of the Red Finnish government of 1918, he had already tried to bring the question of East Karelia into the March 1918 negotiations on the treaty between the Finnish Socialist Workers' State and Bolshevik Russia.[55] Shortly after this, a Finnish Red M.P. in exile in Soviet Russia, Edvard Valpas-Hänninen, devised a personal and political solution of his own. In a Finnish-language newspaper, briefly published in Petrograd, he had suggested that the Finnish White government should be granted East Karelia on condition that parliamentary government be restored in Finland and with it the return of the exiled Red M.P.s allowed.[56] (He did return and got five years' imprisonment. Had he returned earlier, he might have been shot). What is interesting is that both he and other Socialists in exile, such as Oskari Tokoi and Otto Ville Kuusinen, had been in 1918 clearly of the opinion that it would have been in the interest of both Finland and Russia to exchange part of the Karelian Isthmus for East Karelia.[57] They had thus been of the same opinion as J.K. Paasikivi, the

---

[53] Arvo Ylärakkola, *Edvard Gylling*, Helsinki (Otava),1976, p.93.

[54] From 1923 this was known as he Karelian Autonomous Republic.

[55] Hannu Soikkanen, op.cit., p.289

[56] Stacy Churchill, *Itä-Karjalan kohtalo*, Porvoo-Helsinki (Werner Söderström), pp.90–91.

[57] Hannu Soikkanen, op.cit., p.289.

principal negotiator for the bourgeois government at Tartu in 1920! Here were some of the cross-currents of politics, a politics that had to be stemmed for want of structural support but yet contained its own latently gnawing truth.

But the deeply moving story of the Finns relations with their neighbours—and with their kinfolk—over the border was to continue as Edvard Gylling and Santeri Nuorteva tried to build up a second Red Finland in East Karelia.[58] As far as the Finnish Whites were concerned, the loss of the two East Karelian parishes of Repola and Porajärvi was a tragedy, compounded, among other things, by the death of the young Finnish sheriff of the parish of Repola, who, after hauling down the Finnish flag, shot himself. Bobi Siven became almost a saint in Finland and, by his death, an inspiration for the foundation of an Academic Karelia Society, which, in its aims and actions, was far from saintly.[59] However, sympathies sometimes surfaced between the Finnish Communist leaders of East Karelia and the Finnish White establishment. The Conservative politician and banker Antti Hackzell, when Finnish minister to Moscow in 1922, secured wheat from Finland for the starving inhabitants of East Karelia at the request of Edvard Gylling.[60] But such cross-currents, in the name of humanity, were rare. And the situation was to go from bad to worse.

The Åland Islands.

The problems dealt with in the Peace of Tartu (1920) were, *inter alia*, problems of the rectification of frontiers, intermingled with the greater problem of the extrusion of Communism from Finland. In the west, the new Finnish state wrestled, too, with a problem of frontier rectification, which had become intertwined with an even more complex problem of Finnish identity, the solution to which was not to be extrusion but enforced inclusion.

The Åland Islands straddle the seas between Finland and Sweden: where the Finnish archipelago ends, the Åland Islands begin. The Ålanders are Swedish-speaking and by the end of the First World War wanted incorporation in Sweden. When, in 1917, a group of Finnish Activists were in Sweden, one of them, the choleric figure of Jonas Castren, was asked by the Swedish Activist, the explorer and orientalist Sven Hedin, whether he would

---

[58] Both were Finns from Finland and not native East Karelians. Arvo Kostiainen has pointed out that if Gylling was the equivalent of prime minister, Nuorteva was the equivalent of president. There was some tension with the local population. Arvo Kostiainen,*Santeri Nuorteva-Kansainvälinen suomalainen*, Helsinki (SHS), 1983, pp.167 & 174-5.

[59] The death and significance of Bobi Siven is described in Rintala's *Three Generations*, pp.101-102.

[60] Ylärakkola, op.cit., pp.201-203.

like to see Finland restored to Sweden. At that moment, Jonas Castren apparently did want to see Finland restored to Sweden.[61] Had this occurred, it would have solved the Åland problem by putting the islands in the joint state. But Jonas Castren was not an Ålander and this sentiment of his to join Sweden was surely a passing one. It was not a passing one for the Ålanders themselves. They did not want to be with Finland once Russia had collapsed in 1917. As separatists, they wanted to be under the Swedish king, and a strong "independence" movement grew up on the Islands under Julius Sundblom, the founder and editor of the newspaper *Åland*, and the lawyer C. Björkman. A delegation, headed by Sundblom, proceeded to Paris in 1919 to plead for Swedish possession of the Åland archipelago. He was not to get it.

In the previous year, Mannerheim, as head of the White army, had initially in February 1918, stated that he had not taken a position with respect to the future of the Islands, but he rapidly changed his mind as Swedish troops occupied some of them.[62] The essence of the question for Mannerheim was the importance of the islands for the defence of Finland, since their possession enabled a foreign Power to pursue an "island hopping policy" to the Finnish mainland, while between Sweden proper and Åland was a stretch of open water. The Swedes were soon followed by German troops and the former were withdrawn.

Those in the White Vasa government who disliked the increasing pro-German orientation of Finland like Senator Heikki Renvall (of the Vasa government) were none the less angry with the Swedes for having "provoked" the Germans to take Åland. In fact, this German occupation was a consequence of the breakdown in the Brest-Litovsk negotiations between Bolshevik Russia and Imperial Germany.[63] If you were a White of the stamp of the shifty Svinhufvud (then still in the Finnish capital in hiding), you might see this as the start of the German aid for White Finland[64] promoted by Svinhufvud's own visit to Berlin. One figure who did not like these development was Mannerheim, for they put paid to his scheme to have an alternative candidate for the projected throne of Finland taken from the Swedish royal house. This would have been an important lynchpin in Mannerheim's own vision of a rapprochement between the Westward-leaning Scandinavian states.[65] The Swedes did not like losing Åland and thus the Ålanders, who were more Scandinavian-minded than most inhabitants of

---

[61] Matti Lappalainen, op.cit., p.212, following the account of Herman Gummerus.

[62] Stig Jägerskiöld, *Gustaf Mannerheim 1918*. Helsingfors (Schildts), 1967, pp.164–168.

[63] ibid., p.172. Senator Renvall had had enough and became pro-German.

[64] Though Svinhufvud's biographer, Einar W.Juva, *P.E:Svinhufvud*, II, Porvoo-Helsinki (Werner Söderström), p.135 denied that his hero actually offered the Germans Åland.

[65] Screen, op.cit., p.196.

mainland Finland, formed a bulwark against a further development of Scandinavianism as well as a tripwire to blow up another piece of monarchism. But there was an additional factor. At the end of the First World War, Sir Esmé Howard, the British minister to Sweden, undoubtedly backed at this time by the Foreign Office, wished to thwart German expansion into the Baltic region. Howard believed that Åland should go to Sweden, arguing that Finland would be a weak state. These ideas were soon to touch on Baltic League thinking, and concerns, among the British, that a barrier had to be built up to prevent cooperation between Bolshevik Russia and a resurgent Germany.[66] These ideas became weaker as intervention petered out and with it Mannerheim's dream of conquering Petrograd and federalizing Russia.[67]

Yet, in respect of Åland, Mannerheim had done the best according to his lights for his re-adopted Finnish homeland. His discussion with Clemenceau in the autumn of 1919 may well have changed the latter's view that the Åland Islands should go to Sweden.[68] In 1921, the League of Nations awarded them to Finland, while Sundblom and Björkman were released from the penal servitude a vindictive Finnish state had imposed on them.[69] But the matter of Åland and its resolution was to have a wider import still.

Bättre folk

By the early 1920s approximately 12% of the total population of Finland spoke Swedish as their mother tongue. Many of them were farmers and fishers on the coastal mainland. But Swedish was the language of academic culture and it had seemed to bind Finland to the rest of Northern Europe It was, after all, the language of the ancient motherland across the water. The level of education of the Swedish-speakers in Finland was high. But they were a minority that did not like to call themselves by that term.[70] By the 1920s and 1930s they claimed to want equality in language questions, but to many Finnish-speaking Finns this looked rather more like a privilege than a right. Their position in the old Grand Duchy of Finland, when the traditional diet

---

[66] Esa Sundbäck, *Finland in British Baltic Policy*, Helsinki (the Finnish Academy of Science and Letters), 2001, pp. 93–96 & 144. Eino Lyytinen, *Finland in British Politics in World War I and Its Aftermath.*, D.Phil thesis, Oxford, 1973, p.133.

[67] Jägerskiöld, *Gustaf Mannerheim 1918, p.26*; Finland and Poland were to be independent.

[68] Mannerheim, *Muistelmat, I*, Helsinki (Otava), 1951, pp.446–448.

[69] For appealing to Sweden for possession of the islands, they were convicted of treason: Lars Björne, "*syhin ja lakin eikä mielivaltaan,*" Helsinki (Suomalaisen lakimies jukaisuja),1977, pp.46–47.

[70] Göran von Bonsdorff & Frank Jernström,*Från Självständighet till Lappo. Svenska folkpartiet*, II, Ekenäs (Svenska folkpartiet), 1984, p.87.

of four estates still had an influence before the reformed Parliament began to sit in 1907, was not commensurate with their share in the population of their country. Two estates, those of the aristocracy and the bourgeoisie, had been dominated by the Swedish-speakers, while the estate of the clergy and the estate of the peasantry had been broadly Finnish-speaking. Much of the thinking of the top Swedes were that they were a kind of *sanior pars*, the wiser part of the population, a necessary reflective element to leaven a headstrong democracy. On the other hand, many of the top-class Swedish-speakers began to change their names and speech from Swedish to Finnish, as a kind of identification with the majority of the populations, a sort of new source of power. An upper-class, an aspirant upper-class, changed somewhat its character.

But for those who wished to remain Swedish in language and culture the advent of democracy in 1907 and independence on the last day of 1917 presented problems. Some Ostrobothnians felt that they might do better in the Swedish state over the water, but this raised little interest in Sweden.[71] However, there was also the example of Åland before their eyes after the 1921 League of Nations resolution on autonomy for these aberrant islands. Indeed, part of the Finnish case for keeping these islands had been that it would help to swell the Swedish-speaking population of Finland if they remained in the Finnish state.

Unfortunately, it didn't work out like that. Having grudgingly got their autonomy, the Ålanders decided to keep to themselves, not showing much interest in the rest of Finland. The provision of a parallel form of autonomy for the Swedish-speakers of the mainland or the other archipelagos became entangled in the difficulties of boundary drawing. Ernst Estlander and the organs of the *Svenska Folkpartiet* abandoned the idea of appealing to the Peace Conference for their territorial rights—unlike the Ålanders.[72] In the end, the Swedish-speakers were fobbed off with a bishopric at Borgå (Porvoo), their own school administration, and with the *folkting*, an unofficial talking-point of the bourgeois classes, which, in 1941, opened its arms to all Swedish-speakers. By 1924, under the influence of the owner of the Swedish national newspaper, a self-made man called Amos Anderson, *Svenska Folkpartiet* started to tone down its concept of a Swedish nationality in Finland (as a counterweight to Finnish nationalism) and instead to see the opportunities for Swedish-speakers outside the traditional Swedish-speaking home areas.[73] How far this represented a defeat for local self-sufficiency to the advantage of a more

---

71 ibid., pp.94–95.
72 ibid., p.51.
73 ibid., pp.215–216.

dynamically-oriented educated and industrialist class of Swedish-speakers is a touchy subject. On the other hand, the comparatively powerful position of Swedish-speakers in certain national fields such as higher education and military life did not go unchallenged either—by the young Finnish-speakers.

In practice, therefore, though the Swedish People's Party was one of the first parties in Finland to organize as a modern-type party,[74] throughout the 1920s many of the leaders of the Swedish-speaking element who served in political life did not necessarily act in commitment to the Party, and even, as in the case of Amos Anderson, refused to consider themselves as bound by the resolutions of their Party.[75] These figures' personal power *outside the electoral process* was often enough to set them up on high. They were old familiar faces.[76] In the coalition government of Lauri Ingman, a National Coalition Party prime minister, were four Swedish-speaking ministers: Rudolf Walden, the minister of defence, was not a member of Parliament and gained his position because of his close relations to the conservative National Coalition Party and to Regent Mannerheim; Carl Johan Enckell, the foreign minister, was not a member of Parliament either and served in the government as an expert. Readers of chapter I will note that he had once served to destroy a Parliament; neither Enckell, nor Karl Söderholm, the minister of justice, nor Julius Stjernvall, the minister of trade and industry, felt bound by party resolutions and they did not resign when in February 1919 the Swedish People's Party demand for territorial-based institutions went unrequited. The Party did not demand the resignation of these ministers either.[77] In the succeeding ministry of Kaarlo Castren, a Progressive, Söderholm, again minister of justice, and August Ramsay, minister of finance, *did* resign when the Party demands were refused, but yet stayed in office to the end of the brief government! In the government of Rafael Erich (March 1920–April 1921), four Swedish-speaking ministers resigned before time. Leo Ehrnrooth, the minister of trade and industry, said he did not know whether he had the support of his parliamentary group or not. But when still in office, he said he had felt himself to be the representative of the industrial and commercial interests and in that connection had been working to prevent a Left-oriented

---

[74]This party was formed in 1906, was well organized, and had, to its credit, become a party representing a diversity of interests and from the autumn of 1918 it began to comprise many different constituent organizations, including a Left; von Bonsdorff & Jernström,op.cit., p.151. How far this party could stand up to the powerful Swedish-Finnish figures is another matter.

[75]ibid.,p.218.

[76] See this chapter p.44.

[77] ibid., p.98

coalition.[78] Presumably, this had become a legitimate mandate in his opinion. But it did not fit the tenure of the new 1919 constitution.

Constitutional Fragility

The constitution itself was far from fragile. It was primarily the result of a draft worked on by Ståhlberg in 1917 and brought out again by him at the end of the Mannerheim regency. Then Ståhlberg won the presidential election in July 1919 as an embodiment of the new constitution he himself had largely devised. It contained many limitations on parliamentary power and gave the president of the republic many "regal" powers, though not as many as Mannerheim had been prepared to use on the basis of the old Swedish constitution of 1772.[79]

Still, Ståhlberg's constitution was meant to satisfy the Right by giving the head of state strong powers to use where necessary; the next best, in short, to a monarch with some similar powers but without the foreign connection (a danger for Ståhlberg) and the assumed security of a hereditary line. Ståhlberg, who would have preferred himself to continue as head of the Supreme Administrative Court—a post to which he returned in 1925, was a reluctant president and took his time to consider whether or not to run for presidency in 1919. But he could and did use the powers granted by the presidential office he had himself helped to create. Thus was born a dualistic constitution, better known later in the Finnish post-Second World War environment in Merikoski's terminology as a "presidential- parliamentary democracy."[80] There was certainly a double-executive constituted by a president alongside the government. And the president could veto legislation coming up from Parliament. But should Parliament vote anew that same piece of law, then the president had to yield. What was missing was the super-executive previously held by an unyielding Tsardom.[81] In the end, it could be argued Parliament would prevail.

---

[78] ibid., p.101.

[79] See this chapter, pp.41–42. Ståhlberg put the right of making war squarely on Parliament instead of on the supreme executive (in his constitution the president was denied this traditional monarchical power). The matter is of some significance in respect of what was to follow in Finnish history.

[80] Veli Merikoski, *Suomen julkisoikeus pääpiirteittään*, Porvoo-Helsinki (Werner Söderström), 1974, p.93, states that the president had to confirm parliamentary legislation. Merikoski & Eero Vilkkanen, *Suomen julkisoikeus pääpiirteittään*, Porvoo-Helsinki (WSOY), 1983, p.59, mention the president's right to initiate legislation.

[81] Jyränki, op.cit., pp.489–490.

Structurally, the state had become a sort of "ourselves alone" place. For the triumph of Ståhlberg represented a lot of rejection: of the negative aspect of the *arvstat,* the hereditary state of the Grand Duchy. The rejection embraced a monarchy with powers whether Russian or German, or a substitute figure of military calibre in the shape of a Mannerheim; alternatively, the triumph of Ståhlberg indicated the rejection of another kind of close relationship with the new Russia in the shape of joining a federal Russian state of the Bolshevik regime. Small wonder was it that Ståhlberg's Finland did not include East Karelia nor the possible cession of parishes on the Karelian Isthmus in order to get it.[82] The state was neutral and at home it was centrist in endeavour, for the very success of Ståhlberg in the presidential election had been backing from the constitutionalist Social Democrats, the Agrarians and the Progressives. What this meant, in practice, was that Finland was narrowly construed. Headed by a civilian and not by a military man like Mannerheim, the Finnish state had drawn up its boundaries by the Peace of Tartu. Headed by a civilian who was also a distinguished lawyer, the Finnish state was intended now to be a *Rechtsstaat,* as correct internally as it was meant to be externally.

Where the state was fragile, however, was in its very constitutionalism. The fragility did not reside in the form of the constitution, but in the disinclination or sheer incapacity of most of the parties to work with it once they had accepted Ståhlberg's presidency. The governmental politics of the country were to a great degree in stalemate, and an effective political centre did not emerge apart from the often distant and symbolic presidency.

The first problem was that constituted by the Social Democratic Party. After the counter-revolution, only one near Social Democrat M.P. remained in Parliament, the Christian Socialist member Matti Trygg-Helenius. In the spring of 1919, the regent, Mannerheim, was reluctant to allow even the constitutionalist Social Democratic party to fight the election, but the pressure of the Agrarian Union and of the Young Finns, newly constituted as a Progressive Party, made him give way. The Social Democrats emerged, once again, as the largest political grouping with 80 seats and, surprisingly, their participation in government was mooted. Once more, however, the Social Democrats' own self-denying ordinance prevented this participation. They had a minimum programme, whose acceptance they required as a condition of entry. The programme was an attempt to keep the party together, a goal that came before any cooperation in government with the non-Socialist parties. The rejection of this programme (a general amnesty and the abolition of the civil guards) by the latter parties also served to stifle within the Social

[82] Blomstedt, op.cit., p.411.

Democratic ranks any kind of dissension arising around the Kautskyite prohibition on entering government *without* a parliamentary majority, a prohibition that this overvalued guru did not lift till 1926. These manoeuvres failed to prevent the split in the Social Democrat ranks. In 1920 a Socialist Workers' Party began to be formed and by 1922 it had 27 seats in Parliament—to the Social Democrats' 53. It looked as if, therefore, the new Socialist party was destroying, in precise mathematical terms, the comparatively good position the Social Democratic Party had won in 1919 *before the victory of Ståhlberg in the presidential election.*

The relations between the orthodox Social Democrats and the new Socialist Workers' Party were strained by an issue that both parties were in agreement in principle about. This issue was that of the amnesty for Red prisoners still in the camps. It was an issue that cut the Left off from many other matters of practical politics. It was an issue that separated the Left into its own world, a world haunted by revolution and its failure in Finland. Those still in the camps, deprived of civil and therefore also political rights, felt that Tanner and the constitutionalist Social Democrats were indifferent to their needs.[83] This was hardly true. On the contrary, the parliamentary politics of the Social Democratic Party became entangled in the demand for realisation of a full amnesty and the question hindered at the same time the participation of the Party in government.

The retention of the prisoners in the camps (even though at Tammisaari, they gradually succeeded in running a Marxist curriculum of their own) was part of the continuing oppression of the defeated Reds. It gave a considerable boost to the fortunes of the Socialist Workers' Party, however. Considering the repressive nature of much of Finnish society in the aftermath of the events of 1918, it is something of a mystery as to how that party was allowed to arise. OttoVille Kuusinen, a fugitive in his own country now, had been working to found such a party since May 1919 and a year later the foundation meeting was *publicly* held in Helsinki, while a month later the local governmental organization of the Helsinki Socialists declared itself to be a Finnish Socialist Workers' Party (SSTP).

The Party never succeeded in becoming registered.[84] Its problem lay in its connection with the Finnish Communist Party established in Soviet Russia in 1918 by the Finnish exiles. Kuusinen's role had been important, flitting in and out of Finland, once disguised as a woman.

---

[83] Väinö Salmi, op.cit.,p.341: in the beginning conditions in the Tammisaari camp were bad and one of the nurses, a Miss Saleva, was suspected of poisoning prisoners who fell sick, p.263.

[84] Jaakko Mäkelä, "The Radical Left and the Communist Party in Finnish Politics" in *Political Parties in Finland,* ed. Juhani Mylly & R. Michael Berry, Turku (Pol.hist.dept.)1984, p.163.

In the Ståhlberg era, political repression could also occur through the quite long-winded action of the courts. The Socialist Workers' Party members of Parliament sat undisturbed there till 1923 when the court system declared the Party illegal on grounds that the Party's adherence to the Comintern committed it to violent action against the existing Finnish state, that is, presumed treason. Nor did any question of parliamentary immunity for the members arise. They were expelled from Parliament and even imprisoned. President Ståhlberg, in light of a situation in which the number of M.P.s was now inadequate, ordered new elections. Under a new rubric of a Socialist Workers' Party, 18 members were returned instead of the 27 held before the Party's expulsion from the legislature. Harassment was to continue. In the end, an electoral alliance was formed of Socialist Workers and Smallholders with a concomitant name for the parliamentary group.[85] In 1930 with the law on the general suppression of Communism, this public activity disappeared. Two of the alleged Communists were pulled out of a session of the constitutional affairs committee of Parliament.

This opposition movement to the Tannerite Social Democrats lasted as a political activity for ten years. Most commentators seem obliged to call its participants Communists- Wahlbäck makes it quite clear.[86] Upton is less sure.[87] He points, too, to the exasperation among the domestic extreme Left with the interference of the Finnish exiles in the Soviet Union.[88]

Thus, it might be worth considering whether the breakaway party could have been brought closer into the Finnish system by its own undoubted interest in social policy.

An interesting case of this kind was actually provided by the passage of the *Lex Kallio* in 1922. This law, which took the name of the leader of the Agrarian Union, Kyösti Kallio, aimed to provide land for the former crofter population, now liberated, but farming often on too small land-areas. The law was bitterly opposed by the National Coalition Party and by the Swedish People's Party as contrary to the protection of the rights of property laid down in the constitution (the Swedish People's Party were particularly concerned that this was the thin end of the wedge for the finnicization of estates owned by Swedish-speakers).

---

[85] Anthony F.Upton,*Kommunismi Suomessa,* Helsinki (Kirjayhtymä),1970, p.73.

[86] Krister Wahlbäck, *Mannerheimista Kekkoseen,* Porvoo-Helsinki (Werner Söderström), 1968,pp.278–279.

[87] Upton, *Kommunismi Suomessa*: on p.68 saying they were not Communists in terms of the Finnish Communist Party, bu then implying they were a kind of domestic Communists on p. 69.

[88] ibid., pp.74–75.

Kallio himself, a prosperous farmer from northern Finland, was somewhat reluctant to press the changes that bore his name in the first law. The laws provided for the peasant farmer, including the landless, 20 hectares of arable and 20 hectares of forest. Estates of over 200 hectares could be empowered to provide such land—or, estates of over 40 hectares where no serious farming was taking place. The law, for its adoption, needed a two-thirds majority in Parliament as a permanent law. That majority was finally attained (it was passed by 135 votes to 61) by a mixed support from the Centre and Left parties, the latter including the members of the Socialist Workers' Party, who had originally opposed the bill on grounds that it *furthered* the extension of private property. In changing their attitude after the 1922 parliamentary elections, the 27 members of the Socialist Workers' Party secured the passage of the bill. Characteristically, the National Coalition Party had hoped that the Socialist Workers' Party members would have continued its opposition to the bill, and, as a force from the *advocatus diaboli,* would have frustrated its adoption![89] In the end, the Left (Social Democrats and Socialist Workers' Party) preferred to support the private enterprise of the smallholders against the private enterprise of the estate-owners of the Finnish and Swedish Right, who feared that they would lose lands under the terms of the new law. By the way, when, in the following year, the Socialist Workers' Party members were expelled from Parliament, a defence of their position was not a noticeable feature among the Agrarian Union members.

What was going on was a politics of a very different kind from the attempts of one side or the other *to determine the character of the state. Instead, what was in evidence was a politics that aimed, to a great degree, to determine the character of society.* The politics around the passage of the *Lex Kallio* were, from the Agrarian side, a politics that admittedly contained, according to Kallio himself, a restraint on private ownership in which the Agrarian Union believed, for the *Lex Kallio,* as noted above, included provisions on the expropriation of the lands of estate-owners and its accompanying law, the *Lex Pulkkinen.* allowed the disrobing of the timber companies' lands for the purpose of creating peasant farmland. Kallio associated the provision of land with the previous freeing of the crofters from labour servitude for their *rented* land. He was the butt of criticism from the possessing classes for this, but claimed that in this way he was extending private ownership to more and more smallholders, an effective change in the structure of the rural population that increased the efficiency of agriculture.[90] Such a change also, argued Kallio,

---

[89] Sven Lindman, *Parlamentarismens tillämpning in Finland 1919–1926*, Åbo (1937), pp. 198–202.

[90] *Herääväå maaseutu,* II & V, p. 164–164 (Johannes Virolainen's interpretation of Santeri Alkio's "the bread-growing man" who should be the key figure in society).

increased the stability of society since it was brought about by the farming population itself.[91] This was an aside that reminded the rest of the non-Socialist community of the recent revolution (the revolutionary Social Democrats had freed the crofters, who on the whole ignored this concession till better times came).[92] It was a strange situation. The Left had tried to take over private enterprise and had failed. The Agrarians did not fail now in their threat to repossess the land. By 1939, as result of other measures, too, the field hectarage in Finland had increased by 30%.[93]

The workers had had their failed revolution in 1918. The peasants had had theirs in 1596–1597 in the so-called Club War. Then, this had failed, too. The inspirer of the Agrarian Union, Santeri Alkio, had seen the creation of this twentieth century party "as the Finnish peasantry's first independent political manifestation since the Club War." This time the possessing classes had to give, for, as Urho Kittilä in 1956, could proudly point out, on the fiftieth anniversary of the party, "the triumphal urge had been strong."[94]

The politics of the Left in this case were also contradictory to their original principles, which had favoured a peasantry *renting* its lands from a state which had nationalized land for them.[95] Now the Left was engaged in fostering the spread of private enterprise downwards into the countryside community. The Right could not defeat this, but hoped that the Socialist Workers' Party would have done it for them. These tamperings of principles constituted a legislative jiggery-pokery based on the possibilities of tactical voting. The Agrarian historian Kari Hokkanen has seen in this legislation a famous act of state, while, at the same time, decrying its immediate significance.[96]

In the meantime, it is noteworthy that the politics around the legislation produced neither coalition government nor security for the Socialist Workers' Party. The courts started it by playing politics in the summer parliamentary recess of 1923 This hardly redounded to the virtues of the Montesquieuan

---

[91] Quoted by Urho Kittilä in *Herääva maaseutu*, V, p. 93.

[92] Rinta-Tassi, op.cit., pp.205–206 the crofters were freed by the Reds on 31 January 1918, but were in doubt as to whether they had then usufruct or ownership of their lands.

[93] *Herääva maaseutu*,V, p.174.

[94] On Santeri Alkio's and Urho Kittilä's views, *Herääva maaseutu*, V, p.94.

[95] See chap.1, note 136 for Holsti's attack on Gylling in Parliament in March 1914. By the time of the *Lex Kallio* and Lex Pulkkinen Gylling was ensconced in Soviet East Karelia.

[96] Hokkanen, op.cit., p.351. Hokkanen seems to have underplayed nevertheless the significance of the *Lex Kallio* by a superficial reading of the volume *Herääva Maaseutu* VI, Maalaisliitto (1956),where both Urho Kittilä & Johannes Virolainen, stress, pp. 92 & 171, that to avoid expropriation under the law the estate-owners entered into voluntary agreements.

system that Ståhlberg held dear. Nor did it speak of the privilege of Parliament.

Socially-speaking, there was another point to bear with. The Left had lost its cherished position as "the people. " The Agrarians had taken over that role. In Finnish-language politics, they even began to usurp the National Coalition Party in fervour, for the latter could hobnob in Swedish when they wanted. But Kallio could not and the young Agrarian politician Urho Kekkonen did not care to try, a fact he trumpeted in his strident journalism, wanting to relegate the Swedish-speakers of Helsinki University into a separate institution.[97] The essay was also deeply anti-Russian.

In the soul of the Finnish political parties there was an element of sheer irresponsibility. When, in 1922, Vennola's second government fell in the conflict over Rudolf Holsti's foreign policy (a proposed species of alignment with Estonia, Latvia, and Poland), neither the Swedish People's Party, nor the Social Democrats, nor the National Coalition Party were prepared to form a government, though all had voted against Holsti's policy. The situation worsened when President Ståhlberg tried to form a caretaker government (which once created lasted over five months). Both former ministerial holders, whether from the parties or officialdom, refused to head such a government until A.K. Cajander was prevailed upon to leave his post in the civil service to undertake the task.[98] The great problem, Russia, had not been solved, but year in year out it seemed to be weaker, especially with the famine of 1923. Outside Parliament, the military was expected to protect the land, along with the volunteer civil guards of the Right, practising their formulae after Sunday church service. There were also appurtenances like the secret police (for whom, incidentally, Kekkonen and his future wife worked) and a very slow amnesty for those who had been involved decisively in the revolution. And in 1930 "Communism" was forbidden.[99] As Western Europe's interest in Finland waned, it looked as if "ourselves alone" was the best concoction, give or take a few. Leave the worrying to the president?

---

[97] Urho Kekkonen, *Puheita ja kirjoituksia III*,ed.Tuomas Vilkuna, Helsinki (Weilin and Göös), 1969, pp.188–189.

[98] Blomstedt, op.cit.,pp.430–432.

[99] Whether of the classic Bolshevik kind or the extreme Socialism of the revolutionary tradition in the SDP of 1918.

Military Quadrilles

Thus the security of the quarrelsome Finnish society rested *in ultimo* on the obvious power-point of the armed forces, backed up by an internal state-security police

But the armed forces of the new state were not merely an obvious power-point; but they were also a point of vulnerability. The constitution certainly provided a mechanism for controlling this final instrument of coercion, *sed quis cusodiet ipsos custodes? Quis?* Who could do it? The head of the state until 1925, Kaarlo Ståhlberg, *who by the constitution he had largely drafted was head of the armed forces in peacetime,* was a reluctant president, who shied away from the problem and was not to be a candidate for the presidency next time. His successor in 1925, Lauri Kristian Relander, was and has been a somewhat maligned president (in a country full of statues there is no statue to him). His wife was speechless on hearing that he was to become president and she lost a lot of sleep. The children cried and the wife of the outgoing president, Mrs. Esther Stahlberg, sardonically recorded that the family would be in for quite a few crying spells before Relander's presidency was out.[100] But in this case, reluctant president though he too was, Relander was interested in the military and tried to cope with its obstreperous personnel.

The problem was this: the leaders of the Finnish military establishment had been trained in Russia—as Mannerheim had been, though he, at the moment, was in some disfavour. The military commander of the Finnish armed forces, General Karl Fredrik Wilkama (formerly Wilkman) was, in spite of his original Swedish names, a Finnish speaker. He was a man of rectitude, spending some part of his spare time as a Sunday school teacher. But lower down in the military hierarchy were officers a lot younger, trained in Germany with the stamp of Prussia upon them.[101] They were jaegers, light infantrymen impatient to strike. They did not relish "the Russians" over them and especially not Wilkama.

The jaegers were not a united body in their nefarious intrigues, for there were Finnish-peaking jaegers and Swedish-speaking jaegers and the language conflict penetrated their relations with each other. In course of time, however, the two principal sparring partners turned out to be Finnish-speakers, Wilkama and Aarne Sihvo, the young Karelian hero, who had cut such a dash in the victory Parade of 1918. For services in the counter-revolution, the storming of Viipuri, he had become a lieutenant-colonel at the age of 29 and by 1925, when he was 36, he was a major-general. It was not enough.

---

[100] Sakari Virkkunen, *Relander.Hymyilevä presidentii*, Helsinki (Otava), 1979, pp.13–14.

[101] The battalion in which they served was called the 27th Royal Prussian Jaeger Battalion.

When Wilkama was on leave of absence, Sihvo wrote to him, on 25 July 1925, and suggested he should resign as commander and take instead the post of inspector-general of the armed forces, which had been offered to him.[102] In spite of this appalling *faux pas,* Sihvo was not necessarily *then* Wilkama's principal opponent.[103] However, Wilkama had had enough and cleared out and Sihvo got his job. A Finnish-speaker thus remained as head of the armed forces, but this time he was a jaeger. The Swedish-speaking jaegers, who had been equally dissatisfied with Wilkama, had, in all probability, been scheming for Mannerheim to replace him.[104] But, among a large section of the Finnish-speaking population, he was anathema because of his role in 1918. On the other hand, General Lauri Malmberg, the head of the civil guards' organization, also had the support of Swedish-speaking officers.[105]

Relander's decision, in plumping for Sihvo, had a socio-political as well as a military aspect. Relander was an Agrarian, whose wife was Swedish-speaking. Since he secured in the presidential election, the votes of the National Coalition Party, the Swedish People's Party[106] as well as the Agrarians, Relander was a compromise figure, who took in both sides of the Right and blunted the Agrarian onslaught on the Swedish-speakers. All three parties had one thing in common. They were all supporters of the civil guard of part-time soldiers, as was Relander personally. Wilkama, and this accounted for his support among the Left parties and some of the Centre, was not. Malmberg, as head of the civil guards, would have been to these parties and factions almost as objectionable as Mannerheim. A plus for Sihvo was that he had once been a Progressive Party M.P., a Centrist, in short. In all these politics, compromise or not, the Swedish interest took a back-seat and the labile (this time) Agrarians could claim a front-seat.[107]

All these machinations redounded to the credit neither of the military nor political arm. The quarrels went on for years. The basic issue, of the differences in military background between two groups of officers, should never have surfaced in the manner in which they did. It started in Ståhlberg's final presidential years with a threat of jaeger officers to strike, resign, and declare openly the sides they were taking.[108] It continued, after Sihvo's appointment, in the legal farce of the two Laukola brothers, Ilmari and

[102] Vesa Saarikoski, *Keskustajääkäri Aarne Sihvo,* Helsinki (SHS), 1997, pp. 159–160.
[103] ibid., p.164.
[104] ibid., p.168.
[105] ibid., p.170.
[106] George Schauman expressed the view that the Swedish-speakers voted for Mrs Signe Relander rather than for Dr. Lauri Kristian Relander. Virkkunen, op.cit., p.16.
[107] Saarikoski, op.cit., p.148.
[108] ibid., pp.145–152.

Waldemar, who resigned from the army when refused permission to stay longer on an extended course in the Turin Artillery Academy.[109] Sihvo then went on to sue the brothers for defamation.[110] The parties and politicians took sides and the followers of General Wilkama raised their heads in defence of the accused officers.[111] Whatever they thought of Wilkama, the Swedish-speaking interest now scented an opportunity to down Sihvo.[112] President Relander, whatever his initial stand in the whole matter, felt more and more inclined to ditch Sihvo for a more right-wing commander. But in the end he did not dare.[113] As Saarikoski has pointed out, even Kekkonen, in his nasty-minded articles in the student newspaper, could not avoid urging reconciliation between the sides.[114]

So these were the circles that were engaged in drilling the ordinary male citizens into a state of subordination through military service, the horrible details of which are set forth in Haanpää's works.[115] The only thing that can be said is that the wars, which were a decade and a half away, were going to be much worse.

President Relander's *Via Dolorosa*

The difficulties of Finnish parliamentary government having already come out clearly enough, it might be thought that with Lauri Relander as president on a party-backing in the presidential election of three parties previously in conflict with each other in parliamentary politics, then a positive force might spread downwards from presidency to Parliament. It was not to be like this, however. Apart from the new president's family problems (after two and a half years of his presidency, the presidential spouse was claiming that she could not go on),[116] the president himself had the innate suspicion of many Finns that people were against him, and many were, Relander divided people into friends, "friends," and enemies. The middle term was that of "false friends," often people who had not yet had enough practice in the expression of

---

[109] ibid., p.214.
[110] ibid., p.220.
[111] ibid., pp.224–227.
[112] ibid., p.227.
[113] ibid., pp.229–230.
[114] ibid., p.213.
[115] Pentti Haanpää, the collection of episodes of military life written in 1928 and published under the rubric of "Kenttä ja Kasarmi" ("In the Field and in the Barracks").*Pentti Haanpää teokset* 2, Helsinki (Otava),pp.43–123, 1976.
[116] Virkkunen, op.cit., pp.147–149.

hypocrisy and were easily seen through.[117] Strangely enough, Relander's biographer, Sakari Virkkunen, has seen him, in the title of his biography, as "the smiling president." Perhaps it was at best a smile of self-deprecation. The previous president, Ståhlberg, another piece of reluctance, had been asked by the Progressives, the Social Democrats, and an Agrarian delegation to run again, all strictly in accordance with his conviction of a firm Centre coalition. Instead, he had backed Risto Ryti of the Progressive Party. Hearing of the election of Relander, Ståhlberg wished he had run for a second term. The National Coalition Party, on the other hand, had voted for Relander, but the leader of that party, Paavo Virkkunen, had his apprehensions as to whether Relander could really cope.[118] Relander felt the same; but he had a wavering ambition to prove himself. He was a Finn.

The political party with which Relander had the greatest difficulties was his own, the Agrarian Union. It was one thing to be elected president, but to establish his own bearings in the political system he needed a line out to Parliament. The existence of a certain gulf between president and Parliament was less important for Relander than for Ståhlberg, whose model was that of a supreme court justice. Relander, in contrast, wanted to work for a distinct reconciliation between the parties.[119] Within his own party, he first got on best with Juho Emil Sunila, who, like Relander himself, had a doctorate. Less well did Relander get on with Kallio, who had had no higher education and was not even an *ylioppilas*.[120] Relander was aware of the tension between these two leaders and leaned to Sunila since the latter wanted, both as a social and a political matter, a *modus vivendi* between the Agrarian Union and the Swedish-speaking peasantry.[121] On the other hand, Sunila's attempts to relegate Kallio to a governorship or to the speakership of Parliament did not meet with Relander's approval.[122] Sunila had his own quirkiness. In his first ministry, from 1927 to 1928 (it lasted a year), he preferred to be its head as a professional rather than as an Agrarian prime minister and (later) hesitated before deciding (for his second ministry) to become an official Agrarian

---

[117] Lauri Kristian Relander, *Presidentin päiväkirja*, I, 1925–1927, ed. Eino Jutikkala, Helsinki (Weilin & Göös), 1967, pp. 411–412.

[118] Virkkunen, op.cit., p.14.

[119] Ilmari Heikinheimo, *Suomen elämäkerrasto*, Helsinki (Söderström), 1955, p.619.

[120] For those unacquainted with the Finnish educational system, the examination for the *ylioppilas* certificate is the final school leaving examination, entitling one *traditionally* to enter the university, in short "to be a student." But once you have passed it you do not necessarily have to study, but you can call yourself "a student."

[121] Relander, I, op.cit., p.433.

[122] ibid., I, pp. 105–108 & ibid., II, p.29.

premier.[123] Did he need a distance from his quarrelsome party, whose more strident members continued to fight the Swedish-speakers?[124] Kallio, who did not speak Swedish, was thought to be behind this, too, the charge on Relander being that he was soft on Swedish-speakers.[125] Svecoman (Swedish-speaking) or Fennoman (Finnish-speaking) these distinctions from the old Grand Duchy of Finland had not lost their intricate convolutions.

Most of all, Relander detested the Progressives. He told his diary that the they (as well as the Social Democrats, who had been behind the Progressive Party candidate Risto Ryti in the last presidential election), couldn't get along with the idea that "an Agrarian man was sitting in the presidential chair."[126] If not quite a revolution, this was a transformation in Finnish political society that the failed Socialist revolution had helped to pave the way for. The Agrarians had been White and they had reaped what the Socialist revolutionaries had sown. They had become "the people." But Relander, not quite a typical representative of their kind, was now hearing what a fine man Ståhlberg had been and that Ryti should be elected next time.[127]

Many of the Agrarians had once been Young Finns (the party from which the Progressives had sprung) and Relander felt that the Progressives were "political generals" trying to put the Agrarians under tutelage (*holhous)* as some kind of nco's for them.[128] Väinö Mäkinen, an Agrarian from Sortavala, warned him that Ryti was using Kallio to control the Agrarian Union.[129]

A Breather along the *Via Dolorosa*

The key to Relander's vision of politics was there in his *endeavour* to create working relations between the parties. In this he was more active than his predecessor, J.K. Ståhlberg, who was aware of the same problems of instituting government, but solved them by devising caretaker governments under, for example, the official A.K. Cajander. Relander's commitment to parliamentary government was hampered by the unwillingness of the parties themselves to stoop to taking office. They could make and break governments, but they did

---

123 ibid., I, p.451.
124 Note 95 of this chapter.
125 Relander, II, pp.58–60.
126 ibid. I, pp.78–79.
127 ibid., II, p.60.
128 ibid., I, pp.16 & 35.
129 ibid., I, p.438.

not want the responsibility of engaging in government itself, for they were factionist.[130]

In the autumn of 1926, a combination of Progressives, Swedish People's Party representatives, Social Democrats, and Left radicals, defeated Kyösti Kallio's second government, which was based on a coalition of Agrarians and National Coalition members. Defective bullets had been produced by the Riihimäki arms factory and there was corruption in the air. Kallio was surprised when he lost the vote of confidence and suspected that some members of the National Coalition Party had voted with the opposition parties.[131] But the conglomeration of dissidence among those who voted Kallio's second government down had no common bond; the bullets from the Riihimäki factory had, after all, been duds! It was certainly the case that in 1926 Ernst Relander (not President Relander) of the Swedish People's Party, and formerly a very hostile critic of any kind of Social Democratic Party,[132] was, by 1926, beginning to feel that cooperation with the Social Democrats over social policy might be a means of attaining his own party's language demands.[133] Yet on the defeat of Kallio's second government the Swedish People's Party did not participate in a new government with the Social Democrats. In November 1926, the former Progressive Party candidate in the presidential election, Risto Ryti, suggested the possibility of a government composed of Progressives, a certain wing of the Agrarian Party, and the Social Democrats.[134] It did not come off. Since the Left Socialist radicals (known as "Communists") would not enter a government with the bourgeois parties and the SDP did not want them either, and since no bourgeois party would anyway join a government led by a Social Democrat, there were two alternatives: a caretaker government led by a civil servant or a Social Democratic minority government. Relander plumped for the latter. The extreme Left electoral alliance believed that the acceptance of government by the Social Democratic Party was a traitorous act.[135]

[130] Relander, I, op.cit.,on 16 December 1926, a few days after the fall of the second Kallio government, told his diary that of the non-Socialist parties, the Progressives refused all participation in government, the National Coalition Party would only enter a government which had an absolute majority–but would not take the premiership, the Agrarians would not provide a premier for a government in which the other parties were the Swedish or the National Coalition Party, while the Swedish Party would never attempt to form a government.

[131] Hokkanen, I, p.468.

[132] von Bonsdorff & Jernström, op.cit., p.101, when, in March 1920, Ståhlberg wanted them in the government, to smoothen out the path to peace with Russia, Estlander demurred on their participation.

[133] ibid., pp.307-308.

[134] Hokkanen, op.cit., p.468.

[135] Tanner,op.cit., pp.82-83.

In accepting the proffered choice of government, after an election in which they gained as many seats as the parliamentary election of 1924 (60), the Social Democrats, with a previous refusal behind them,[136] now assumed a degree of parliamentary responsibility: but only in theory. They were already hemmed round. A believer in what later became known as *eheyttäminen* ("making whole")[137] in Finland, Relander had automatically excluded the Left Socialist radicals from participation in Väinö Tanner's Social Democrat government. Radicals of this kind both Relander and Tanner himself called "Communists." Lookng back a year later on Tanner's minority SDP government, President Relander felt that without this chance on their own, the Social Democrats and "the Communists" might have drawn closer.[138] It was therefore quite natural that, having decided to trust the constitutionalist Social Democrats as legitimate, he nonetheless went round the other legitimate parties to see if he was right. Pehr Evind Svinhufvud of the National Coalition Party simply gave the laconic comment "let them try."[139] To secure, among the Swedish People's Party and the Progressives, a minimum of support for the minority Social Democratic government, Relander warned that the government's programme had to be as narrow as possible.[140] This might be thought good advice for a minority government. But the speaker of Parliament, Paavo Virkkunen,[141] a distinguished theologian of the National Coalition Party, who had checked the programme of Tanner's forthcoming government, had a more cynical interpretation, illustrating the ruling out of the use of Parliament as a means of promoting consideration of broad

---

[136] In 1919 the possibility was mooted by the Progressives that the Tannerite Social Democrats would join the government, but the Progressive prime minister Kaarlo Castren, would not accept two of the most important parts of the SDP programme,an all-round amnesty and an end to the civil guards:Hannu Soikkanen, op.cit., pp.338–339.

[137] Relander I, op.cit., p.27 stressed, in his first presidential speech, the need to improve the economy as a means of strengthening political *eheyttäminen*. For other significant references, ibid., pp. 63,88,188, & 460. But on p.71 with respect to the Social Democrats' opposition to the civil guards, he asserted—somewhat curiously—that *eheyttäminen* should not take place at the cost of "justice." This view is comparable to his rejection of *eheyttäminen* with the "Communists."

[138] Relander, op.cit., p.484

[139] ibid., p.361.

[140] ibid., p.347 & 353–355. The general line of the Progressives was that they had not caused the fall of the government and therefore had no responsibility for creating a new government; a couple of Progressives were, however, suspected of approaching the Social Democrats for governmental office, but had not consulted their own party group. The National Coalition leaders, Paavo Virkkunen & Eemil Nestor Setälä, had the nerve to recommend that the Progressives should join the government.

[141] Heikinheimo, op.cit., p.830,tells how Virkkunen's dissertation dealt with the beginning of the disputes among the Arians—presumably a good training for Finnish politics!

alternatives.: "nothing will come of this, and if it does come, it will not last."[142] He was not quite right, for the Social Democratic government secured, helped by the votes of some Leftist members of the Swedish People's Party and the "Communists," an amnesty for those still in prison for their part in the 1918 revolution. But otherwise Virkkunen *was* right. Tànner's plan for a national health insurance was defeated and as he himself noted, it was to take almost forty years to get it achieved.[143] The parliamentary parties did not like being usurped in government by a caretaker government of officials,[144] and so, suspiciously tolerant as Relander had seemed in asking the Social Democrats to form a minority government, he had really had no alternative, for the other parties needed a break from the tiresome business of government. This then was the real political background to Tanner's taking the salute on 16 May 1927.

Relander, in spite of his desire to be a mediator between the parties, did not trust the rank and file of the Social Democratic Party. Should war occur with the Soviet state, the party would abandon Tanner and support the Russians, he believed.[145] In spite of these deep misgivings, Relander, in his discussions with Tanner, began to search for a way out of the continuing oppositional stance of the Social Democratic Party. This is what he thought up. The Social Democrats might even join a bourgeois government provided that government would alter the tax structure and go in for social security, while on the other hand the Social Democrats would agree to accept subsidies to industry and agriculture. On the workability of this model, Relander had more detailed proposals: the Social Democrats should agree to maintain the bulk of the agricultural duties and in return the financial tariffs (for government revenue), the sugar and coffee duties, should be abandoned.[146] Though a minority government, the Social Democrats did not follow this advice. They fell from office because they tried to alter the tariff on rye imports in the name of cheaper bread, an urban piece of politics. The Social Democrats remained, with the Progressives, a party of urbanization. As a whole, they were not ready to make compromises, though Tanner apparently was.[147] The Social Democratic- Agrarian alliance, foreshadowed by Relander, was still a long way off. In fact, in 1928, the Social Democrats, in the election of the speaker and deputy-speakers of Parliament, voted for the chairman of

---

142 Relander I,op.cit., p.354.
143 Tanner, op.cit., pp. 86–87.
144 Relander I, op.cit., p.165.
145 Relander, I, op.cit., p. 441.
146 ibid, I, op.cit., p. 442.
147 ibid., I, p. 470.

the Swedish People's Party, Ragnar Furuhjelm, who became deputy-speaker, thus knocking Kallio out by one vote. Tit for tat.

Relander, though he had sought to sponsor, a Social Democrat-Agrarian rapprochement, called this "a great victory for Tanner."[148] In terms of the interplay of multi-party constitutionalism, Relander might have had a point. At the same time, it was surely from this sort of politics that he was trying to find a way out. Others of a very different sort were soon going to try to find that way, too.

Tanner's minority government hardly illustrated the success of the Ståhlberg constitution's permissive outlook towards coalition government, nor was Relander the strong executive force to knock heads together so as to serve this aspect of constitutionality. The constitution was wavering and, the achievement of a final amnesty apart, the Left was divided, while even the kindly Relander was afraid of its members.

The Lapua Movement

In terms of the general criteria of economic performance beloved of the economists and some economic historians, Finland had become increasingly prosperous by the mid-1920s, once, that is, the disturbances caused by revolutionary Reds and the costs of the newly-independent state had been smoothed down into a bearable plateau. The best way of smoothing down was found, by 1920, to be devaluation of the mark. This had, as its inevitable consequence, the growth of inflation, but the positive side of this was that the smallholder population (most of the farmers) could pay off more easily any debts contracted by payments for the land assigned to the crofter population or got as a result of the *Lex Kallio*.

Since the funds for land purchase were originally provided by the state, the financial burden on the state was considerable, particularly when inflation reduced the real value of the peasants' repayments. In 1920, a new law for income and property tax was introduced since the state needed an increase in fiscal funding for its needs. Nonetheless, these taxes did not fall heavily on the smallholder. The state continued to draw the bulk of its income from tariffs, which in turn protected the agricultural sector from the competition of cheaper food imports—to the chagrin of the urban working-class population.

One of the advantages for the smallholder freed from the crofter system was that he received not merely arable and meadow land, but also a stretch of timber, which he had not had previously as part of his rented land. This

---

[148] ibid., II, pp. 29–30.

enabled him to sell his wood for export in a postwar world engaged in massive efforts to reconstruct from war damage and wartime neglect. In this way, the smallholder was enabled to pay off his own debts to the institutions (state or savings bank) that had loaned him funding.[149]

But the export of sawn timber from Finland, mainly to Western Europe, was facing by 1928 strong competition from other timber exporters elsewhere, particularly from Sweden and the Soviet Union. In addition Left Socialist and Communist workers in the Finnish ports conducted an over- ten-month long strike in the same year, which was ultimately broken by non-union labour, most of which was drawn from southern Ostrobothnia. What these Ostrobthnians probably did not know was that the Finnish wood industry had entered into an agreement with both the Swedish and Soviet exporters at least as far as the British market was concerned (the main market) to share out the market.[150] To the Ostrobothnian farmers the scenario appeared simply as a combination of local Communism and aggressive international Communism now expressed through the politics of international trade. The basic situation was, however, that the Soviet Union was now doing a deal with the international traders of the capitalist world. As the market was becoming saturated, after the postwar reconstruction boom was over, a monopolistic share-out of what remained of the market was an inevitable reaction. The Soviet export companies had competed, but then joined the system. The enemy was the same for the striking port workers as for the Ostrobothnian farmers, namely fluctuations in the capitalist system.

Then the two sides of the citizens' divide, having fought in the ports for some time (the strike-breakers' organization *Vientirauha* ("Export Peace"), had been founded by the employers in 1920), now started up a wider campaign against each other, which was to threaten in its outcome the presidential-parliamentary system of their country. The symbolic act was a piece of near-sacrilege as far as the pious Ostrobothnians were concerned. On November 1929, a group of Young Communists, dressed in red shirts went to Lapua (a centre of Lutheran Pietism, though not yet a bishopric) and outside the workers' hall made Communist propaganda. An enraged group of local citizens then manhandled them and stripped them of their shirts. Nevertheless, the Communists had had permits for their meetings. A few days later, the Agrarian-led government of Kyösti Kallio (of the thirteen ministers in his government two came from the Progressive Party and the one "professional" minister was the former Swedish People's Party member, the ambitious Hjalmar Procopé: the rest were Agrarians) introduced legislation

[149] Virrankoski, op.cit., pp. 202 &204.
[150] Virrankoski, op.cit., p. 211.

abolishing the right of free association for Communists.[151] As David Kirby has pointed out,[152] measures to bridle the Communists had been planned by the government of the day for some time. That government might well have given voice to a similar statement to the one shortly to be forthcoming from a noisy politician in a somewhat larger country in speaking to the people: "we know what is in your mind." For a section of the Finnish political system was already thrashing round and blaming the radical Left for the doldrums into which the economic situation was drifting in Finland. But in seeking to thwart the Communists, the government and the populace involved were dealing with the symptom not the underlying cause.

After the events in Lapua, support groups sprang up over the south and west of the country and a Lapua Movement was formed.[153] It began to put pressure on the government, which, in the opinion of the movement, was not acting readily enough against "Communism and Russian slavery." A Law of Lapua was devised to "by-pass the written law."[154] With the aid of this "people's will"-.type of thinking, illegalities could be condoned. Communists, Social Democrats, even Progressives, were harassed[155] and, on 14 October 1930, former president Ståhlberg and his wife were kidnapped, the intention being to dump them over the Soviet border.

While this movement had started in the basically agricultural area of Ostrobothnia, it soon attracted a motley band of Pietistic clergymen (like the vicar of Lapua, Kaarlo Kares), civil guards (often themselves farmers), serving officers (like Major-General K.M. Wallenius, a former Jaeger, who planned the abduction of President and Mrs. Ståhlberg), academic supporters (like the historian J.R. Danielson-Kalmari, the former chancellor of the University of Turku, who believed, like President Relander,[156] that in the event of a war with Russia, the Social Democrats would not defend their country)[157] and politicians like the chairman of the National Coalition Party parliamentary group Professor Kyösti Haataja, expert on land legislation and inevitable

---

[151] Rintala, op.cit., pp. 164–167.

[152] Kirby, A *Concise History of Finland,* p.177.

[153] It was not formed till June 1930 after dissatisfaction with a previous organization, *Suomen Lukko,* which was for the Lapuans too close to the existng party system. Rintala, op.cit., p.197.

[154] Rintala, op.cit., p.165.

[155] The "flying columns" of the Lapua movement mainly targeted alleged "Communists," but Väinö Hakkila, a leading Social Democrat politician from Tampere was also taken "for a ride." He had spoken against both the Lapua movement and Communism. Juha Siltala, *Lapuanliike ja kyyditykset 1930,* Helsinki (Otava),1985, pp.284–287. In the localities Social Democrats were often so terrorized as to be unwilling to sek redress in the courts:ibid., p.411.

[156] See this chapter, note 145.

[157] Rintala, op.cit., p.185.

committee member).[158] The head of the Lapua Movement was a comparatively well-off farmer, Vihtori Kosola, who attacked at the same time both Marxism and "party power." "Others do what they can. We do what we like."[159]

On 7 July 1930 a march was held in the capital. This time it was farmers' march, though it was marshalled and organized by leading military figures, including two former jaegers. The men were, many of them, armed[160]—or, as the historian Vesa Saarikoski puts it, "the men marched with their mausers on their hip under their raincoats."[161] They were welcomed by General Mannerheim, President Relander, and by the outgoing prime minister, Kyösti Kallio, whose resignation they had activated, and by the new prime minister, Pehr Evind Svinhufvud, who was to become president a year later. Whatever was going on?

The authorities had been kind to the marchers, granting them half-price tickets on the railway. This at least showed that many of the marchers were regarded as being men of modest income. Undoubtedly, many of them were Agrarian Union voters. The president was an Agrarian, the prime minister of yesterday an Agrarian, while the general had always praised his peasant soldiers in the counter-revolution and now continued to praise them, as they praised him.[162] From this point of view therefore what was happening was a property-owning democracy in revolt against its democracy. It was in revolt because the property it owned was often too small.

The Agrarian leaders had felt that they had done their best for their own in the previous decade, ending the crofter system (even though this had not been a common system in Ostrobothnia) and by developing a system that would have allowed the buying of extra land on easier terms. But the capital for this—and for agricultural improvements in general- depended on the international pricing of timber. International trade did not care if the Soviet Union dumped timber on the world market in a period in which the demand for timber slackened, but the Finnish farmers could not stand up to this and their resentment against everything to do with their eastern neighbour only grew. That resentment included the alleged or real supporters in Finland of the Soviet Union in the continually-striking trade union movement.[163] Many

[158] ibid., p.181.

[159] Heikinheimo, op.cit., p.404.

[160] Rintala, op.cit., p.177.

[161] Saarikoski, op.cit., p.241.

[162] Rintala, op.cit., pp.178–179.

[163] But now at this critical moment the trade union movement split and in 1930 the Social Democrats formed their own umbrella organization, the SAK distinct from the SAJ, a movement in which Social Democrats and "Communists" had struggkled to work together:

Finnish farmers had difficulty in living solely from agriculture. On the other hand, as the world slump hit the saw mills and paper mills in Finland, if you could manage on your land you were saved from the threat of unemployment that might be the factory workers' lot. The statistics seem to show that Finland came out better in the world slump than many of the more industrialized countries. But the livelihood of many farmers in Finland was a tough one. Until the price of timber rose again, the solution was to protect agriculture still more.

Hence the true heir of the Lapua movement was not the abortive and aborted Mäntsälä revolt of a section of the civil guard in 1932[164] nor the development of a fringe Fascist Party under the leadership of Vihtori Kosola:[165] Svinhuvfud, on becoming president in 1931, would not countenance the former, and his party, the National Coalition Party, took care of the latter manifestation by running for some time an *electoral* alliance with it. The true heir of the Lapua movement was the movement known in Finnish as the *pulaliike*,[166] a movement of discontent in that hitherto allegedly-favoured section of "the people," the peasantry.

Meanwhile, the under-privileged in Finnish society, trade unionists on the one side and smallholders on the other, remained in conflict with each other. When international circumstances changed, the constitutionalist state had difficulty in solving the problems of either group, but it was the latter group it was more concerned with. But in listening to this protest in terms laid down by the Lapua Movement, constitutionalism itself became damaged. Two days before the farmers' march the two members of the radical Left Party who were its representatives on the Constitutioanl Committee of Parliament were dragged from the Committee meeting. Shortly afterwards, by executive decree of the Ministry of the Interior, all "Communist" election activity was

---

Lauri Haataja et al, *Suomen Työväenliikkeen Historia,* Helsinki (Työväen Sivistysliitto), 1976, esp. pp.165–172.

[164] On 27.2.1932, when Dr. Mikko Erich was speaking in the workers' hall at Mäntsälä, his meeting was disturbed by local civil guards and later more travelled from other parts to start a rebellion. Some top military officers were implicated, but Svinhufvud, now president, and the conscript armed forces, stood firm against them. Antero Jyränki believes that this is a recommendation for an army based on military service.

[165] The IKL was a continuation of the Lapua movement. It was fascist black-shirt movement that disdained the term "party" though it fought in the parliamentary elections and in 1933 was even in an electoral alliance with the National Coalition Party, whose then political leader was J.K. Paasikivi! Kari Selen, "Tasavalta hakee suuntaa,"in *Itsenäisen Suomen historia,* 2, Helsinki (Weilin & Göös), 1991, pp.241–243.

[166] The term *pula* refers to the then economic depression, while *liike* means "movement."

banned[167]. This was the end for over fourteen years of the parliamentary representation of the extreme Left.

These events occurred against a background of the loss of parliamentary authority. The Agrarian prime minister Kyösti Kallio resigned in early June though he had received a vote of confidence from Parliament.[168] It seemed as if he had no confidence in the vote of confidence. Svinhufvud was waiting in the wings and took office without an election, forming a Centre-Right government.

Svinhufvud, who had stood up well against Russian oppression before the First World War,[169] was, however, by now only part-constitutionalist and he offered seats in his cabinet to the Lapua Movement. Its leaders refused. On his becoming president in 1931, he was succeeded as prime minister by Juho Sunila, an Agrarian, who continued with a Centre-Right government. But Svinhufvud's first choice for prime minister had been Rudolf Walden, a powerful industrialist and crony of Mannerheim's. He could have spoken for exports, whose interruption by Left-wing strikers had been one of the factors in the rise of the Lapua Movement (in his paperwork no unions were allowed).[170] Walden, who was not a member of Parliament, had the sense to refuse the offer.[171] Mannerheim, on the other hand, did not refuse the offer to become head of a reconstituted Defence Council. This gave a sense of stability to the Right, whose members from Svinhufvud's government of 1930–1931, to Kallio's government of 1936–1937, were prepared to negotiate with the Agrarians for ministerial positions, a possibility that soothed the *kykypuolue* (the party of all talents, namely the National Coalition Party). (This party held the presidency under Svinhufvud from 1931–1937, while the Agrarian Kallio held it from 1937–1940).

The *Pulaliike*

In Finnish historical writing, Kallio's work, in fostering the cultivation of extra land for the farming community of peasant stock through measures like the

---

[167] Rintala, op.cit., pp. 171–172 & 183.

[168] ibid., pp.175–176.

[169] In the autumn of 1914, he objected as a jurist to the appointment of a Russian to the post of procurator in Finland. Svinhufvud was exiled in consequence to Siberia, returning home after the March revolution of 1917. Juva, I, op.cit.,pp. 474–481.

[170] But housing for workers was provided at reasonable cost. On this patriarchal system, *without mentioning the prohibition on trade unions in many inter-war Finnish factory complexes,* see the appendix on Finland in R. Seebohm Rowntree & G.R. Lavers, *English Life & Leisure. A Social Study*, London (Longmans Green), 1951, esp. p. 457.

[171] Mauno Jääskeläinen,*Valtioneuvoston historia,* I, p.492 & E.Juva, *Rudolf Walden,* II, p.446.

Lex Kallio of 1922 and comparable reforms, has been overestimated. Kallio himself was a comparatively prosperous farmer: his handling of agrarian issues in the depression of 1928 to the mid-thirties was inept as far as the needs of many of the less affluent members of the peasant class were concerned. It had been estimated that a plot of 9–10 hectares would be sufficient to provide a reasonable standard of living, but by the early 1930s three-quarters of the peasant class were living on plots of less than this hectarage, so that extra work, for example, in timber flotation, was essential for this class.[172] They were even more dependent for their survival on the sawn timber export trade (before the depression jut over 50% of Finnish exports)[173] than were the large firms of the forestry industry, which years before had been going over to paper and pulp This is not to say that the middle-rank farmers (who might grow their own timber) were also exposed and one authority holds that the majority of forced sales of farms occurred in this latter class.[174]

The *pulaliike* grew out of the failure of the Lapua Movement to do anything substantial for agriculture. That movement had knocked the Left off its perch,[175] in the course of which action the Lapuans helped the constitutional forces to suppress an officially-alleged "Communism." But that was small beer. The Lapua Movement was a political movement that lost its way in politics. It was anti-parliamentary and anti-party demanding instead Fascist-type "coalitions" of interests, but its "march on Helsinki" turned out to be another "march in Helsinki," a patriotic demonstration that put Svinhufvud back in power. He had offered their leader, Vihtori Kosola, and their main religious figure, Kaarlo Kares, the Vicar of Lapua, seats in his government. But since the Movement as such was not a constitutionalist movement, it seemed as if a self-denying ordinance was enduring almost of the same strength as Kautsky's old imposition on the Social Democratic Party's participation in power with the bourgeois parties. Hence, the Lapua Movement used the narrowly-constitutionalist Right and the narrowly-constitutionalist Right used the Lapua Movement and ultimately swallowed most of it up. Svinhufvud paid off

---

[172] Jorma Kalela, *Pulapolitiikkaa*, Helsinki (Työväen taloudellinen tutkimuslaitos), no.13, 1987, p.80.

[173] ibid., p.23.

[174] ibid., p.96. This may have been because the smallholders were unable to get loans and the middle-rankers had mortgaged their farms. On the other hand, Kari Selén has maintained that the enforced sales hit all ranks of farmers—there were 15,000 between 1928 and 1936: Kari Selen, "Tasavalta hakee suuntaa," in *Itsenäisen Suomen historia*, 2, Helsinki (Weilin & Göös), 1991, p.235.

[175] Upton, *Kommunismi Suomessa*, pp.85–86, believes that the extreme Left failed to persuade the smallholders in the late 1920s that they could offer them anything. It may be argued that the legitimate parties and the anti-parties were equally useless.

the guards to go home. Thus, in so far as Parliament and parliamentary government was maintained, the Social Democrats could live in hope. They had supported Ståhlberg in the presidential election of 1931 as they had done in 1919. He did not make it in 1931. It may still be argued that the SDP had, in their maintenance as a legitimate party, reaped the fruits of the Ståhlbergian concept of *political* centrism. But they had also suffered an emasculation in terms of their *economic* policy and the means of achieving it.

Ståhlberg was a Progressive, but so, too was the head of the Bank of Finland, Risto Ryti. And the president was a very conservative Pehr Evind Svinhufvud, standing by to prevent the realization of disturbing ideas. In December 1932, Svinhufvud broke the Agrarian-led government of Juho Sunila by refusing to accept that government's proposal to reduce the interest rate and thus provide cheaper money.[190] The "centrism" as originally envisaged by Ståhlberg was, after all, a piece of political manoeuvering, however well-intentioned it was meant to be as a preservation for liberal values. Two parts of the equation, the Social Democrats and the Agrarians, were not *in strictu senso* bourgeois parties, but the third part of the equation, the minor but dominant fraction, the Progressive Party, was. It might equally well line up with the other bourgeois parties, particularly in economic issues. Both Social Democrats and Agrarians were therefore liable to find themselves trapped. Representative committees of Parliament permitted this to occur. On the Retrenchment Committee of Parliament (*supistamislautakunta)* set up in March 1931 sat Väinö Tanner of the SDP and Tyko Reinikka of the Agrarian Union (admittedly a Right-wing Agrarian who needed no incentive to cut state expenditure—but others of his party would have wanted a more expansionist credit policy). These two figures signed a report for retrenchment along with Alexander Frey (of the Swedish People's Party), J.K. Paasikivi (of the National Coalition Party) and Risto Ryti (of the Progressives).[191] All five were sitting on bank boards of one kind or another, Ryti as head of the Bank of Finland.

In the latter capacity, Ryti resisted calls for a reduction in the interest rate. He was more or less supported by the representatives of the private banks.[192] It is true that within both the Agrarian Union and the Social Democratic Party voices were heard for a reduction. But since the chairmen of the two latter parties, Kallio[193] and Tanner, were prepared to follow Ryti when it came to it,

---

[190] Mauno Jääskeläinen, "Demokratian kriisi" in *Valtioneuvoston historia 1917–1966,* I, Helsinki (Valtioneuvoston historiatoimikunta), 1917-1966.

[191] Kalela, op.cit., pp.63-65. Also, p.77.

[192] On the other hand, Ryti was not above lambasting the private banks for their too-extensive network of local branches. Martti Turtola, *Risto Ryti. Elämä isänmaan puolesta,* Helsinki (Otava), 1994, p.157.

[193] ibid., p.156 quoting Heikkilä, on Kallio's support.

the Ståhlbergian centrism turned out to be a triumph of conservative banking against somewhat discontented political parties. The experts ran the democracy into the ground. The problem of the Finnish political community was not simply that of a threatening *political* dictatorship from the side of the Lapua Movement. There was another sort of dictatorship in being–albeit temporary. This was what Ryti, its chief servant, called the "dictatorship of the empty purse."[194] Farmers should bear their own mistakes and all should make sacrifices,[195] though it is difficult to see what kind of sacrifice Ryti himself made. Was it that he had taken his country off the Gold Standard?

Since this regulation of the currency had failed, at first glance it may be equally difficult to estimate what exactly his Bank policy really was. It sometimes looked as if he just wanted to let things alone, finding their own natural level as it were, an interpretation that both Kalela and Turtola, from their different standpoints, seem to be in a certain agreement about.[196] However, Ryti's financial conservatism now came to his aid. Having once taken Finland into the Gold Standard in 1926 (at a time when the Finnish mark had fallen 70% on its prewar value and on entry Ryti had it undervalued even further),[197] his cautious policy enabled both the Bank of Finland and the commercial-industrial sector in Finland to take up short and middle-term loans from both the Bank of England and the City of London. These credits were for the financing of Finnish exports, especially to Britain[198]–and were not for the stimulation of Finnish domestic consumption. In 1931, when many farmers were losing their land, Finland had a foreign trade balance of 1000 million marks.[199] In 1933, Ryti led the country into the sterling area,[200] the next best thing to leading it into the Gold Standard? So, in spite of the Second World War, Ryti's reputation, at least among British historians and bankers, has remained quite high.[201]

Patrick Salmon has been at pains to show that while Ryti entered the Bank of England's governor Montague Norman's "professional caste" of consulting central bank heads, he was not averse to politicians (as Norman was) nor even

---

194 Turtola, op.cit., p.151.

195 ibid., pp.155 & 151–152.

196 Kalela, op.cit., p.243 & Turtola, p.157.

197 Patrick Salmon,"The Bank of Finland and England during the inter-war period," in "*Muille maille vierahille . .* " *Kalervo Hovi ja yleinen historia*, Turku, (Turun historiallinen yhdistys), 2002, p.134.

198 Turtola, op.cit., pp.164–166.

199 ibid., p.167.

200 ibid., p.147.

201 Patrick Salmon, op.cit. esp. pp.145–146, and Mervyn King, "Risto Ryti ja Englannin keskuspankki," *Kanava*, no.6, 2006, pp.368–369.

to becoming one.[202] This interpretation overlooks several factors. The Progressive Party was in continuous decline from 1930 (22 seats), 1933 (11 seats), 1936 (7seats), till 1939 (6 seats). Much more than the National Coalition Party, it was a *kykypuolue* of well-educated representatives. Ryti's empire was the Bank of Finland, which put Parliament and politicians in their place, as Salmon himself shows.[203] In 1932, when the Sunila government fell, Ryti was invited to head the next government but he preferred to stay on as head of the Bank.[204] Above all, when Kallio was no longer capable of holding presidential office in 1940, Ryti was to take it up—as a patriotic chore.

Tacit Alliance

The Progressive Party, as it were, filled in the gaps in the democracy. When Ryti preferred to be a banker rather than lead a government, another Progressive, the lawyer, Professor T.O.M. Kivimäki stepped in. His government was to last for close on four years. Like Ryti, Kivimäki had certainly done a stint in Parliament (Ryti from 1919–1924 &1927–1929 and Kivimäki in 1922, from 1924–1927, and from 1929 onwards). But in his economic policy, as prime minister, he deferred to the Bank of Finland, that is, to Ryti. This is exactly what President Svihufvud wanted: a tight working between the two bourgeois parties without any hindrance from troublesome Agrarians who wanted cheaper credit. But in the new government there were also Agrarians, two of whom came in outside the parliamentary party but with the blessing of the Agrarian Union itself,[205] and one of them, Professor K.T. Jutila, was minister of agriculture and the other, Dr. Eemil Hynninen, was minister of social affairs. But only towards the latter part of the Kivimäki ministry did they exert their influence. Kivimäki did not actually have a parliamentary majority[206] and ruled with the help of the Swedish People's Party. The National Coalition Party was against the government, but four of its members came in without the blessing of the party.[207] The Agrarian Union waited for better times and would not take part in Kivimäki's government, which, had replaced Sunila's government. So Kivimäki ruled with the help of professionals outside Parliament, most noteworthy of all, H.M.J. Relander, his

---

[202] Salmon, op.cit., pp.135,137, & 145–146.
[203] ibid., p.138.
[204] Jääskeläinen, op.cit., p.511.
[205] ibid., p.511.
[206] T.M. Kivimäki, *Suomalaisen poliittikon muistelmat*, Porvoo-Helsinki (Werner Söderström), 1965, p.75.
[207] ibid., pp.75–76.

old mathematics teacher and a Ph.D, who had been minister of finance before (in 1924,1925, and 1929), without sitting in Parliament. He was a well-known skinflint,[208] calculated to follow Ryti right to the end, who was the real power in the finances of the state.[209]

But most interesting of all was the role played by the Social Democratic Party. As stated above President Svinhufvud would have nothing to do with them in the government, though he had said in 1926 "let them try."[210] But the SDP nonetheless decided to support Kivimäki's government, a line of "responsibility without power," provided that the government continued to hold out against the Lapua Movement.[211] Here was the crux of the alliance created by Ståhlberg.

Legitimacy in politics thus meant for the SDP protection against the illegitimacy of, say, a violent movement such as that created by the men of Lapua. This was guaranteed by Ståhlbergian politics, whose protection of the Left was the source of the hostility of the Lapuans against him. Equally, for the sake of maintaining the rest of the community's conviction, that after all, the SDP had accepted bourgeois constitutionalism, the Party had to toe the line when rejected for government by the Svinhufvud presidency. Hence the SDP had to tack not merely to the Centre, but also to the Right. Svinhufvud's view being based upon a considered opinion that the SDP was really a Marxist party inspired by a doctrine of class war. What fed this was his experience of Tanner's government of 1926–1927, which, he averred, had wanted to cut military service to 9 months, slice the military budget, while at the same time raising the property tax to 100% and making the local tax progressive. Svinhufvud believed also that talk of a popular front against Fascism was a mere cover for an intriguing politics to establish a class-dominated state. Tanner was an exception and was being side-tracked by the radicals of the Party.[212]

So Svinhufvud made out his case and at the end of the Kivimäki ministry repeated his prohibition on having the Social Democrats in the new government, now led by Kyösti Kallio, mainly Agrarian and Progressive with the dissident Conservative, Arvi Oksala. He was undoubtedly bolstered in keeping the SDP out by the revelations of the secret police that the Communists were penetrating various Finnish institutions—the name of Professor Jutila (the minister of agriculture) cropped up. He resigned but the

---

[208] ibid., pp.77–78.
[209] ibid., p.78.
[210] this chap., note 139.
[211] Jääskeläinen, op.cit., p.513.
[212] Einar W. Juva, *P.E. Svinhufvud*, II, Porvoo-Helsinki (Werner Söderström), 1961, pp. 524–528.

Kivimäki government lost the vote of confidence, partly because a couple of Progressives preferred to go out and drink coffee when the vote was taken.[213] One of them became the next prime minister.

While there was much that was farcical and *intrigant* about all this, a few serious points could still be made. Svinhufvud himself was party responsible for stimulating the conspiratorial elements in the extreme Left by forbidding their party in Parliament. It is certainly true, however, that certain public scenes, such as hoisting the red flag in Tampere in 1933, easily gave rise to the fear that red extremism was just as bad as the black extremism of the IKL that it was claiming to oppose. Kivimäki had been introducing legislation to tighten up on spying and revolutionary activity. It was the Social Democrats who brought in a motion of no-confidence in consequence. The Agrarians did not like this and, in forming under Kallio, a new government, refused at this point to take the Social Democrats into it in spite of previous *pourparlers* with them.[214]

But more important still was the fact the Svinhufvud maintained his opposition, too, to the inclusion of the SDP in the new government. Was there no way out for the Social Democrats? There was.

Finland had a double executive, which, under Svinhufvud, interfered with the executive formed, in greater or less degree (often the latter), through Parliament. Kivimäki's government was not based on a direct representation of a majority. It was ultimately frustrated by the very party that had initially claimed to give it support *without representation*. It was watched over by the senior executive, the presidency, and in economic affairs by the Bank of Finland. In the general election of 1933 the SDP received 78 seats (66 earlier) and in 1936 they received 83 seats. But, as prime minister, Kivimäki did not believe that elections necessarily meant the resignation of government.[215] His government was not a truly parliamentary government: it was a sort of constitutionalism, which President Svinhufvud was backing up, in his narrow constitutionalist way. The way out of the trap into which the SDP had fallen was therefore to change the president.

So began the great institutional conflict in Finland that was in many respects detrimental for the political parties who were engaged in it. It was an internal conflict about how to govern the Finns, about where the hub of power was, in the presidency or in parliamentary government. In 1937, in the presidential election of that year, the Social Democrats, fed up with their patient waiting since 1932, decided to unseat Svinhufvud. In practice, this led

---

[213] Kivimäki, op.cit., pp.103–106.

[214] Jääskeläinen, op.cit., pp. 538–539.

[215] Kivimäki, op.cit., p.105.

to tactical voting. At first, the Social Democratic electors of the electoral college voted,[216] as traditionally, for Ståhlberg. But he received only half of the votes, one short of the simple majority needed. The SDP electors then joined the Agrarian electors and chose the Agrarian leader Kallio.

As it turned out, there were two consequences from this: for the first time in independent Finland, both halves of the people, countrymen and industrial working-class, had a president in common, for tactical voting had produced a presidency representing an alliance between the SDP and the Agrarian Union, which then formed the basis of the new government, even where the new prime minister was a Progressive.[217] The SDP and Agrarian Union alliance formed a cement in Finnish society, invaluable in the critical time to come. But, in the second place, tactical voting had produced a weak president, whose knowledge of the world was of the slightest. Svinhufvud certainly did have that knowledge, but he did not have the attitude nor the appropriate conviction to be able to unite "the people," nor were the international conjunctures favourable initially to his outlook on Europe. To sum up, however: a tension existed between the domestic and foreign policy of Finland.

The former was doing quite well. By the mid-thirties, the stability of the Finnish mark, Ryti's work, now served the opportunities provided by the more favourable economic trends in the world, in spite of the earlier sacrifices required in the name. of this currency. The Finnish sociologist Heikki Waris estimated that in the period 1926–1939 real wages rose 28%, though admitting that this general trend had witnessed some unpleasant shortfalls at certain times.[218] Unemployment had been dealt with by adding wherever possible to the funds used by the local government councils,[219] but as prime minister Kivimäki admitted in 1933 of the over 90,000 unemployed only slightly over 31,000 could be helped and a substantial alleviation did not occur till 1935.[220] On the whole, however, until the advent of the Red-Earth government of 1937, most of the provision of government funding for the less favoured classes of society went to agriculture or ancillary work: both Kivimäki

---

[216] The presidential elections until 1994 were not direct votes of the people, but electors were chosen for an electoral college, which out of an electoral body of 300 members had to produce a president by simple majority–and vote on until this was attained. The person ultimately chosen could therefore often be something of a surprise.

[217] The new prime minister was A.K. Cajander, one of two who had preferred to drink coffee rather than vote for the government of his party colleague, T.O.M. Kivimäki. Kivimäki, op.cit., p.105.

[218] Heikki Waris, *Suomalaisen yhteiskunnan sosiaalipolitiikka,* Porvoo-Helsinki (Werner Söderström), 1961, p.102.

[219] ibid., p.152.

[220] Kivimäki, op.cit., p.80.

and Kallio eased the redemption payments of farmers and by the end of 1937 some 2,700 farms had been redeemed, the greater part of them regained by their former owners. Where distraint still did occur, it became no longer possible to confiscate agricultural equipment.[221] For forest work, a tripartite system (employee, employer, and government representatives) was set in motion in 1935 for the determination of minimum wages.[222]

All these measures improved the situation *gradually* after Ryti's too tardy a retreat from the gold standard in 1931. Nonetheless, thousands of farmers had in the meantime lost their farms. The well-thought out experiment of Professor Jahnsson to cope with this crisis of capitalism by pursuing a policy of cheap money had not been tried, though it was meant to be a controlled experiment, releasing unused production capacity by a note- increase just great enough to have a multiplier-effect without excessive inflation.[223]

With the advent of the Red-Earth government, measures to support the development of agriculture continued, particularly with respect to corn growing[224]—fortunately, in the light of what was to come. But more general measures applicable, too, to urban workers or those in the *ruukit,*[225] were brought in: paid annual holidays,[226] for example. It was true that the leading Social Democrat newspaper, *Suomen Sosialidemokraatti* of 14.3.1937, on surveying the Red-Earth government's programme, drafted together by Tanner and Agrarians, said that there was little Socialism in it.[227] But that was the price to be paid for cooperation with the bourgeois and non-bourgeois centre, Progressives and Agrarians together. Majoritariainsm was not an option for the SDP.

The Second Finland

What, in the meantime, had been happening in the other Finland, where a form of Socialism *had* prevailed? The other Finland was the region of East Karelia, which had never belonged to the old Grand Duchy, but had been coveted by the independent state. Inhabited by a Finnic people, Karelians who spoke the Karelian language,[228] they were considered by Finnish intellectuals

---

[221] Jääskeläinen, op.cit., p.545.

[222] Waris, op.cit., p.103.

[223] Kalela, op.cit.,pp.234–237 for a critical review of Jahnsson's theorizing.

[224] Jääskeläinen, "Keskustan ja vasemmiston yhteistyö" in *Valtioneuvoston historia,* I, p.567.

[225] These were industrial establishments founded in the countryside where there was abundant water-power.

[226] Jääskeläinen, "Keskustan ja vasemmiston yhteistyö, p.567.

[227] ibid., pp.561-562.

[228] The Karelian language was also spoken in the Finnish border parishes such as Suojärvi.

and politicians as suitable subjects for a true Finnicization. For there, indeed, a form of majoritarianism did, indeed, prevail.

In 1920, Edvard Gylling, the last leader of the Red defence of Viipuri, was called from his Swedish exile by Lenin to run a Sovietized East Karelia. He went and ran the place well, bringing in Finnish-Americans with their capital equipment and dollars to develop the whole area, which became perhaps the most prosperous part of the Soviet Union. But the system fell foul of the Stalinist terror,[229] which was if anything far worse than the White terror of the counter-revolution in the Finland of 1918 and after, for there was no Ståhlberg in East Karelia nor in the Soviet Union to plead for reconciliation. Those Finnish Communists who survived, such as Otto Wille Kuusinen, did so by mouthing the justice of the fate of the accused. It was called rehabilitation.[230] Kuusinen's second wife, Aino, was in the labour camp (twice). He sent her some food and soap.[231] Thousands of Finns died, ordinary devoted believers and leaders like Gylling, Kullervo Manner, and Hanna Malm.[232] In general, this persecution was known in Finland, even if the knowledge filtered out gradually about particular individuals. The brutal irrationality of Russia and its politics was confirmed. A crude joke began to be circulated in Finland according to which Stalin was a good man because he killed a lot of Communists. As far as East Karelia was concerned, the twist of fate, was, in its irony, soon to be even greater.

---

[229] A partial explanation of this terror may have lain in the fact that, as an ageing Molotov later revealed in a TV interview (his wife was once in a camp), foreign Communist refugees in the Soviet Union (later the Spanish refusgeees) were felt to be in danger of introducing ideas at variance with Stalinist doctrine.

[230] The film *Mies varjossa* (1), shown on Finnish TV1, on 8.8.2006. Epidem.

[231] *Mies varjossa* (2) shown on Finnish TV on 14.8.2006. Epidem.

[232] Aino Kuusinen, *Jumala syöksee enkelinsä. Muistelmat vuosilta 1919–1965*, Helsinki (Otava), 1972, pp.224–225, revealed that Kullervo Manner, the former Finnish Social Democrat M.P. and Dictator in the final period of the Finnish Revolution, ended up in Soviet camp sweeping the floor in the camp's barber's shop: his wife Hanna Malm, another Soviet concentration camp victim, drowned herself.

CHAPTER 3
A RESTORATION OF POWER?

It was 16 May 1939. A parade was being held in the streets of Viipuri, the principal city in the Karelian Isthmus, then still in Finland, and not yet a part of the Soviet Union. Watching the parade was Mrs. Kerttu Kalenius from Kouvola. She was heavily pregnant and did not see much of the parade, having to be rushed to hospital to give birth to her daughter Helena. Mrs. Kalenius might just have had the time before the birth to hear the words of the army chaplain Sillanpää who recalled the words of the Epistle of Paul to the Romans, 8: 31, "If God be for us, who can be against us?" In the forthcoming war, there were to be plenty against the Finns, but in the long run, perhaps Apostle Paul, Chaplain Sillanpää, and the Almighty were going to be proved right. The short run was to be different.

Had Mrs. Kalenius seen the whole parade, she would have seen Major-General Taavetti Laatikainen, an old jaeger, and now head of the Viipuri garrison, marching at the head of his infantry, some coastal artillery, a naval contingent, planes flying overhead, and some anti-aircraft guns being trundled along, and she would have heard a lot of about the fortifications and the spirit of those who had volunteered to extend them.[1] *Eheyttyminen* (for the Finns, of course) was the name of the mood. That latter mood was to be demonstrated by the Finns in the forthcoming war. But the parade, on the ground and in the skies, was rather deceptive. On the outbreak of the war, on 30 November, there was still a shortfall of almost one-sixth as far as rifles were concerned, the Finnish artillery was predominantly former imperial Russian artillery from 1918, the country had only 13 modern tanks, and hardly any anti-tank weaponry.[2] Many Finnish soldiers had never seen a tank until compelled to fight one. Above all, there was a grave initial shortage of automatic weapons.[3]

The mood was intensifying, even among the Left, for preparing a defence of the country. In the *Suomen Sosialidemokraatti* of 14.3.1939, a statement already drawn up for the May meeting of the Party spoke for a strengthening of the armed forces as the League of Nations, ran the statement, was

---

[1] *Maakansa* (the Agrarian paper, then published in Viipuri), 17.5.1939.

[2] Ohto Manninen, "Suomi toisessa maailmansodassa" (*Itsenäisen Suomen historia*, 3), Vantaa (Weilin & Göös), 1992, pp.18–19.

[3] Anthony F.Upton, "The Winter War" in *History of the Second World War*, London (Purnell), 1966, pp. 127 & 130–131.

weakening. The strengthening of the armed forces was to take place "even if it could not be expected that the defence establishment of our country could fully protect our country against an attack from the forces of a Great Power." The statement also embodied a decision to repel the plans of any "irresponsible elements" to exploit an international situation as possibly favourable to them "if an attack occurred." Presumably, this meant Communists. The statement spoke out against Powers that were building up bases outside their own territory. Presumably, this meant the Soviet Union. It was a statement of neutrality, not militarism.

But it was a statement that implied that a declaration of neutrality might not be enough and that even the action of the country's own defence forces might be inadequate. The hidden question was who might the allies be: in other words, what use-value had Finland that would bring the forces of a foreign Power to its defence?

With its declaration of neutrality, reinforced in 1935 by prime minister T.M.Kivimäki,[4] Finland had no easy way into alliance politics. But it did have a military-naval policy of a defence of neutrality. Since he early 1930s, the two shores of the Gulf of Finland were guarded by Finland and Estonia at the mouth of the Gulf so as to box in the Soviet fleet in the eventuality of war. A foreign fleet would then have time to come into the Baltic to defend the two states.[5] But which would be the foreign fleet?

An Independent Finland. Of Use to Whom but the Finns?

Independence is to be on one's own. Yet the independent states, however jealous they are of their integrity, wish to provide something for others. In 1918, in the first few months of its existence, Finland had been of apparent use to Imperial Germany, in respect of which the White Finnish government was prepared to turn the country into a quasi-colony of Germany so as to take advantage of Ludendorff's drive eastwards. In fact, there was something deceptive, even panic-stricken in the Finnish White civilians' wish to take in the Germans. Mannerheim did not want them, even if he valued the Finnish jaegers the Germans had trained. Nor did Finland expand its borders with German aid–the Germans did not bring East Karelia to Finland. Their aim was to defeat Russia and control it. This most certainly embodied a stripping away of territories on Russia's Western borderlands, a colonization that also formed a barrier- but a *penetrable* one–between Germany proper and Russia

[4] George Maude, *The Finnish Dilemma*, London (Royal Institute of International Affairs & OUP), 1976, pp.7-8.

[5] Osmo Apunen & Corinne Wolff, *Pettureita ja patriootteja*, Helsinki (SKS), 2009, pp.41-42.

proper. After Brest-Litovsk, which laid down that the Russian troops should leave Finland—the shadow of a Russo-German rapprochement was in the air, and this in spite of the revolutionary aims of Lenin's government, which in its turn harboured the vain hope of helping to provide for the Socialist transformation of German society.

As to the Finns, the German defeat in the First World War and its suddenness in the final weeks overwhelmed them, flushed as they nevertheless were with their own victory over the Finnish Reds. But already in November 1918 Finland was recognized by Britain as a neutral country for trading purposes.[6] By this time, the British had come to their own rapid conclusions. For the Foreign Secretary, Arthur Balfour, Finland and the would-be independent Baltic States might also form a barrier, and the British minister to Sweden, Francis Howard, even toyed with the idea that Sweden should join in, though the Foreign Office expert on the north, Professor James Young Simpson, felt that because of the Åland dispute, Sweden could not join if Finland came in. But this, and other variations on barrier formation concocted by the British, had a dual purpose, for they aimed to prevent not merely Bolshevik expansion, but also the growing German hegemony in the eastern Baltic and, once more, the threat of Russo-German understanding.[7]

In all this tentative British planning, the planning of a victor, there was some local help. In January 1918, Rudolf Holsti became official representative of White Finland in Britain.[8] He was a declared Anglophile, had studied at the London School of Economics prewar, been a correspondent in London for the newspaper *Helsingin Sanomat*, worked for the passive resistance movement in those years and by his return to Britain in 1919 was already a rising star of the Young Finn-Progressive Party movement. In April 1918, he was instrumental in furthering a visit of an Estonian delegation to the British Foreign Office to plead for the independence of Estonia.

Holsti did not like his own country's connection with Germany, feeling already in spring 1918, that Germany had lost the war. But he managed to explain this German connection to the British Foreign Office as a means of getting rid of the Russians. On the other hand, his championship of Estonian independence and his emphasis to the British that the Baltic peoples wanted to get the Germans from their soil began to form part of a larger picture in which Finland's own identity was seen in terms of a linkage with independent

[6] Esa Sundbäck, *Finland in British Baltic Policy*, Helsinki (The Finnish Academy of Sciecnce and Letters), 2001, pp.274 & 326.
[7] ibid, pp.179–181.
[8] ibid., p.181.

Baltic states, a counterpoise to both Germany and Russia.[9] A construction of such a kind was not alien to British thinking since the British chargé d'affaires Francis Lindley, after meeting Estonian and Latvian representatives in January 1918, suggested to the British prime minister that the future of any Baltic states lay either in a relationship with Russia or with Finland and Sweden and possibly Poland.[10] The British views were, however, far from clear as yet: in the Foreign Office, the new Europeans, of whom Simpson was one, were inclined to think that the best bet for the Baltic lands was a Russian federation, assuming the development of a more liberal Russia.[11]

But while Holsti, back in Finland in 1918, was working on the alignment of Finland with the Baltic states and possibly Sweden, Svinhufvud and Paasikivi were binding Finland ever more to Germany, as the year went on. Two different foreign policies were working through at the same time. And the differences were party differences, *though how far Holsti's scheme were to represent the core policy of Progressivism was a more complex question.* These two lines were to continue to exist in Finnish foreign policy. They were ideologically based in origin, though historical circumstance was to overshadow this distinction. Actually, by 1919, the Finns even had a third foreign option, that of invading Petrograd under Mannerheim. But, as noted, neither the Finns themselves, nor the White Russians, nor the West felt up to undertaking this. The British prime minister, David Lloyd George, had already groaned at the expense of war operations in Russia,[12] and by 1921 was committed to the traditional Liberal line of trading with Russia as a means of softening relations with that troublesome state. As noted by Sundbäck, this was in political, military, and naval terms, a policy of withdrawal.[13] It was only the French who had a strong connecting point with the Baltic world as demonstrated by their support for Poland against the invasion of the Red Army in 1920": the miracle on the Vistula."

At the same time, back home in Finland, and foreign minister from 15 August 1919 to 20 May 1922, Holsti was stuck with the other side of British involvement in postwar Baltic affairs, namely the encouragement of alignments and even political unions between the smaller Baltic states, the politics, in short, of the barrier. But as both Germany and Russia were now considerably weakened states, this aspect of things had little urgency and,

---

[9] Heikki Roiko-Jokela, *Ihanteita ja reaalipolitikkaa. Rudolf Holstin toiminta Baltian maiden kansainvälisen de jure-tunnustamisen ja reunavaltioyhteistyön puolesta 1918–1922*, Jyväskylä (Jyväskylän yliopisto–Studia historica jyväskyläensia no.52), 1995, pp.64-67.
[10] ibid., pp.59-60.
[11] Sundbäck, op.cit., pp. 171-172.
[12] John Charmley, *Churchill. The End of Glory*,London (Hodder & Stoughton), 1993, p.157.
[13] Sundbäck, op.cit., p.228.

more importantly, with Sweden indifferent to matters on the other side of the Baltic, and the general uncertainty of life of the new states created there, the environment was not one in which Holsti could call up British involvement. Holsti, in the early autumn of 1921, asked the British Foreign Office as to whether it would be advisable to enter into a military alliance network with Estonia and Latvia. He was advised by a junior official to avoid such entanglements.[14] The head of the Northern Department, John Duncan Gregory, did not want to give any advice, for fear of binding Britain.[15] By 1927, the British foreign secretary, Austen Chamberlain, was telling the Latvia foreign minister that British involvement in Europe stopped at the Rhine.[16]

On the whole, official Britain seemed to look upon Finland as a new state with a strong chance of obtaining internal stability in spite of its recent civil conflict. There were therefore strong reasons for preferring Ståhlberg and Holsti as the architects of reconciliation. But by 1920, as far as the British were concerned, Holsti's dalliance with Poland was regarded as equally precarious since a section of Finnish public opinion did not approve of it. The British were well informed on the internal politics of Finland in the early 1920s and they had their preferences.[17] But this did not mean commitment. From the British side it was sympathy *without the sense of formal obligation* for the political grouping in Finland that most resembled in outlook the ideals of the British system.

In the early months of 1922, Holsti brought his plan to the fore, a political arrangement between Finland, Estonia, Latvia, Lithuania and Poland. It fell on several grounds. It was divorced even from the moral backup of British power, as Gregory in 1921 had made clear. In Finland itself, politicians were divided. President Ståhlberg was not enthusiastic since he feared that Poland would constitute a nuisance: on the other hand, Mannerheim and the aged politician J.R. Danielson-Kalmari were wanting only the Polish connection. Mannerheim's crony, General Rudolf Walden, somewhat strangely this time, did not go along with Mannerheim, but the National Coalition Party prime minister, Lauri Ingman, after an earlier hesitation, was prepared to go for the whole treaty. The Social Democrats were opposed to it for fear of worsening relations with Russia.[18] In Parliament, largely because of

---

[14] ibid., pp.229–234. Merja-Liisa Hinkkanen has charted in some detail the withdrawal even by 1920–1921 from British commitment to the Baltic states, though Holsti continued with his plans to 1922. Merja-Lisa Hinkkanen-Lievonen, *British Trade and Enterprise in the Baltic States 1919–1925*, Helsinki (SHS,. Studia historica no.14), 1984, esp.pp.94–95.

[15] Sundbäck, op.cit., p.233.

[16] Hinkkanen, op.cit., p.94.

[17] Sundbäck, op.cit., pp.197–199 & 224.

[18] Roiko-Jokela, op.cit., pp.256–259.

clause VII ("to act sympathetically to a member-state under attack"), the treaty was voted down. The proposed treaty had an inner weakness, two antagonistic member-states, Poland and Lithuania, were dissatisfied with it.[19] Many in Finland also felt that the treaty was liable to drag Finland into a Polish-German conflict.[20]

Holsti's idea had originally been to produce a large belt of states stretching from Norway to the Ukraine, a conglomeration that would be powerful enough to prevent Russo-German rapprochement[21] This view was Western. It rested on the conviction that the old empires, Russia and Germany, were the real imperialists. According to Holsti,[22] these Powers were weakened, but might be strong again. This view was, indeed, Western, but Holsti was trying to do the work of the West that the Western Powers were sceptical about.

As noted by Heikki Roiko-Jokela, following Jukka-Pekka Pietiäinen and Mauno Jääskeläinen, the policy envisaged by Holsti was not a policy of neutrality.[23] But, it might be added, its rejection reinforced Finnish neutrality. On 13 May 1922, Holsti resigned.

The post-First World War security schemes promoted by Holsti had come crashing down. In spite of many attempted variants, the states of *Zwischeneuropa*, the "Europe in-between," could not jell together in a security complex. The weaknesses were at all ends. The admiration for the Scandinavian example, held by many, did not in any way open up the possibility of an adherence of the Scandinavian states to East and South Baltic security proposals.[24] In the south, the revival of Poland brought with it a revival of traditional aspirations from the old state of 1772, albeit at first in the form of Pilsudski's federal schemes, but nonetheless taking in the Ukraine and White Russia—and Lithuania, the relations of which with Poland remained, particularly over Vilna, irreconcilable.[25] In between, Estonia and

---

[19] ibid., 258–259.

[20] This alienated the Social Democrats as well as the Right: Jukka-Pekka Pietiäinen, in *Itsenäistymisen vuodet 1917–1920*, vol.3, *Katse tulevaisuuteen*, Helsinki (VAPK), 1992, p.411

[21] Roiko-Jokela,op.cit., pp.260–261 & 277.

[22] ibid., p.277.

[23] ibid., p.270. Also Jukka-Pekka Pietiäinen, op.cit., p.400.

[24] Roiko-Jokela has pointed out that the Norwegians made it clear, early on,their standpoint was "Atlanticist." The inspiration that the Estonian liberal Jaan Tönisson found in the Scandinavian experience was not reciprocated by any concrete measures from,e.g., Sweden. See Kalervo Hovi, *Intressensphären im Baltikum. Finnland in Rahmen der Ostpolitik Polens 1919–1922*, Helsinki (SHS- Studia historica no.13), 1984, p.29. When Holsti's own endeavours began, the Åland question was still upsetting Finnish-Swedish relations.

[25] Hovi, op.cit.,esp. pp.65 (a proposed Polish federation with Lithuania) p. 121 (federation as a form of interest-sphere division),p. 132 (the suggestion of a Polish protectorate over the Ukraine), & p. 143 (Zeligowski's solution of the Vilna question).

Latvia quarrelled, by force of arms, over possession of the town of Valk, while Latvia alternated between calling in Polish aid against Russia and distrusting Polish influence.[26]

These problems constituted, in practice, a geopolitical mess. Poland became over-extended eastwards in the Ukraine and White Russia, while Lithuania, which had used Soviet forces–briefly–to regain Vilna, made its own treaty with Soviet Russia, a secret clause which would facilitate the advance of Russian troops westwards.[27] Lithuania thus remained the weakest link, a natural road for invasion–or linkage with[28]–Germany. Politically, the quarrel between Lithuania and Poland inhibited the Finns, in October 1920, from following up the proposals of the Polish Foreign Minister Eustachy Sapieha, welcomed by both Ståhlberg and Holsti, for a military agreement with Poland, Romania and the Baltic States.[29]

The very aim of a Baltic security system was protection against the eventuality of a hostile Great-Power alignment even where the priority of the emphasis, whether upon Russia or Germany, was different for the different potential members: for Finland it was primarily Russia, for Estonia it was Germany.[30] But common to all was the fear of a German-Russian rapprochement. Tragically, it was this fear that had also animated the interest of the Western Powers in such arrangements in respect of which, however, they gradually withdrew from any shred of the little responsibility they had once vaguely showed. They left Russia to its devices once it became clear that that country would not transform itself into a liberal state and satisfy the original solution for the Baltic provinces, autonomy within a Russian federation.[31] The one Western Power that did show a fairly consistent policy towards the states of *Zwischeneuropa* was France, which chummed up with Poland defending it in the "miracle of the Vistula" against the Red Army, but

---

[26] Hovi, op.cit., pp.87–94 (on Valk) & pp.114–121 & 145–151 (on Polish-Latvian relations).

[27] Seppo Myllyniemi, *Baltian kriisi 1938–1941*,Keuruu (1977), pp. 74 & 84.

[28] Hovi, op.cit., p.140.

[29] ibid., p.139.

[30] Svinhufvud in early autumn 1918 favoured a joint monarchy over Finland and Estonia, headed by a *German* prince, partly for the sake of gaining East Karelia for Finland. At the same time, the Estonians wanted, first of all, to be freed from the German invader and the power of the local German estate-holders. Hovi, op.cit., pp.34–36. Pietäinen, op.cit., p.405. In their reception of Sapieha's proposal, the Finns did not want a military alliance directed ostensibly against Germany, Hovi, op.cit., p.139.

[31] Hovi, op.cit., pp.26–28: this solution arose out of hopes immediately after the Russian revolution of March 1917. The French, in favour of a big and united Russia (with the exception of Finland and Poland) maintained well into 1919 their belief in putting back the Baltic provinces into Russia. Pietäinen, op.cit., pp.387 & 410.

showing little interest in the Baltic region otherwise[32] and seeing Poland more and more in terms of a French policy towards a Little Entente of the less northerly states. In a sense, the French broke into the policy of Holsti, who, by the summer of 1919, had developed the idea of gaining East Karelia for Finland by a utilization of the British-led Murmansk Legion.[33] The British, the Americans and the Italians might have backed this, but for the opposition of the French, who wanted all resources put together for Mannerheim's projected attack with the White General N.N. Yudenitch on Petrograd, after which a united non-Bolshevik Russia would be restored.[34]

The attitude of the West was thus crucial, but divided. There was no centre. It disappeared with war weariness and quarrels over Germany. These were—apparently—big enough problems of the moment. The future could take care of itself. Nor could a Baltic League produce its own centre. The Polish proposal of spheres of interest, with Finland in the north and Poland in the south as the two hubs, could not serve either to cope with the problems of *Zwischeneuropa's* own states in-between. Between the two hubs communications would have been difficult and rapidity of action equally so. Zeligowski's one-sided action in seizing Vilna and Mannerheim's persistence in thinking that a conquest of Petrograd was still a possibility for him after he had lost the presidential race were signs of internal weaknesses in the political structure of both Poland and Finland.[35]

The Retreat to Geneva

With the departure of Holsti from the foreign office in 1922, Finland faced two policy alternatives. The one was that of a carefully-considered and clearly-defined neutrality. This depended on an objective geopolitical factor, namely that in war there was no particular use-value of or in Finland. The other alternative was directly the opposite: it saw that Finland just *might* be involved in war and that the opportunity to call up additional aid in hostile circumstances was worth ensuring. The two alternatives were not necessarily of

---

[32] Though by the April of 1919 supporting at least the idea of a Polish-Lithuanian Federation, a non-starter from the Lithuanian side. Hovi, op.cit., p.70.

[33] The Murmansk Legion was formed by the British from Finnish Reds who had crossed the border into Bolshevik Russia, but were sceptical of the system developong there.Their leaders hoped that the British would use the Legion to establish a Socialist Finland. This was not to be, but the rank an d file and their families were allowed back into Finland as a result of British pressure.

[34] Pietäinen, op.cit., p.401.

[35] On Zeligowski, see Hovi, op.cit. pp.140–145. On Mannerheim's persistence, see Pietäinen, op.cit., p.413.

a mutually exclusive kind: a neutrality breached by a Power might be defended by other Power(s), as was the case with Belgium in 1914 (a grim example admittedly). But, in any case, prior engagements or understandings were risky: a nervously aggressive Power might see them as damaging the very neutrality the smaller state was pretending to maintain.

The over-arching League of Nations might be thought of as proving a way out of this sort of dilemma. Finland had done well out of the League of Nations, which confirmed Åland as Finnish in spite of the wishes of its inhabitants and the claims of Sweden that went with them. The League had thus helped to make Finland and its continuing purpose was to guarantee states' rights. In its Covenant, the two most important provisions were those of article 8 and article 16. Article 8 aimed at reforming the world. It would do this by changing the circumstances under which the diversity of states lived. They would *all* have to cut their armaments to the minimum required by national security and international obligations. Article 16, on the other hand, laid down the culmination of developments that would occur if a bellicose aggressor sought to breach the reformed world system: in the name of every state's right to self-defence (article 12.1), article 16: 2 envisaged as a last resort the use of military, naval and air force measures against the aggressor state once resort to sanctions had failed.

The weaknesses in the system were at once apparent. Learned Swiss authorities pointed out that the whole thing was a creation of the victor states of the War. Even that was defective since the United States did not join and Japan felt that the "White Powers" were ganging up against it and left in 1931, after a decade of unhappy presence in Geneva. An equally significant weakness resided in the working out of the relationship between articles 8 and 16. These were meant to be complementary, but, as it turned out, they were competing approaches, the British preferring armament reduction, while the French wanting to ensure, first, an adequate defence, the swift use of sanctions against an aggressor, and, as an inheritance from the war, a guarantee agreement from the British and Americans.[36] The latter demand did not come to pass, while sanctions proved difficult of effective attainment. As to the distinction between defensive and aggressive weaponry, it proved to be an impossibility to draw the line.

Finland was closer to the French League of Nations position and in 1926 succeeded in getting the League to adopt a proposal for aid for a state under attack and even *under threat* of attack. Primarily, it was British opinion that got this measure linked to a disarmament agreement, and, failing the latter, the

---

[36] Kari Selen, *Genevestä Tukholmaan*, Helsinki (Otava), 1974, pp.16–25, on the differences in approach between the French and the British.

Finnish proposal ceased to have any effect. Nonetheless, the Finns succeeded in leaving out of the manpower statistics (and thus cuts) the civil guards, whose constant military training was to prove an invaluable asset in the wars to come.[37]

These specifics of armament and disarmament apart, the League continued to show its greatest weakness at the political level. It could not resolve the problem arising from the Russo-German nexus, a problem vital, the most vital to Finnish security. When in 1926 Germany was taken into the League, the Soviet Union was not a member. When in 1933 Germany left, the Soviet Union came in. The League could provide no forum for resolving their relationship. It was created for status-quo Powers and for new or restored states made out of the remains of failed great Powers.

But Russia and Germany were potentially revisionist states—revisionist Powers—Russia working through revolution, and Germany, long before Hitler's rise to fame, by attacks on the injustice of Versailles. The core of the threat was contained in the Rapallo Treaty of 1922, when Soviet Russia offered training grounds for a new German army in return for technical assistance in, *inter alia,* military know-how from the German side. These revisionist Powers were thus *potentially* quite ready to take back what they could of their losses, though there were phases in their foreign policy that did not always reflect this. Finland's problem started with Russian revisionism, a revisionism which, because it was a branch of revolution, had an internal dimension for the Finns.

At times, however, Soviet suggestions took on a colouring from what was going on in the League in Western Europe. This became another option. In 1926, the Soviet Union proposed separate non-aggression agreements with Finland, Estonia, Latvia, Lithuania, and Poland. This was the maximum of what the Soviet Union could do. It would have dominated were an alliance to have been created—or, in the worse case, exposed its own internal weaknesses. And it would not have gone well with Germany. Non-aggression was a term to suit the times: it was not against any specific state. But yet it was. For in the Soviet draft the participants were to agree not to assist in any attack by a third party against either of them. This could have been a Western state or could have been Germany.

This was the start of a lengthy Soviet process of deliberation. Nothing came of this first, detailed suggestion. Finland wanted a guarantee of the relinquishing of revolutionary activity by either party on the other party's territory. The Soviet government ignored this. It was a reference to the Finnish official standpoint that domestic communism was simply fostered from

---

[37] They went for their training after Sunday church.

without. There was also a vaguer Finnish demand to have a "geopolitical area" covered. This, too, was ignored by the Soviet government, presumably because it did not want to be faced by "a bloc within a bloc."[38] But in 1928 the Soviet Union signed the Kellogg-Briand pact (with the USA, both states being outside the League) for the peaceful resolution of international disputes

By 1931, Soviet policy had clearly changed. The impact of the 1925 Western European Locarno Agreement (the prelude to Germany's entry into the League in 1926) seemed to be granting equality of status to Germany, while the failure to create a corresponding "Eastern Locarno," due to Germany's opposition to adopting the Versailles Treaty changes in Eastern Europe, could be interpreted as presaging a revival of the *Drang nach Osten*. In the east, the Japanese takeover of Manchuria seemed to be a threat to the Soviet Union's Siberian borders.[39] The Soviet government began to produce a series of measures destined to reassure its immediate neighbours in the West. In 1932 therefore Non-Aggression treaties were signed with these neighbouring states, including Finland, and, in consequence of the Kellogg-Briand Pact, the Soviet authorities presented proposals for the definition of aggression. These were signed also by the adjacent states.

Among these states was Poland. Poland was worried, primarily by the failure of an Eastern Locarno system—a failure that kept the borders of eastern Europe unstable. The Poles were not reassured by Mussolini's declared hope of seeing the creation in Europe of a directorate of Britain, France, Germany, and Italy, a proposal viewed favourably by the British prime minister Ramsay Macdonald. It was all apparently leading to the relegation by the Powers of *Zwischeneuropa*. The change in Poland's attitude to the Soviet Union was illustrative of the dilemma of handling any potential Russo-German nexus. Poland needed help in this and urged Finland to join in the Soviet suggestion for a definition of aggression. The French minister in Helsinki, G.A. de Vaux, wanted Finland to adhere.[40]

The crux of the matter was clear enough. The smaller states of Eastern Europe were the creation of the Allied cause in the First World War. But the Allied cause did not hold; even their League policy was divergent. And in themselves, the new states showed aggression to each other, exploiting selfishly what they could of the Allied victory of 1918. There was no hub of power in this disparate mess. But the shadow of the Rapallo agreement of 1922 was always available to be dredged up to frighten the scared. The joint name for this scary phenomenon was revisionism.

---

[38] Kejo Korhonen, *Naapurit vastaan tahtoaan*, Helsinki (Tammi), 1966, pp.130 & 139–155.,

[39] Selen, op.cit., p.83.

[40] ibid., pp.83–89.

Neutrality—a Refuge.

The Finns were suspicious of the above-mentioned Polish demarche. Reasonably so, for on 26 January 1934 the Poles entered into a ten-year non-aggression pact with Germany.[41] In spite of this, they had approached Finland in December 1933, as had the Soviet foreign minister, with a suggestion for a Polish-Soviet plan for a declaration of intent relating to the preservation of Finland and the three Baltic States.

The Russians kept on trying and in March 1934 fetched up another scheme, a Baltic Protocol by which a German-Russian agreement could, at last, be entered into, which would guarantee the Baltic States and possibly Finland. The Germans were not buying, referring instead to the 1926 German-Soviet treaty with its vaguer protestations of friendship. The Finns, in their turn, did not want anything to do with protection,[42] not even *then* by Russo-German rapprochement. This they seemed to fear even more than Russo-German hostility.

All measures of this kind were now to fall finally apart in another abortive attempt to create an Eastern Locarno Pact. This seems to have started as a Franco-Russian move to box in Germany by an agreement between France, the Soviet Union, Poland, Czechoslovakia, and Finland as a result of the rise of the Nazis in Germany, not to speak of the increasingly threatening attitude of Japan in the Far East. The idea of the Pact was soon widened to other states—Belgium, Latvia, and Estonia. However, Poland demanded the inclusion of the principal enemy, Germany. Britain also wanted Germany in and the whole idea linked with disarmament. Thus the conceptualization rapidly changed and it reflected more and more the core of the Western Locarno, the guarantee of frontiers. Since Germany's problem with Versailles was precisely its dissatisfaction with its eastern frontiers, Germany demurred. The German refusal then frightened the Poles into withdrawing.

The Finnish foreign minister, Antti Hackzell (foreign minister from December 1932–December 1933) also demurred, having already told the Soviet foreign minister, M.M. Litvinov, that Finland was not pro-German in outlook. But for Hackzell things were deeper than that. He had not been attracted to the inclusion of Poland, which the Finns regarded as an unstable element. Nor did he want anything stronger than the existing non-aggression pact with Russia. He felt, too, that both neutrality and Finland's Nordic links would be weakened since Sweden would most certainly not join.

---

[41] ibid., pp.98.
[42] ibid. p.101-102.

But the deepest factor of all related to the safeguarding of national identity. The parameters that now bound Finland together were the narrowing out of the extreme Left and the narrowing out, wherever possible, of the extreme Right. Hackzell feared that joining a coalition of whatever sort led by the Soviet Union would stimulate in Finland the extreme Left and provoke an equally disturbing reaction from the extreme Right. Since the two non status-quo Powers, Russia and Germany, appealed respectively to extreme Left and extreme Right, they might seek intervention, at an appropriate moment, were the Finnish political climate to be disturbed and altered further. The increasingly centrist solution to Finland's internal political development would be challenged in any case *as a guide for the conduct of foreign relations* by the shift in the external alignments of the Powers. Here lay the threat of a Finnish dilemma long before the present author used the term to cover Finnish post-World War II politics.[43] The centrist solution did not have an external arm with it, for the West showed reluctance in Baltic affairs.

Within Finland a deal had been made in connection with the Lapua movement. The Finnish establishment had stifled "Communism" in return for an acceptance of an Agrarian will, or, as the National Coalition politician Hackzell put it, the Agrarians were able "to terrorize the country."[44] At that time, it was something of a piece of exaggeration. But, they were nevertheless, "the people" and the Lapua movement had shown *their* need (not that of the extreme Left) to be conciliated

As to *external* relations, it is hardly surprising that under this set of circumstances Hackzell, like many another responsible Finnish politician before and since, enjoined upon every citizen the task of showing discretion in the discussion of foreign policy and was prepared to avoid even parliamentary debate, instead preferring to communicate about developments in the field of foreign policy to each of the parties in turn.[45] This phenomenon was later, after the Second World War, to be dubbed Finlandization.

Was there, however, no possibility of a sudden intervention from above to save the sorry state of Europe? By the turn of 1934, a *deus ex machina* did appear on the horizon in the shape of an aged French politician, now foreign minister, by name Louis Barthou. This gentleman of discretion produced a much more important version of the use-value of secrecy than the fumblings of Finlandization (whether before or after the Second World War). Barthou concocted the idea of drafting two complementary treaties for saving Europe. Treaty A would offer reciprocal aid in case of aggression against Germany, the

[43] Maude, *The Finnish Dilemma*, chap. 2.
[44] Selen, op.cit., p.162.
[45] ibid., pp. 226–227 & 241.

Soviet Union, Finland, Estonia, Latvia, Poland, and Czechoslovakia. This would mask a Treaty B, which would be a pact of Franco-Soviet mutual help, involving Soviet adhesion to Locarno and the League of Nations. In early June, Barthou discussed these treaties with Litvinov.[46] But in October, on the visit of King Alexander of Yugoslavia to France, both Barthou and the royal guest were assassinated in the streets of Marseilles by a Macedonian terrorist. Barthou was succeeded by Pierre Laval, a characterless figure with not a shred of the divine in him.[47]

Nordic Succour?

By the mid-nineteen thirties, a still open alternative for aid in travail might, it was envisaged, be found in cooperation with like-minded Nordic countries. This choice would not so easily be thought to compromise neutrality, for all the Nordic states had a neutrality tradition of their own. Their wariness towards the outside world was rooted in a common apprehension that even a guarantee of the Power(s) might draw their states into conflicts between the Powers—as Rickard Sandler the foreign minister of Sweden expressed it. A Nordic defence league, he came to think, might obviate this.[48] But Peter Munch, the Danish foreign minister, was warier than most. Summoning a Nordic conference to Copenhagen in 1935, he left Finland out, partly because of what he felt was the French orientation of Finland, though the fact of the matter was that the Franco-Soviet rapprochement was already disturbing Finnish confidence in France.[49] The truth was that Denmark's problem was Germany. That was not Finland's prime problem.

Indeed, it might coarsely be argued that the force of circumstance, embodied in the Anglo-German naval agreement of 1935, was bringing the German fleet into the Baltic as a counterweight to the Soviet fleet. The Swedes were less sanguine than the Finns were about this prospect, fearing an aggressive breakdown between these two revisionist Powers. However, the Finnish foreign minister Antti Hackzell, who liked to think in these terms of balancing off Russia, had not been averse either to sharing in the German *Grossraumwirtschaft*, but suspected that the Finnish Agrarians would not allow

---

[46] Selen seems to think that Litvinov had originated the idea. As to Treaty A, neither Germany nor Finland expressed any interest. Selen, op.cit., pp.107–108.

[47] Louis Clerc, "La Finlande dans la diplomatie francaise," II, original text of the doctoral dissertation, presented at the Univ. of Strasbourg, 2007, pp.465–466. Clerc regards this treaty as "French- born."

[48] Selen, op.cit., pp.143–144 & 153–155.

[49] ibid., pp.153–155.

it.[50] There is always a listening post. Thus, in spite of what Hackzell had done to try to convince the Russians, that pro-German feeling was not all that strong in Finland[51] by 1935 the Soviet emissary Assmus was threatening that in the event of European war the Soviet Union would march into Finland.[52] His motivation may have been rumours of a Polish, Finnish, and German naval accord.[53] This—and other misconceptions about Finnish opinion—drove Hackzell into further attempts to control the flow of information—now with regard to loose talk appearing in the international press.[54]

In autumn 1935, the Finnish minister of defence, Arvi Oksala, made the classic statement on the need for a strong Finnish army until help came from abroad.[55] More specifically, such help seemed only possible from Sweden alone. A defence of Åland might serve as bridge with Sweden.

For some time the demilitarization of the Åland Islands had been a source of worry to both Sweden and Finland. Rickard Sandler, the Swedish foreign minister, had first urged Rudolf Holsti, Hackzell's successor, to work for the inclusion of the Soviet Union (now a member of the League) among the states guaranteeing the demilitarized status of Åland and had denied the Swedish minister in Helsinki, von Heidenstam, permission to raise the issue of the defence of the islands. Hackzell, when still foreign minister, had not wanted the Soviet Union among the guarantors for fear of giving the potential enemy an excuse for intervention thereby.[56] But Sandler began to depart from a simple reliance on League policy, and discussed with the Swedish military projects for the defence of the islands. One such project the General Olof Gerhard Thörnell, head of the Swedish general staff, presented for the joint meeting of foreign and defence ministers of the two countries in September 1937.[57] Even before the Anschluss, Östen Unden of the Swedish foreign office, had come to the conclusion that demilitarization offered no guarantee of security any longer. A few days after the Anschluss, which took place on12 March 1938, the Swedish air force General Torsten Friis told himself that

---

[50] ibid., p.162 (the German economic and commercial union, the agricultural exports of which were considered by the Finnish Agrarians as a threat).

[51] ibid., pp.156-158. Hackzell himself was careful not to identify too closely with Polish attempts to come closer to Germany. On the other hand, as noted, he was impressed by the economic power of the *Grossraumwirtschaft*.

[52] ibid., p.157

[53] ibid., p.241.

[54] ibid., p.255.

[55] ibid., p.245.

[56] ibid., p. 259 & Krister Wahlbäck, *Veljeys veitsenterällä*, Helsinki-Porvoo (Werner Söderström), 1964, p.60.

[57] Wahlbäck, op.cit., p.56.

Germany and the Soviet Union could send their planes to Åland in two-three hours and that the weak Finnish air force would not be able to resist.[58]

But at this point the Åland question began to illustrate all the problems of Nordic and Finnish security. The Ålanders themselves were not happy with their projected defence and while there was a difference of intensity between their two powerful leaders, Julius Sundblom and Carl Björkman, it was the former who led the field, in Sweden (where an Åland Committee was set up) and Åland, and in opposing the Finns.[59] The question was one of the imposition of military service upon the Ålanders, as a back-up to Swedish and Finnish aid should the "enemy" arrive. The Ålanders, however, feared Finnicization by the strengthened grip of the Finnish military, even though alternatives were thrashed out by which, for example, the language of command might be Swedish.[60] The kernel of all this was that the local folk wanted to see no change, apparently fearing the Finns as the immediate danger! They stuck with demilitarization. Hostile to the Finns as they were, the Ålanders' reactions were but a microcosm of what the Finnish folk themselves on the mainland were declaredly feeling against any change in their own environment. The intensity of Nordic democracy revealed itself in a sense of place and locality of culture.

But this whole question related in another way to the existence of the newly-independent Finland. It related to its shape. The Finns had tried to form a state on the basis of the old Grand Duchy with, wherever possible, *extended* borders, as in the Petsamo region or in East Karelia. The maintenance of the old Grand Duchy was seen in the continuing need to keep Åland with Finland, a historical claim but containing a defence of the Swedish-speaking minority in Finland by not losing the Swedish-speakers of Åland either to Sweden or their own independence. Such a defence of minority rights went down well with the League. In practice, after the League's favouring of Finland, the solution did not work out: the Ålanders remained aloof from contacts with the Swedish-speakers of the Finnish mainland, and their autonomy, as noted in the previous chapter did not serve either as a model for "a state within a state" as wanted for a time by the Swedish-speakers of mainland Finland.[61]

The better solution would presumably have been to let the Islands go to Sweden as the islanders themselves in the early 1920s most certainly wished.

---

[58] ibid., pp. 63 & 65.

[59] ibid., chap.V and chap.VI (esp. pp.139–154)

[60] ibid.,p.118.

[61] By the spring of 1939, the greater part of the Swedish language press in Finland had, reciprocally, become antagonistic to the Ålanders.: Herbert Tingsten, *The Debate on the Foreign Policy of Sweden 1918–1939*, London (OUP), 1939, p. 251.

Sweden was in no sense a potential invader of Finland proper and the defence of Åland would have been on firmer ground if it had been run exclusively by Sweden with the loyal help of the Ålanders, too, as Swedish citizens.

Nevertheless, between 19-21 May 1938, serious negotiations began between Sweden and Finland for the defence of the Åland Islands.[62] But a year later, in June 1939, Sandler was compelled to admit that he did not clearly know what the Soviet position was.[63] Throughout 1938, the NKVD emissary Boris Yartsev had told the Finns that they could themselves fortify Åland *alone*, providing that the Soviet Union would have a controlling voice in the Åland question.[64] But in October 1938 Yartsev raised the possibility as well of a Soviet fortification of Suursaari in the Gulf of Finland,[65] and thereafter the question of the islands *in the Gulf of Finland* became linked with the prospect of fortifying Åland. Gradually a Soviet use of these islands in the Gulf dwarfed the importance of Åland, the Soviet foreign minister Maxim Litvinov proposing in March 1939 that Suursaari and three other Finnish islands in the Gulf of Finland be exchanged for Soviet territory in East Karelia.[66]

The latter offer was crucial in two respects. It seemed to take the weight off the Åland demand. But it also offered a solution in terms of an exchange of border territory (the first Soviet proposal had been comparatively mild: to lease the four islands for only 30 years simply as observation posts). But on neither count was there to be any Finnish yielding, even though Mannerheim was in favour of doing a deal over Suursaari.[67] Erkko countered the question of the islands of the Gulf by saying that if the Soviet Union received such concessions, the Germans would demand similar privileges.[68]

The Finnish government had a few days earlier emphasized that the islands in question in the Gulf of Finland had been neutralized in the 1920 Peace of Tartu.[69] These arguments geographically pushed the expressed Soviet

[62] Wahlbäck, op.cit., p.75.
[63] ibid., p.196.
[64] ibid., pp.178–179.
[65] ibid., 179–180.
[66] ibid., p.182.
[67] Once he heard of it. Though head of the Defence Council, Mannerheim was not told by foreign minister Hol sti of the Soviet emissary Yartsev's proposals about Suursaari (Hogland) in 1938. Mannerheim believed that this was due to the threat that he might immediately demand additional military appropriations. In March 1939, when Boris Stein, repeated the demand for Suursaari and other islands in the eastern Gulf, Mannerheim immediately suggested that a deal should be made with the Soviet Union. Max Jakobson, *The Diplomacy of the Winter War*, Cambridge, Mass., 1961, pp.49 & 63–64.
[68] Wahlbäck, op.cit., p.182.
[69] ibid., p.182.

needs either back to Åland or on to the Finnish mainland. It was becoming very dangerous. Anyway, the Soviet Union had not given up even on the islands in the Gulf of Finland and, what was more, Mannerheim understood them.[70] The latter was even prepared to shift the border on the Karelian Isthmus farther away from Leningrad. Really, the question of Finnish security had now been transferred to another plane. Instead of a search for allies or co-partners at least (with Sweden over Åland), the Finnish security position was suddenly at the level of territorial concession. And there it was going to stay.

But there were plenty of other untied ends. When, in 1939, the Soviet Union made its deal with Estonia and established bases on the big Estonian islands of Saaremaa and Hiidenmaa, General Thörnell, the commander of the Swedish defence forces, believed that the chances of a Soviet surprise attack on the Åland Islands had greatly increased. But the Finnish foreign minister, Eljas Erkko, for his part, felt that since, with the Estonian concessions, the Soviet fleet was now established on the Baltic, there was much less of a Soviet need for an Åland base or for control of that area.[71] Perhaps this was so, but the threat of an attempted control of the Åland area by the Germans could hardly disappear from the Soviet mind, nor, as far as the Gulf of Finland was concerned, were the Soviet military and naval authorities going to relinquish the succession of defensive lines that protected the great city of Leningrad and which required some kind of Soviet control of parts of the northern shore of the Gulf of Finland.

Things were changing rapidly. The rapprochement between Germany and the Soviet Union that emerged in the Nazi-Soviet Pact of 23 August 1939 was one of the most remarkable *coups* in the history of international relations. But not everyone had closed their eyes to the chances of its emergence. Four years earlier the then Finnish foreign minister Antti Hackzell had quietly warned of the dreaded possibility of a German-Soviet working arrangement.[72] It would cut the ground from under the feet of the smaller states.

This development was now occurring. Apart from the Swedes' own desire to protect their eastern coast, a Swedish involvement in the defence of Åland had been *politically* motivated by a desire to keep an allegedly pro-German Finland away from an even closer relationship with Germany. In practical terms, too, however, should the Finnish armed forces need more material support, the obvious place to get it was Germany. By 1938, the Germans also made it clear that they had nothing against the fortifying of the Åland

[70] Jakobson, op.cit., pp.64–65.
[71] ibid., p.208.
[72] Selen, op.cit., p.156

Islands.[73] Knowledge of this admission undoubtedly strengthened the Soviet fear that military measures on Åland were a confirmation that the whole of the Swedish-Finnish project for Åland was one that was favourable to Germany.[74] Yet the Swedish political interest in Åland was a means of serving the goal of keeping Finland out of the Russian-German conflict by presenting the Russians with a programme that put this delicate area under the protection of two Northern neutrals who would guarantee its neutralization. It was a pity that the Soviet decision-makers could not see this, being unwilling either to see or trust Sandler's basic reasoning that Finland was better off with Sweden than with Germany.[75]

Thus, the defence of Åland was not merely to be justified in itself, but working with the Finns to do this would have drawn the Finns away from the German embrace. It would also therefore have been a *political* move. Sandler counselled the Finns, in consequence, in May 1939 to stay clear of the German offer of a non-aggression pact.[76] And because it had this wider, political dimension, the question of Swedish aid to Finland was *speculatively* and to some extent practically extended. This became not merely a question of mining the sea lanes or of sending military equipment to the Finns, but the question of the use of Swedish troops in the north to repel a Russian advance was also discussed.[77] All these schemes fell apart as world war started again, the West against Germany once more and Russia as a passive spectator and partner of Germany in the carve up of *Zwischeneuropa*. The Swedish prime minister, Per Albin Hansson, had never been too keen on commitments to Finland and by October 1939 he was pulling Sweden back on the plea that avoiding involvement in the world war was preferable to defending Åland.[78] Later in the same month Defence Minister Pehr Edvin Sköld, expressing the traditional Swedish fear of a German attack on southern Sweden if Sweden got entangled in the war by helping the Finns, reinforced the caution of the prime minister.[79]

Was Åland therefore an irrelevance? It had been the core of a Swedish attempt to reduce tension for war in the Baltic area, but as the Russian

---

[73] Wahlbäck, op.cit., pp. 173–175.

[74] ibid., p. 187.

[75] ibid., pp.135–136. His statements in the Swedish Parliament and to a meeting of his own Social Democrats were made in January 1939.

[76] ibid., p. 169

[77] On the question of mining the sea- lanes, ibid., pp. 227, 230, 246, & 270 esp. On the inadequacy of the supply of equipment to be sent, ibid., p.230,on the possibility of the use of Swedish troops in northern Finland, ibid., p.236.

[78] ibid., pp. 220–221.

[79] ibid, p. 240.

demands changed their emphasis, concentrating more on the Gulf of Finland and the Karelian Isthmus, the raising of a Swedish-Finnish defence of the neutralization of the Åland Islands was not big enough to counter war tensions—but only big enough to draw Sweden itself closer to war involvement, particularly if the above-mentioned wider defensive measures were to be carried out.

Instead, the Åland Islands began to take on a somewhat greater significance for the Germans. Once the war was on, the Swedes had made an agreement between the Western Powers and Nazi Germany for the division of iron ore exports.[80] At that moment, therefore, the Germans did not necessarily need to occupy Åland for the sake of ensuring any seabound transport of ore through the Baltic from Luleå. But in December 1939, shortly after the start of the Winter War, the Germans offered to occupy the Åland Islands should the Finns so desire this,[81] but they apparently did not desire this. (nor did the Swedish premier Hansson).The German offer could, nonetheless, be seen as an indication of German willingness to help the Finns, a prospect that was later to be utilized. Additionally, the German-Soviet rapprochement of that time had of course two aspects, a temporary peace between the two, and the taking up of positions for a war between them, in which Åland might serve as a submarine base. Once again, however, the German attitude can be understood as being much wider than the case of Åland, for in the previous October Hermann Göring had told the Finns that if the Russian demands upon Finland became too onerous, Germany might intervene to try to alleviate them.[82] These demands *were* onerous for the Finns and there is no evidence that they asked for German intervention, but perhaps at a later date they kept this in mind.

In any event, Paasikivi, who always felt that the Finns should have given way to these demands, was of the opinion that Göring had expressed his sympathies to the Finns by encouraging them to give way in territorial concessions and avoid conflict *at that time* with the Soviet Union.[83]

Before looking at the blundering policy that brought Finland into the Winter War on 30 November 1939 (till 13 March 1940), it will be worthwhile looking at yet another previous attempt to impose a security system on an already tense Europe.

---

[80]Gunnar Hägglöf, *Svensk krigshandelspolitik under andra världskriget*, Stockholm (P.A.Norstedt & Söners Förlag), 1958, pp.14–98. This was a peculiar form of neutrality, sending raw material (iron ore) to both sides in ostensibly equal shares.

[81] Wahlbäck, op.cit., p. 271.

[82] ibid., p. 220.

[83] Letter of 26.12.1940 from Paasikivi to Väinö Tanner in Tanner's *Kahden maailmansodan välissä*, Helsinki (Tammi), 1966, p.266.

The British, French and Russian Abortive Alliance and Its Alternative

This was a security system that was to be imposed on the Finns: they did not want it. But they did not need to frustrate it since another member of *Zwischeneuropa* did the job for them. And then the Finns had to face their enemy, alone.

The British and French were, in this project, the suitors of the Russians, and what they tried to play upon were the fears the Russians had of the Germans. With or without the Western allies, the Russians had two possibilities of dealing with the German threat. The first was by war-fighting, where necessary outside Russia, for example, in Poland. The second was by doing a deal with Germany, for example, by splitting up Poland together. Both possibilities envisaged war, for example, in Poland or against Poland. The British and French position was more complex: its aim was, as far as possible, the maintenance of the status quo in Europe. Britain and Frances showed a concern for third states, for example, Poland, Finland, Estonia, and Latvia. These countries expressed a certain sense of reciprocity with the West, but to the Russians they were potential enemies to be watched with some degree of apprehension. For they might also throw in with Germany. The Russian suspicion that Finland was basically pro-German has already been noted. Even more important to the Russians was the ambiguous attitude of the Poles. The former president, Pilsudski, had laid down the alternative policy for Poland of working with Germany. In January 1939, Col. Joseph Beck had followed this line in offering to join in a German-led crusade eastwards against Bolshevism and as late as 25 March Count Joseph Lipski, the ambassador, had assured the Germans (on instructions) that Poland was committed to an anti-Soviet policy.[84] The French, too, had their suspicions. Paul Cambon, the French ambassador in London had already expressed the view, on 20 March, that any talk of Soviet assistance to Poland might drive the Poles into the arms of Germany.[85] This standpoint was only the reverse side of the Soviet line that, where necessary, Poland and other recalcitrant nations had to be forced into an accommodation with the potential alliance of the West and the Soviet Union.

The result of this was that while Russia, on the one side, and France and Britain on the other, dreaded Germany, their respective attitudes to the third states *under the assumed protection of the alliance* would be different. The two

---

[84] Anita Prazmowska, *Britain,Poland, and the Eastern Front, 1939*, London (Cambridge University Press), 1987, pp.34 & 49.

[85] ibid., p.43.

Western allies did not assume that these states would change: the Soviet side feared a change for the worse in them (towards Germany) and, in turn, wanted to force them into a change in the opposite direction. This Soviet idea became crystallized at its high point (or low point) in the concept of "indirect aggression." According to this interpretation, the third states might be liable to change their governments into governments more favourable to Germany and were thus potentially aggressors. The Soviet position was to allow intervention to oppose such a political change in a third state. The Western allies could not accept such assumptions damaging to the integrity of what were, in the Western opinion, basically Western-type states and needing protection. This difference of opinion between the West and the Soviet Union was to affect Finland.

But towards the end of the negotiations for this unsuccessful attempt at a Western- Soviet alliance, it had certainly become clear that the Poles were heading for a conflict with Germany. The dismemberment of Czechoslovakia (in which the Poles had initially taken part by seizing Tessin), the shameful treatment of President Emil Hacha of Slovakia, and the constant Nazi aggravation over the fate of Danzig, were clear enough evidence of the intensity of German hostility towards the Slavic states of *Zwischeneuropa*. And the Poles were not the sort of people under all this to renege on the chance of fighting back.

But what were their prospects of succeeding if they did this? By July 1939, the French Premier Edouard Daladier was urging Georges Bonnet, the French foreign minister, to tell the Germans that if they went to war with the Poles, the French would come to the assistance of the Poles.[86] In effect, this was bluff as far as both Germans and Poles were concerned. The latter had been guaranteed by the West, which, in military terms, we now know, was an empty gesture in respect of action on the Western front. But, at this juncture, the role of the Soviet Union in Western eyes became crucial. It was the Soviet Union that was intended to back up the Poles in their resistance to Nazi Germany. Lord Halifax, the British foreign secretary, had said to Sir Nevile Henderson, the British ambassador in Berlin, "it would be folly for us not to conclude an agreement (with Russia) in view of our commitments in Eastern Europe."[87] Nor did this role find, as such, dissent from the Soviet government. In the vitally important period of July-August 1939, the Soviet Union, as far as Poland was concerned, seems to have forgotten its obsession with "indirect aggression" (that is, the emergence there of a pro-German government) and

---

[86] *Documents on British Foreign Policy, Third Series,* vol.VI, no.212, Sir E. Phipps to Lord Halifax, 1.7.1939, pp.236–238.

[87] ibid., no.94,30 June 1939; p. 220.

instead come to the swift conclusion of military aid, meaning Soviet troops, coming over the Polish border to help the Poles. In this sense, the Soviet position was a simple one: how to help Poland and the other weak states mentioned in the negotiations with the West.

This simple solution was predicated upon the reception of Russian troops on Soviet soil *in advance* of a German Blitzkrieg on Poland. It was agonizingly simple. For the British and the French, Russia was a potential ally, but for the Poles a potential enemy. They had two enemies, Germans and Russians. *Frustrating one enemy might make the way for conquest by the other.* Thus, the Poles demurred to take Russian troops in what would nowadays be called "the crisis period." The French diplomat Bonnet forcefully urged that the Poles were refusing "the only immediately efficacious help that could reach them in the event of a German attack."[88] Lord Halifax, the British foreign secretary, believed that Col. Beck had given away his own case": if Poland could bring herself to accept Soviet help once war had started, it is not clear why she cannot agree to contemplate such assistance when war is imminent."[89] But General Jules Doumenc's draft of the Anglo-French-Soviet Military Agreement had only stated that Russian troops could go into Poland through the Vilna corridor to attack East Prussia and defend Roumania on the Galician front "if and when Poland shall be at war with Germany."[90] Three days before the signing of the Nazi-Soviet Pact, Beck gave way: he accepted Soviet material help, but in wartime only Soviet technical help and the passage of Soviet troops "if Poland has her back to the wall,"[91] a situation to be determined, presumably, by the Poles themselves. That was one point of view from Poland, but there was another point of view from Poland. General Stachiewicz, the Polish Chief of Staff, on the same day that Beck gave his statement, told the British as follows": in no case could admission of Soviet troops into Poland be agreed and that the mind of the Polish Government was made up."[92] Thus, the Soviet government changed its partner and went in with the Nazis. Poland was carved up.

If Poland had been for the Soviet Union a weak state that needed, in a possible war with Germany, direct Soviet aid in the opinion of the Soviet leaders, so Finland, too, was in a general sense in the same category as far as the Soviet Union was concerned. But here the issue was *seen* only partially as one of land war and very much concerned in Soviet eyes the naval protection

---

[88] *Documents on British Foreign Policy, Third Series,* vol. VII, no.80, 19.8.1939, pp.77–78

[89] ibid., no.91, 21.8.1939, pp.114–115.

[90] ibid.,no.6, copy of a letter from General Heywood of 17.8.1939 (the copy is dated 23.10.1939), pp.600–605.

[91] ibid., no. 90, 20.8.1939, pp.87–88.

[92] ibid., no.87, 20.8.1939, pp.84–85.

of Leningrad. Had the Soviet Union helped Poland as under the Anglo-French-Soviet Treaty, there would have been Russian troops and military equipment on Polish soil. But Finland was expected to give bases on the shore and islands of the Gulf.

According to the draft of the military Agreement made by the Western Allies, it was intended to send a Franco-British squadron into the Baltic (thus reversing the stipulations of the 1935 Anglo-German Naval Agreement) for the occupation of certain ports and islands belonging to Finland, Estonia, and Latvia so as "protect the neutrality of the Baltic States" while helping to interdict Swedish-German navigation (presumably the Baltic ore traffic from Luleå).[93] So far so good, but Russia was demanding the same rights for her fleet. Already on 30 July Sandler, in a speech at Stocka, had, however, warned the Finns against joining any guarantee scheme of Russia, Britain, and France, and his views were soon echoed by several of the leading Swedish newspapers.[94] The Finns actually needed no such warnings.

Their position can be succinctly defined in the later expression, used after the Second World War, of "a defence against aid." They really did not want to be protected. For one thing, both they and the British were surprised at the listing of Finland by the Russians as a "Baltic State."[95] This had, however, an obvious connection with a *Soviet* defence of the Gulf of Finland, Estonia being controlled on one shore and Finland controlled on the other. No longer would the Soviet fleet be boxed in: it would burst out. In addition, as Johan Nykopp later pointed out in the context of the bilateral negotiations between Finland and Russia in the autumn of 1939, the classification of Finland as a Baltic state emphasized the difference between Finland and the rest of the Scandinavian states.[96] With he collapse of the Western alliance negotiations, those matters were postponed for approximately three months.

The Finnish minister in London, Georg Achates Gripenberg, was one of the few Finns who was *vaguely* aware of what was now going on. In early July, he called on the British foreign minister, Lord Halifax, and expressed his disquiet at certain rumours according to which the British government "would recognise the Soviet government as a guarantor of the independence and neutrality of Finland, or as having the right to guarantee and take steps to protect Finland, or . . . they would admit that Finland was within the Soviet

---

[93] See this chapter, note 91.

[94] Tingsten, op.cit., pp.269–270.

[95] Sir William Seeds, the British ambassador to the Soviet Union, was firmly of the opinion that Finland was not a Baltic state and should be treated separately. Martti Häikiö, *Maaliskuusta maaliskuuhun. Suomi Englannin politiikassa 1939–1940*, Helsinki (Söderström), 1976, p.29.

[96] Johan Nykopp, *Paasikiven mukana Moskovassa*, Helsinki (Kirjayhtymä),1975, p.36.

sphere of influence." Gripenberg said he did not believe these rumours.[97] He had talked earlier with Halifax, who had then been disingenuous enough to compare Finland's position vis-à-vis the Russians with the British attitude towards the Netherlands, a comparison Gripenberg rejected on grounds that the Dutch did not fear the British but the Finns most certainly feared the Russians. That was true, but Gripenberg's conclusion that "nothing could be more disastrous than a German-Soviet understanding" (with which Halifax agreed) since "the consequence would be to drive the Finnish government into the arms of Germany"[98] was too rapid a conclusion. A German-Russian understanding, on the contrary, was soon going to put Finland into the arms of Russia, though Gripenberg's own prediction about the German embrace, was, indeed, to come true two years later.

In 1939, it was the proffered alternative of being included in the British-French-Russsian amalgam that seemed to be "the more disastrous" for Finland, since the British and French were distant and weak. In the Anglo-German naval agreement of 1935, the British had signed the Baltic Sea over to the German fleet!

Soon Gripenberg called in again, asking why the British had brought in the Baltic States (meaning here, Finland, too) when the simple option of a tripartite agreement between the three Powers would have been possible.[99] That had been the starting-point of the Western allies, too, and the British continually hovered over it, even arguing, *in the light of the discussion with Gripenberg,* whether there was too much pressure being exerted on the "Baltic States," which might lead to their "going over to the other side." The Soviet ambassador in London, Ivan Maiski, said that this was all show on the Finnish side, too.[100] In answer to Gripenberg's own query, Halifax replied that "the immediate application to the local problem of Poland and her interests" had brought in *from the Soviet side* "the Baltic States," which for Russia were as important as the Low Countries were for the British. Gripenberg then left, saying that he would have no holiday this year and wishing that the British fleet would enter the Baltic,[101] presumably without the Russians.

The problem of a security arrangement between Russia, France and Britain was the problem of the smaller states in- between At the crunch, it was

---

[97] *Documents of British Foreign Policy, Third Series,* vol.VI, no.243 Halifax to Snow, 5.7.1939, pp.264–266. Gripenberg had visited Lord Halifax on 5.7.1939.

[98] ibid., no.278, Halifax to Snow, 8.7.1939 pp. 307–308. Gripenberg had visited Halifax on 27.6.1939.

[99] ibid.,no.373, Halifax to Snow, 20.7.1939, with an *aide-mémoire* from the Finnish Legation in London, pp.373–375.

[100] ibid., no.253, no.253, Halifax to Seeds, 6.7.1939, pp.277–278; no. 255, pp.279–281.

[101] See note 102.

not a problem of the defining of what constituted indirect aggression, upon the assessment of which one of the Powers (inevitably Russia) could intervene in the states on its eastern border. The key problem was that of helping Poland against Germany, of how to get Soviet troops and aid in quickly enough and thereby of overcoming Polish hesitations. It was the Soviet Union that brought in a list of other states and thus encouraged the West to build up a comparable list of the smaller Western European states it also wanted in the protective system so as to build up a cross-European collective security pattern. The endeavour was not in itself without merit, but it led to wrangling between the West and the Soviet Union, both on the definition of what constituted internal aggression (that is, when a Power could intervene to protect its own interests) and what states could be listed. But in the latter question, at least, the British and French were being somewhat ingenuous. They had not wanted a list of protected small states but when the Soviet negotiators insisted, their Western counterparts put into the package a number of Western European states, which, initially, had to be kept secret, presumably because they had not been asked.[102] By the third week of July, Sir William Seeds, the British ambassador to Moscow, was in a state of exasperation with the Soviet negotiators, noting already that the Soviet government had an alternative: a deal with Nazi Germany.[103] It was easier for the Soviet Union to make this deal with the Germans on the basis of a sphere of influence division of eastern Europe without worrying about touchy democracies, major or minor. Without a fight, the Soviet Union gained an advance on territory for its future war-fighting. All this left Finland on its own and bilateral negotiations opened between Finland and the Soviet Union in the autumn of 1939.

Now the citizenry of Finland were confronted with the reality of the defence of neutrality. They began to work on the fortifications of the Karelian Isthmus. Over their heads another world war began, though at first it did not take them with it. Nevertheless, the decisions of security-state megalomaniacs and the all-pervading influence of the military were soon to obscure the daily life of people who were content with modest goals like love.

---

[102] On the discussions between the British and French on this subject (should Luxembourg be included?) and the wrangling with the Russians, see ibid., Enclosure no.160,Letter from the French ambassador to Sir Orme Sargent, 28.6,1939 pp.183–184 & no.171, Halifax to Seeds, 29.6.1939, pp.193–194.

[103] ibid.,no.376, 20.7.1939, pp.422–426.

Ourselves alone

But, initially, the reactions to the Nazi-Soviet Pact of 23 August 1939 were sometimes surprising in Finland. On the opening of Parliament on 2 September, President Kallio assured the parliamentarians that the international situation had now improved as far as Finland was concerned. The suspicious Paasikivi dismissed this as rubbish.[104] However, things did *look* better. A change in the international conjuctures was just what the Finns needed *in so far as this meant that the coming together of the two Great Power adversaries had suddenly transpired without Finland having to lift a finger.*

But it soon became clear that more than a finger was at stake for Finland. Many months after the Winter War was over, Paasikivi, now Finnish ambassador to Moscow, and probably the finest analyst of Soviet policy the country had, admitted to Väinö Tanner, his co-negotiator in the autumn of 1939, "who knows Stalin's thoughts"?[105] The question, in the negotiations preceding the Winter War, was not of what Stalin wanted, but of what he really wanted. For if the Finns themselves are not exactly the best communicators in the world, the Russians are a lot worse. How to read Stalin's mind? At this point, it may at once be said that the pessimistic Paasikivi, in the autumn of 1939, was more optimistic than most of the rest of the Finnish elite, for Paasikivi's optimism was always grounded in a large dose of the acceptance of the truth of his own pessimism. It is worth looking at the mistakes the rest of them made therefore. They had forgotten that a German-Russian *modus vivendi* was a potential prelude to acts of hostility towards small states simply because the Germans and the Russians did not trust each other.

As to Paasikivi, when minister in Stockholm in 1939, he had known nothing of Boris Stein's proposal in April, until Mannerheim's crony, General Rudolf Walden, alerted him.[106] Yet it was Paasikivi who was subsequently expected to pull the government's chestnuts out of the fire a few months later when relations with Russia began to be critical.

Stein's 1939 proposals were, indeed, discussed in the government, where closure was called with a decisive statement by the Progressive prime minister A.K. Cajander, following the line of the grand old man of the Progressive Party, Ståhlberg, that not an inch of Finnish territory could be yielded.[107] The small Progressive Party thus dominated the foreign policy of the Red-Earth

---

[104] Tuomo Polvinen, *J.K.Paasikivi. Valtiomiehen Elämäntyö*, vol.3, Porvoo-Helsinki, 1995, p.5

[105] Letter of J.K.Paasikivi to Väinö Tanner, 26.12.1940, in Tanner, op.cit., p.255.

[106] Polvinen, *J.K Paasikivi. Valtionmiehen elämäntyö*, vol. 2, p.489.

[107] ibid., p.489. Ståhlberg repeated this doleful advice on 1.10.1939: ibid., vol.3., p.9, shortly before Paasikivi embarked on his first trip to Moscow before the Winter War broke out.

government. And it bound Paasikivi's hands when he was entrusted in the autumn of 1939 with the task of negotiating with the Russians. The president of Finland, who had the ultimate say in foreign policy, was the Agrarian Kyösti Kallio, who was not up to the task. But, having said this, Paasikivi also told Tanner in a confidential correspondence that the end-product would have been the same even if Svinhufvud or Ståhlberg had held the presidency: "only Mannerheim as president could have prevented the war."[108]

Curiously, especially considering the agonies of its independence and subsequent civil strife, Finland had now attained a certain state of beatitude, the simplicity of which disturbed only the troubled souls like Paasikivi, or those who were occasionally troubled, in between their extensive periods of leisure, like Mannerheim. The beatific mood of state and society arose from the working of a compromise, which was so great- and so gratefully received—as to have engendered a sort of national will and, what is more, to have bridged the gulf between the internal and external politics of the country. The bridge was called neutrality.

Its party-political embodiment was the little Progressive Party, following the Ståhlbergian lines laid down for a Centrist Finland, of a reconciliation between the constitutionalist Left, the land-hungry Agrarians, and a well-organized capitalism of forest-industry exports with a high-tariff barrier against imported manufactures and agricultural products. In foreign affairs, the pursuit of neutrality did not require any more land for Finland. But it did require the safeguarding of the land the Finns already had. This was particularly significant for the Agrarians, whom the Kivimaäki government's foreign minister Antti Hackzell had regarded as the key Finnish party. Land meant farms, with the bulk of the country living and/or working on farms—more likely only working on them or in the adjacent forest. Territory was sacred soil, especially so in the Agrarian-dominated Karelian Isthmus. In a way, the educated elite was close to all this, too. The towns were small and people with a bit of money had a summer cottage. A strengthening of the link between national and educated elite, then as even today, could be found in military service, a male-bound and bonded service done in defence of neutrality, a duty urged on the male sex by the womenfolk, who at the end of the 1930s were also volunteering for constructional work on the military positions on the Isthmus (the Mannerheim line). The citizenry served. They were not asked their views on the cession of territory (with compensation in other territory) to avert war. Subjectively, it was impossible to ask them. Their leaders had not prepared them for an exchange of territory (the amount

---

[108] Letter to Tanner of 26.12.1940 in Tanner, op.cit., p.268.

offered by the Soviet Union in East Karelia was more than twice as large as that to be lost by Finland under the failed negotiations).

But this buoyant picture of what a Rousseau might have divined to be an expression of the general will was, alas, not quite so general as it might at first glance have seemed to be. Approximately up to one-fifth of the population were said to owe allegiance to another will. They were said to be Communists. This radical Left in Finland had been suppressed not only by the counter-revolution of 1918 but also by the impact of the Lapua movement, which had succeeded in outlawing the radical Left, after which the Lapuans having done their job, some shrank away into a minority Fascist movement, the IKL. The faint possibility of a parliamentarian radical Left, represented in part by the Socialist Labour Party of the 1920s and its variously named successors, was extinguished by 1930. What remained for the task of urging on a dialogue with Russia were only pockets of the intelligentsia, who were unable to start a wider debate.[109] As to the loyal members or rather supporters of the Moscow-based Finnish Communist Party, they were either in Russia or in a Finnish prison. They might well have been in a Russian prison, too, or shot already by Stalin's henchmen. The terror he started from the mid-1930s destroyed the image of Russia as a progressive state in any case. But, failing massive military support, some kind of *modus vivendi* with Russia had to be attempted.

The man who tried hardest was Paasikivi. And, as it was to turn out, even his way was to be fraught with doubt. He was a staunch anti-Communist. He believed that the worth of his country rested on the rejection of Communism by the populace in the country's internal politics.[110] At the same time, he believed in 1939 in concessions to Russia, in respect of which he had no constituency in the Finnish population as far as its expressed party-politics were concerned He certainly did not have support for a concessionary policy towards Russia from his own party, the National Coalition Party. Paasikivi was, in fact, a man of the last resort, a monarchist, not a democrat, and for whom the intricacies of negotiating with Russia he could not reveal because, *inter alia,* the masters of Finnish democracy would not allow him to do so.[111] Painfully and unsurely, Paasikivi was searching for a key, the turning of which would unlock relations with Russia from any identification with a party of the extreme Left in Finland. This outlook did not speak for party politics, whether imposed by revolution or democracy.

---

[109] The magazine *Soihtu* was but a flickering image of this outlook.

[110] Letter to Tanner of 26.12.1940 in Tanner, op.cit., p.260.

[111] On this, Rintala's essay in *Four Finns*, Berkeley & Los Angeles (Univ. of California Press),1969.

Officially, the stumbling- block for Paasikivi was his own foreign minister, Eljas Erkko. The latter had already set the tone in a speech of several months earlier on 6 June 1939 in which h he lambasted those Powers who offered Finland a guarantee *without its wish* as being tantamount to aggressors.[112] It was a tough speech, but the minister was not tough enough to go to Russia and do the job he foisted on Paasikivi in October. For after the Nazi-Soviet Pact of 23.8.1939, Molotov began to demand bases in Estonia, casting scorn on Germany's previous non-aggression guarantee with Estonia and Latvia. In October, 21,000 Soviet troops entered Estonia to garrison the conceded Soviet bases there.[113] Soviet power was no longer boxed into the straits of the Gulf of Finland, but the northern shore of the Gulf was still held by the Finns.

The concessions Paasikivi was prepared to undertake, as the principal negotiator with the Russians, were territorial. He rejected, in the name of his own government, the possibility of a mutual aid treaty and was opposed to a guarantee, both forms being in his opinion straight roads to the interference in Finland's internal affairs by the Soviet government and the consequent replanting of Communism in Finland. Territorial concessions on the Isthmus would instead mean a loss of traditional Finnish parishes and the rural way of life there, but thereafter the rest of Finland could remain in the purity of its neutrality. Thinking back on the negotiations he had had with Stalin in the autumn of 1939, Paasikivi praised Stalin's moderation, forgetting for the moment, that after his rejection of Stalin's offer of a mutual aid agreement or localized defence agreement, the next time Stalin's demands for territorial concessions had swelled to take in the Finnish defence line on the Isthmus.[114] Nonetheless, since Stalin offered the two vast parishes of Repola and Porajärvi in the "Second Finland" over in East Karelia, areas of extensive economic resources–both of timber and water-power, the offer in material terms was a good one. And–may it be mentioned that in *spiritual terms*–East Karelia meant a lot to the Finns–or so they said. It soon dropped out of the talks.

The sticking-point was, however, the base at the entrance to the Gulf of Finland, Hanko or one of the islands off it. Though Stalin stabbed quite a few islands off Hanko as the great map was spread on the table before the negotiators, Paasikivi could not get Erkko to agree to yield on any: Hermansö, Hästö-Busö, Kvö, Jussarö, and Russarö (it is not clear whether Mannerheim's suggestion of Öröhön was ever put before Stalin).[115] A subsequent Finnish

---

[112] *Turun Sanomat*, 7.6.1939.

[113] Seppo Zetterberg, *Viron historia*, Helsinki (SKS), 2nd. Ed.,2007, pp.608–611.

[114] Tanner, op. cit., pp 255–.256. Tanner, who accompanied Paasikivi, on the second and third trips to Moscow, did not seem to think that loss of this defence line could not have beeen compensable.

[115] ibid., p.256

historian has pointed out that possession of these islands by a Soviet fleet would inevitably also have meant an automatic use of the waters of the Hanko peninsula:[116] in short, Hanko by other means. But the major point was this: such territorial concessions or leases would have given Finland a breathing-space in which to rearm[117] or even, at a later date, to accept a Soviet recognition of Finnish neutrality. But the refusal of Erkko to endorse a cession or leasing of any of the islands in the immediate vicinity of Hanko enabled him to avoid conflict with the Agrarians over the cession of any part of the Karelian Isthmus. It was an unusual kind of Pyrrhic victory. It did not occur in the war: it precipitated the war.

In talking to the Finns about the need for territorial concessions, the Soviet negotiators were prone to paint a picture of a naval attack on the Soviet Union, whichever state won the war, Britain or Germany.[118] Swedish attempts to mediate with Moscow on behalf of the Finns were dismissed as an attempt to build up a bloc against the Soviet Union.[119] It cannot have escaped the attention of the Soviet leaders that some of the smaller states of Europe, including the Nordics, had met in a conference in Brussels on 24 August to suggest peace between the West and Nazi Germany,[120] one day after the Nazi-Soviet Pact had been signed. Soon the "Phoney War" was to begin, a war in which the "peace option" between Germany and the West might still be open.

The core problem was still Germany. Stalin fought a war against Finland to keep Germany at bay, in the zany world of international politics this was an aspect of a peace between Germany and Russia. One may sympathize with President Kallio for his failure to understand what was going on. War with Finland was part of a breathing-space granted to Stalin by the pact with Nazi Germany It was less of a breathing-space than Stalin had anticipated, since the courageous stand of the Finnish citizen-army nearly brought Stalin into conflict with the West, when Britain and France decided, late in the day, to help the Finns. Fortunately, this help, which might have plunged the West into world war with both Russia as well as Germany, was rejected by the Finns. But the offer from the West might on the other hand have frightened the Soviet leaders into making peace with the Finnish government. *The Finnish army saved Finland from the mistakes of its civilian leadership.*

---

[116] Ohto Manninen has made this point. The author is grateful for a discussion with Professor Manninen about this on 25.8.2009.

[117] Tanner, op.cit., p.258.

[118] Jakobson, op.cit., p...109.

[119] Polvinen, *J.K.Paasikivi*, vol.3, pp.50–51.

[120] ibid., p.4

In the Winter War (30.11.1939–13.3.1940) the Finns lost 23, 000 men[121] killed, and in territory the Karelian Isthmus was taken and Hanko had to be leased for 30 years. There were also territorial changes in the north, but not (regrettably) Petsamo.

In-between

Unfortunately, the relief that followed was taken too seriously by the Russians themselves. taken too seriously by Stalin. As the year 1940 drew on, relations between Finland and the Soviet Union began to deteriorate again.[122] Finland sought to lean on Germany, while Stalin was caught off guard by Barbarossa, the German invasion of the Soviet Union, in June 1941.In May 1941, the leader of the Red Orchestra, Leopold Trepper, learned of this invasion—and of its revised date, 22.nd June and informed Stalin: so, too, did another agent of his, Richard Sorge. Stalin's biographer, Isaac Deutscher, while admitting Stalin's appalling neglect, could not explain it. Trepper did better at this:"he (Stalin) preferred to trust his political instinct rather than the secret reports piled up on his desk."[123]

In the negotiations with Finland in 1939, the Soviet Union feared a German influence. In early June 1939, the Leningrad Military District and the Baltic Fleet command expressed their sense of danger that Finland might throw in with Poland and Germany and take part in the invasion of Russia.[124] These were, of course, the days when the Soviet Union was still toying with a Western alliance. A little latter, Molotov, true to his principles of ideology and capability for producing a self-fulfilling prophesy, analysed the situation in the Baltic States, including Finland as one in which "governments and ruling classes as distinct from the rest of the population" were "about to compound with Germany."[125] This was to occur in the Continuation War in 1941. Molotov's prognosis had been made roughly two years too soon, but he helped to make the prophesy come true. The fundamental situation was that both Finland and the Soviet Union were, at a crunch, not averse to courting Germany. In both cases, it was to mean a marriage of convenience. For by

---

[121] Mortality list taken from *Tietosanakirja*, vol.5, Helsinki (Weilin & Göös), 1994, p.1879.

[122] Antony F. Upton,*Välirauha* (the Finnish version of *Finland in Crisis 1940–1941*), Helsinki (Kirjayhtymä),1964, pp.129–131.

[123] V.E. Tarrant, *The Red Orchestra*, London (Cassell), 1995, pp.131–13.2 Isaac Deutscher, *Stalin*, Porvoo-Helsinki (Werner Söderström), 2nd.ed., 1979, pp.388–395.

[124] Nikolai & Vladimir Barysnikov, *Terijoen hallitus*, Helsinki-Petersburg (Johan Beckman Institute,) 2001, p.17.

[125]*Documents of British Foreign Policy, Third Series, vol.VI*, no.139,24.6.1939, pp.160–163.

1941, the Nazis were able to satisfy both at the same time, since while bigamy is outlawed in marital relations, it is not similarly outlawed in international political relations.

Perhaps, after all, however, the simpler model of monogamy will serve best to illustrate the situation. In August 1939, the Nazis succeeded in courting Russia. When it was time, in 1941, for a divorce in this partnership, they had already courted Finland on the sly. But, in spite of an undercurrent of sympathy for Germany in Finland, divined by both Molotov and the Germans themselves, only the faintest hints of future support were uttered from the Nazi side in the tense autumn of 1939,[126] since Hitler was not then ready for his divorce from Stalin.

The Winter War and Consequences

Molotov's analysis of the Finnish situation was connected in part with the Soviet fear of "indirect aggression," that is, of a change of government for the worse should Finland agree to go along with Russia, in short, a fear of a military *coup* of pro-German forces. As noted, this was a stumbling- block to making a deal with the Western Powers, who disliked such intervention, and were prepared to trust Finland as a Western-type state. The concept of "indirect aggression" was an outgrowth of an even deeper analytical tool, namely the application of the potentially changing nature of what the Soviet authorities called, variously, "the relation of forces" or "the alignment of forces" in the politics of a non-Communist state. Should the working-class forces and their allies fail to exert sufficient control of the alien state in question, then the defence of the Soviet homeland might require military action against that state.

Once Finland failed to concede the territorial changes required by the Soviet Union, the Soviet government tried a maximalist solution, that is, invasion by the Red Army with the purpose of conquering Finland. The latter state was to be replaced by a Karelian-Finnish Republic, which would cover Soviet Karelia and Finland together and with which the Soviet state signed a treaty as if the new state were now formally independent. The invading Red Army was expected to arrive in Helsinki in three days time.[127] The prime minister of this puppet state was none other than the old Finnish revolutionary in exile in the Soviet Union, Otto Wille Kuusinen. And the Finnish workers would joyfully throw off their chains and welcome Kuusinen and the Soviet Red Army liberators. In the fact of the matter, both armies

[126] The clearest case was the offer to occupy Åland in Dec.1939: this chap,p.99

[127] So foreigners were told: Jakobson, *The Diplomacy of the Winter War,* p.168.

fought each other to exhaustion and Finland lost large parts of its territory, but not its independence. Hence Max Jakobson's magnificent final chapter "Victory in Defeat" in the English version of his work. For the delaying action of the Finnish army, had forced the Soviet Union to negotiate and forget the Kuusinen puppet state.

The Soviet interpretation of the relation of forces had thus proved wrong, for the Finnish populace fought with the upper-classes to defend both its state and society. In a book written in the middle of the Continuation War, O.W. Kuusinen was compelled to admit that in the Winter War a section of the Finnish working-class, too, had fought against the Soviet army.[128] Kuusinen did not deign to provide an explanation of this, but the usual explanation, the lack of a developed class consciousness among the workers, was hardly applicable: in Finland in 1918 the Red revolution, partly led by Kuusinen himself, had shown ample class consciousness and the families of the revolutionaries, decimated as they often were, still harboured plenty of sense of class. Men of military age from known Red families were not in this war called up: they landed in prison. But many of the rest of the working-class and peasantry were certainly by the summer of 1939 aware of the Stalinist terror of the middle and later years of the 1930s.There was quite enough about it in the Finnish press.[129]

What is even more important in Kuusinen's propagandist work was his recital of opposition to the Continuation War. In this war, Communists in Finland *were* called up, often into the penal battalion of Nikita Parma. The populace, as a whole, undoubtedly went dutifully to war, but in places reluctance about the war surfaced. Kuusinen refers to demonstrations on May Day in 1942 and, in general, to the discontent of part of the inhabitants of northern Finland about the war. Some Communists were shot for sabotage. People who had been active in the period between the Winter War and the Continuation War in the Finnish-Soviet Friendship Society were jailed–Dr. Mauri Ryömä for seven years.[130]

---

[128] Kuusinen, O.W. *Suomi ilman naamiota*, Moscow (Karjalais-Suomalaisen SNT:n valtion kustannusliike), 1944 (though written in 1943), p.6.

[129]The execution of Marshal Tukhashevski and his colleagues for traitorous relations with Nazi Germany in June 1937 was reported in some detail, including the fact that all confessed in the "in the Soviet- Russian style": *Turun Sanomat, 6.6.1937,12.6.1937. 16.6.1937, & 16.6.1937.*

[130] Kuusinen, op.cit.,p.50. But *Suomen Sosialidemokraatti* of 3.5.1942 refers with disdain to the pamphlets of a "*Suomen kansan vapausliitto*" distributed by a child who received pocket-money for doing it. Dissatisfaction with the war in parts of the north was a more complex matter: Kuusinen, op.cit.,pp.67–68, even tells of joint Norwegian and Finnish partisans operating under the leadership of an H.Larsen. On the persecution of radical Left figures, Kuusinen, op.cit., p.47.

But there was nonetheless a sufficiency of the national will to carry the war through for three years to the final defeat. Kuusinen argues that the populace were persuaded intentionally by the Finnish authorities that the hostilities were aimed at getting the lost lands back. But that the populace were betrayed by the invasion of East Karelia so that the issue was that of an imperialist war in respect of which many Finnish soldiers refused to cross the frontier into Soviet territory—another sign of restraint in the exercise of the national will.[131]

War as Trauma[132]

By implication, Kuusinen seemed to see even the matter of the returning of the lost lands as a piece of trickery, however. It is difficult to see why, however, since once again he gave no explanation as to why this should be, except that the new war was a part of a wider act of imperialism, for Finnish hostilities were by now linked with German hostilities as a kind of extra arm to the invasion of the Soviet Union known as Barbarossa (and had gradually been linked since August 1940).[133] Finnish propaganda claimed that the Continuation War was a separate war, a piece of "co-belligerency," but Finnish propaganda from the same nest of academics also drew up vast plans for the possession and exploitation of East Karelia as well as the Kola Peninsula. Academic patriots produced not merely ideas like "co-belligerency," but also the concept of a "Finnlands Lebensraum," the joint identity of Finland and the Kola Peninsula and East Karelia, proved "scientifically" by geographical and racial ("historical") reasoning.[134]

The Finns had appealed to the Germans on 9 October 1939 for help in the negotiations with the Soviet Union, and on the outbreak of the Winter War, they appealed to the United States and then to Sweden.[135] Now they were back with Germany, this time with a strong German response, having in the meantime rejected late in the day (at the end of the Winter War) the help of the Western Powers (fortunately) and, immediately afterwards, tried to

---

[131] ibid,p.135 et seq.

[132] Using here definition 3 of the *Concise Oxford Dictionary*, Oxford Dictionary, Oxford (Clarendon Press), 1990:"emotional shock following a stressful event."

[133] Per G. Andreen, *Finland i Brännpunkten mars 1940–juni 1941*, Stockholm (Lindfors), 1980, pp.167–169,regards the Veltjens visit to Finland in August 1940 as the decisive factor, two months after Hitler had decided to invade Russia.

[134] Väino Auer (a geographer), Eino Jutikkala (a historian), & Kusta Vilkuna (an ethnographer), *Finnlands Lebensraum*, Berlin (Alfred Metzner Verlag), 1941. According to the film on Auer's life, shown on Finnish TV2 on 7.6.2009, the title was the publisher's.

[135] *Talvisodan historia* I, Porvoo-Helsinki, (Werner Söderström), 1977, pp.37,42,& 45.

court Sweden—to the anger of the Soviet Union. Thus, the German cause seemed a godsend, bearing with it the chance of a final extirpation of the Russian threat, actually to be guaranteed by a German-occupied strip of land that would cut Finland off for ever from Russian territory,[136] once, of course, the Germans had won the war.

It was the neatest of designs all round. Paasikivi, too, side-tracked for some time as Finnish minister in Moscow, was temporarily convinced, though as a decision-maker this time his views were not required and he was not kept informed of the growing network of military relations with Germany. But the fact was that a Finnish attack on the Soviet Union at the time of a massive German invasion of Western Russia suited his own version of the operation of "the relation of forces" laid down in his letter to Tanner of 26.12.1940. Or, it ought to be said that it more than fulfilled his expectations, for the scenario he sketched out to Tanner was one in which Germany, presumably by conquest or negotiation, had made peace with the West and then stood confronting the Soviet Union. Paasikivi did not see this as a start of a new war, but as a peace in which Germany stood all-powerful and could, should she so wish, help Finland as, he said, it was rumoured that in the autumn of 1940 she had pressured the Soviet Union to leave Finland alone.[137] When, a few months later, Barbarossa occurred, and Finland went back into its own war, Paasikivi sat back in astonished satisfaction and turned once more into the Activist he said he had been in 1918. His satisfaction was not to last long.

The Soviet Union, with its clumsy policy, had produced the result it had always pretended to fear, a Finland working alongside and then fighting alongside Germany. To the Soviet leaders, this development was one they had come to see as almost as "natural" as "fearful." Some part of their ideology always justified this, as noted above. But the Finns had been more hesitating on this route than they had been given credit for.

Their immediate response to the Peace of Moscow that ended the Winter War and stripped Finland of one-twelfth of its territory had been to engage in negotiations for a defence union of the three Nordic States, Norway, Sweden, and Finland. This idea was soon abandoned due to the opposition of Molotov and the action of Nazi Germany in beginning to conquer Norway. In April 1940. A milder form of this plan soon surfaced, however, in a proposal for a Nordic *political* union. This type of scheme was hardly new. It had come up even before the independence of Finland and a Finnish Activist, Rafael Erich, had, in 1915, been involved in its drafting.[138] He was still around—in fact, a lot

---

[136] Apunen & Wolff, p.132.

[137] Tanner, op.cit., esp.p.266.

[138] Ohto Manninen,*Toteutumaton valtioliitto,* Helsinki (Kirjayhtymä), 1977, p.173.

of people were around, working on the idea, which, even in the 1930s, had kept making a fitful appearance.[139] Now it seemed to be "a way out" for at least three of the Nordic states. Its protagonists in Sweden, the *Decemviri*, as they were called, even adjusted to putting occupied Norway into their scenario They set the proposal within the existing framework of the Nazi-Soviet Pact, the preventive mechanism against a war on two fronts for Germany, and aimed to be build up—in the current *modus vivendi* between the two Powers—a strong Northern Europe that would prevent further change in that area.[140]

That, in itself, was interesting. There was a lot of background to the proposal. One aspect that might be mentioned is the fact that the commander-in-chief of the defeated Norwegian forces was later to withdraw from the defence of northern Norway (Finmark) against the Germans, partly in the light of his worrisome conviction that the Soviet Union *at that time* was "almost allied to Germany."[141] Putting Norway into a Nordic Union proposal would have ignored this suspicion of any alleged Soviet intentions in the North. In any case, the victorious Germans began to occupy Finmark, not leaving it to the Russians.

Historically seen, there might have been a British element in the background to the Nordic Union proposal, at least as it concerned Sweden and Finland.[142] Twenty-odd years before the British ambassador to Sweden, Esmé Howard, had first thought of a solution to the Finnish problem by placing Finland back under the Swedish crown.[143] The current proposals envisaged a joint state, with one of the heads of state being the King of Sweden.[144] This monarch had already offered his services as a mediator in the war between Britain and Germany. The British minister to Finland continued to be involved, off and on, in the half-hearted negotiations to make a peace between Britain and Germany for several weeks in the summer and early autumn of 1939. These attempts were known and appreciated by the Finns, including the acting President Risto Ryti, an Anglophile.[145] At the turn of

---

[139] ibid., p.10.

[140] ibid., esp.pp.75–77.

[141] General Otto Ruge, *Krigens Dagbok. Annan Verdenskrrig*, Oslo (Halvorsen & Larsen Forlag), I, 1946, pp.396-397. H.Peter Krosby, *Finland, Germany, and the Soviet Union*, Madison (Univ. of Wisconsin Press), 1968, p.24, is adamant that Ruge (the Norwegians) preferred the Germans in northern Norway to the threat of the Russians.

[142] The group known as the *Decemviri* in Sweden, who included Major- General Axel Rappe, the Chief of Staff of the Defence Forces, were basically pro-Allied and in favour of the participation of Norway. Manninen, op.cit., p.179.

[143] See chapter I, note

[144] Manninen, op,cit.,pp.246–247 reveals the existence of a draft constitution found in the Ryti archives in which the two heads of state were the Swedish monarch and the Finnish president.

[145] ibid., pp.58–62.

1940–1941 the Finns even sent their own emissary to England, Henrik Ramsay, to suggest the opening of peace negotiations between Germany and Britain, but to no avail.[146] Meanwhile, the Nordic Political Union began more and more to take on the appearance of a Nordic Defence League.

It is clear that among the Soviet leaders the idea easily arose that peace between Britain and Germany meant the danger of an attack on the Soviet Union, by one or both Powers. The Nordic Political Union was declared to be an adjunct of neutrality in the form of cooperation with Sweden, another neutral state, by Professor Jarl Wasastjerna who believed in it—yet feared what the Soviet leaders feared, the growing shadow of Germany.[147] This would be a Germany in defence of Finland against Russia and it presupposed a breakdown in German-Russian relations. By early 1941, the British did, indeed, seem to be believing that the Soviet attitude towards the Nordic Political Union was changing.[148] But it was too late in the day.

Molotov had shot down the idea in the early days after the close of the Winter War, while an attempt to revive it was rejected by Hitler in the spring of 1941 on the grounds that the Swedish heir to the throne was pro-Allied and that the proposal would turn Finland into a mere province.[149] This was interesting, for it put Hitler into a defender of Finnish independence, *something he had already demonstrated.*

Göring had influenced Hitler to send arms to Finland and the Finns had been glad to respond by allowing leave troops to pass through Finland to Norway[150] and then by the discussions between the military staffs of Germany and Finland. The Nordic Political Union was overwhelmed by this. Sweden began to withdraw, fearing once again that, for Sweden, Germany not Russia was the enemy, but that a British landing in the North in conjunction with a Russian onslaught on the Kalott area (the tip of Northern Europe) might bring the Germans into southern Sweden. The Swedish army would be preoccupied by this defence and would have no troops to spare for a defence of Finland. The feeling in Sweden and Finland for the *independent* defence of *their own* neutrality died hard. In September 1940 Ryti had succeeded in

---

[146] ibid., pp.209–212.

[147] ibid., p.237. 25.4.1941.

[148] ibid., pp.228–229.

[149] Ohto Manninen, "Saksa tyrmää Ruotsin-Suomen unionin," *Historiallinen aikakauskirja*, vol., 1975, pp.218–238. Hitler warned the Finns that if hey went with Sweden, they would forfeit German protection: Manninen, *Toteutumaton valtioliitto*, p.207

[150] As a matter of fact, the German troops began to pass through Finland on 21.9.1940, while he Russian troops garrisoning the Hanko base were not *entrained* till 25.9.1940:Mauno Jokipii, *Jatkosodan synty*, Helsinki (Otava),1987, pp. 117–118. These Soviet troops had previously arrivede at Hanko by sea.

defusing the demand of the pro-German foreign minister Witting that Finland should join the Axis Pact, a very astute rebuttal by referring to the British naval response of shipping coming out of Petsamo if this occurred. He also told a National Coalition Party group that German aid had to be done secretly.[151]

As relations with Germany became tighter, Hynninen in January 1941, had told Assarsson, the Swedish ambassador in Moscow, that the Finns would probably not have to go to war on the German side, if a break occurred between Germany and Russia: without going to war, they could hold down forty Soviet divisions. But Hynninen also said that if active participation were required, the Finns would fight alongside the Germans.[152]

These glosses on neutrality would have been on great importance had the Finnish decision-makers cared to reflect a little more when the German-Russian understanding collapsed, for at that stage—the stage of *Barbarossa*—Molotov asked the Finnish government whether the country was going to remain neutral, in the light of the fact that Hitler had just declared war on the Soviet Union and told the world, in a broadcast of 22 June 1941, that Finland was with Germany in this enterprise. Molotov called P.J. Hynninen, the Finnish *chargé d'affaires* in Moscow, over to the Kremlin, a day later on 23 June 1941. Hynninen didn't know, but tried to ask his government. But the Russians delayed Hynninen's telegram for almost 24 hours, while the Soviet minister, Pavel G. Orlov, had, in his turn, already cut communications with Finland.[153] So they received no answer to Molotov's request. This was a fundamental mistake of policy in a vital crisis period. It is, by the by, worth noting that similarly Molotov appealed to the Hungarians to remain neutral.[154] A second mistake was the assumption that Finnish planes had bombed the Hanko base (then leased to the Russians) and had flown over Leningrad. Subsequent research has shown that they were German planes flying from East Prussia, some of which sowed mines between Kronstadt and Leningrad.[155] These were probably the German planes which Kuusinen mentioned as bombing Kronstadt on 21,22, 23 June and which he erroneously thought had flown from Finnish airfields.[156] A third mistake of the Russians was their bombing of Turku on 25 June. This was the excuse used by Ryti to tell the

[151]Manninen, *Toteutumaton valtioliitto*, p.97.
[152]ibid., p.214. Manninen thinks that this may have come from Halder via Talvela.
[153] Heikki Jalanti, *Suomi puristuksessa 1940–1941*, Helsinki (Tammi), 1966, pp.356–357 &.367.
[154] Nikolaus von Horthy, *Muistelmat*, Helsinki (Otava), 1955, p.267.
[155] Jalanti, op.cit., pp.357–358.
[156] Kuusinen. *Suomi ilman naamiota*, pp.29–30.

people that their "hereditary enemy" had once again *attacked them* and therefore they were at war.[157]

Apart from the constant Soviet haranguing of Finland between the Winter War and the Continuation War,[158] which soured the confidence of the Finns (Soviet propaganda and Soviet insecurity), the mistakes of organization, as above-mentioned, point also to the basic lack of coordination in security policy, behind which was the unbelievable crassness of Stalin to have been caught unawares by the German invasion. His simplicity was even greater than that of Eljas Erkko towards the Russians in the period before the outbreak of the Winter War, since Erkko had the defects of his belief in keeping to one's word, while Stalin was an expert in betrayal.

At this stage in the argument of this text, it is pertinent to look at Finnish policy at its widest and first to recall what Väinö Tanner said at the Elanto meeting of 19 June 1941. Tanner was not then in the government, having resigned from the government in August 1940 after pressure upon Finland from Molotov.[159] This was another Russian mistake, for the Menshevik Tanner was on the cautious side when others were carried away—as in 1918 when he refused to go with the revolution.[160]

In June 1941 Tanner was head of the great cooperative, Elanto, and his audience on 19 June were members of Social Democratic organizations, whose sympathies *ceteris paribus* was with the West, the forthcoming ally of the Soviet Union. Indeed, quite a lot of them were Marxists, though not Marxist-Leninists. In May 1942, for example, one of the columnists in *Suomen Sosialidemokraatti* was to defend everything in Marxism except the concept of the increasing pauperization of the working-class—a grave omission for the purists, but there was plenty left that the columnist found fruitful in directly rebutting the IKL charge that the SDP should forget Karl Marx.[161] As to Tanner, for years he had played his original Marxism down. It was his caution, his pragmatism that now needed listening to. With that, he could have taken a lot of domestic Marxists with him, many of them undoubtedly attending his meeting on 19 June 1941.

This is what he advocated in the war that was coming: essentially a defensive war by holding down a large number of Russian divisions without much of a need for a more active engagement of Finnish troops. He did not

---

[157] Ryti's radio speech to the Finnish people was not given till 25.6.194, at 20.25 p.m., after the bombing of Turku, Helsinki, Lappeenranta, Joensuu, Rauma, and Nokia.

[158] Upton, *Välirauha*, chap.6.

[159] Kalle Lehmus, *Kolme kriisiä*, Helsinki (Weilin & Göös), 1971, p.118.

[160] He was stopped on the road by the revolutionaries and asked to run the finances of the revolutionary government.

[161] *Suomen Sosialidemokraatti* 5.5.1942.

reveal what Ryti had already told him about Hitler's message to be delivered on 22 June. The German troops already in northern Finland (having moved in from Norway) could do the fighting up there, the Finns isolating or even emptying Lapland), but in the south encircling and conquering Hanko and stopping the further transit of Russian troops there. The next day, 20 June, a delegation, chosen at the meeting, saw civilian and military leaders: on this occasion Mannerheim doubted the wisdom of Tanner's view about Lapland and said that public opinion would not support such views. It needs to be said that the lost lands on the Isthmus of Karelia would, in Tanner's view, be restored in the course of the Germans' *Blitzkrieg*. Incidentally, Mannerheim later said that he did not know the date of Barbarossa until the evening of 21 June. Notwithstanding, it is believed that both Ryti and Mannerheim were aware of the Barbarossa plan by 13.6.1941.[162]

These views of Tanner recall the views of Hynninen that the first hope would be to get the lost lands back by serving the Germans in holding down Russian divisions without engaging in much actual fighting. In expressing them, the question arises as to how far Tanner was genuine in his statements to the Elanto meeting and how far he wanted to reassure the constitutional Left about participation in the next stage of the war.[163] Note that Tanner seems to have known more accurately about the onset of Barbarossa than Mannerheim. In any case, with the start once more of war, Tanner re-entered the government on 3 July1941. In that position, he was borne along by the course of the war. A *Blitzkrieg* did not occur. Loss of life and policy change did.

The new bout of hostilities lasted a long time—from 26 June 1941 to 9 September 1944. The war aims of Finland were never officially defined. Finnish propagandists devised the idea that the war was a "co-belligerency," something of a nature of a separate war, though alongside that of Germany. Much later Max Jakobson defined it as an expression of neutrality,[164] for his argument rested on the idea that the war had been from the Finnish side a limited war, *without* an alliance and therefore "the essential ingredient of neutrality" was there. In Ryti's radio-speech, the war was said to be a defensive war, but, naturally enough, once a war has been started the distinction between defence and aggression easily loses meaning.

The preliminaries to the alignments for war were confused, embodying a series of alternatives that were far from clear even to the national elites that engendered them. For Finland did not exactly start the war and some of the

---

[162] Lehmus, op.cit., pp.54–55.

[163] In a public discussion in the Univ. of Turku with the author of this text, the late Professor Jokipii asserted that Tanner, on this occasion, was being "less than truthful."

[164] Max Jakobson, *Finnish Neutrality*, London (Hugh Evelyn), 1968, p.54.

projected alignments were meant to stand as alternatives to war, such as the *holding down* of Russian divisions.

It can hardly be said either that Finland, as the historian Arvi Korhonen[165] once tried to argue, was a log in a current that bore it forward into war. But certain demands had been smouldering between the Peace of Moscow of 13 March 1940 and the 26 June 1941. One was the return of the lost lands, the other was a desperate feeling for security in case the Russians took the rest of the country.

When solutions were mooted, these demands might conflict. The idea of a Nordic Political Union in its later form of a Swedish-Finnish joint state did not, *as far as the Swedes were concerned*, comprehend a war for the return of the lost Finnish lands. This was crystallized in the statements made in April and May from the Swedish side according to which Sweden would be willing to help Finland if it were attacked by the Soviet Union, but not to join in an attack *on* the Soviet Union.[166] Thus, though the Nordic Political Union project had rapidly taken on a military character, as Molotov in the autumn of 1940 had divined,[167] and the Swedish high command had been prepared to see Swedish troops *defending* the Finnish frontier against the Russians at Salla,[168] the Finnish belief as expressed by General Paavo Talvela in October 1940 that Swedish support would be a means of easing into German support[169] was not swallowed by the Swedes. The third Power to be taken into account was Britain and it was rumoured in the spring of 1941 that the British might strike down from northern Norway, thereby provoking a German counter- move up through Sweden leading to a German occupation of that country—a vision that once again confirmed that if Russia were Finland's main enemy, Sweden's was Germany.[170] By March 1941, the bulk of the Swedish army was in southern Sweden in the event of a German attack.[171] This was not a reassuring development for the Finns.

---

[165] Arvi Korhonen, *Barbarossa suunnitelma ja Suomi*, Porvoo-Helsinki (Werner Söderström), 1961, p.340: the final word of his text is "driftwood."

[166] Manninen, op.cit., p.235.

[167] ibid., pp.91 et seq. & 195–196. Molotov was well able to play on the Swedish fears that a Swedish-Finnish Political Union might easily lead Sweden into a war for the return of the Finnish lost lands: C.L.Lundin, *Finland in the Second World War*, Bloomington (Indiana Univ.Press) 1957, p.158. A transfer of guilt.

[168]ibid., p.228. And also the defence of Åland: March 1941.

[169] ibid., pp.151–152.

[170] ibid, p.224.The British attacked the Lofoten Islands on 4 March 1941.

[171] ibid., p.226.

Deutschland macht frei: Another War. The Continuation War

But, in any case, behind this haze of the on-and-off military relationships with Sweden, the Finnish military and civil authorities were building up a nexus with Nazi Germany. The key factor was the rebuttal of Molotov's proposal, in November 1940, that the Soviet Union should take Finland over; this would have been quite in accordance with the sphere- of-influence deal made with Germany in the 1939 Nazi-Soviet Pact. But times had somehow changed And so, in a very back-handed kind of way, Germany under Hitler was upholding Finland as an independent state! The Finns were now moving towards an alignment with Germany.

But how far to go? That was the problem of the fortunes of war. Blitzkrieg was a deceptive word Even the cautious Paasikivi was deceived. He was hoisted on the petard of his own concept of "the relation of forces." In his letter to Tanner of 26 December 1940 he had urged his Social Democratic colleague to show patience until in the future "events independent of ourselves should come to our aid" while in the meantime the country should develop its military preparedness for such an eventuality.[172] By June 1941, the right conjuncture, the Nazi invasion of the Soviet Union, seemed to be about to occur (to all, that is, except Stalin). Paasikivi had no part in Finnish decision-making at this time, but he felt he had got hold of another truth. In the next few months, he was to make a few pro-German speeches.

The most notorious of these was in the Exhibition Hall in Helsinki on 13.3.1942. Here he spoke with Tanner, justifying the new war "with the powerful Greater Germany by our side." The significance of this was that both Paasikivi and Tanner had been the negotiators with the Russians in the autumn of 1939 and had been prepared to trade territory for the sake of peace. Now (eating humble pie?) they pronounced determinedly for a new war.

If Paasikivi felt that the truth had now revealed itself, as a mega-act of history, the Finnish decision-makers had nevertheless had some difficulty in finding what was going to be the appropriate moment of truth. In short, the question was going to be that most delicate question of military politics, the question of when to strike and of how far to strike. A small country that had in the recent Winter War lost over 23,000 soldiers and was burdened with more than 400,000 refugees mainly from the lands of the Karelian Isthmus[173] had reason to be hesitant. Yet it will be contended in the following pages that, when all is said and done, Finland, alas, was not hesitant enough.

---

[172] Tanner, op.cit., letter from Paasikivi, p.262.
[173] Korhonen, op.cit., p.33.

The question is still a bitter one in Finland as witnessed by the furore that arose at the end of 2006 on the publication of the Swedish journalist Henrik Arnstad's book *Spelaren Christian Günther*, a work on the role of the Swedish foreign minister in the period of the Continuation War, which at the same time is a critique of the Finnish foreign policy of that time.[174] This provoked the Finnish journalist Leo Pugin to affirm that the Swedes, in general, were sadly ignorant of Finnish affairs.[175]

What hurt the Finns was Arnstad's statement that Finland was the only democratic country to join in the Second World War on the Nazi side and that there was no such thing as co-belligerence. The usual answer to the charge of Finland's having ganged up with the Nazis was once again brought forth. The answer to this was that there was no alternative. It was brought forth by a member of the Finnish foreign office, Pertti Torstila, who criticized the book in Sweden. The Finnish historian. Markku Jokisipilä said that all this had been discussed already in Finland years ago. Arnstad admitted that he did not know about this. Actually, it may be worth mentioning that the pro-Finnish Norwegian-Canadian historian Hans-Peter Krosby once wrote a book called *Suomen valinta* (Finland's choice) to show, too, that Finland had had no choice.[176]

In the previous section of the current text, however, it has been shown that on 23 June 1941 Molotov asked whether Finland would remain neutral now that the Nazi invasion of Russia had started, while on 19 June Tanner had described a limited engagement in war for Finland. On the other hand, it is true that Finland was already by June 1940 bound by certain considerations to Nazi Germany. These were limited but to some extent unclear. This existing German connection and the Finnish entanglement in it need first to be untangled.

The Finnish Leadership Could Not Get Out Because They Wanted To Get In

By the summer of 1940, Nazi Germany appeared to be the most powerful state in Europe. It had by then taken over a large part of Western Europe: France, the Benelux states, Denmark and Norway. In central and eastern Europe, it had taken in Austria, occupied, divided, and controlled the former state of

---

[174] Henrik Arnstad, *Spelaren Christian Günther*, Stockholm (Wahlström & Widstrand), 2006.

[175] *Helsingin Sanomat*, 2.12. 2006.

[176] Hans-Peter Krosby, *Suomen valinta*, Helsinki, 1967, esp. the final chapter, pp.232–237. The English version published a year later is called *Finland, Germany, and the Soviet Union*. See this chapter, note 141.

Czechoslovakia, and had conquered half of Poland. Its relations with the Soviet Union were good. But Germany faced a problem. And because of this problem, its policy was in the crucible. It had not defeated Britain and yet, at the same time, it wanted to defeat the Soviet Union. The sense in this was, according to Hitler's thinking, that because of the isolationism dominant in the United States,the only possible ally for Britain was the Soviet Union: the latter had to be knocked out so as to defeat Britain.[177] Hitler had therefore misunderstood the United States, where a president, wanting to get into the war, is more powerful than a legislative organ.

In terms of Hiler's own war-fighting, the resolution of this problem in his mind was a nexus for disaster. It portended a war on two fronts for Germany, in short, a repetition of the scenario that had proved to be too much to cope with in the First World War. Hitler's way out was the prosecution of war as *Blitzkrieg.* Against Britain, the *modus operandi* was air power, which was to be understood in the terms laid down in the Italian general Giulio Douhet's dictum: "the bomber will always get through."[178] The success of the British in the Battle of Britain proved the limitations of Douhet's assertion and Hitler did not dare to risk a sea invasion and offered the British a peace that was rejected. His advisers, especially those on the naval front like Admiral Raeder, insisted that Britain was the main enemy and should be downed first.[179] As to the *modus operandi* to be employed against the Soviet Union, *Blitzkrieg* meant pre-eminently land warfare, an enormous operation to knock out the Western Russian heart of the country. In terms of economics, the attack on the Soviet Union known as Barbarossa was an absurdity since the Russians were supplying Germany both with oil and foodstuffs and an invasion to conquer the oil wells required a rapid deep thrust into the Caucasus and thereafter the creation in hostile territory of an extended pattern of logistics. There were, as it turned out, doubts in Hitler's mind about all this. In the autumn of 1940, he conceived the idea of offering the Soviet Union a place within the framework of the existing tripartite pact between Germany, Italy, and Japan, scheming to direct Soviet attention towards the Persian Gulf and Indian

[177] Korhonen, op.cit., p.59

[178] On Douhet's doctrines and influence on Hitler and Göring, see Robert Wohl *The Spectacle of Flight,* New Haven and London, (Yale Univ.Press), 2005, esp. pp. 228–229 & 319. An alternative explanation for the failure of the German Blitzkrieg on England is that put forward by Bevin Alexander in *How Hitler Could Have Won World War II,* New York (Crown Publishers), 2000, p.41, according to whom the fault was not in the bomber but in the change of target from war industries to civilian population—but that, too, was a mistake originating in Douhet.

[179] Korhonen, op.cit., p.176 and 182–183.

Ocean.[180] It did not work. And Hitler had to continue his cosy relationship with the Soviet Union a bit longer, always, however, with the fear that (by his own estimation) the United States would enter the war, after all, in 1942.[181] He had to be quick therefore. But he was already trapped by his *Blitzkrieg* fantasies into the characteristic illusion of all German policy, the possibility of winning a war on two fronts. He had to be quick to do that, too. If the *Blitzkrieg* worked against Russia, while leaving the defeat of Britain till later, Hitler actually avoided a war on two fronts. If it did not work, Hitler was up against a losing campaign of attrition in Russia and a base in a Britain increasingly ready, and waiting for the United States.

After the Winter War, the Finnish military were, indeed, quick off the mark in seeking German military contacts. General Leonhard Grandell, in late March 1940, planned to meet the German general, Georg Thomas, in May in respect of the supply of additional military material for Finland. The talks were somewhat non-consequential.[182] This was before the German defeat of France.

From his side Hitler was slow to take the Finnish civilian leadership into his confidence. The Finnish minister in Berlin, Tauno Kivimäki, asked Weizsäcker in August 1940 what the German reaction would be if a conflict broke out between Finland and the Soviet Union once more. He received no answer.[183] Hitler's option of working with the Soviet Union was still available at this point.[184] Yet as early as July 1940, Halder had been working on the plan to invade Russia, with the possible help of Finland and Turkey.[185] By December 1940, these plans included not merely the possible use of Finnish forces but even the protection of Swedish forces for German troops coming in from Norway,[186] and in military discussions in Helsinki in February 1941 more detailed plans for the invasion of the White Sea area and Murmansk were discussed by the German and Finnish military.[187]

---

[180] Molotov showed an interest in the Persian Gulf, but had an additional set of counter-demands a base on the Turkish Straits, Bulgaria to be in the Soviet sphere, and the withdrawal of German troops from Finland. ibid., p.153–154.

[181] ibid., p.177.

[182] Jokipii, op.cit., p77.

[183] Korhonen, op.cit., p.52.

[184] ibid., pp.153–154.

[185] ibid., p.70 & 73. At the Berghall meeting of 31.7.1940, Hitler sketched out the possibility of a Finland stretching to the White Sea. But in the plan drawn up on 5. 8.40 by General Erich Marcks Finnish divisions should first simply hold down by their existence 15 Russian divisions and two motorized brigades, though the possibility was mentioned that *later* the Finns might take part in the attack on the Murmansk railway. See also note 202, however.

[186] ibid., p.171.

[187] ibid.,p.228.

As noted by Korhonen, Hitler was playing a well-worked out plan of bluffing the Russians that preparations were proceeding for the defeat of Britain. In this question one of the dangers was that if the potential Finnish ally was told too much, it might percolate through to the Russians.[188] Even Finnish mobilization plans might give the game away.[189] Yet the gap between Finnish and German commitment persisted. At the important Salzburg negotiations in May 1941, the Finnish General Heinrichs and aides were careful to avoid committal since, as they told the Germans, the German plans and demands were not known to them.[190] This was blatantly untrue since at the Salzburg discussions in May 1941 the Finns military agreed to send troops with the German forces against both Murmansk and Kantalahti (Kandlaksha on the White Sea), but in the latter case only as far as the old frontier after which German troops were supposd to carry on. In fact, Mannerheim on 5 June said that Finnish troops would not stop at the old frontier but would strike for Kantalahti. In the south, it was agreed at Salzburg that Finnish troops would strike for Lake Ladoga in support pf the German attack on Leningrad.[191] These measures were *offensive.* Additionally, it is worth notimg that in the closely connected Berlin negotiations, the German general Halder took it for granted that in these operations the Finns would not merely regain their lost lands, but would gain a bit more.[192]

Vice versa, when Karl Schnurre, Hitler's emissary, visited Finland in May 1941, and asked Ryti what the Finnish demands were (not necessarily should war break out), he was informed of a Finnish need for compensation in East Karelia *as an apparent acceptance of a loss of territory on the Isthmus in the light of Leningrad's defence needs!*[193] How ironic–this was the very basis on which Russian conciliation was offered in the negotiations before the Winter War!

But, overall, there was a more subtle point. The Finnish claim for "co-belligerency" and not "alliance" with Germany was reflected in the concept that the Finns were fighting a limited war.

In turn, the heart of the concept of limited war was somewhat greater than anything reported about Tanner's Elanto meeting on 19 June. It was not even merely to conquer the lost lands, a goal the cautious Swedes were apt to

---

[188] ibid.,on the extent of Hitler's policy of bluff, pp. 70 &300- 301.

[189] ibid.,p.267.

[190] ibid., pp.257-258.

[191] Jokipii, op.cit., pp.301-302.

[192] ibid.,p.313.

[193] ibid., pp.253-255.

equate with a "war of revenge."[194] Since the Finns did cross the old frontier and did not stop there as many of their troops wanted,[195] the goal was even greater than the re-conquest of the lost lands. The goal became extended into the securing of natural frontiers.[196] This was ironic since Mannerheim's goal was to take East Karelia, two enormous parishes of which had been offered to the Fins in October 1939 in the negotiations with the Soviet Union and considered by the Finns as not constituting a defensible frontier. The term "natural frontiers" could cover a lot and easily became entangled with the vast dreams of the "Suur-suomalaiset" or of "the march to the Urals" (!). And that, in itself, became mixed up with progress in the fortunes of war; why stop the advance now?

In deep contradiction, the element of fighting a limited war did not, however, disappear. Curiously, it had also been agreed to by the Germans. In March 1941 Hitler expected the Finns only to attack Hanko and for the rest to pin down Russian troops by their presence.[197] It was presumably a reflection of *this* view of Hitler's that Tanner was still peddling in the Elanto meeting of June 19.[198] Quite close to the start of Barbarossa, it had been agreed that Finnish mobilization should take place as late as 14 days after the German attack and as late as the Helsinki talks, the possibility was left open that the Finns should join in the hostilities later: in early June 1940, Heinrichs stated that Finnish troops should not necessarily attack with the Germans unless Finland itself was attacked.[199]

Korhonen, in his well-researched work has produced plenty of evidence. But it hardly leads to the conclusion that he came to, of Finland's drifting into war What his evidence shows is that there were difficulties in adjustment

---

[194] Manninen, op.cit., pp. 138 & 193. Korhonen, op.cit., pp.238 & 241 (as late as April and May 1941, in the latter case the Swedish foreign minister was expressing his doubts about Finnish intentions).

[195] Helge Seppälä,*Suomi hyökkääjänä 1941*, Porvoo-Helsinki (Söderström),1984, p.153 points out that even in respect of going over the old frontier on the Karelian Isthmus (told to the troops as a means of attaining a more natural frontier) several hundred initially refused to cross the frontier. Some persisted in their refusal and were sentenced to hard labour.

[196] This became fused with the idea that the gaining of natural frontiers was the culmination o f a defensive war. Note the leader in the *Helsingin Sanomat* of 4.5.1942.

[197] Korhonen, op.cit., p.192, Heusinger's report of 25.3.1941 to General Halder on Hitler's encapsulation of Finland's role in Barbarossa.

[198] See page 118 of this chapter.

[199] Korhonen, op.cit., pp. 271, 305, &282. Even in respect of operations in northern Finland, it was said, after all, that the North Finland division should only have covering duties: op.cit., p.323.

between Germany and Finland and that the Finns' own war aims were not clearly declared[200] and were even contradictory.

Tanner tried to sort it all out in a meeting in the Social Democratic Party headquarters on 5 September 1941. He affirmed that the Finns were not going to attack Leningrad, but presumably holding down Russian troops on their part of the Leningrad front and that Finland should get out of the war at the first possible opportunity. In the meantime, the search for the suitable natural frontier should go on, but no decision could really be taken till Leningrad was attacked, apparently by the Germans alone! The radical Left in the Social Democratic leadership disagreed with much of what he said: Mauno Pekkala, J.W. Keto, and Eino Kilpi all expressed their regret that the old frontier had been crossed and what was more claimed, in their critique, to be reflecting the ideas of the common soldier.[201]

These soldiers who refused to cross the old frontier were expressing their convictions by disobedience. But disobedience was not recognized in Finnish society. The Social Democratic Party had tamed itself into constitutionalism, which, in party-political terms, meant coalition. This gave the SDP important ministries, but of an economic and social nature, not directly connected with the prosecuting of the war. Mauno Jokipii was right to point out that as far as the latter was concerned.

It was the province of a Camarilla, an inner cabinet of president, prime minister, foreign minister (Rolf Witting), and Mannerheim's bosom friend, the soldier in the cabinet, General Rudolf Walden.[202] To this may be added what Paasivirta called "the military government" at Mikkeli, composed of Mannerheim and his soldiers.[203] Professor Edvin Linkomies of the National Coalition Party affirmed just before the outbreak of the Continuation War that defence issues should not be dealt with publicly and that in the press they should have as little attention as possible.[204] What did all this mean in war-terms? It meant that the country waited for a German victory or, its alternative, as expressed by General Walden in a cabinet meeting, "that we

---

[200] Tuomo Polvinen, *Barbarossasta Teheraniin. Suomi kansainvälisessä politiikassa I: 1941–1943*, Porvoo-Helsinki (Söderström), 1979, p.109, points out that the Finnish foreign minister, Rolf Witting, thought that the same was true of the more powerful states. Polvinen seems to think Witting was right.

[201] Lehmus, op.cit., pp.118–121.

[202] Jokipii,op.cit., p.28.

[203] Discussion between the author and Juhani Paasivirta in the 1980s

[204] Jokipii, op.cit. p.101.

keep our army equipped in battle-shape as long as possible."[205] To bring it all to a fighting-finish.

Getting on and Gainfully Getting Out

One of the strangest acts of duplicity in the approach to war in 1941 was the exploitation of the talents of J.K.Paasikivi, a person who could work well with the Russians, as minister in Moscow—and then keeping him uninformed as he continued to protest the neutrality of Finland.[206] In this post, Paasikivi, to keep the peace with Russia, even suggested that the nickel mines of the Petsamo area should be transferred to the Soviet Union. He did not know what President Ryti was doing.

This fitted in with Hitler's own policy of bluff, namely that Germany was arming all the time against Britain, and was preparing to "defend" the North against a possible onslaught from a British seaborne landing. This was not entirely bluff since it was something Hitler feared so greatly that he forced his own armed chiefs to pay particular attention to the Arctic coastline.[207] Hitler's concern also, however, encompassed the frustrating of a possible link between the two enemies, the current enemy of Britain, and the future enemy, the Soviet Union.[208]

Anyway since Hitler was preparing an invasion of Russia in as secretive a manner as possible,[209] the Finns sought to emulate this approach. They made a protestation of neutrality, but saw the real alternative in the prosecution of war.

Thus, the Finns joined the invasion of the Soviet Union under the German plan *Barbarossa*. Once again, Jokipii made the point that only a small group of leaders made the decision: they consulted neither the foreign affairs

---

[205] *"Faktillisesti tämä tarkoittaa antautumista,"* ed.Kauko Rumpunen & Ohto Manninen, Helsinki (Edita), 2009, p.105.

[206] Korhonen, op.c.it., p.159. Juhani Paasivirta, *Suomi ja Eurooppa 1939–1956*, Helsinki (Kirjayhtymä), 1992, pp.133–135, emphasizes the conflict between Paasikivi's policy of concessions to the Soviet interest esp. over nickel and the general Finnish rapprochement with Germany. Paasikivi resigned his post in February 1941.

[207] ibid.,p.201

[208] Ziemke, Earl F. *The German Northern Theater of Operations 1940–1945*, Washington (Dept. of the Army Pamphlet no.20–271), 1959, p.124.

[209] Extreme secrecy was demanded of the few commanders let into the planning of Barbarossa in December 1940, whose subordinates were to be told that the plans were only in case the Russians themselves began to change their policy. Korhonen, op.cit., p.181. Until November 1940, the Germans pursued measures of bluff in Norway (Plan "Harpune Nord") so as to indicate that they were still planning for an imminent invasion of Britain: Korhonen, op.cit., p.214.

committee of Parliament, certainly not the whole of the government, nor Parliament.[210] On 12.6.1941 the Social Democratic parliamentary group made a declaration of support for the defence of the boundaries of Finland, but in no way to go over them.[211] But on 5.6 1941 Mannerheim had already said that the 12th Finnish division *would* go over the frontier and drive for Kandalaksha (Kantalahti) on the coast of the White Sea.[212] The Germans made the big plans.

And the biggest plan was that of the *Blitzkrieg*, which would destroy the nerve-centres of the Soviet Union in its western one-third. The plan ignored not merely the two-thirds of the Soviet Union that were left, but also the fact that the western one-third of the Soviet Union was not like Western Europe where the *Blitzkrieg* had worked (apart from the obstinate case of Britain). The three upsetting factors for an invasion of Russia were climate, terrain, and the backwardness of the infra-structure. Visually, this negative combination is often seen in terms of bogged-down motorized transport on an autumnal or wintry steppe. But equally the same three factors affected operations on the Arctic coastline.

After the Winter War, Finland had retained an Artic port, Petsamo (with an outpost at Liinahamari), but under the terms of the Peace of Moscow, that area had had to be neutralized. The Finns could not defend it and, in the coming conflict with the Soviet Union, the Germans intended to occupy Petsamo—with the consent of the Finns. According to plan, they would then advance with the Finns along the coastline and capture Murmansk, one of the few ice-free ports in the Soviet Union and through which the Russians could receive aid from the West. Another advance was planned further south on Salla (an area taken by the Soviet Union by the Peace of Moscow) so as to strike ultimately at Belomorsk (Sorokka) and Kandalaksha on the White Sea, thus threatening transport from abroad to the port of Archangel. These operations were also meant to cut the railway, whether in respect of the mainline from Murmansk to Leningrad or in respect of the spur that connected Belomorsk with Moscow. Though the Murmansk-Leningrad line was once or twice cut, these operations in the north (known as *Silberfuchs*) were, as a whole, failures. The railway continued to function for the benefit of the Russians, who were able to transport their troops to other vital and threatened areas by its means.[213] As to Hitler's hobby-horse, the coastline attack, one of the most capable of the German field-generals, Eduard Dietl,

---

[210] Jokipii, op.cit., p327.
[211] ibid., p.334.
[212] ibid., p.324.
[213] Ziemke,op.cit., p.187

had doubted all along the wisdom of endeavouring to strike along the coast, but had then swallowed his doubts.[214] *In toto,* these northern operations- three-and-a half months in duration—cost the Germans 21,500 casualties and the Finns over 5,000.[215] As far as the advance along the coast was concerned, it had gone 15 miles.[216] Murmansk was still more than 40 miles away.[217]

Participation in *Silberfuchs* was the first of the military mistakes committed by the Finns, for though it was mainly a set of operations conducted primarily from German forces coming in from conquered Norway the Finns were also involved. Unlike the Germans, they had knowledge at least of climate and terrain; as to infra-structure over the border, Salla had formerly been theirs (less than a year before) and the Finnish military must surely have had some intelligence, particularly as the Russians were compelling them as a peace condition to build a railway from the frontier deep into Finland. In respect of the coastal area, the German force when it crossed the border used maps with roads marked on it that did not exist.[218] Surely the Finns could have supplied them with better maps or at least intelligence—or, best of all, have dissuaded them from these attempts. On the other hand, the Germans themselves, in the honeymoon period of the German-Russsian Non-Aggression Pact, had actually had a submarine base on the Litsa river over on the Soviet Murmansk coast, from which to attack British shipping (this fact was the probable source of the Norwegian c-in-c's belief in 1940 that the Germans were in Murmansk and might—he possibly thought- bring Russians into Norway).[219]

This brings the countervailing arguments a stage further. Were there institutional defects in the Finnish relationship with the Germans? The preliminaries were discussions between leading members of the military in both countries (bearing in mind that a large number of politicals in Nazi Germany, like Göring or Hitler himself, were anyway to be considered as military leaders). From the Finnish side, General Paavo Talvela was Mannerheim's personal representative not merely in Germany but, where necessary, with the German forces in Finland. He it was who discussed with the Germans the initial thrusts to be made over the Russian frontier in the very north of Finland.[220] Why did he not warn the Germans to use greater

[214] ibid., p.155.
[215] ibid., p.184.
[216] ibid., p.154.
[217] ibid., p.141.
[218] ibid., p.141-142.
[219] See this chapter note 141.
[220] In visiting Germany as Mannerheim's personal representative in the early December of 1940, Talvela's commission was to sound out German views on the possibility of Mannerheim's becoming president of Finland: Korhonen, op.cit., pp.171-172. Talvela, op.cit., I, p.266 On his

resources up there once they insisted on making the attempt? Perhaps he did so warn, as his memoirs are even more secretive than is usually the case with military men- and saying that says a great deal. But having said that[221] it is worth making a contrary point. Were both Talvela and Mannerheim carried away by the impress of a *Blitzkrieg*? In any case, there does not seem to have been, in this particular aspect of the Continuation War, any special Finnish negotiating stance.

In one aspect, however, the Finns appeared to excel. In the practice of war, they had been able to cut the Murmansk railway on 8 September 1941 and several times thereafter. It may be said that this work, *had it continued*, would have constituted a military operation in respect of which small groups of Finnish guerrillas, first-class forest fighters, might have performed well. Yet Mannerheim stopped it. For on 27 October 1941, the US government warned the Finnish government that any interruption from Finnish territory or Finnish-controlled territory of US war material to the Soviet Union would create a crisis in US-Finnish relations.[222]

These declarative words added a new content to "co-belligerence." Finland could be on the side of Germany against Russia, but not where it upset the biggest Western Power, which was still technically at peace with Germany. When, after Pearl Harbor, the US entered the war against Japan and Germany obliged by declaring war on the US, Germany once more tried to get the Finns to cut the Murmansk railway. But Mannerheim refused. This brought in another feature of "co-belligerence," for now, in the summer of 1942, the Germans asked the Finns to do something they had hitherto refrained from doing, that is, to attack Leningrad from the Karelian Isthmus side instead of simply holding down Russian troops in that area. Mannerheim answered by

previous visits in the autumn, Talvela had also discussed Finnish military matters, especially with Halder. These issues were couched in *defensive* terms. In mid-December, Talvela pointed especially to the inability of the Finns to protect Petsamo should the Russians invade. He requested that where needed the German army in Norway could do the job, Talvela I, op.cit, p.257. In February 1941, he visited the German armed forces in Norway, ibid.,p.268, and thus must have been aware of German plans to invade along the coastline to Murmansk.

[221] Talvela, according to his editors who furnished the reader with the information, made no references in his diary about his visits to Norway in early 1941. This was characteristic of the caution enjoined on him by Mannerheim as far as his diary and other reports were concerned. Talvela, op.cit., I, p.240, in the words of his editors, Vilho Tervasmäki & Sampo Ahto. Seppälä, op.cit., p. 61, recounts how Talvela in the middle of Deecember 1940 discussed operations involving both Petsamo and Salla with General Franz Halder, the chief of the German general staff. A few days later General E. Heinrichs, chief of the Finnish General Staff, discussed with Halder, *inter alia*, the possibility of operations in the Petsamo area and towards the White Sea port of Kantalahti: Seppälä, op.cit., pp.67–68.

[222] Ziemke, op.cit., p.182.

saying that he would order the Murmansk line to be cut if the Germans would take Leningrad first.[223] This was actually a reverse of German policy, which still conceived of cutting the line as a means of ensuring a weakening of the defence of Leningrad.

In the popular Finnish version as to why the Finns did not attack Leningrad directly from the side of the Karelian Isthmus, the whole matter is slotted into the construction of a limited war, which was the heart of co-belligerence. It has been argued that Mannerheim was aware of the force of a future argumentation arising from any postwar reconstruction: that the next Russian government would once again blame the Finns, as in the negotiations before the Winter War, of encroaching too closely on the vital city of Leningrad.[224] This was an argument from the "Russian" aspect. But traditionally the argument also had an "Allied " content since Leningrad-St-Petersburg was known in Petrine terms as "the window to the West." By 1943 the Germans were convinced that Finnish restraint vis-à-vis an attack on Leningrad was due to the fact that the Finns did not want a complete break with the US.[225] The argument does not have all that much to recommend it. The civil arm, as represented by President Ryti, had already by this time come to the conclusion that Finland should possess the Kola Peninsula and East Karelia with the Germans controlling a wedge of territory that would separate for ever Finland from the future *truncated* Russian state.[226] Contradictions in Finnish policy were, of course, not unknown—and existed even between the military itself, some members of which wanted a frontal assault from the Isthmus on Leningrad.[227] Screen seems to find a lot of merit in an argument drawn from General Erik Heinrichs, according to which the stationary period

---

[223] Screen, op.cit., p.330.

[224] ibid., p.314.

[225] Ziemke, op.cit., p.249.

[226] Lundin, op.cit., pp.261–263. This standpoint included a reduction in the significance of Leningrad so that it would become a German trading post and loading bay.

[227] From listening to Mannerheim on 5. June 1941, General Talvela had come to the conclusion that Mannerheim was going to send Finnish troops against Leningrad. Talvela regretted that this did not occur; if it had occurred "world history would have taken another turn." Talvela, op.cit., I, pp.269–270. (This was probably written later in 1959—which makes it all the more appalling). It is fair to say that many Finnish generals at the front did feel that Leningrad should have been attacked from the Isthmus side: Lundin, op.cit., p.375. But in the second volume of his memoirs, published in 1952 (p.269), Mannerheim tells that as late as the Salzburg and Berlin negotiations of May 1941 General Heinrichs, the principal Finnish officer present, insisted that Finland wished to remain neutral (unless attacked), did not have the troops to attack the Murmansk railway, and did not intend to join in the attack on Leningrad, not even if attacked first by the Russians. Some troops might be spared for participating in the attack towards the White Sea. Quoted by Lundin, op.cit.,p.193.

of war had already begun for Finland, with a necessary release of troops back to civil employment.[228] Additionally, it may be argued that where military resources *were* to be used, other sectors (a drive to Belomorsk) were more important for Mannerheim's strategic goals. Since this would, if successful, upset the Western supply route into Russia, there was the other apparent contradiction hovering in the background, fighting a war along with Germany and trying to please the West whose principal enemy was Germany. A more cruel conclusion can be drawn. If the Germans could have managed on their own to conquer Leningrad (and it should be remembered that among their schemes was no solution to the problem of the starving civil population),[229] then all well and good. The hands of the Finns would be clean. According to the analysis of Earl Ziemke, Mannerheim expected Leningrad to fall, after which he could have at his disposal eight or nine additional brigades, whether German or Finnish, so as to strike to Belomorsk in a winter offensive in 1941.[230] This looks as if, for Mannerheim, this is further evidence that Leningrad could fall as long as the Germans did the job.

There were, however, many ways of strangling Leningrad. Talvela has spoken with regret of the inability of the Finnish forces to come round the northern shore of Lake Ladoga and meet with the German forces at Lotinanpelto. A pincer move would have closed and Leningrad as a city would have died.[231]

It is worth repeating that the war aims of the Finns were never officially defined. Both Ryti and Mannerheim certainly wanted the extinction of Bolshevism. Ryti also wanted a re-writing of political geography so as to produce a permanent solution for the security of Finland. This included a fairly substantial shift of population, moving the Russians out of large tracts of northern Russia and letting the Finnic peoples occupy these areas, working in the forest industry under German control.[232] How far Mannerheim knew about these plans is unclear. But in 1942 the Finnish military told General Wilhelm Keitel that they regretted the failure to get to Belomorsk in the previous winter offensive since, *inter alia*, the postwar frontier ("a natural frontier") was to be fixed at this point.[233] For an operation of this intent, it is difficult to imagine the military's views being anything other than a reflection

[228] Screen, op.cit., p.330.

[229] Talvela II, p.133 tells simply how Hitler admitted to him that the conquest of Leningrad would present the Germans with the problem of what to do with its population of four million.

[230] Ziemke, op.cit., p.206 & 210.

[231] Talvela II, pp.227–228.

[232] ibid., pp.159–160 & 166–167. This aspect of "reconstruction" seems to have originated in the mind of the National Coalition Party politician Antti Hackzell.

[233] Ziemke, op.cit., p.230.

of Mannerheim's. Meanwhile Mannerheim told his Russian friends abroad that he was not against Russia, but only against Bolshevism.[234] His crossing of the old frontier and drive into East Karelia was suspect and his proclamation of 10 July 1941, recalling his promise in 1918, to liberate this area, seemed to put him in the camp of the Academic Karelia Society. Yet he claimed he had not wanted the incorporation of this vast area into Finland- it was not ready for it, from 10–15 years had to pass.[235] The additional argument of establishing a natural frontier for Finland over there seemed to mean therefore Finnish control of the vast region as a kind of colonialism until the Finnic population had reached the status of *évolués.* Assuming that Mannerheim, after all, was not so impressed by Greater Finland propaganda—and this is still an open question, an additional explanation for his going over into East Karelia may lie in the fact that he intended to work with the Germans and therefore came down on the eastern side of Lake Ladoga. An explanation *in terms of* Greater Finland goals may thus, as Seppälä seems to suggest,[236] be covering his intention *at that point* to work with the Germans for the destruction of Leningrad.

So far as is known (there was no vote or poll on this), the bulk of the population of Finland felt the legitimacy of getting their lost lands back, an aspiration particularly strong among the Agrarians. The re-settlement of the Isthmus Karelians after the Winter War was causing tension in many parts of Finland. Once the Continuation War started, a further cause for discontent among the Karelians themselves arose from their astonishment that Mannerheim did not immediately prosecute the war by driving down into the Isthmus, but preferred to attack along the north shore of Lake Ladoga, apparently as part of a pincer movement that would connect with German troops coming from the southern shore of Ladoga. This coordination ran into difficulties. By 21 August Mannerheim decided that the Isthmus was instead to be recovered by his forces.[237] Whether through the Isthmus or along the northern shore of Ladoga to Lotinapelto on the river Syväri, Mannerheim realised that he had not the troops to invest Leningrad and that the Germans

[234] Screen, p.308

[235] According to Heinrichs II, p.272–276, quoted by Lundin, op.cit., p.270, Mannerheim could never imagine that East Karelia could be stripped from Russia, which, in Heinrichs's view of Mannerheim's outlook, would always remain a great power! Talvela, however, *Muistelmat* II, Helsinki (Kirjayhtymä), 1977,p.81, sees that Mannerheim's belief was still the ultimate incorpration of East Karelia into Finland.

[236] Seppälä, op.cit., pp.108–109.

[237] Screen, op.cit., p.314. Opinion in Finland was confused at this delay. Polvinen, op.cit., p.22.

were equally devoid of sufficient forces, recognizing instead that they could not overwhelm Leningrad but had to besiege it.[238]

The value of the Finnish participation in Barbarossa has been estimated at 16 divisions,[239] but the total impact of the invasion into Russia showed that the resources were inadequate for it and the concentration of the resources that did exist imperfect.

The Continuation War was itself detrimental to the practice of democracy. That war, hardly surprisingly, provided opportunities for those who commanded its forces. Then, the doctrine of *carpe diem* became an overwhelming lure, especially when coupled with the conviction that the *Blitizkrieg* was bound to triumph. Thus "the fortunes of war" became an even greater attraction for a country that had previously felt itself to be under the threat of extinction. The factor of bluff, primarily in the German policy of deceiving the Soviet Union that Britain was continuing to be Germany's principal enemy along with a brief period when it seemed as if the Soviet Union might be persuaded to pursue its own interests elsewhere in the world and even join the Three-Power Pact as a fourth member, began to be matched by a similar Finnish policy of deception towards Russia and the West (neutrality) but with an underlying expectancy that something was going to turn up.

These were the elements that produced a secretiveness that cut down the power of the constitutional organs, of the military negotiators, who even as late as May 1941 were not allowed to commit themselves to the extent of making Finnish aims too closely known, and led in turn to the relegation and partial exploitation of the Finnish diplomats both in the Soviet Union and the United States. This policy was not the policy of a piece of mindless driftwood, but of an armed boat coasting to the Russian shore under German protection. In summing up the moves to be taken in the forthcoming Continuation War. Helmuth Greiner, who kept the *Kriegstagebuch* for the German high command, asserted that it did not matter whether the Finns themselves had given an explicit commitment to particular measures. It surely did matter. For on 3 February 1941, Halder assumed that the Finns would detach five divisions "for the attack on Leningrad."[240] Fortunately, they did not do so and Leningrad held out. But, unfortunately for the Finns, the general lack of commitment and, when it came to it, of covert-commitment in many operations, confused no one as much as the Finns themselves and the friends they had elsewhere in the world. On 25 June 1941 President Ryti told

[238] ibid., pp.24–25.
[239] ibid., p.31.
[240] Lundin, op.cit., p.213.

Parliament "today begins a new defensive war"—the Russians had already bombed a number of points in Finland. War was thus a *fait accompli*. Parliament agreed to endorse the war as was their right and duty under article 33 of the Constitution. But what they endorsed was a circumstance that had already happened. No wonder Professor Ragnar Furuhjelm of the Swedish People's Party blamed the government for lack of information up to this state of affairs and wanted to know what *commitments* the government had made.[241] For the circumstance that had brought the Russian bombing was the cooperation between the German military and the Finnish military, *non-committal* as it had apparently been, and known to the Russians if not to Professor Furuhjelm.

Getting out

The total number of Finnish dead in the Continuation War was 58,000, but of these many thousands were killed as a result of the Soviet offensive that started on 9–10 June 1944. Hostilities went on for three months until 4 October (a day later from the Soviet side).

The Finns, using the good offices of the United States (which had not declared war on Finland) and Sweden (a Nordic neutral), had been deliberating on the chances of seriously withdrawing from the war since 1943. They had failed to pull it off. Stalin himself seemed to value the maintenance of diplomatic relations between Finland and the US.[242] So did the Finns, but by June 1944 their handling of these relations slipped badly. At a critical point in the Finns' attempts to get out of the war, they preferred to come to a temporary accommodation with the Germans rather than trust the West, that is, use the intermediary help of the United States. This final tragedy will be recounted below.

A somewhat unstructured peace movement had by then been in existence for over two years. It was composed of dissidents from many parties and included from 1943 Paasikivi. Members of this group refrained from setting-up an alternative government in Sweden: yet their r role was often ambiguous and sometimes dangerous—Nils Meinander was arrested in Finland and sent to a penal battalion.[243] Urho Kekkonen of the Agrarian Party continued to

---

[241] ibid., pp.223–224.

[242] R. Michael Berry, *American Foreign Policy and the Finnish Exception*, Helsinki (SHS), 1987, p. 408. Messages from Harriman to Roosevelt on 11 & 12 June 1944.

[243] Apunen & Wolff, op.cit., p.300

write war-propaganda, while speaking of the need for peace in Sweden. [244] These people had contacts with Madame Aleksandra Kollontai, the Soviet minister in Sweden, who was pro-Finnish and wanted Mannerheim to be left alone to lead his army into peace [245] The Finnish government gingerly made probes for peace, too. But somehow the "peace opposition" and the government could not jell on this vital question.

The failure of US pressure on Finland to make peace with the Soviet Union in the summer of 1944 (after several previous attempts)seems to have been due in part to a probable misunderstanding in the Russian terms for surrender connected with the Russian term used, namely "capitulation." This was interpreted by the Finns in the same sense as the Rooseveltian demand for "unconditional surrender."[246] Generaly speaking, however, the term "capitulation" is, apparently, stronger in Russian than the Anglo-Saxon equivalent. In fact, the word "capitulation" in the Anglo-Saxon sense means, on the contrary, "surrender on conditions." It is always possible to think that had the US maintained diplomatic relations with Finland, it might have been possible to insert some conditions into the Finnish surrender to the Russians.

The conditions offered previously up to the end of April by the Soviet government did not seem to suit the Finns. The United States government, having tried for three years to encourage the Finns either not to go to war with the Russians[247] or to make peace as quickly as possible with them, had, by the end of April, lost a lot of its interest in fostering peace between Finns and Russians and began to move to break off relations. This was done to reassure the Russians and to avoid participation in "involvement in the final settlement which must take place between Finland and the Soviet Union." But still it was also felt that a breaking off of diplomatic relations with Finland might help the formation of a new, more peace-loving government in Finland.[248] This did not occur, though it was discussed.

---

[244] In a speech given in Stockholm to the Swedish Agrarian Union on 7.12. 1943, Urho Kekkonen presented a future of "Good Neighbourliness with the Hereditary Enemy," a speech which to some extent blamed Russia, but was as nothing to the propaganda he wrote under the name of Pekka Peitsi ("Peter the Lance"). The Stockholm speech is in his writings called *Neutrality:the Finnish Position,* London (Heinemann), 1973, 18–31.

[245] Apunen & Wolff, op.cit., p.294.

[246] As interpreted by the Americans (Gullion's statement to Cordell Hull of 25.6.1944), the Soviet meaasge to the Finns was simply to "capitulate" meaning "giving up." FRUS, 1944, vol. III, p.603.

[247] In the spring of 1941, the US warned the Finnish government not to get involved in a German attack on Russia. This is referred to in *Foreign Relations of the United States,* vol.iii, 1944, p.581, in Hugh Cumming's report of 24.3.1944.

[248] ibid., p.596. Memo of Secretary of State Cordell Hull to Pres.-Roosevelt of 28.4.1944.

The Soviet offensive against Finland in June produced a panic reaction. Panic drove Ryti to accept an additional promise of aid from Germany in return for a promise not to make peace without a German endorsement of it. Ribbentrop arrived in Helsinki on 22 June and the deal was done. It is worth stressing once again that the breaking of diplomatic relations by the United States was regrettable. In practice, this was a bit of a bungle. But starting measures had been taken before Ribbentrop had arrived. On 16.6.1944, Cordell Hull told the American chargé in Helsinki, Edmund Gullion, that the Finnish minister to Washington, Hjalmar Procopé, was to get out along with three other members of his staff (in the case of Urho Toivola, this was rescinded). Curiously, Hull said that even this did not constitute "a rupture of diplomatic relations."[249] In turn, the American legation in Helsinki was reduced to one man, Edmund Gullion, by 29 June 1944. The US ambassador in Moscow, Averell Harriman, had discussed this move with Stalin on 27 June. Stalin then stated that the only thing the Americans might now try was to suggest informally that the Soviet Union had no designs to take over the country.[250] This was remarkable and far from a demand for "unconditional surrender". But the badly-drafted Soviet note demanding "capitulation" had already been sent on 23 June.[251] What to do in the new context of Stalin's milder version in the changed context of the by- now reduced and low-level diplomatic connections between the US and Finland? The Americans, exasperated by the Finns, had cut down their own facilities for influencing events. How could Harriman get a message effectively to President Ryti? Through Sweden? He does not seem to have tried.

On the other hand, Washington appears to have had little faith all along in the Finnish legation in Washington: the minister, Hjalmar Procopé, before leaving his post in early June, seems to have antagonized Roosevelt by consorting with the anti-Roosevelt (and deeply anti-Soviet) faction and, among other things, ridiculing Roosevelt's D-Day poem.[252] (!) On the other hand, the press attaché, Urho Toivola, who was pro-Allied, did not have the confidence of the government of his own country. His book, *Amerikka varoitti,* is a lament for lost opportunities, of his country and of his own.[253]

---

[249] ibid.,p.601.

[250] Berry.,op.cit., pp.412–413. FRUS, 1944, vol. III, pp.603–604.

[251] Kimmo Rentola, "Stalin, Mannerheim ja Suomen rauhanehdot 1944," *Historiallinen aikakauskirja, 1/2001, p.52.*

[252] ibid., pp.409–410.

[253] *Amerika varoitti*, Helsinki (OY Suomen kirja), 1946.In January 1942 a Harvard professor told Toivola that Finland had not taken advantage of the US approaches in the previous autumn:Toivola, op.cit., p.25, 39, & 109–110.Toivola noted, on 27.10.42, that Wendell Wilkie, the Republican presidential candidate, had been told by Stalin that the Russians were

Meanwhile, the fighting between the Finns and the Russians was at its fiercest, while the latter waited for a change of government in Finland and the opening of direct peace negotiations in consequence. To add to the tragic irony of the situation, Gullion, in a report from Helsinki to Cordell Hull of 27 June 1944,affirmed that the Finnish government had decided to break with Germany, but that "the hesitation of the headquarters" had slowed things down and Ribbentrop had stepped in.[254] The latter offered the bait of *direct* help as opposed to the *indirect*–and one seemingly less elusive than the help of the Americans.

In the end it was all to be left to Stalin and his need, the need to transfer troops from Finland to get to Berlin before the West did. On 3 July, Pravda changed its tune and mid-July the remaining Soviet troops in Finland were in a defensive position.[255] The plan for a Soviet occupation of Finland, drafted perhaps first in 1943, was never used, though the date 28.6.1944 was imposed on it.[256]

As far as US sympathies for Finland had been concerned, there had been throughout a problem of synchronising US peace initiatives with the actuality of the position in Finland. US warnings, given in the spring of 1941, indicating a possible entry of the US into the European war, were made to Finland at a time when the Finnish government and high command were already deep in investigating the possibilities provided by cooperation with Germany. It was assumed in Finland, as in Germany, that Russia would be knocked out before the United Sates came into the war. The value of Lend-Lease both for Britain and the Soviet Union (the latter from October 1941)[257] was ignored.

Thus, American attempts in August and October 1941 to stop the Finnish advance came to naught. The United States was not yet in the war And only very gradually did the Finnish act of "playing both sides" come into being, when Mannerheim (for whatever *prime* reason) pronounced a halt to any advances on Leningrad and, somewhat more reluctantly, to the further cutting of the Murmansk railway: a policy of continuing to fight Russia, while letting

---

prepared to make peace with the Finns and accept the 1939 frontiers: ibid., p.83. Two weeks later, Toivola noted that Admiral Standley, Roosevelt's special envoy to Stalin, was convinced that the Russians wanted peace with the Finns:ibid.,pp.102–103. As to the obstacles placed in the way of Toivola's own communications homewards, ibid., pp.83 & 91 (entries of 27.10 &1.11.1942), in respect of the suppression of his letters to Mauno Pekkala and Ragnar Nummelin, and pp.202–203 in respect of the information he garnered from American newspaper men on Cordell Hull's views on Russia and Finland (entry of 27.10.1943).

[254] FRUS, 1944, vol.III, p.605.

[255] Rentola, op.cit., pp,56–57.

[256] Turtola, op.cit., pp.294–298.

[257] Robert Dallek,*Frankilin Roosevelt and American Foreign Policy 1932–1945*, New York (OUP), 1979, p.299.

the Germans do most of it, and keeping a potentially friendly West on the hop. This policy of "playing both sides" became a key element in Finnish postwar security policy, but in the Continuation War it was staggering and unsuccessful. Vital links in the chain, such as the Finnish Legation in Washington, were largely antagonistic to the dominant American political scenario and were not close enough to the authorities back home to serve as a channel of communication. Urho Toivola felt differently, but his attempts to communicate his views to dissident politicians in Finland such as Mauno Pekkala were frustrated.[258] Within Finland, the constant emphasis on the threat of civil war, should disagreement about the course of the war with the Soviet Union burst forth, served as a form of self-censorship and "the peace party" could not force its way forward, when in early June 1944, Ryti decided against a change of government.

The emphasis on loyalty, however, worked both ways. Talvela, a general sympathetic to the Germans, recalled in his memoirs how Heinrich Himmler, encouraged him to become head of a resistance movement in Finland against the supposedly-impending Russian occupation of the country. At this time, as Talvela indicated, there were over 200,000 Germans in Finland.[259] But he refused that part of the leadership Himmler offered. As noted earlier in this chapter, Talvela had previously wanted a Finnish assault on Leningrad but he did not go against Mannerheim's wishes on this question either.

War breeds a politics of its own, a politics that rests on loyalty in the face of an enemy from abroad. Toivola picked up from an American newspaperman a brief summary of how the Russians regarded Finnish political society: "a formal democracy where in practice an oligarchy rules."[260]

How far this pertains in peacetime is part of the theme of this text, but in wartime there is to that extent truth in the picture bearing in mind the closed nature of the Finnish governments of the war years, a system in which the ministerial body tends to have more in common with each other than with their own party whose exertions brought them into politics and into the government. While all parliamentary governments in Finland are coalition governments (even when resting on a minority in Parliament), the tendency of a government to jell together is greatly accentuated in wartime. Party differences do not disappear, but they do not so easily break governments and re-make governments.

---

[258] Toivola, op.cit.,pp.83–86 & 91. Toivola also wrote to Ryti in the autumn of 1942, but this letter, too, was returned unopened. His letter to Pekkala tells, from US sources, that the Russians were willing to accept the 1939 borders for Finland.

[259] Talvela, op.cit., vol.II, pp.483–484.

[260] Toivola, op.cit., p.214.

In the Continuation War, the classic cases emerge with the Social Democrat politicians Mauno Pekkala and Väinö Tanner. Both were opposed to the crossing of the old frontier, but Pekkala did not resign until 22 May 1942 and Tanner, for whom the Continuation War meant a place in the government,[261] did not resign at all, only leaving the government on the approaching defeat of his country in August 1944.At the start of the war, Tanner shared the view of many Social Democrats that the Finnish armed forces should not move beyond the old frontier, but later swallowed, seemingly as a temporary measure, war operations beyond the old frontier as a means of safeguarding the Finnish position.[262]

It can hardly be denied that the impress of the unity of the Winter War was a factor in impeding open dissent in Finland and joined to this Toivola himself saw the effect of a censorship so that the citizenry had no clear picture of what was happening.[263] Dissent among the citizenry easily ran into disloyalty about the country's relationship with the Powers–pro or contra Germany or Russia. But Toivola's point was the third alternative, the West, which meant pulling away from power. This, too, were it to occur from the citizenry, bore with it the imputation of disloyalty. And while the threat of civil war was exaggerated, strong internal political dissension might occur between Agrarian interests–wishing to fight on for the Isthmus where many of their farms lay–and the urban working-class. In wartime, the party wishing to fight on for a solution had the upperhand. And, in the person of Tyko Reinikka, it spoke in the government. Yet only the elite (the oligarchy) could form the essential peace-loving government.

But the elite was not only a ministerial elite. There was also an elite of the high command of the Finnish armed forces. On 27 June 1944, Edmund Gullion, the American *chargé d'affaires* in Helsinki, wrote to Cordell Hull, the US Secretary of State, that the government had actually decided to break with Germany, but that the "hesitation of headquarters" "prevented developments" and Ribbentrop flew in.[264] The main hesitant was Mannerheim; the main

---

[261] Russian pressure had forced him out of Ryti's first government in March 1940 in which he had been foreign minister and out of Ryti's second government in August 1940 in which he had been minister of supply.

[262] On the twists and turns in Tanner's outlook, see Ilkka Hakalehto, *Väinö Tanner. Taipumaton tie*, Helsinki(Kirjayhtymä) 1973, pp. 231–232. The subtitle of Hakalehto's work (it means "unyielding road") can, in this case, be challenged.

[263] Toivola, op.cit., pp.79–80 & 287–288, where Toivola calls censorship "a double-edged sword."

[264] FRUS, vo.III, 1944, p.605.

dissident was Heinrichs—who, true to form, gave way.[265] Hesitancy meant, in this case, a continuance of war-fighting, fostered by the image of German help (actually important only in the battle of Talin-Ihantala).[266]

But Heinrichs was not the only one who had given way. President Ryti gave way, too. He had never wanted to be president (nor had Ståhlberg, nor had Relander—possibly only for a second time after he had once got used to the job). Ryti succeeded a president, Kyösti Kallio, who was not up to the demands of the office. After a few months of presidency, Ryti led his country into war, but he could not compete with Mannerheim, who took his forces over the East Karelian frontier (Turtola thinks that Ryti "accepted" this).[267] Mannerheim had "military reasons" and did not want the place put into Finland, yet still wanted to fight on in June 1944, though Ryti had sanctioned the formation of a peace-loving government under Mannerheim- who refused- and then Ryti back-tracked, under military pressure, to make his deal with Ribbentrop.[268]

Urho Toivola, still in Washington, sketched out as one possibility, that Finland might even be thinking of fighting on till Germany itself was defeated "whereafter the western Allies, believed by the Finns to be disposed to maintain Finnish independence, might make such views prevail over Russian plans for the absorption of Finland."[269] Fortunately, things were not quite as bad as this.

But they were bad enough. Ryti's action in holding off a change of government and Mannerheim's decision to continue fighting until the Russians abandoned what Mannerheim himself thought was a demand for unconditional surrender lost a lot of lives.[270] Though Finnish peace moves began in mid-July, the essential change did not occur till August, when the Finns finally changed their government and president. Contacts were then made with Madame Kollontai, the Soviet minister in Stockholm, on 25 August. In the Moscow negotiations, the British insisted that only an armistice be made and the peace left till later. Both were onerous. The Americans, not having declared war on Finland, were only watchers.

---

[265] Markku Jokisipilä,*Aseveljiä vai liittolaisia?* Helsinki (SKS, Bibliotheca historica 84), 2004, p.333.
[266] ibid.,363.
[267] Turtola, op.cit., p.266.
[268] ibid., op.cit. pp.282–283
[269] FRUS, 1944, vol.III, p.599–600. Memo of Conversation by Arthur Schoenfeld with Urho Toivola, 13.6.1944.
[270] Kalle Lehmus, op.cit, p.193, maintains that the mortality was much less in this period than in the opening stages of the Continuation War, but that the number of wounded (largely through shrapnel) was heavier in this final stage of the war.

A recent doctoral dissertation in Finland has shown that the extra aid supposedly brought by Ryti's avowal not to come to terms with the Soviet Union without German endorsement was not, in material terms, significant. [271] This being the case, it is all the more tragic, considering the losses in life involved at the front. American knowledge that the Soviet Union was not going to take over Finland could not be transmitted to the Finns once relations broke down as a result. In this sense, the deal—a personal one—covering only Ryti's word was hardly a heroic act, nor was it, in spite of its insignificance in material terms, of minor importance. It prolonged the war and was therefore in human terms a disaster. Mannerheim followed the viewpoint he had undoubtedly impressed on Walden: to fight on so as to keep the army intact.[272] It was to be needed in the next war, the Lapland War, throwing the Germans out, a matter that cost another one thousand Finnish lives, mainly of the young. It might be added that had Mannerheim led a "peace government" in June that job might have been even harder. Thus, it behoves the author of this text to suggest that at what point an alternative form of the Continuation War might have been possible.

A Better Alternative for the Continuation War

This alternative was not as such meant to be an alternative to war, for it was sketched out by the enthusiast for war, Adolf Hitler. In March 1941, Hitler, in continuing to work on his plans for Barbarossa, found for the Finns the following roles: the return of Hanko by force, and then the pinning down of Soviet troops in the north by a mobilization of Finnish divisions.[273] It was presumably the hearing of this that encouraged Väinö Tanner to give his talk at the Elanto meeting of 19 June on the moderate role to be engaged in by the Finns.[274] The key to the policy of "playing both sides" was not primarily keeping the lines open to the West. It was keeping them open to Russia. Mobilization of Finnish troops would certainly have had negative

.[271] Jokisipilä, op.cit., argues that it was the German aid previous to the Ribbentrop agreement that was significant, p.362, with the exception possibly of the battle of Tali-Ihantala, p.363. Jokisipilä seems to believe that Mannerheim was able to pull the country out of the war at the right time *in any case*—a view not shared by the current author. See note 272.

[272] Note that J.K.Paasikivi, before becoming prime minister in autumn 1944, blamed Ryti. for not making peace in spring, which would have saved Porkkala for Finland (not returned till the end of 1955) and saved, too, 20,000 men killed or wounded. The role of Mannerheim was implicit in this critique: J.K.Paasikivi, *Päiväkirja*,I,pp.35–36 (entry of 30.9.1944).

[273] See this chapter, note 197.

[274] See this chapter, page 130. Lehmus, op.cit., p.58 takes seriously the original proposal of Väinö Tanner.

consequences for the Russians in compelling the maintenance of Russian troops on the other side of the Finnish-Russian border (a policy of benefit to the Germans), but mobilization without an attack on the Russians would have been preferable to an invasion of their territory. A modest variant of this policy would have been an advance to the old frontiers—and no further.

Molotov asked the Finns on 25 June whether the country was going to remain neutral[275] and this, in spite of the fact that Soviet planes had already bombed Finland and that German planes and minelayers were using Finnish territory:[276] Finnish policy might have been described as a "defence of neutrality" with a continuing mobilization, but no more serious operations than mine-laying and defence of airspace. The Finns had already told the Germans that they could not defend Petsamo, which was neutralized by the Peace of Moscow. German occupation of this port, which occurred, could have been told to the Russians as a regrettable concession to *force majeure* in an indefensible area. In short, Finnish decision-makers might have tried here, too, to play off both sides.[277]

In the writings of the anti-revisionist school, those, that is, who feel that history in the sense of the Continuation War was right, the question of Petsamo and its outport Liinahamari, is also seen in connection with the existence on the Arctic Highway that ran from Rovaniemi to Petsamo of the nickel mining area at Kolosjoki, an area that could reasonably be included in the Petsamo area. Since nickel is a steel-hardening substance of meteoric origin, it is, especially in war, important, its importance being enhanced by its comparative rarity. It is therefore somewhat surprising that the Soviet Union did not take this area after the Winter War. It was their mistake (one of Paasikivi's last ideas as Finnish minister to Moscow in 1941 was to suggest to his government that the area should be given to Russia).[278] It is possible to argue, however, that at the Peace of Moscow, they thought more of avoiding any further antagonizing of Britain and America (Finnish trade through

---

[275] Heikki Jalanti, *Suomi puristuksessa*, Helsinki, (Tammi), 1966, pp.356–358. Molotov also asked the Hungarians the same question: Nikolaus von Horthy, *Muistelmat*, Helsinki (Otava), 1955, p.267. Jalanti, op.cit., p.358.

[276] Antti Juutalainen, in *Aspects of Security*, pp. 156–157.

[277] Urho Toivola,*Amerikka varoitti*, Helsinki (Suomen kirja), 1946, p.27, endeavoured to make a similar point. Unfortuntaely, his comparison from a presumed Allied standpoint, between a German occupation of France and a German occupation of Petsamo may seem a bit stretched, but the acceptance of the latter by the Finns on grounds of *force majeure* might still have been mediated by the United States to Britain. The French from 1940 onwards were a divided nation in respect of which Allied policy was not an acceptance of German control but an attempt to overthrow it by an Allied *force majeure*, not by withdrawing France from the war. Toivola was no guide here.

[278] Polvinen, *J.K.Paasikivi*, 3, esp. pp.271–273.

Petsamo with these Powers was a lifeline for Finland), while the mining and industrial company at Kolosjoki was a Finnish company (Petsamon Nikkeli Oy) but a subsidiary of the British Mond Nickel Company, which, in its turn, was a subsidiary of the Canadian International Nickel, whose headquarters were in New York.[279] Since the Soviet Union was now rapidly expanding its own nickel production, the conclusion drawn by the Norwegian-Canadian historian Hans-Peter Krosby is that the whole question by 1940 had become one of strategic control of the area, once the Germans occupied Norway.[280] Further Russian pressure on Finland did, indeed, concern the mines, including the Soviet demand for the licence to be given to Russia and for the appointment of a Russian managing director, which was interpreted by the Finnish authorities as a means of quiet control by the transforming of the mine area into a nest of Communism.[281] Nonetheless, under these circumstances, the Russians were prepared to consider even 75% of the production going to Germany.[282]

Germany's was the greater need, for the Germans did not have the potential capacity on their own soil that the Russians had. They anticipated that by 1942 they could satisfy from the mine 70% of their needs and would thereafter be independent of the world nickel market for (mainly under North American control) for the next twenty years.[283] As early as 26 August 1940, Hitler had said to Field Marshal Walther von Brauchitsch that if the Russians conquered Finland, the German army would take the Petsamo region.[284]

It is difficult to say which aspect of the Petsamo region was uppermost in Hitler's mind; the chance of striking along the coast to Murmansk or the mines lower down, below Petsamo, on the Arctic highway. Krosby gives evidence from German sources that both the defence of the Norwegian coastline and the possessing of the nickel mines were of prime importance.[285] But this by no means destroys the argument that Petsamo as a total area if occupied by the Germans in 1941 (and it was discussed among the Finnish top-brass as to whether or not to leave the whole of northern Lapland in German hands)[286] could have been quietly interpreted to the Russians by the Finns as a limited and unavoidable concession to *force majeure*. An additional option for he Finns would have been to warn the Germans and their *Blitzkrieg*

---

[279] Krosby, op.cit., p.17.
[280] ibid., pp.19–23.
[281] ibid., pp.50, 133, & 181 esp.
[282] ibid., p.56.
[283] ibid., pp.98 & 125.
[284] ibid.,p.99.
[285] ibid., pp.176 & 223.
[286] Manninen, *Toteutumaton valtioliitto*, esp.pp.149–152.

from trying to get to Murmansk. Surely the Finns knew the tough nature of that area.

As a matter of fact, the Finns did attempt to play a double game in another aspect of the hostilities, by refusing to cut the Murmansk line after the first few attempts and by holding back from the assault on Leningrad, measures that helped both Russia and the West. What is important is that the Germans, though disappointed on both counts, did not retaliate out of exasperation with these Finnish reservations. The war was for a considerable period one of co-belligerence, but the reservations that this implied should have been made clear in the beginning, especially in regard to the thrust along the Murmansk coast and crossing the old frontier. On 18 August 1941, the US secretary of state, Sumner Welles, told the Finnish minister to Washington, Hjalmar Procopé, that the US was prepared to try and mediate between the Finns and the Russians with respect to territorial concessions from the side of the latter.[287]

It is fair to add that the historian Juhani Paasivirta was of the opinion that this approach was not in itself "an actual peace initiative" from the US side, but a diplomatic contact-point simply. Yet Paasivirta admitted that Welles repeated his démarche in October.[288]

And the instigator of this particular attempt to turn events round was none other than Joseph Stalin, who on 4 August 1941 had addressed a letter to President Roosevelt asking him to pressure the Finns to go back to their neutrality and wriggle free of the German connection. This was known to the British a day later and a further request was put to the British on 3 September. Vague hints were made about territorial concessions (not specifically on the Karelian Isthmus, by and large).[289]

With the Finns' involvements in the war almost running away with themselves at this time, it is difficult to imagine any possibilities of taking up these overtures. And, in the summer and autumn of 1941, the danger was ever-present that the Germans might have turned round and conquered Finland if these feelers had been taken seriously by the Finns.[290] But in them a certain fund of goodwill was evident, in the United States, which was still neutral, and in the Soviet Union, which was now fighting for its life. As to the latter, a change had been noticeable in its relations with Finland even in the late spring just before the Finns went to war. In the struggle between the

[287] Korhonen, op.cit., p.343.
[288] Paasivirta, op.cit., pp.184–185.
[289] Polvinen, op.cit., pp.101 &106.
[290] ibid., pp.109–110.

Germans and the Russians for the control of the Balkans, the Russians were beginning to feel that they were losing out. One spin-off from this was a slackening of Russian propaganda against Finland.[291] Had the Finns been concerned only for the regaining of their lost territory (or some of it) and otherwise, in the spring of 1941, kept their commitments to Germany limited strictly to mobilization, they might have retained a certain leeway and been able to re-occupy something they had previously lost. By the time Stalin was writing to President Roosevelt and the British, in the summer and autumn of 1941, the war was already on. The Russians—once again in their history—had changed too slowly, while the Finns had committed themselves to a non-committal policy with the Germans that the Germans then filled in.

It was too late in the day, considering also that the Finnish military and President Ryti were already keyed up about the prospects to be gained by participating in the *Blitzkrieg* on Russia. These prospects were entrancingly vague but exciting, too. The entry into the Continuation War was not merely to right the wrongs but to see what else turned up so that you could might achieve the permanent security solution. The vision of war in 1941 among the leaders of war in Finland was akin to the vision of revolution of the exasperated militants among the Finnish Left in 1917–1918. By one fell swoop you put not merely unjustified wrongs to right but you change, once and for all, the direction of reality. In 1941 the words "opportunity" spelled for the Finns "Germany." Subjectively speaking, this seemed to open out a spectacular prospect in a hitherto friendless world.

The Finns could share in the megalomaniac vision of reconstructing Russia, once and for all. Objectively seen, however, the Finns might instead have produced specific and limited plans for what they wanted, not for what they could seize with the help of their racist[292] ally, an ally intent on destroying Leningrad and its people. The Finnish propagandists produced a concept of a separate war, which was contradicted by aspects of Finnish military policy. Fortunately, nonetheless, Finland got its separate peace.

The human cost of war balanced on the scales the goal of maintaining an independence in respect of which there were other possible tools available. Such a policy would not have taken in East Karelia, let alone dreamt of the shore of the White Sea. No wonder caution has subsequently been enjoined on the Finns.

Those who, in the earliest weeks of the Continuation War, refused to cross the old frontier—or were compelled reluctantly to do so—were

---

[291] Seppälä, op.cit.,pp.76–77.

[292] On the racism of the Finnish wartime administration in East Karelia, see Maude, *Historical Dictionary of Finland*, 2nd.ed. Lanham (Scarecrow),2007, p.67.

nevertheless expressing a certain *nimis nimium* ("nothing too much") folk wisdom. In the beginning, Tanner, too, believed that the old frontiers ought not to be crossed. Holding the Russian divisions down on the other side of the old frontiers without further action unless challenged was a feasible politics. It fit the talk about the defence of Finnish neutrality, of which there was plenty. Per Andreen has seen that the failure lay right at the top of the military structure, in Mannerheim, whom he sees as having not wanted to use the opportunity accorded by the third article of the Peace of Moscow which ended the Winter War (12 March 1940).[293] By this article, both parties had agreed not to attack the other nor join coalitions against the other. A capable leader would have built upon it and prevented the sort of anti-Soviet hostility from emerging that Upton has recorded in his book *Välirauha*. But could Mannerheim have been that leader? If Mannerheim was, "the father of the FCMA treaty" as Polvinen, Screen, and Timo Soikkanen seem to be arguing, this change occurred after acceptance of defeat, a defeat prolonged by his own obstinacy. The moral of all this is the one drawn by the later Kautsky: not to let the military man (or the would-be military man) usurp the civilian leader—always providing that there is a strong enough civilian leader. Ryti was not.

So, in this weird world, Mannerheim had to play yet another role. Ryti had wanted him in the summer of 1944 to head a peace government. He refused and more young men died. Then Ryti retired from the presidency and Mannerheim took it over. The Soviet Union had wanted this as it guaranteed, apparently, the support of the armed forces for the cessation of hostilities against Russian troops and the turning of Finnish forces against the Germans. And, as Juhani Paasivirta has emphasized, it guaranteed, too, the acceptance by Right-wing Finland of an armistice. Civil war did not ensue.[294]

---

[293] Andreen, op.cit., pp.343–345.

[294] Paasivirta, *Suomi ja Eurooppa 1939–1956*, p.255.

CHAPTER 4
THE INTERSTICES OF POWER

On Independence Day, 6 December 1944, there was no military parade, as there was to be in future years when the parade was switched from a less contentious date than 16 May. There *was* a celebration, but a rather quiet and sad one. The Helsinki town band did, indeed, play the rousing March of the Men of Pori at 9 o'clock on the hill of Tähtitorni overlooking the harbour, but at 10 o'clock there was a service for the fallen at the Hietaniemi cemetery. This was attended by the President, Mannerheim, with his Marshal's baton. With General Martola, the Marshal also attended a service of memorial for the Jewish fallen. In the evening, at the Exhibition Hall, Uuno Takki, the new Social Democrat minister of education, spoke for reconciliation between the different elements in the Finnish community, while the prime minister (the only Conservative in the government), J.K. Paasikivi, spoke, from his knowledge of the writings of Thomas Carlyle, for the recognition of facts.

What facts were they? That Finland was a defeated country and had to adjust itself to the Soviet Union. Though Paasikivi did not underline in his speech that this had an internal dimension requiring change in the relations between political forces in Finland, it was significant that at Malmi, on the outskirts of Helsinki, the radical Left also held a mourning ceremony for those Finnish Reds killed in the counter-revolution of 1918.[1] Only a few months before Reds had been shot while armistice negotiations were expected with the Russians.[2]

The new mood of reconciliation between disparate political elements in Finland contained much that was artificial, forced, limited and downright unfair. But the microcosm had once more to adjust to the macrocosm. The great world around Finland struggled to break out of tri-polarization (the West, Germany and Japan, and the Soviet Union) into—what? A unitary world (the United Nations) or its own version of bi-polarization (the West versus the Soviet Union)? In the meantime, Finland, once more, had to develop another version of bipolarization of its own. It was all too clear that the Soviet connection was now to replace the German connection.

---

[1] *Helsingin Sanomat* and *Suomen Sosialidemokraatti*, 8.12.1944.

[2] Olavi Laiho and several others in September 1944. Maude, *Historical Dictionary of Finland, 1st. ed.*, Lanham & London (Scarecrow), 1995, p.202.

It was a *déjà-vu* phenomenon. The microcosm of Finland had tended to feel the bi-polarity of international politics. Neutrality had been a response to it, hewing out, as it were, a microcosmic haven in a potentially disturbed world. In the time of Leo Mechelin, before the First World War, the Finnish passive resistance movement had envisaged a an enlightened but powerful Western Europe holding Russia back until change occurred there,[3] or, alternatively, among the more compliant of Finnish politicians, the policy arose of trying to make the best of what the Russian connection offered Finland. Towards the end of the First World War, in the period of Ludendorff's eastern policy, Finnish monarchists even planned a German monarchy for Finland. In the Second World War, Germany, by 1941,had come up again, transformed by Nazi-ism in a tri-polarized world, the triune nature of which seemed to afford a possibility of Finnish survival. Now, after defeat in 1944, the necessity was apparent to certain Finnish leaders of having to lean once more on Russia, a *modus vivendi et operandi* pursued in the hope of not being swallowed by that Power

It is an interesting curiosity of history nevertheless that the two leading figures in the making of the latter transition were Conservatives. These two, the President, Mannerheim, and the Prime Minister, Paasikivi, got on less and less well, for they were Conservatives of a different kind. Truly, both were monarchist[4] and both, behind their fascination for royalty, had a certain sense of the *Realpolitik* in international relations and this included, too, a comprehension of Russia's traditional strategic needs. Clearly, by 1944, Finland was never going to have a monarchy. It had a President instead and it was Paasikivi who had persuaded the reluctant Mannerheim to take that post in the summer of 1944. Thereby, it was intended to bring the conservative forces in Finland, including the top echelons of the army, into acceptance of peace with Russia. Unfortunately for Mannerheim, the Soviet leaders wanted social and political changes in Finland, too, and Mannerheim, while he might respect Russia and its historic culture, detested Bolshevism. This detestation of Bolshevism overrode Mannerheim's understanding of the strategic needs of Russia. He saw no accommodation possible with a victorious Bolshevism. "Power" had long since ceased to be negotiable by statesmen. It had fallen into the hands of revolutionary forces, and in his Continuation War policy of

---

[3] Mechelin attempted to hasten change in Russia by drafting a Russian constitution with Prince Peter Dolgorukoff in the early twentieth century. Sigurd Nordenstreng, *Leo Mechelin*, II, Helsingfors (Mercator), 1937, p.192. The attempt was futile.

[4] As a former general in the Tsarist army, Mannerheim lived much less easily with "democracy" than Paasikivi did. See Rintala (below), p.38.

using one revolutionary force to constrain another (Nazi-ism to crush Bolshevism), Mannerheim's expectations had failed. It was the Bolsheviks who won. A crafty exploitation of tripolarization politics in the Second World War had failed Finland. The developing bipolarized world would do nothing for the country either. These deep feelings in Mannerheim brought on a growing tension with Paasikivi, who, as prime minister, was prepared to cope with the politics of negotiation.[5] Deep down, Paasikivi blamed Mannerheim, too, for having kept on with the war, and, thus, for the 20,000 dead and wounded that the extension of the war into summer 1944 brought with it.[6]

One service Mannerheim did perform. The president was commander-in-chief in peacetime, who delegated this function to a soldier in wartime. Since Mannerheim was a soldier, he could serve to be commander-in-chief as president and in this role, until 1 January 1945, led the Finnish army, by a prestige that compelled obedience, to fulfil article 2 of the armistice agreement, namely the expulsion and internment of the German forces from Finland, where necessary with Soviet help.[7]

Paasikivi had helped to catapult Mannerheim into presidential office, but there was no reciprocity from the latter for Paasikivi in his struggles with the parties. For Mannerheim, Paasikivi was not an automatic choice for the prime ministerial post. He was not even an automatic choice for any ministerial post. The first two governments appointed by President Mannerheim were headed by Conservatives, the government of Antti Hackzell before the armistice and the government of Urho Jonas Castren after the armistice were headed by men who had no conviction in political change. In talking to Castren, Paasikivi expressed his amazement at the lack of President Mannerheim's political acumen, pointing out that Mannerheim had even suggested Tanner or Kivimäki (both later to be tried for war guilt) as possible prime ministers, while ignoring the merits of Paasikivi himself.[8] The historian Tuomo Polvinen has pointed out that it took time for Mannerheim to come round to the idea of putting Paasikivi in this position. An invitation to supper helped on 2 November, in the presence, too, of Mannerheim's kindly yes-man, General Rudolf Walden; on 11 November Mannerheim asked him to form a

---

[5] Marvin Rintala in *Four Finns*, Berkeley and Los Angeles (Univ. of California Press), 1969, brings out well the difference between Mannerheim and Paasikivi by describing the former as an "aristocrat in politics" and the latter as "a politician in politics": chapters 2 & 5 respectively.

[6] J.K.Paasikivi, *Päiväkirjat 1944–1956*, I, Porvoo-Helsinki (Werner Söderström),1985, pp.29–30 & 35–36. (entries of 8.9.1944 & 30.9.1944).In the latter statement, he maintained that the peace terms of April–My 1944 should have been accepted and Porkkala would not have been lost.

[7] The Russian forces took part in this task only briefly and only in northern Finland.

[8] Paasikivi, *Päiväkirjat*,I, p.36 (entry of 2.10.1944).

government and on 17 November Paasikivi formed his government, almost two months after the armistice.[9] He had refused to be a minister in anyone else's government. Paasikivi's last and greatest decade of power had now commenced.

In justifying this hero of his, the Finnish-American historian Marvin Rintala, pondering on the role of the powerful individual in history, saw such persons as "representatives of the deeper needs and tendencies of human nature."[10] In this way, they linked with the rest of their community. The process of linkage was one of extreme difficulty for Paasikivi—it had been easier in the Second World War for Mannerheim, leading a nation that felt itself, in one way or another, compelled into war—even by fate—a war in which Mannerheim was the destined leader rather than the *causa proxima.* The compulsions of the dawning peace were less straightforward. But Paasikivi, if anyone, was the puppeteer to string along the relation of the forces. And so much so, that Walden declared him to be "the only man who could now form a government."[11]

This was an exaggeration. In the SDP, people like K.A. Fagerholm, a wartime minister with Leftish inclinations and Eero Wuori, the trade union leader, who had supported the war, but was equally in favour of political change,[12] were apparently ready and waiting. Both had served as ministers in the short-lived Castren government and thus, in spite of their Left leanings, could not have been all that objectionable to the Right. And there were also the inevitable Agrarians, a party hungry for power and able to straddle the divide between Left and Right. In this deeply patriotic party of property were men like Kaarlo Hillilä, the governor of Lapland and a minister in the transitional governments of Mannerheim in the summer and autumn. He like Paasikivi was prepared to take the Communists into the government, at least one of them. (!) So Hillilä may be seen as another potential non-Socialist leader of a government of national unity. His thinking was so close to that of Paasikivi that the latter praised him in his diary, a rare if momentarily concealed commendation.[13] Then, from that same party, was the clever Dr. Urho Kekkonen, though he was distrusted by its more conservative members,

[9] Tuomo Polvinen, *J.K. Paasikivi. Valtiomiehen elämäntyö 4*, Helsinki (WSOY), 1999, pp.18–25.
[10] Rintala, op.cit., p.7.
[11] Paasikivi, *Päiväkirjat 1944–1956*, I, p.48 (entry of 12.11.1944).
[12] By December 1945, Zhdanov was telling Stalin and Molotov that had Wuori been prime minister here would have been less trouble with the war-guilt trials: Polvinen, *Paasikivi*, 4, p.230.
[13] ibid., p.48.

and intensely disliked by the National Coalition Party. His merit lay in the other direction: he would not serve *without* the Communists.[14]

The problem of the Right in general was not simply that the latter were still trying to lead the country. They certainly *were* still trying, but during the Second World War, through patriotic associations and the sheer fervour of war, the official Right, embodied in the National Coalition Party, had seen that some Rightist views were not the prerogative of their own party. Since Finland had been defeated in the war, the ethos in the name of which Finland had fought, had to be maintained instead in the political system, and even, if possible, in the person of a prime minister who had come to oppose the war.[15] Politics had become trickier for the Right.

On 10 November Paasikivi was visited by a parliamentary delegation, consisting of Väinö Hakkila of the SDP, Anssi Kukkonen of the Agrarian Union, and Toivo Horelli of the National Coalition Party. All three were on the Right of their respective parties, even if Hakkila, a former speaker and deputy-speaker of Parliament, had once been mauled by fanatics of the Lapua movement. Kukkonen, a clergyman by training, had been a minister of education: he was shortly to stand trial for his part in promoting the Continuation War. Horelli had been Minister of the Interior for two years during that war and had been responsible for sending eight Jews (one of whom had fought for Finland in the Winter War) into Nazi hands. These men now approached Paasikvi as representatives of their parliamentary parties and asked him to form a government, whereas four days previously the Conservative (National Coalition Party) prime minister Urho Castren had only wanted Paasikivi in his own government as another minister.[16] This, too, had been Mannerheim's line when inviting Paasikivi to supper on 2 November. But Mannerheim had had to give way. Paasikivi was adamant. He would form and lead a government, but not serve under anyone else.[17]

---

[14] ibid., p.49. He was also ruthless, an aspect of the man Paasikivi was to commit to his diary, when he later felt that a stronger prime minister than himself might be needed. ibid., p.161 (entry of 3.7.1945). Before Paasikivi formed his first government, the parliamentary groups had also discussed the possibility of a government led by Kekkonen–or Hillilä or Wuori: Juhani Suomi, *Myrrysmies*, Helsinki (Otava), 1986, p.531. On the change in Kekkonen's attitude to the Communists, see Suomi, op.cit., pp.518 et seq.

[15] The idea that Paasikivi had always been in favour of close relations with Russia reflects a misunderstanding of his *Realpolitik*. In 1941–1942 (as noted in chap. 3 of this text),he had spoken in support of the connection with Germany. The point was, when necessary, to acknowledge the need to come to terms with some "greater Power."

[16] Paasikivi, *Päiväkirjat*, I, p.46 (entry of 6.11.1944).

[17] Juhani Suomi, op.cit., p.530, has maintained that on 28.10.1944 Kekkonen met Yeliseyev, (Yelisei Sinitsin) of the Control Commission and then Kekkonen through the mediation of Svento and Pekkala, had informed Paasikivi that the Russians did not want him to join

Paasikivi's position was complicated. He had the support of Rightist feeling among many parliamentary groups, including the National Coalition Party. But the previous Conservative prime minister and the conservative-minded president were stalling when it came to giving him power. General Walden, who does not seem to have openly supported him even as late as 2 November at the presidential supper-table, had the clue. He told Paasikivi not to reveal to President Mannerheim that he, Paasikivi, had ever talked directly to Communists, but that he had heard from others that the Communists were willing to enter a government.[18] Here was the rub: the suspicion among a section of leading Right-wing opinion that Paasikivi might be too soft towards domestic Communism, which would then take the country over, backed by the Russians.

At that moment, at any rate, this was, however, a misconception of the underlying scenario: the Russians were far more likely to take the country over if the Finns failed to create a political system that in some way adapted to them. For as the weeks passed, the Soviet-dominated Control Commission (there was a silent British member, who was told by his superiors in London to do what the Russians wanted) was becoming increasingly restive at the delays in fulfilling the demands of the armistice agreement. Yet already at the end of October the Left-wing Social Democrat trade union leader Eero Wuori was speaking to the Castren government and to Mannerheim himself of the need for a change of government, being prepared with Paasikivi's agreement to suggest the latter's name for the prime ministerial post.

As noted above, Parliament was also stirring. But it was an old Parliament once elected in 1939 when the Communist Party had been outlawed and thus had no parliamentary members. Using the latter fact, President Mannerheim felt that Communists could not therefore enter the government before a new election was held.[19] This was a delaying tactic and a highly dangerous one as Paasikivi sought to build up as quickly as possible a caretaker government *before* the general election to keep both domestic Communists and the Control Commission happy about the fact that changes were on the way.

The Communists and their sympathisers were now forming an umbrella organization, the Finnish People's Democratic League (henceforward SKDL), in respect of which Mannerheim was all too aware. In discussing with Paasikivi the nature of the future government, Mannerheim expressed a particular

---

Castren's government. Paasikivi, in rejecting Castren's offer of a post in his government, made his decision on the 28.10, too: Paasikivi, *Päiväkirjat* I, p.42. But it remains so far unclear as to the precise time, even day, when Paasikivi learnt of Yeliseyev's opinion.

[18] ibid., p.48 (entry of 12.11.1944).

[19] ibid.,p.43.(entry of 30.10.1944) pp.43–44 (entry of 2.11.1944).

objection to Johan Helo, a Social Democrat who was moving to SKDL membership. But Paasikivi ignored this, claiming that Helo had to be taken into the government "to keep the Communists under control."[20] Nor did Paasikivi stop there. He also brought into his government two other formally educated members of the Left-wing of the Social Democratic Party, both of whom were moving towards the SKDL, Mauno Pekkala, and the journalist Reinhold Svento. These were matched, as it were, by a real Communist from the trade union movement, namely Yrjö Leino. His was the most controversial appointment. Mannerheim objected, but then dispiritedly gave way—on the very day the composition of the government was announced.[21]

Paasikivi had now produced a very complex version of his own for handling the relations of the forces. He had actually tried the model before in his work for reconstructing—a few weeks earlier—the Finnish-Soviet Friendship Society. Meeting Mauri Ryömä, a former Social Democrat who had spent four years as a political prisoner in Finland and become a member of the Finnish Communist Party and Aimo Rikka, the secretary of the Finnish-Soviet Peace and Friendship Society in the period between the ending of the Winter War and the start of the Continuation War, Paasikivi found that both were in favour of a substantially different sort of society henceforward. They had discussed the refounding of a Finnish-Soviet Friendship Society with the Soviet minister Pavel Dmitrievich Orlov (also a member of the Control Commission) and he had recommended that the Society be re-established "on a wider basis" than had previously been the case. Paasikivi was delighted to hear this acknowledgment of Finnish diversity from the Soviet and domestic-Communist side[22] and thereupon, hearing this, Walden began to think of recruiting a few Finnish businessmen for membership of its board.[23] As it turned out, Paasikivi himself was to become the honorary chairman, sitting in front of the audience in a big chair. And so, unknown to the worried president, Paasikivi had talked with the Communists. But a few days before this, he had also talked to Reinhold Svento, a member of the SKDL but not of the Finnish Communist Party, who had sounded out Yeliseyev, a member of the Control Commission, on the need for such a society, and the agreeable Yeliseyev had also spoken of a *widely-based* Friendship Society.[24]

But how did the model fit Finnish constitutionalism? The basis of the answer was to be found in the replacement of Mannerheim as president by

---

[20] ibid.,pp.46–47.(entry of 10.11.1944). &

[21] ibid., pp.47 &51, & 53–56 (entries of 11.11.1944, 15.11.19444, & 16–17.11.1944)

[22] ibid., pp.38–39. (entry of 6.10.1944).

[23] ibid., p.40 (entry of 14.10.1944)

[24] Paasikivi, *Päiväkirjat* I., p.37 (entry of 3.10.1944).

Paasikivi. In practice, this occurred quite soon since Mannerheim was falling more and more into physical as well as into a kind of mental illness. Because of Mannerheim's treatment and convalescence abroad, Paasikivi, as premier, took on at the same time the presidential duties. He was able to do this as Mannerheim's military role ceased on 1 January 1945 when the German troops in Finland were left only with the redoubt of Kilpisjärvi in the far north-west of Finland. Though it was not until 11 March 1946 that Paasikivi became officially elected president, he was in the saddle long before that.

Paasikivi was elected by Parliament and not after an election campaign among the people, as the Constitution would normally have decreed through a popular election of an electoral college of 300 members who would then vote for a president. Out of a parliament of 200 members, he received 159 votes and another veteran, ex-President Ståhlberg, received 14. The rest of the M.P.s were absent or did not vote.

At first glance, this form of election of president by parliament might seem to redound to the power of the parliamentary organ. In fact, it spoke for the power of the presidential organ and for the person who held it; the best possible president if not the only possible president. The wars with Russia as well as the subsequent attempt at friendship with Russia fostered executive decision-making, but in the case of the Paasikivi use of presidential powers, the executive itself had become ever more complex in form, a fact which in turn complicated the operations of the executive. Finland, since its inception as an independent state, had had a double executive of president and prime minister. In the early period of Paasikivi's last decade of power, the double executive had often been fused when, as a prime minister exercising presidential duties owing to the illness of President Mannerheim, Paasikivi had to do the latter's work. But all the time in the background there lurked still a third executive, and one well known in Finnish history. This was the foreign executive, the Russians in the Control Commission and ultimately the Russians in Moscow. And Paasikivi was, indeed, the best possible Finn to deal with this phenomenon since he had belonged to the Old Finn Party in pre-First World War days, a party that had tried to temper the difficulties between Finland and the Russian Empire. He spoke Russian. And more than that: he had a model in his mind, which he did not reveal to the Finnish people except posthumously through his diary. The model was based on the Russo-Finnish period of 1809–1899 when the old Grand Duchy had lived in comparative tranquillity with the Russian Empire.[25]

In him the past lived in the present: Paasikivi's thinking was a thinking in terms of a return of history that justified *his* own role. It was as if he turned a

---

[25] ibid., p.69 (entry of 11.12.1944).

retrospective view on its head, Finland having to go through again a Grand Duchy period because this was the only way to live alongside "an autocratic Russia."[26] Most of the Right faced this prospect reluctantly. For the National Coalition Party, the view held of Russia was like that of Mannerheim's (without his old nostalgia for the Tsarist days). Russia was Bolshevik, Communist, and could not be trusted to leave Finland in peace. What lay in Paasikivi's genius, however, was the chance of using *domestic* Communism against the possible intrusions of *Great Power* Communism.[27]

It was one of the paradoxes of Finnish history that in 1944 the victory of autocratic Russia against Finland pressured the Finnish parliamentary system to open its doors to the suppressed one-quarter or one-fifth of the population whose political views had not been represented in the so-called representative organ. Paasikivi's (and Kekkonen's) political sagesse resided in the conviction (or at least hope) that parliamentary representation would exert its cachet over the extremes of Communist doctrine. But, both as prime minister and later as president, Paasikivi would give the process a helping hand, endeavouring to manipulate wherever possible the highly complex relation of forces.

What Paasikivi had to do was to try to exert control *and* engender confidence. His power was to be based on consultation and not *Diktat*. Within his own country, he behaved—in so far as he succeeded in controlling his temper[28]—like the diplomat he had been in Sweden and Russia.[29]

In approaching problems, he did not always necessarily work by going straight to the potentially sensitive party. Thus, as noted above, he talked to Svento on Yeliseyev's opinions about a Friendship Society. But when it came to the formation of a government, he also expected Svento to be able "to handle the Left." General Walden told Paasikivi he had another candidate for this task; somewhat curiously it was Eero Wuori head of the great trade union organization, the SAK.[30] But then Wuori had, during the war, worked with the industrialists' organization to keep peace on the labour market. Svento and Wuori were "Left," but not quite Communist Left. They were, among other things, journalists with a lot of erudition behind them. And both were able to serve as diplomats, Svento in Berne and Wuori in London. By

---

[26] ibid., p.69 (entry of 11.12.1944).

[27] ibid., p.52 (entry of 15.11.1944).

[28] Note the last sentence in Rintala's portrait of him, op.cit., p.120: "a hot-tempered, foul-mouthed old banker, who taught the Finns—and others—what it means to have Finnish politics as a vocation."

[29] He had been Finnish minister in Stockholm from 1936–1939 and minister in Moscow from 1940–1941.

[30] Paasikivi, *Päiväkirjat*, I, p.38(entry of 6.10.1944 note that this was over a month before his becoming prime minister).

exploiting these gradations in personalities, Paasikivi, on becoming prime minister on 17 November 1944, was able to rule by networking, particularly as his first ministry did not have to follow party strengths since they were not currently known—the last election had been in 1939 when, *inter alia,* the illegal Communist Party had been unable to take part in it. In his first ministry, Paasikivi formed a balance by personal choice, using professional ministers from the bourgeois side, such as the *vieux routier* Carl Enckell as foreign minister and General Walden as defence minister (a choice pleasing to Mannerheim). In fact, Paasikivi stood up for Walden against the accusation by Helo, the Left-wing minister of finance, that Walden was a war-monger. To this, the ever-articulate Paasikivi replied that Walden had successfully opposed during the Continuation War the making of a treaty with Germany. Helo was thus pacified.[31] And, as noted previously,[32] Helo could now go on, *as an educated man,* to serve the role marked out for him by Paasikivi of "keeping the Communists under control." Here was the core of Paasikivi's own politics of power. It lay in the utilization of shades of difference: in education, and, partly in consequence, in the difference between the non-Communist minority in the SKDL (radical Socialists) and the grass-roots of the Communist majority.[33] Helo was set to play a double role, accepting in Paasikivi's pre-election government Mannerheim's crony, Rudolf Walden, while being able to caution the Left-wing extremism he was himself allied to. If this was a policy of *divide et impera,* it was a very clever version of it, involving accommodations in both directions, Left and Right, and through the manipulation of the same person. The potential loss, however, was Leftwards.

Once the election at last came on, in March 1945, Paasikivi's task did not appear, at first, to be becoming any easier. For what he feared, most of all, was not a pro-Soviet electoral outcome, but an anti-Soviet election.[34] He need not have worried. On the eve of Paasikivi's first (caretaker) government, Helo had told him that when the election was held "the Communists" would gain at least 35 seats.[35] In fact, the SKDL itself got 49, almost a quarter of the parliamentary seats. Zhdanov, the head of the Control Commission (and thus the representative of the third, the foreign executive) was satisfied,[36] once the results were counted (it took several weeks).

---

[31] ibid., p.50(entry of 12.11.1944).

[32] note 20 of this chapter.

[33] For most non-Socialists in Finland, the SKDL *were* Communists. Note that so sophisticated an observer as Krister Wahlbäck has occasionally fallen into this trap in *Mannerheimista Kekkoseen,* Porvoo- Helsinki (Werner Söderström),1968, pp.278–279.

[34] Paasikivi, *Päiväkirjat,* I, p.113 (entry of 1.3.1945).

[35] ibid., p.49 (entry of 12.11.1944).

[36] ibid., p.125.(entry of 20.3.1945)

In the same election, however, the Social Democratic Party won even more seats than the SKDL, only one more to a total of 50. But this meant that the Left in Parliament now had almost half the parliamentary seats. Since the two Left parties had nonetheless been competing (the SDP not wanting to go into an electoral alliance with the SKDL), Paasikivi's role in moulding a government was not a straightforward task. Throughout the country, the Left was numerically strong. But it was divided. Indeed, it might be said that a part of the Left was actually Right! Väinö Tanner, the SDP leader, whom the Russians wanted tried for war guilt, still rode the roost and among the younger generation the influence of the wartime "Brothers-in-Arms" association (a patriotic association of servicemen stretching across the parties) was clearly in evidence as an anti-Communist force.

On the one hand, Paasikivi, a deep—dyed Conservative, might have been expected to be overjoyed at this division of the Left. But his task was also to produce a government formation that would not upset the third executive, the Russians. He had further to plough on with the duty of trying to fulfil the more arduous of the demands laid down in the Armistice Agreement. The Left would support him in this, but the Right and the SDP Right would wish to frustrate his efforts in that direction. With great patience therefore, Paasikivi, still prime minister but doing much of the presidential work in Mannerheim's absence or moods of despair, built up a government by a variety of means. The end -product was a national government that did not necessarily reflect the strength of the political forces whether inside or outside Parliament. Finland, in the *persona* of Paasikivi, was steadily moving towards a presidentially-dominated state as Paasikivi himself came nearer to gaining the presidency, the official mediating point of the Finnish state with the third executive. On the way to this goal, while still prime minister, he received one of the greatest accolades of his life from a Finnish politician. "Whatever the merits Mannerheim might have had in getting Finland out of the war," said this politician, "if he resigns the presidency we shall have no regrets: it is the present prime minister we trust." The politician who made this statement was Yrjö Leino, then in the key position of minister of the interior. He was a Communist. And he added that his political group did not seek to have one of themselves in the presidential office.[37] Paasikivi's gossipy secretary saw that a certain bond had grown up between the SKDL (including the Communists) and Prime Minister Paasikivi.[38] But this was far more than the exercise of a personal chemistry. Leino (and Helo) were hand-picked into his caretaker

---

[37] ibid., p. 174 (entry of 27.7.1945).

[38] Toivo Heikkilä, *Paasikivi perämisessä*, Helsinki (Otava), 1965, p.67.

government to keep the Communists off the street in noisy meetings in the square.[39]

In the meantime, Paasikivi formed a government. It could not reflect the strength of the parties in any proportional sense. Yet Paasikivi committed himself to a most ambitious endeavour: "I will have to have in some way unanimous support."[40] Having won the confidence of the Communists,[41] Paasikivi continued his policy of balancing them by awarding ministerial positions to the more educated members of the SKDL: Communist trade union ministers such as Yrjö Murto and (later) Matti Janhunen were offset in Paasikivi's scheme of things by—once more—Reinhold Svento, Johan Helo, and Mauno Pekkala, as well as by Pekkala's brother, Eino, all of whom had now more or less moved from the traditional SDP. Whatever their social origin, these were educated men. Even President Mannerheim found he could swallow Svento on hearing, additionally, that he was married to the sister of Antti Hackzell, a former Conservative prime minister.[42] Education and class affiliations had not lost their significance in these postwar political shifts.

A certain blurring of identity was now also occurring among the Left parties, as Eino Pekkala had also left the Communist Party on his way to joining the SKDL![43] This was hardly much of a problem for Paasikivi, rather the reverse. But the Tannerite heart of the SDP, who were inclined to pre-empt the right to leadership of what was, after all, the largest party, constituted a problem for Paasikivi's conciliatory politics, since conciliation in internal politics was a pre-condition for conciliation with the Soviet Union. The Tannerite Social Democrats, on the contrary, felt that the requirements of conciliating the Soviet Union were preventing the development of internal political conciliation. Paasikivi solved this problem by taking into his government members of the internal opposition in the SDP such as the trade union leader Eero Wuori and the friendly go-between Onni Hiltunen, who sought to straddle the gap between internal opposition and those of a more traditional persuasion.

Outside the intricate politics of the Left, the pliable centre, principally, the Agrarian Union, including the aggressive Dr. Kekkonen, were always willing to serve. But a centrist politician of Progressive persuasion, Sakari Tuomioja, also

---

[39] Paasikivi, *Päiväkirjat* I, p. 85.(entry of 4.1.1945, showing that the Communiste minister of the interior used his authority to keep the Communists away from street demonstrations).

[40] ibid., p.112 (entry of 1.3.1945).

[41] On Paasikivi's confidence in the Communists and SKDL, see ibid., pp. 134 & 136 (entries of 12.4.1945 & 13.4.1945)in which Paaskivi finds that the Communists were following parliamentary and legal ways)

[42] ibid., p.38 (entry of 6.10.1944)

[43] Hannu Soikkanen, *Kohti kansanvaltaa*, 3, Helsinki (SDP-puoluetoimikunta), 1991, p.61.

joined the government for a period, though not with the backing of everyone in this fractious little political group.[44] He was replaced by a Swedish People's Party member, Ralf Törngren. Paasikivi even hoped to get into his government a member of the National Coalition Party in the light of his own (earlier expressed) conviction that the party should know what was going on.[45] A leading female politician of that party, Kyllikki Pohjala, could not be persuaded to come in, however.[46] Instead, Paasikivi, as far as a Rightist presence was concerned, worked with the old stand-by arrangement of Finnish politics, ministers who were professedly non-political experts, the old foreign minister Carl Enckell and the previous minister of foreign trade Åke Gartz. Both were gentlemen of the old school. Speaking Swedish, they looked westwards, but speaking Russian, they could look eastwards, too.

What Paasikivi had now to do was to lead this motley collection of personalities and parties into an acceptance of the more stringent demands of the Armistice Treaty with Russia. Paasikivi's solution was a political one, an exercise of executive power. He was helped in this by the fact that increasingly as prime minister from November 1944 to March 1946, he acted, too, as president, as Mannerheim commanded the operations of the Lapland War till the end of 1944 and thereafter sank into what can only be called despair. Meanwhile, Paasikivi had, most often a double executive position. Since his main concern was dealing with a third executive, the foreign executive of the Soviet Union and the Control Commission, he could spread the presidential function of running the country's foreign policy over quite a vast panorama.

As has been made aware, his exercise of power included a large dose of duplicity. To answer the question put in a later work written by one of Finland's leading constitutionalist lawyers, Paasikivi was not a president who behaved *neutrally*,[47] though he was prepared to make use of the concept of neutrality in foreign policy to gain his ends. His principal end was to prevent the new friendship with the Soviet Union from leading to internal Communism. In picking his governments, he selected with care, far more

---

[44] Polvinen, *Paasikivi,4*, p.25.

[45] Paasikivi,*Päiväkirjat*, I, p.52 (entry of 15.11.1944—before forming his caretaker government).

[46] ibid., pp. 134,136,154, & 204. Paasikivi, who now considered himself non-party, had, however, to content himself by going to the National Coalition Party's parliamentary group to explain his position at their request: ibid, p.154 (entry of 7.6.1945). Pohjola was interested in the working conditions of nurses and had graduated from Columbia University with a degree in health care. With Mauri Pekkala, then a Social Democrat, she had visited the Delaware Tercentenary Celebrations in 1938: in 1946 Pekkala, then Prime Minister and a member of the SKDL, asked her to try to secure a loan from the United States:Kyllikki Pohjala, *Kuljin tietäni*, Helsinki (WSOY), 1966, pp.62,70, &150.

[47] Antero Jyränki, *Presidentti*, Porvoo-Helsinki (Werner Söderström), 1981, p.2.

sophisticatedly than Mannerheim would have done if left to himself. And Ståhlberg's assumption that the ministerial occupants should require the confidence of Parliament,[48] was, to say the least, somewhat stretched.

The Caching of Arms

By article 2 of the Armistice Treaty, the Finnish army was to enter upon a third war. It was to expel the former German *Waffenbrüder* from Finnish territory. After resisting in a bloody battle a German attempt to capture the Finnish island of Suursaari in the Gulf of Finland, the German armed forces conducted a measured retreat through Finland to northern Norway. With the initial collusion of the Finnish army, the *Wehrmacht* retreated gradually without further hindrance until the Soviet command demanded hostilities and even sent troops of its own into northern Finland. The Finns then tackled the Germans courageously and 1 January 1945 only a pocket of German resistance remained in Enontekiö in north-western Lapland.

In spite of this war, a large part of the Finnish army was demobilized in the autumn of 1944. In this connection, a section of the Finnish military began to prepare for the eventuality of still another war. The war they envisaged was the one that they believed was going to occur between the West and the Soviet Union. Either as a preliminary to this or in conjunction with it, the Soviet Union would, these Finnish officers felt, try to occupy Finland. Instigated by the operational section of the Finnish high command with at least the knowledge of General A.F. Airo,[49] arms began to be buried in the course of the demobilization of the bulk of the army. Arms were hidden in the archipelago or in the forest areas with the help of the foresters, sometimes they were stored in official depositaries but uncounted in the book-keeping, while in one place petrol for the military was stored in the Shell depot, while in northern Savo weapons from demobilized troops to equip two battalions were left under the control of the local civil guard.[50] As a matter of fact, what greatly helped in this clandestine activity was the existence still of the network of the civil guards associations in the localities supported by members of the wartime Brothers-in-Arms movement. Not merely therefore was this activity clearly anti-Soviet but it was being conducted by members of associations that were prohibited by the Armistice Treaty. It did not take long for Andrei Zhdanov, the head of the Control Commission, to get wind of a certain revanchism in

[48] ibid., p.119.
[49] Screen, op.cit., pp.355–356.
[50] Matti Lukkari, *Asekätkentä*, Helsinki (Otava), 1984, pp.129, 121, 122, & 108–109. Lukkari engaged in this activity.

some Finnish circles and he was already complaining to Kekkonen, then minister of justice, about this in the autumn of 1944.[51]

The revelation of actual arms caching led to the resignation of General Eric Heinrichs, who had succeeded Mannerheim as head of the military establishment in 1945, and ultimately to imprisonment sentences on 1,488 persons, Lt. Col. U.S. Haahti receiving six years penal servitude and Col. Valo Nihtilä five years penal servitude.[52] Others, including General A.F.Airo, were freed on grounds of time served during their arrest period. Airo had been detained for somewhat under three years.

Arms caching had its bizarre features. Because of his knowledge of it, General Heinrichs had resigned: but because of his military expertise he was consulted at length before the security treaty between Finland and the Soviet Union was made in 1948. Even stranger was the position of Mannerheim. General Airo told him of these plans at the end of September 1944, when Mannerheim was already president. Mannerheim only urged caution.[53] A few weeks later, however, in January 1945, Mannerheim was discussing with Zhdanov the possibility of a security treaty between Finland and Russia![54]

As time went on into the spring of 1945, Paasikivi learnt more and more about Finnish arms caches sometimes from what Zhdanov's deputy, General Grigori Mihailovitch Savonenkov, had told other Finnish ministers.[55] As cracks in the Western-Soviet alliance began to show, Paasikivi eschewed all desperate choices and stuck to his line that Finland's only choice was to develop as far as possible relations of trust with the Soviet Union.[56] He had confidence in Zhdanov, who, whatever his private thoughts might have been,[57] expressed nonetheless to Paasikivi that, in Soviet eyes, Finland should remain "independent and economically successful."[58] As to economics, Finland had become increasingly important to the Soviet Union, through its war reparations and ordinary trade, as a workshop supplying war-devastated Western Russia. On the other hand, the intelligence service of the still

[51] Paasikivi, *Päiväkirjat*, I, pp. 62 (entry of 27.11.1944).

[52] Polvinen, *J.K.Paasikivi*, 4, pp.165–166. Matti Lukkari, op.cit., pp.270–272.

[53] Screen, op.cit., pp.355–356.

[54] ibid., p.351.

[55] Paasikivi, *Päiväkirjat*, I, p.159–160, when Gartz told him about Savonenkov's complaints (entry of 26.6.1945).

[56] This was the advice he had given Prime Minister Urho Castren in the beginning of October 1944:"for us only Russia is meaningful." ibid., p.36 (entry of 2.10. 1944).

[57] According to Milovan Djilas,*Conversations with Stalin*, London (Penguin Books), 1962, p.120, in early 1948 (at the time of the negotiations for the Finnish-Soviet security treaty) Zhdanov expressed his regret to Molotov that Finland had not been occupied; Molotov replied that the country was not important enough: it was "peanuts." But he had tried earlier; see chapter 3!

[58] Paasikivi, *Päiväkirjat*, I, p.148 (entry of 12.5.1945)

unreformed political police had already picked up in the autumn of 1944 that Russia was not going to take over Finland. Partly, this may have been not unconnected with the low opinion held by the Soviet authorities of the Finnish Communist Party, who were often dismissed as "windbags."[59]

The issue of arms-caching tells much about the relation between the civil and military arm in Finland. The latter did not necessarily trust the former and embodied, once more, a power in reserve in case the civil arm proved itself disastrously wrong in its estimation of Russian policy. Many of the officers engaged in the concealing of arms were retained in the military forces, and one of them, Major Yrjö Keinonen, ultimately became head of the Finnish armed forces. Like Keinonen, these officers were to serve loyally under the aegis of the 1948 Russo-Finnish security treaty. Others have felt that these two factors, the caching of arms and the 1948 treaty, actually dovetailed, the conspiracy contributing to warning the Russians against an attempt to take the country over.[60] The treaty recognized a *separate* Finnish army. But beneath the surface anti-Soviet feeling survived in that army. Capt. Magnus Haaksalo, when adjutant to General Aarne Sihvo, the head of the Finnish armed forces, declared to the American chargé d'affaires, A. Randolph, that should war break out in Europe the Finnish army would first fight alongside the Russians but would switch sides if the West invaded the Soviet Union by way of Murmansk.[61] *Such officers were waiting upon another war.*

The idea was undoubtedly fostered by the rapid emergence in the West of the Cold War. But, as an exercise in wish-fulfilment, it even went deeper than that, as many Finns who had supported the Continuation War regretted the gulf between Germany and the West, and hoped that the former Power would have knocked the Soviet Union out of the picture after which reconciliation between Germany and the West could occur. In 1941 and early 1942 Paasikivi himself may have been haunted by this vision. In early June, he recorded in his diary that Sir Stafford Cripps had told the Swedish ambassador in Moscow (Vilhelm Assarsson) that if Germany invaded Russia, Britain might make peace with Germany.[62] Straws in the wind?[63]

In any case, almost three years after the signing of the Finnish-Soviet Security Treaty ion April 1948, Paasikivi, in a discussion with the minister of

---

[59] Osmo Jussila, *Suomen tie 1944–1948*, Porvoo-Helsinki (WSOY), 1990, p.55.

[60] Lukkari, op.cit., pp.298–301.

[61] Quoted in Hannu Rautkallio, *Suomen suunta 1945–1948*, Helsinki (Weilin & Göös),1979, pp.176 & 291. The date given is 6.2.1948, the period in which the Russian-Finnish security treaty was being negotiated.

[62] J.K.Paasikivi, Dagböcker 1941–1944, (translation by Frank Jernström), Borgå (Söderström Förlag),1991, p.p.66 (entry of 3.6.1941).

[63] What did this say about Cripps' mission to the Soviet Union?

the interior, the Agrarian Kekkonen, came to a resolution of what the current author has called "the Finnish dilemma."[64] The treaty enjoined Finnish repulsion of an attack "from Germany or its allies" through Finland against the Soviet Union. Paasikivi now argued that if in a future war, the West won, its leaders would understand the treaty obligations which Finland had committed itself to perform for the Soviet Union. If the Soviet Union won, however, the Finnish position would be quite in order, for having faithfully followed the same obligations.[65] As will be noted later, Paasikivi's interpretation was somewhat simplified.

Leaving aside for the moment these aggressive undercurrents about Finland's foreign-political position, there is another aspect of the arms-caching issue that merits attention, bearing, as it does, upon the legality of the would-be constitutionalist state that Finland wanted to serve. What was the crime that these soldiers had committed? The law that enfolded the crime of "preparing for illegal armed activity" was not actually passed till January 1947. By this time, for example, General Airo had been more than two years in prison awaiting trial for a crime that had not yet been determined upon. So this law was truly retroactive, hardly the mark of a constitutionalist state. Additionally, it may be argued that, whatever, the nature of the state, the army is expected to be prepared for any external eventualities that might threaten the state it serves. Further, it acts by orders and commands from higher echelons of its own and only the top brass has the luxury of discussion. In this case, the middle-ranking officers had mayhap taken the initiative, but they had told the commanding circles, one of whom was president of the country (then Mannerheim) and exercising his legitimate powers as commander-in-chief, too. He had been told what was going on and had only advised caution.

Article 13

The constitutional problem that the country faced was that it had to live under a top-heavy and lop-sided executive structure. The Russians were waiting for the fulfilment of one of the most important articles of the Armistice Treaty—article 13—and were disagreeably surprised at the time this was taking, and even more disagreeably surprised at the revelation of arms-caching. Paasikivi struggled on, whether as prime minister or as president, conceiving his main work as creating a reformed political society, meaning a working government and a working Parliament that would reflect better

---

[64] Maude, *The Finnish Dilemma, pp.38–45.*

[65] Paasikivi,*Päiväkirjat, II, p.209 (entry of 11.4.1951).*

relations with Russia and thus enable Finland to survive—as far as possible on its own terms.

But for the foreign executive of the Control Commission, this meant—by article 13 of the Armistice Treaty—that those who had been involved in instigating the Continuation War had to be tried for war guilt.

In historical terms, in terms of the chronology of history, this demand was a corollary to Paasikivi's control of the Finnish political scene. Paasikivi did not see it that way and he sought to avoid resort to the trials. In actuality, the projected trials were not a corollary to Paasikivi's accession to power. They were meant to be a precondition of it. When, in August 1944, argued Paasikivi, "Mannerheim, Ryti, Tanner, Ramsay, Linkomies, etc.," crudely ignored him, and then turned "towards himself," a little later, this only showed up the failure of their policy.[66] But who—which forces—turned to him? Within the country, he was supported by thoughtful businessmen like Holger Nysten, the former managing director of the Nordic paper cartel Scancraft,[67] Åke Gartz of the Ahlström Paper Company, Ralf Törngren, a liberal-minded member of Parliament for the *Svenska Folkpartiet,* and Carl-Olof Frietsch, an M.P. for the same party,[68] while from the side of the Agrarian Union both the Governor of Lapland, Kaarlo Hillilä, as well as Kekkonen. Then there were the members of the fragmented Left, like Reinhold Svento and Mauri Pekkala. And there were the Russian generals on the Control Commission and the Russian minister P.D. Orlov and their relations with a very important go-between of the SKDL, the Estonian-born Finnish citizen, Hella Wuolijoki (née Murrik). Slightly before Paasikivi formed his first government, she arrived with a ready-made list of ministers, having talked with Orlov and Yeliseyev previously, and the list. included three SKDL ministers.[69] Since these Finns and "one foreigner," as Paasikivi called Madame Wuolijoki,[70] were intriguing with the Russsian dignitaries in Helsinki, this was clearly dictation from the third or foreign executive. For on 10 November, Paasikivi had already decided that since the Communists had been unable to fight an election in prewar days their representation in the government should wait till after the election in the course of the New Year. After seeing Hella Wuolijoki a day later, Paasikivi went to Mannerheim and stated that at least one Communist should

---

[66] ibid.,I, p.294 (entry of 14.4.1946).

[67] ibid., I, p.20: (entry of 29.7.1944—he had been in Paasikivi's private discussions for peace three weeks before the Armistice was signed).

[68] ibid., I, p.20 (entry of 29.7.1944).This collection of pals assembled several months before Paasikivi formed his government.

[69] ibid., I, pp,43 &47 (entries of 31.10. & 11.11.1944) Jussila, op.cit.,p.99.

[70] Hella Wuolijoki (the writer *Juhani Tervapää*) narrowly escaped execution in the Continuation War for harbouring a Soviet parachutist.

now be taken into his pre-election government. The taking- in of the SKDL Helo would not be considered sufficient nor would Helo come in without the Communists and neither would Kekkonen and Hillilä.[71]

All these Finns had divined what the Soviet authorities had wanted and they pressed each other for the desired result. But they had equally seen that the previous government of Castren could not stand up to dealings with the Soviet Union. The group around Paasikivi willed a better future for their country in trying to accommodate with the Russians—as opposed to what they heard of the mad defiance of Tanner's attitude—"let the Russians (try to) occupy the country if they want."[72]

The scenario had become more complicated. In the best manner of Plekhanov's individuals, exerting their role in history,[73] the Finnish individuals, native-born or naturalized, behind Paasikivi were pushing him forward at a speed he did not like but in the direction he was going anyway, that is, cooperation with the Communists and the SKDL. What they had in common was a sense of working with historical change.

The key situation was that of the development of a special but limited relationship with Russia—as was previously said of the relationship with Germany. But the latter relationship had been in war, based on a miscalculation in the minds of the national and foreign military, while the new one, with Russia, was meant to be in peace. No one knew, however, what might transpire. There were people on both sides of the divide in Finland, some in various degrees of pro-Sovietism, others deeply fearful and hostile, but Paasikivi was to sense the patriotism in the Communist leader, Yrjö Leino, a figure whose socio-economic viewpoints he could never endorse.[74] The change that Paasikivi and his kind embodied for Finland was an international relationship, the extent of which Paasikivi was to be increasingly troubled about.

Fortunately or unfortunately, Paasikivi had more friends within the Finnish political system than he knew. True, he now found Tanner and his statements an embarrassment, but there were those who in general supported a less strident Tannerite line and who endorsed a certain traditionalist line within the Finnish system. One such was Unto Varjonen, an adherent of the

---

[71] Paasikivi, *Päiväkirjat*, I, p.47, (entry of 11.11.1944).

[72] ibid., I, p.45 (entry of 5.11.1944).

[73] G.V.Plekhanov, *The Role of the Individual in History*, London (Lawrence & Wishart), 1950, p.49 "influential individuals can change the individual features of events and some of their particular consequences, but they cannot change their general trend, which is determined by other forces." p.62 "not only for great men is that broad field of activity open."

[74] Paasikivi, *Päiväkirjat*,I, pp. 58,85,130, & 140 (entries of 20.11.1944, 4.1.1945, 1.4.1945, & 20.4.1945).

"brotherhood-in-arms" wartime movement, a movement that had sought to comprehend soldiers of Social Democrat and non-Socialist background. Varjonen was sceptical about changing the details of the Finnish political system, particularly the original SKDL proposal to put together Communists, Social Democrats and Agrarians into one broad political swathe. (Another leading Social Democrat, K.A. Fagerholm, joined it—and left it). Varjonen had the nerve to quote José Ortega y Gasset on the dangers of "hyper democracy" and he preferred the politics of negotiation: his example, the alliance between the Finnish SDP and the Svenska Folkparti. He was troubled by excessive majoritarianism, and quoted, in disdain, rule by a party with a majority of six seats (two times three), a remainder of the majoritarianism of his own party when it gained a majority of three seats in the 1916 election.[75]

Articulate people like Varjonen were now open to a politics that repudiated all talk of issues like East Karelia and the bundle of demands that went under the rubric of a Greater Finland. But there were, naturally enough, other wider issues that Varjonen's carefully demarcated politics had to leave on one side and with less justification than the case of East Karelia.

What both Paasikivi and Varjonen were accommodating to were a series of gaps in the over-arching power complex in which defeated Finland had to live. One might call these gaps the interstices of power.

But East Karelia was anyway coming up when those who had brought into being the German connection for Finland had to be on trial. And the rejection of this connection had to be done by a court of law in Finland. The use of a court and the fact that the court was to be situated in Finland and with a totally Finnish staff gave a semblance of legitimacy to the whole business, but, apart from the extremely difficult problem of the *composition* of the court, (it was a mixture of law-learned and pure politicians like Hertta Kuusinen, the Communist leader) a basic problem arose of how to try politicians for questions relating to the expediency of their wartime politics. Paasikivi, when still prime minister, argued with Yrjö Leino that there was no law in Finland by which to judge these people. Leino's response was laconic: "If a political change occurred you can be sure that you and I will be convicted and that paragraphs of the law will be found for this."[76]

The War Guilt Trials

Paasikivi had tried to avoid the eventuality of trials by encouraging those liable to be tried to withdraw, voluntarily, from politics. It was the politics of the self-

---

[75] Unto Varjonen, *Todellinen demokatia*, Porvoo-Helsinki (WSOY), 1945, esp.pp.52–56.

[76] Paasikivi, *Päiväkirjat*, I, p.131 (entry of 6.4.1945).

denying ordinance. Some of them like Risto Ryti and Väinö Tanner followed this line, the latter reluctantly. But the Control Commission still insisted on trials. There was to be no avoiding the Armistice Treaty. It could only be made more palatable by Finnish acceptance of it, either through Parliament or by the actions of the courts. In this way, the foreign executive was to cut down the former constitutionally-elected executive of the Finns and to isolate the new Finnish executive from a tradition. Yet the new politics from the Soviet side would actually tend to restore civilian leadership in Finland, even though the top brass itself was not to be tried. Instead, it was as if the old political leaders were to be punished for *giving way* to the military, whether Finnish or German.

There were objective reasons for Paasikivi's dilatoriness in this question. The Yalta Conference, at which the Soviet Union, the US, and Britain discussed, *inter alia,* the war guilt of the German leaders, did not occur till February 1945 and even then the definition of this guilt was not of the clearest. The London Conference, where the "greater war crimes" were defined more closely in terms of military aggression, did not begin till 26.6.1945.[77] But Paasikivi's reticence—and the reticence of many others—had little to do with these parallels. Two weeks before the start of the Yalta Conference, the "Six" members of the Finnish Left who had opposed the war and suffered imprisonment for doing so demanded that the war-guilt trials should begin.[78] On 15 January a 15-man delegation from the Finnish-Soviet Friendship Society had also "demanded" that trials of the war guilty should start. Paasikivi quoted back at them the statement already given by ex-President Ståhlberg, with which Paasikivi himself was in complete agreement, that under Finnish law politicians could not be tried for "wrong and detrimental policy."[79] The problem was aggravated further by the lack of a close definition even in the armistice agreement. The relevant article, article 31, simply read:

"Finland undertakes to collaborate with the Allied powers in the apprehension of persons accused of war crimes and in their trial."[80]

Being a lawyer as well as a historian, Paasikivi had, however, a yet greater juridical element to worry over. He could not abide the idea of retroactive law. Thus, in contrast to his better judgment as a history-bound politician, he sought out the British member of the Control Commission, Francis

---

[77] Jukka Tarkka, *13.artikla*, Porvoo-Helsinki (Werner Söderström), 1977, pp.103 & 115–117.
[78] ibid., p.103.
[79] Paasikivi, *Päiväkirjat*,I, p.90 (entry of 15.1.1945).
[80] This is from a rare copy of the English text recovered from the British Public Record Office and reproduced by Tuomo Polvinen in *Between East and West*, Porvoo-Helsinki (WSOY), 1986, Appendix I, pp.289–298.

Shepherd, and discussed the problem with him.[81] Shepherd was of the same opinion: that, as far as Finland at least was concerned, retroactive law was unnecessary. He saw the war trials as something like this: Ryti, for example, might be charged over the Ryti-Ribbentrop agreement if he could be found to have neglected in making it the provisions of *existing* law.[82]

But it was not to go like this. Paasikivi has assured Zhdanov that the old "war guilty" politicians would not be re-entering Parliament,[83] and still the Soviet Union pressed on with the arraignment of these politicians—and further, after serving his sentence, one of the most important, Väinö Tanner of the SDP, did come back into Parliament. And the law under which Tanner and the others were charged and convicted *was* retroactive. And since, in Ryti's case, in Tanner's case and several others, the sentences were deemed too low by the Control Commission, they had been increased by Soviet Diktat.[84]

The necessity of having to have Finnish war guilt trials was a shock to the tripartite division of the Constitution upon which the Finnish constitutional system claimed to be built.

Since this obligation arose from article 13 of the Armistice Treaty, it was convenient in Finland to think that the imputation of war guilt had been made under duress. That was true enough. What was being imposed on Finland was a consequence of defeat. At the same time, there were those in the country, and even in the government, who felt that as a condition of the armistice, article 13 was in itself law.[85] The question was penetrating the internal political system and disturbing it. Relations between the president (Mannerheim), the government (Paasikivi), Parliament, and the citizenry slumped. Worst of all was the fact that relations *between* the citizens were being damaged. SKDL (this time read Communist) members of the government (Paasikivi II), Matti Janhunen and Yrjö Murto, were ready to insist on the

---

[81] Bearing in mind, Paasikivi's previously expressed conviction that Finland's diplomatic dealings were to be with Russia and not significantly with the West (see note 56 of this chapter), his discussions with Shepherd might be considered to have been somewhat risky. The same might be said about Foreign Minister Enckell's talks with Shepherd, e.g. on 8.12.1945 as reported in Paasikivi's *Päiväkirjat*. Nevertheless, Shepherd's ultimate conclusion was that the Russians had treated Finland well, Paasikivi, *Päiväkirjat*, I,p.427 (entries of 17 & 18.3.1947).

[82] Paasikivi,*Päiväkirjat*, I, p.101 (entry of 10.2.1945).

[83] ibid.,pp.96–97 (entry of 2.2.1945).

[84] The pressure came from Zhdanov's deputy Savonenko: Ryti's sentence, e.g., was increased from 8 years to 10 years and Tanner's from 3½ to 5½.

[85] One such was Johan Helo, who was minister of finance in the first Paasikivi government and minister of education in the second until the end of December 1945:Paasikivi, *Päiväkirjat* I, pp.183,186, 189 & 261.(entries of 8.8.,10.8.,12.8., & 15.12.1945). Helo had forgotten that Finland had a dualistic system, requiring additionally the passing of Finnish legislation. The author is grateful to Antero Jyränki for a discussion of this topic.

discontent among the people because the war-guilt trials were not coming on, while Paasikivi himself was disgusted with the assertion that *torikokoukset* ("meetings in the square") were representative of the people's will. In his opinion the only representative voice of the people was Parliament.[86]

But from his standpoint—which was increasingly that of the unavoidability of war-guilt trials—Parliament itself constituted a problem. In August 1945, a deputation of Social Democrat members of Parliament went to see President Mannerheim to protest not merely against the trials but against the proposal to put a special law through Parliament to give the kind of covering legality for starting the trials, in short, the national law that Helo had not found necessary.[87] Mannerheim said that he agreed with the protesters. But—characteristically—they had admitted that they represented only the smallest of majorities, one obtained by a final casting of the lot.[88]

Politics of this kind were undermining Paasikivi's own politics of trying to find a solution that would at least reflect a semblance of constitutionalism. But it was beginning to look as if the whole of the Finnish constitutional system was now pitting itself against him. Much debate had already passed within the Finnish leadership as to whether the war-guilty could be tried under *existing* Finnish law. The legal community had quite early pondered over the matter and the Chancellor of Justice, Toivo Tarjanne, had decided that Finnish law would not provide a means of dealing with the problem. The judges themselves might simply acquit.[89] Signficantly, the historian Eirik Hornborg, entrusted by the government to draw up a report on the whole question was thinking in the same way. The burden of his report ran counter to the idea that the governmental policies of expediency connected with entering and pursuing the Continuation War could be judged in a court of law. [90] Further, irrespective of Hornborg's reasoning, two of Finland's leading judges came to the conclusion that they could take no part in war-guilt trials. Hjalmar Neovius resigned as president of the Supreme Court, while Urho Castren, who had served as prime minister in 1944, refused to move from the Supreme Administrative Court to take Castren's place. Paasikivi's intention in wishing to appoint Castren to the presidency of the Supreme Court had been to entice him to try the war guilty. Paasikivi pleaded the politics of patriotism, while Castren stuck to the oath he had taken as a judge and refused to be entrapped.[91] He nevertheless later agreed to serve as the legal member of the

[86]ibid.,p.188 (entry of 11.8.1945).

[87] See note 83.

[88] Paasikivi, *Päiväkirjat*, I, p.194. (entry of 16.8.1945).

[89] ibid., p.172 & 175.(entries o f 25.7.1945 & 27.7.1945).

[90] ibid., p.179 (entry of 4.8.1945).

[91] ibid., pp.234,242–243, & 251 (entries of 19.10.1945, 16.11. & 17.11.1945, &3.12.1945).

jury that was set up otherwise on party political grounds (12 members plus a jurist).[92]

Paasikivi thus went ahead to get his "enabling act" passed through Parliament. This required patient talks with the parliamentary parties, a clear enough case of the executive interfering, this time, with the parliamentary will,[93] in the hope that the law being passed it would enable a more pliant member of the judiciary to try the politicians for a war in which almost 60,000 of their fellow-countrymen had lost their lives. The act, known as the "protection law" (*suojelulaki*), required a five-sixths majority in Parliament for its passing *as a constitutional law*! To obtain this, Paasikivi won the accord of the leader of the National Coalition Party's parliamentary group to the abstaining of 48 M.P.s, mainly of the National Coalition Party, when the bill came to be voted on in Parliament.[94]

This was not the end of the affair, for then Paasikivi had to act as a go-between, in communicating Savonenkov's commands for several increased sentences, to the chairman of the court, the new head of the Supreme Court, Oskar Möller, who had been described as a "strong anti-Fascist."[95] Thus, the foreign executive had directly interfered with the independence of the Finnish judicial organ and Finland's leading politician had been his dogsbody.

Whatever may be thought about the wisdom of throwing in with the German invasion of Russia in 1941 and the continuance of the Continuation War in the summer of 1944, the trials of the politicians for pursuing these bungling policies were as inept as the policies themselves. Paasikivi told his diary that the Russians attacked the Finns in 1939 and split up Poland with the Germans.[96] Ryti, in his defence, tried to argue that the Continuation War came out of the Winter War, which in its turn emerged from the disregard of Finnish neutrality evinced by the Soviet Union and Nazi Germany in the Nazi-Soviet Pact of 23 August 1939 as well as by Soviet behaviour towards Finland in 1940–1941.This defence was disallowed.[97]

---

[92] Polvinen, *Paasikivi* 4, p.232.

[93] Paasikivi did much of this work himself, talking to both the Progressive and National Coalition parliamentary groups: ibid., pp.190–191. Erkki Koivisto, a Lutheran clergyman and National Coalition M.P., did not see eye to eye with Paasikivi: ibid., p.196. In general on the need to secure Parliament's backing, ibid., pp.246–248.

[94] Polvinen, *Paasikivi*, 4, p.196.

[95] ibid., pp.252 & 280 (entries of 4.12.1945 & 17.2.1946).

[96] Paasikivi,*Päiväkirjat*, I, p.198 (entry of 22.8.1945).

[97] The defence was later printed as *Risto Rytin puolustus*, Helsiniki (Tietokalervo), 1989 more than forty years after his trial. Ryti argued that the Soviet Union and Nazi Germany destroyed the efficacy of Finnish neutrality a first time by the pact of 23 August 1939—with its consequence in the Winter War, while the Soviet Union harassed Finnish neutrality a second time in 1940–1941 by interfering in Finnish internal affairs: pp. 13,15–16, 23, & 25.

The politicians had acted under the impress of the military men, including the then Marshal Mannerheim. But none of these men were charged, though Heinrichs resigned.[98] It was as if the Soviet authorities wanted to maintain a sort of fiction about the "neutrality" of the armed forces—which possibly "next time" might serve the Russian interest.

As to the politicians, it is the contention of Hannu Soikkanen that the Russians were gunning for VäinoTanner.[99] He had not been in the government when the country went to war: but Mauno Pekkala had been in the government, yet he was not charged. Now of the SKDL, he was shortly to become Prime Minister. He had resigned from the government, however, in 1942. Even more extreme was the case of Kekkonen, the minister of justice at the time of war-guilt trials. During the Continuation War, under the name of Pekka Peitsi ("Peter the Lance"), he had been a vociferous supporter of the war, but turning against it in 1943, while still writing *for* the war until somewhat later.[100] He is the classic example of a certain truth in Risto Penttilä's theory of the importance of the "turncoat" in Finnish history.[101]

The war-guilt trials created consternation in Finland. Newsreels, some of them made by the well-known photographer "Heddy" (Hedengren), show well-dressed men agitating in disgust outside the venerable building where the trials were being held (the building was that in which three estates of the pre-1907 Diet of Four Estates used to meet). Up and down the country, the pictures of the sentenced politicians were exhibited in the shop windows under the rubric "They Served Finland."[102]

The war-guilt trails with their denial of the defeat of Finland by the Soviet Union in the Winter War, the selecting of the politicians chosen to stand trial, and ignoring of the military personnel involved in planning the war with Germany, were a distortion of the history that had just occurred.

In this sense, a lie was forced on Finland. But in another sense, there was a lurking truth in the trials. President Ryti's acceptance of a German destruction of Leningrad and the shifting of population in the areas planned to be controlled by Finns and Germans along with the whole concept of

---

98 Mannerheim was the Soviet candidate for leader of a peace government in the summer of 1944 and the guarantor that the army would obey. Heinrichs resigned in connection with arms-caching (the army top-brass did not want to obey!)

99 Hannu Soikkanen, op.cit., pp. 69 & 71.

100 In popular parlance, Kekkonen was known as "the weather vane." Maude, *Historica Dictionary of Finland,* 2nd.ed.,p.138.

101 Penttilä, op.cit., esp. pp.73–74.

102 Maude, *Historical Dictionary of Finland,* 2nd.ed., Lanham, Toronto, & Plymouth (Scarecrow Press),2007, p.302.

Finnlands Lebensraum,[103] was a distortion set out for the future of a Europe under the aegis of Nazidom.

Impact—No Socialism

There were two forces wanting war guilt trials. The one was the Soviet Union, the other was the internal political force that felt it would emerge into power after the Soviet victory. They were not identical even if connectable. Essentially, the Soviet authority was working for the creation of a *broad-* based support in Finland for friendship with Russia and to that end, in the usual heavy-handed way, it wished to destroy the power of those who had led Finland against Russia. The former had committed an act of aggression by turning their country into a *plasdarm (place d'armes*–"military springboard") against Russia. (It is worth pointing out that the dreadful expulsion of émigré Russians from Finland–including some of the Kronstadt refugees from the 1921 rising–was part of the same policy imposed on the Finnish government. Finland was not to be a centre for anti-Soviet propaganda.).[104]

As to Finland's internal politics *otherwise,* the choice seemed to be for a mix of forces, including but not solely the radical Left that suddenly emerged once more. The historian Hannu Soikkanen has seen that this was so important a factor as almost to have forced Zhdanov to bring on the war-guilt trials.[105] The Soviet victory had, as stated, released the suppressed radical Left from the consequences of illegality, but a much wider consequence for the Left was the persistence of its division, and the extreme Left apparently assumed that spectacular war-guilt trials would redound to their own credit.

This division of the Left did not arise from disputes over the direction of internal economic policy. Both the SKDL and the SDP were committed to strong-sounding statements about the nationalization of key industries and commercial banking. In January 1945 in the Finnish Parliament SDP speakers, including Unto Varjonen of the "Brothers-in-Arms" association, began to ask about proposals for nationalization and support for this came also from the SKDL side, including Atos Wirtanen.[106] On 20 April 1945, Karl Wiik, now an SKDL M.P. after several years of imprisonment on security

---

[103] See chapter III of this work. Regrettably when the part-author of this work, Eino Jutikkala, died in 2007 the *Helsingin Sanomat* obituary did not mention this publication of his and Veikko Auer's.

[104] Jussila, op.cit.,p.53.

[105] Hannu Soikkanen, op.cit., pp.69 & 71–72 gives plenty of evidence to show that the extreme Left pestered Zhdanov for action in this question—even from the autumn of 1944.

[106] Soikkanen, op.cit., pp.115–116.

grounds, stood up in Parliament and asked the government to investigate at the earlier possible opportunity whether the "big capitalist section" of the wood and paper industry as well as the war industry could be brought under the control of the state. Wiik argued in terms of a prewar capitalism that had led to intermittent economic collapse and war, postulating the need for democratic control, particularly of the large-scale industries of Finland, which had broken both export workers and smallholders. Somewhat paradoxically, Wiik went on to say that collective agreements were only introduced because of the tense time of the Winter War![107] In general, Wiik's stand, even though it contained a lot of recent historical truth, could be faulted for its absence of comment on the immediate prospects of the labouring classes—the work in postwar reconstruction, the re-settlement of the predominantly smallholders from Karelia, and the prospects for work in the reparations industries, privately run or not.

However, the grim fact for the Left was that with the Soviet Union in political control on top of the country (a third executive) the *economic* transformation that was occurring in many parts of Western Europe was not going to take place in Finland! In November 1944 Wiik had personally asked Zhdanov whether the collectivisation of agriculture could begin by taking over the big estates. Zhdanov said that the was "premature."[108] In the local government elections of the autumn of 1945, where the SKDL and the SDP were in electoral alliances, demands were voiced for nationalization at the municipal level.[109] On 5 October Väinö Leskinen of the SDP stood up in Parliament and repeated the need for "social economic planning" as voiced by the SDP in January. He recounted the experiences of England and France and the need for Finnish state control of the reparations going to the Soviet Union, asking, too, for governmental reactions to the January SDP proposals. He was brushed off.[110]

As the war guilt trials came on, however, this cooperation between the two sides of the Left became overshadowed by the patriotic reactions of the

---

[107] *Valtiopäivät* 1945. *Liitteet I-XII*, pp.185–186. The motion of 20.4.1945 was signed also by Ville Pessi,general secretary of the Communist Party and an SKDL M.P., and Cay Sundström, an SKDL M.P. The author is grateful for the brief reference in Lasse Lehtinen's *Aatosta jaloa ja alhaista mieltä*, Helsinki (Söderström), 2002, p.100.

[108] Polvinen, *Paasikivi* 4, p.32.

[109] Hannu Soikkanen, op.cit., p.93. In Finnish terms these demands were reasonable since municipally-owned institutions were characteristic of Finnish municipal enterprise. The initiative for a local electoral alliance seems to have been a tactical move from the SDP side that only proved the point that in this type of situation the SKDL had the advantage, as it turned out: ibid, pp.91 & 94.

[110] *Valtiopäivät. Pöytäkirjat*, 1945, I, pp.1072–1073.

traditionalists in the SDP. Far from working to the benefit of a *joint* Socialist cause, it made the division deeper. The existence of the SKDL had drawn away into their fold a part of the Left opposition within the SDP, which in consequence strengthened its right-wing character.[111] Instead of leading to a Leftist takeover therefore, the impact of Soviet demands on Finland, in particular the war guilt trials, strengthened Finnish traditionalism. Soviet demands also strengthened Finnish *economic* traditionalism. Leskinen's point about the fortifying of private enterprise through the reparations system was an apt one. The Soviet authorities wanted to utilize the products of the *existing* facilities in Finland; they did not have the time nor the inclination to promote economic change in Finland.

But even in connection with the war-guilt trials, Zhdanov had a couple of points against the SKDL, as Polvinen has revealed. Among the mix of forces that Zhdanov was working with was a section of the bourgeoisie and a section of the Agrarian Union. When therefore the SKDL asked for the replacement as prosecutor in the war-guilt trials, that is, to have the Marxist Eino Pekkala instead of Toivo Tarjanne doing the job, Zhdanov reminded them of the need to prevent Paasikivi from resigning in anger or, as Zhdanov put it, let the bourgeoisie serve us. As to the Agrarian Union, he said, that along with the SDP they formed with the SKDL "the big three" that were running the country. This bloc should not be upset.[112]

But it was to be upset. The apparent unanimity between two sections of the Finnish Left for nationalization projects was dwarfed by the antagonism of the SDP over the war-guilt trials especially the trial of Väinö Tanner. If the traditional enemy of the Socialists was the capitalist system, many Social Democrats in Finland would have answered the question "who is the enemy" by saying "the Soviet Union." The needs of maintaining parliamentary democracy had constrained their will for economic change.[113] This did not mean that the SDP had discountenanced nationalization, but it began to take second place. The Soviet demand for war-guilt trails awakened the feelings of Finnish wartime unity. The association called "The Brothers-in-Arms" had been suppressed on 25 January 1945 in accordance with the requirements of article 21 of the Armistice Treaty on the prohibition of associations of a

---

[111] Tarkka, op.cit., p.257.

[112] Polvinen, *Paasikivi*, 4, pp.188–189.

[113] Doubts came early. Unto Varjonen, a member of the "Brothers- in- Arms" but initially after the war a believer in nationalization expressed in *Sosialistinen aikakauskirja* 3, 1946,a certain bewilderment over the fact that in both the SDP and the SKDL a reticence was occurring in regard to nationalization projects (quoted in Armas Äikiä, *Kolmas tie*, Helsinki, (Kansankulttuuri), 1948, pp.35–36.

"Hitlerite or Fascist nature,"[114] but its spirit was not quenched and its adherents took on a pronounced character of the defenders of parliamentary democracy.

Politics therefore was operating in Finland at several levels. It was felt by the SDP that the key question was, after all, that of the defence of the institutions of constitutional government. This view penetrated their standpoints in the nationalization discussion. If nationalization occurred, the SDP did not want the Communists controlling it. They did not want to go too far for fear of promoting a Communist system that would spread over the whole of society, stealthily. The Social Democrats thus eschewed too ideological an approach. Nonetheless, government backing of industry was traditional in Finland And it was even a part of a national capitalist system. After the Second World War, with a Socialization Committee in being and founded by the government, its composition required all-party representation. Such stalwarts of the capitalist system as Heikki Huhtamäki ("the sweet man") and Esa Kaitila were sitting on it,[115] and by 1947 the committee was receiving the usual Finnish expert opinion, according to which (Kastari) expropriation in terms of "a general need," expressed in terms of law, could hardly apply to the committee's recommendations and therefore an expropriation law would have to have *as a constitutional law* a five-sixths majority of Parliament (an impossible attainment since even in the 1945 election the National Coalition Party gained 28 seats, the Swedish People's Party 15 and the Progressives 9 -in short a potential blocking minority of over a quarter of Parliament)—while another expert (Merikoski) doubted whether the real cost of compensation could ever be estimated nor even whether a firm destined for nationalization could ever be required to supply information about itself.[116] Article 6 of the 1919 Constitution provided explicitly for the protection of the property rights of the citizenry. Thus, Finnish constitutional law was a sufficient instrument for frustrating what had what had been more easily done in Britain and France.

All this notwithstanding by September 1947, Väinö Liukkonen had produced the report of the Socialization Committee. A graduate of the Social Sciences Institute in Helsinki, Liukkonen was a Social Democrat somewhat under the influence of the teachings of the Austrian Socialist, Otto Bauer.[117]

---

[114] Maude, *Historical Dictionary of Finland*, 2nd ed., p.36.

[115] *Komiteamietintö A 1950*, 7, p.3 Huhtamäki was patron of rune singers and told one of them that when she came to Turku she should ask for the "sweet man," as this is what he manufactured ("candies").

[116] Experts' opinions to the cabinet, 1947:no.15. (Parliamentary archives).

[117] *Sosialitoimiskomitean mietintö* (typescript), 1947; pp.3 & 7, and sympathetically pp.26–31 (historical section). For Finland, Liukkonen did not seem to advocate, however, Bauer's model

He produced a lengthy report recommending the nationalization of a large part of Finland's greatest export industries, the forest industries, including paper, on grounds of efficiency, the profit to be gained for society, and increased employment in a postwar world crying out for wood products.[118] The scope of Liukkonen's enthusiasm for nationalization was vast and went far beyond the key sectors of the economy. Once a particular branch had become monopolized, it became in his opinion ripe for a takeover by the state in accordance with the strict tenets of Marxism: this included cigarette manufacturing and the comparatively small sugar industry and sugar imports.[119] At this point, nationalization ran into further opposition—from the SKDL, who, true to their manoeuvering towards the Agrarians, now opposed the nationalization of the latter branch of industry.[120]

Liukkonen's work was in vain. When it came to it, the *party-* political will was lacking. After their initial enthusiasm in late 1944-early 1945, the SKDL backed off the question, intent as they were to work with the Agrarians in a "big three" party-alliance they, the Communists thought they could control. The Agrarians, in their turn, feared that nationalization might start with industry, but would end with the collectivisation of agriculture, a fear that Kekkonen was not above exploiting.[121] "The country" did not want "experiments."[122] Liukkonen, in his 1950 report, argued that the nationalization of the cigarette industry would bring a substantial profit to the state, but where was the initial and compensatory capital to come from to carry through the nationalization? State bonds, for example, were hardly an attractive proposition in the postwar inflationary situation. The Communists and the SDP quarrelled over the prospects of control that any nationalized industries might afford them.[123] Individual politicians in general were not above intriguing for jobs in any of the to-be nationalized industries. But only a section of the SDP expressed, among other things, a party-political interest in the question. These included members of the "Brothers-in Arms" group like Penna Tervo, the chairman of the Socialization Committee. Perhaps their interest was a genuine desire to establish a Social-Democrat bureaucracy to counter the extra-parliamentary agitation of the Communists. But waiting in the wings were the experts of bourgeois persuasion, all ready to tell the

---

of a troika board of one-third state representatives, one-third workers' representatives, and one-third consumers' representatives.

[118] ibid., pp.43–45.

[119] ibid., pp.50–51.

[120] Lehtinen, op,cit., pp.100–101.

[121] Juhani Suomi,*Vonkamies*,Helsinki (Otava), p.301.

[122] Lehtinen, op.cit.,p.100.

[123] ibid., pp.100–101.

Cabinet what the Constitution would not allow to happen.[124] The world-weary chairman of the Social Democratic Party, Karl August Fagerholm, summed it up best: "our constitutional law in all its stiffness guarantees that big and sudden turnabouts cannot be made. . . Nowhere else in Europe are there so old-fashioned a set of laws as those we have."[125]

What was left after all this was a certain pragmatic approach, for example, in regard to the establishment of a state-funded national telephone system or for the nationalization of the apothecaries of the country, each of which had a monopoly over a certain area.[126] The latter still have it, since nothing came of these proposals. In 1950, when Penna Tervo, a Tannerite Social Democrat, had been chairman of the committee for three years, the sugar industry was still being laboriously examined. The opponents of nationalization argued that the industry was mainly owned by the farmers themselves (the sugar-beet growers). In fact, their share was only 60%, while 32% of the shares were owned by the state(the rest by various foundations).According to one opponent of nationalization, this gave the state sufficient control, though his suggestion of state control by threat of a *reduction* of the state's interest in the industry was hardly convincing. What was convincing was the reverse of this: that the state could buy into companies without the heavy burden of nationalization. This was traditional in Finland, the Finnish way, as it were.[127] And there was another Finnish way, the subsidy of agriculture, including the growing of sugar-beet. This support, in that time, was not going to be threatened in the slightest, though "the dissenting opinion" seemed to have it in mind—as an argument only, without a basis in the Finnish reality.

Constitutionalist economics

A demand for justice pervaded the air. But in the parliamentary sphere there were now three parties contending with each other for their own and their followers' interests. These parties, the SKDL, the SDP, and the Agrarian Union became known as "the Big Three" after the three big states in world politics. All governments, from the spring of 1945 until the summer of 1948, contained representatives of these parties (as well as non-party ministers like

---

[124] Their views, quoted above, were not included in Liukkonen's texts.

[125] Lasse Lehtinen,*Fagerholm. Kekkosen tasavallan kakkonen*, Porvoo-Helsinki (Södersröm), 1981, p.148.

[126] The proposal to take over the apothecaries was particularly reasonable since existing rights were safeguarded until the expiry of the current owner's right. *Komiteanmietintö* 412, 1950 & *Sosialisoimiskomitean lausunto valtionneuvostolle*, 31.3.1950.

[127] ibid., p.15 & the dissenting opinion of Viljo Venho thereafter.

Paasikivi before he became president and Carl Enckell the foreign minister and, on occasion, members of the smaller centre parties). These coalition governments ran from 17 November 1944 to 29 July 1948 (Paasikivi I and II, and then the government of Mauno Pekkala). Under them, governing the Finns became—apparently—a Finnish problem and not a Soviet one in so far as the Finns continued to pay up their reparations to the Soviet Union and saw to it that their wartime leaders (except Mannerheim and most of the generals) stayed out of politics and took their sentences for war guilt.

On 8 July 1946, Penna Tervo, a rather important member of the SDP, made a significant statement in Parliament about a shift in constitutional politics that was then occurring. He referred to the on-going inflation and its causes: a rise in prices because of a rise in wages, but without a subsequent price ceiling. In politics, the cause was quite clear, he said. It was due to the "illicit relations" between the SKDL and the Agrarians. They had accepted that an increasing share of agricultural products would be sold on the free market. In this, Tervo saw a disturbing feature for the constitution. Instead of Parliament having to have a confidence in the government, the government had sought to win the confidence of Parliament by a series of deals with the powerful parties[128] (two to one).

The fragmentation of the Left, a factor which brought the SKDL nearer to the Agrarian Union, did not simply exacerbate the tactical nature of Finnish parliamentary politics. The Left in general still had a concern for the rural proletariat working in agriculture and forestry—indeed, that was where the greater part of the proletariat still worked. But the Agrarian Union stood between the Left parties and this proletariat. Many of its supporters were now evacuees from the Russian-occupied Karelian Isthmus. They needed land from the rest of the Finnish community and they were going to get it.[129] This re-settlement strengthened the smaller peasantry[130] and with it the belief in the

---

[128] Hannu Soikkanen, op.cit., p 115, has drawn attention to the importance of Tervo's interpellation. For the full version, see *Valtiopäivät.Pöytäkirjat*,I,1946, pp.1138–1142 & 1146. Note also the section on the war-guilt trials in which Paasikivi courts the parliamentary groups so as to obtain a five-sixths majority for the "protection law."

[129] It is difficult to know how far the costs of this re-shifting are really calculable. The re-settlement after the Winter War was only in process, when most of the Karelians went back after the successful start of the Continuation War. They all left again in 1944, and Paasikivi's view that some of them should stay in the Isthmus was a non-starter.

[130] K.U.Pihkala, "Siirtoväen ja rintamamiesten asuttaminen" in *Itsenäisen Suomen taloushistoria 1919–1950*, ed.Eino Jutikkala *et al*, Porvoo-Helsinki (Söderström 1950), p.247 points out that, after the second re-settlement, the average number of farmers with only 2.5 hectares of cultivable land increased 32% and those with only 5–15 hectares of cultivable land increased 32%, while correspondingly those farming on a larger hectarage were declining considerably in numbers—those having between 25–50 hectares by almost 20%, e.g.

economic salvation of property at a very basic level, so basic, in fact, that the small land units were not viable without additional aid. This came in the form of toleration for a certain level of a free market and in subsidy payments.

Thus, the Agrarian Union's support for an independent, land-owning peasantry often conflicted with the interests of a rural proletariat that did not have any land. Immediately after the Armistice, the Finnish Parliament passed a law for a degree of price control of basic agricultural products, but only in so far strikes were to be outlawed, a matter intended to circumscribe the trade unionists of the urban areas and of the *ruukki*,[131] but which also affected the rural proletariat working in forestry, for example. When Parliament passed a law on working hours, the Agrarian Union saw to it that those working in forestry and in the flotation of timber would be exempt from its provisions.[132] As to the anti-strike law itself, Paasikivi and Tanner (before the latter had left Parliament) discussed the issue together and Tanner seems to have come to the conclusion that it would be better to accept this in return for a continuance of rent control in the towns.[133] In October 1945, however, in the parliamentary debate on wheat growing in Finland, two SDP back-benchers queried whether the Agrarian spokesman, Johannes Virolainen, was right in asserting that wheat could not be got from abroad and one of these M.P.s suggested that the laying down of agricultural policy was in the hands of big estate-holders, while the other M.P. was inclined to encourage smallholders to switch to dairying [134] The SKDL was undoubtedly aware of a problem, even of a contradiction in its own policy, for it accepted with reluctance the division of big estates into smaller plots.[135]

On the other hand, the leading force in the agitation for better wages of the agricultural workers were the Communists in the SKDL. The chairman of the land workers' union was Eero Antikainen, who had come back from the Soviet Union after the war. On 10 May 1946, in over 200 places in Finland, the land workers struck, but particularly on big estates.[136] In vain did the minister of agriculture, Erkki Härmä, a Social Democrat, rail that this was a strike against the whole country. The prime minister, Mauno Pekkala,

---

[131] The *ruukki (bruk* n Swedish) was a large factory installation in the rural areas. As noted previously, trade unions had been forbidden in some of them, e.g.,at Myllykoski.

[132] Hannu Soikkanen, op.cit., p.113.

[133] Paasikivi, *Päiväkirjat*, I, p.74,(entry of 19.12.1944), & Soikkanen, op.cit., p.107.

[134] *Valtiopäivät I, 1945*, pp.1085 & 1086. Statements of Paavo Leskinen & Eeno Pusa. By 1946, the conflict had escalated and a Kotka Social Democrat, Olavi Karttaavi, pointed to the tension in the relations between the Agrarian Union and the urban working-class. These views were also expressed in the grass-roots of the SKDL: Hannu. Soikkanen, op.cit. pp.110–111.

[135] ibid., p.114.

[136] *Suomen Sosialidemokraatti*, 11.5. & 134.5.1946.

condemned the strike equally. It was time, he said, for sowing: three-quarters of Finland's food was provided by Finnish agriculture. Imports would be an intolerable strain on the economy if the land was not tilled.[137]

As a matter of fact, Mauno Pekkala was a member of the SKDL so that Communist trade unionism was in clear conflict with the over-arching would-be *national* outlook of the SKDL-led government.

The Communists were also in supposed to be in cahoots with the Agrarians, who were claiming to lead the farmers' interests. But the Agrarian Union opposed the strike, asserting sarcastically that the national trade union organization, the SAK, had approved the hitherto-*existing* wages of the land workers.[138] The principal organ of the SDP called for a continuance of a tight price control, but the settlement of the strike was a 25% wage increase for the agricultural workers, to be paid for in increases in dairy product prices and in the sales of *surplus* agricultural produce on the free market outside the rationing system.[139]

Less than a year later, however, the government of "the Big Three" was again in trouble due to internal dissension. The Agrarian Union members threatened to pull out when the Cabinet voted for a wage increase for members of the lorry-drivers' union, a fact which, said the farming interest, substantially added to their costs.[140] Attempts were thereafter made to create a new government with another prime minister instead of the SKDL's Pekkala. Sakari Tuomioja of the Progressives was given the chance of forming a government of the Left, but this simple scheme foundered on the insistence of the SKDL that the Agrarian Union should be in any future government. These politics were curious since the SKDL was being blamed by the Agrarians for stirring up the lorry drivers, yet the SKDL wanted to sit with the Agrarians in the government![141] *It was another teasing effect of coalition government.*

What was at stake? In large part what was happening was a spinning away of the trade union movement from the delicate balancing within the government of the parliamentary forces. In fact, the SKDL or the Communists within them were not the only political forces working in the lorry-drivers' union: many of the members of the union were Social Democrats, who also supported the strike. *Hence in practical issues of the workplace Communists and the SDP collaborated; this was not, however, reflected necessarily in political alignments, let alone parliamentary forces. Often therefore politics did not reflect a basic realities.* But,

---

[137] ibid., 12.5.1944.

[138] ibid., 11.5.1944.

[139] ibid., 13.6. & 21.6. 1946.

[140] Hannu Soikkanen, op.cit., p.197.

[141] ibid., p.197. Hannu Soikkanen maintained that the Finnish Communist Party did not *instigate* the strike.

in any case, the SDP could not supply a prime minister: the inheritors of the Brothers-in-Arms faction ducked the issue, and the SKDL would not take Fagerholm. Yrjö Leino, the minister of the interior, tried to work unofficially for his own candidature for the premiership, but other parties would not have this—apparently, to the relief of Leino's own party. Pekkala was kept on by Paasikivi as prime minister.[142]

But trade union agitation had by no means disappeared. And it was operating at many levels. The lorry-drivers' strike had fallen foul of the SDP campaign in the umbrella organization of the trade union movement, the SAK, that is, to challenge the Communists with the slogan "Now it's enough." But in practice once strikes occurred, at grass-roots level supporters of both branches of the Left had to work together. There was another aspect of this that challenged the SAK itself. If the SAK did not support strike action, then unofficial strikes occurred. The problem of the share-out between urban working-class interests and farming interests was a real one, which the organizations vying for power had to address. But if their demands were too greatly conceded (as Tervo argued in his theorizing about governments that were constantly seeking the confidence of Parliament),[143] then the economy would collapse under inflationary pressure and, whether by this pressure or the pressures of constant strikes, reparations to the Soviet Union would be endangered.

But by autumn, strikes in the engineering industry and in the harbours (the latter promoted by Communists) led the SAK to threaten a general strike unless wages were once more adjusted. In October 1947 wages rose 25% with a promise that when prices rose 5% then wages would rise 5½%.[144] The cabinet had given way to trade union pressure. For the Constitution this was worse even than Tervo's scenario: he had seen that government would cringe to Parliament: but now Parliament had been by-passed yet another time by a direct threat from the trade unions' top organization, which was itself conscious of its own precariousness as unofficial strikes occurred. Grass-roots democracy had narrowed down into the pursuit of immediate interest, the wage-packet, the key feature of democracy at the workplace.

Strikes were an expression of special interests in the face of the special interests of increasingly flourishing sections of the market such as those of the larger food-producers or consumer goods importers. The cost of reparation payments to the Soviet Union absorbed 16.1 % of the government's budget in

---

[142] ibid., pp.198–199.

[143] See this chapter note 128. Also note 86: Paasikivi's point that Parliament was, however, the representative organ—not meetings in the square.

[144] Hannu Soikkanen, op.cit., p.206.

1945 and even by 1948 this was as high as 14.8% of the budget.[145] It was difficult to see how any government could establish a national policy of economic restraint: the Agrarian Union policy of demanding tax cuts as an alternative to wage spiral[146] meant equally the creation of an augmented purchasing power for the *individual* that would at the same time deprive the *government* of part of the wherewithal to pay off the reparations.

But one solution was being found. In the autumn of 1947 children's allowances were introduced as part of wage settlement policies. This approach, based on Swedish experience, helped the family economy, while serving, too, as a means of wage restraint since childless employees did not of course qualify for the benefits.[147] However, as the system began to be extended to cover all families, including those in the countryside, the system grew in overall costliness and was thus included in state expenditure.[148] It remained a positive outcome of the conflictual politics of the later 1940s. It was nonetheless a part, too, of a wage restraint policy, and, as time was soon to show, part of the alternative to a socialist transformation of Finnish society.

Unholy Alliances—Still No Socialism

In his contemporary analysis of post-Second World War Finnish politics, Armas Äikiä, a Communist and former Soviet broadcaster to Finland during the war, who had returned to Finland in 1944, described the breakdown of relations between the SKDL and the SDP in terms of "evil men" and their ideology. They were both inside and outside the country. In his opinion, the SDP was not a Third Force alternative ("*Kolmas tie*" was the ironic title of Äikiä's book) as the SDP itself pretended to be. The Third Force, Äikiä said, was a servant of capitalism, ever ready to listen to officials like Matti Virkkunen[149] and his litany of the threats of withdrawal of American credits if the Finnish government nationalized industry and banks. According to Äikiä, Unto Varjonen, K.A. Fagerholm, and Väinö Leskinen of the SDP, who had formerly championed nationalization, had gone soft on the issue after their own contacts either in America or Britain. Later research has suggested that

[145] B.Suviranta, "Sotakorvaus 1944–1952 ja sen vaikutukuset" in *Itsenäisen Suomen taloushistoria 1919–1950*, ed.by Eino Jutikkala et al., p.263.
[146] ibid., p.205.
[147] Lauri Hyvämäki, "Valtioneuvosto 2.maailmansodan jälkeen vuoteen 1957", *Valtioneuvoston historia 1917–1966*, II, Helsinki (Valtion painatuskeskus), 1977, p.316.
[148] Heikki Waris, *Suomalaisen yhteiskunnan sosiaalipolitiikka*, Porvoo-Helsinki (1961), p.225.
[149] Matti Virkkunen was to go on to be the National Coalition Party's candidate in the 1968 presidential election. In 1947, when Äikiä noted his statement, Virkkunen was in the important position of chief of the Commercial Dept. of the Finnish Foreign Ministry:Äikiä, op.cit., p.37.

there may have been some truth in Äikiä's allegation.[150] An even more striking criticism in Äikiä's text relates to the postwar inflationary situation in Finland, which Varjonen argued was due to excessive wage demands, while Äikiä himself argued that the failure to nationalize the banks was the fundamental cause and with it the growing conviction of the SDP, by 1948, that the "key elements in the economy" had to be left alone.[151]

In regard to the politics of the day, however, Äikiä's version of events was ingenuous or at least partial. After the previously-noted initial enthusiasm in late 1944 and early 1945, the SKDL's own enthusiasm for nationalization waned. Jussila does not mention this initial stage, however. But goes on to point to the advice given by Otto Wille Kuusinen when a cultural delegation visited him on October 1945. The delegation included members of the non-Socialist parties, one member being Sakari Tuomioja, head of the Bank of Finland. Kuusinen seemed to stress wage restraint and played down the significance of nationalization, possibly just for water-power and for an insurance company. He told the delegation not to "romp around" too much with Socialism, but to use capital, *whatever its ownership might be.*[152] This advice would certainly be in the line of Soviet policy to Finland in these years, namely to use Finnish industrial capabilities to serve the reconstruction of Russia.

As Jussila shows, but cannot adequately explain, the pioneers of Socialist solutions at this time (1945–1946) were the SDP.[153] Only in 1947–1948 did the SKDL once more renew its concern for nationalization at a time when the SDP had become somewhat more cautious about it.[154] This lack of synchronization between the two Left parties doomed the schemes for a thoroughly- grounded "planned economy."

What was constant was the over-reaching indifference of this question in the eyes of the Soviet leadership, whose basic concern was the security-political

---

[150] Äikiä, op.cit., p.36 & Jussila, op.cit., p.121.

[151] ibid., pp.102–107 & 43. since the Bank of Finland raised the exchange rate of the Finnish mark three times in 1945 to the tune of 176%, there is a *prima facie* case for the assumption that Äikiä had a point. In 1946 prices were rising more rapidly than wages, which pushed ever upward a wage- rate spiral in the attempt to compensate for price increases (here, Varjonen had a point). Into this context, Suviranta placed the *additional* inflationary consequences of reparations, op.cit.pp.266–26, a factor that, naturally, Äikiä dared not touch.

[152] Paasikivi,*Päiväkirjat,* I, p.232 (entry of 16.10.1945).

[153] Jussila, op.cit.,p.169. Jussila's astonishment at this fact can only be explained by his ignoring of the Socialist core of the SDP's outlook.

[154] The change of heart of the Finnish Communist Party, in their support for nationalization in the period, roughly, 1946–1947, is explained by Jussila as a change of heart in Otto Wille Kuusinen and therewith the Soviet Union's own strategy, ibid., p.170, while the rapid fading away of this interest Jussila explains by the failure to stimulate in Finland a mass movement to produce it, ibid., pp.172–173.

relationship with Finland. The contempt with which the extreme pro-Soviet grouping in the Finnish Communist Party viewed, for example, the British Labour government's nationalization policy[155] reflected only too well the Soviet leadership's conviction that the road to Socialism could not come through "piecemeal *economic* engineering," to adapt Karl Popper's phrase(in a manner he would not himself have approved).What this meant was a denial of the use-value of cooperation with Social Democracy—except, of course, when the Communists were in a controlling position in a coalition with the Social Democrats.

But in Finland the coalition was that of the "Big Three," which, by 1948, had become a laconic comment on the Finnish microcosm's disjointed position vis-à-vis the relation of forces in the outer world. Finland's role for the Soviet Union had been filed down to that of a tame but loyal state on the border, the loyalty of which rested upon an *internal* political relationship between three political parties, two of which were, by 1948, not interested in fundamental economic transformation of their country—nor countryside, for the third element in the combination was an Agrarian Party, fiercely wedded to the maintenance of privately-owned agriculture. Since at least the Communist section of the SKDL associated the economic outlook of the SDP in terms of a linkage with the aggressive imperialism of the Anglo-Saxon dominated world, the SKDL and the Communists who formed its core were drawn ever more into an understanding with the Agrarian Union.

The Finnish Communist Party could easily dress this relationship up from the standpoint of class ideology. To the chagrin of the landowning classes, the Communist Party had, as noted, supported the strike of farm workers in 1945. but its solution to the problem of the rural proletariat was no longer that advocated by SKDL members to Zhdanov in 1944, that is, of collectivisation. Matti Janhunen, the Communist Minister of Social Affairs, drafted a bill for solving the working-hours of farm wage-earners (left out of the general law) by provisions that allowed longer working hours in summer and shorter in the winter work season.[156] Yet the longer-term solution was instead very close to the solution of the Agrarian Union itself, that is, of the granting of land to the landless. So close was this to the Agrarian Union's policy that the Agrarian leadership lived in fear of losing out to Communist initiative.[157] The Communists had a ready programme and it did not essentially differ from that

---

[155] Äikiä, op.cit., pp181,183, &192–194.

[156] ibid., pp. 134–135.

[157] Both the Agrarians and the SDP conducted propaganda in the Finnish countryside, asserting that the Communists would collectivise the land; in fact, the SKDL programme was to take land from the industrial companies, banks and the larger landowners:Äikiä, op.cit., pp.128–129.

of the Agrarian Union—except that the Communists were bolder in their planning of the sources from which the expropriated land was to come.

Communist Party policy would also have allowed the farmers to sell their surplus produce on the open market in this period when, under the continuance of wartime legislation, deliveries of farm produce were priced and delivered legislatively, a system that created a thriving black market in farm produce surpluses. The legalizing of a surplus-produce market would, so it was hoped, end the illegal activity of the black market and benefit both producer and consumer. But it was not to be either. The SDP, sticking to standard and fixed price policy, and the Agrarian Union, sticking to a free market (and subsidies) ran the proposal down.[158]

But the main question remained that of the expropriation of land. This matter was difficult enough as far as the re-settlement of the Karelians was concerned. But it became a large part of the solution, in spite of the initial opposition of President Mannerheim and Prime Minister Paasikivi, both of whom feared not merely for loss of agricultural production if the larger land units were broken up but also the burden of compensatory costs (article 6 of the then Constitution guaranteed property of the citizens and compensation for its expropriation) in a country already struggling to pay off war reparations.[159] Paasikivi's original stance had been to adopt the model of the forest pioneer, carving new agricultural land out of the vast wooded areas of the country.[160] Parliament opposed him on this and in the parliamentary solution the existing fields of the larger land units were apportioned to the Karelian refugees. But this solution remained separate from the granting of a plot of land to those who had served in the war (for the construction of a house) and separate, too, from the solution originally proposed by the government of Urho Castren, whose committee (the Nissinen committee) planned a wider land settlement that would have included others than the dispossessed inhabitants of the Karelian Isthmus.[161]

At any rate, after the Second World War government was faced with an "agricultural front." This by no means consisted solely of the political party known as the Agrarian Union, which had almost one-quarter of the seats in Parliament. For in existence, too, was the powerful interest-group organization, the MTK, of farmers and forest owners, founded in 1918, some of whose most active members were supporters or members of the National

[158] ibid., p.132.

[159] Silvo Hietanen, "Voiton ja tappion saralla" in *Paasikiven hirmuiset vuodet*, Helsinki (Tammi),1986, pp.49–53.

[160] ibid., p.46.

[161] ibid., p.46 & for the criticism of the Nissinen committee's proposal—p.49.

Coalition Party and an organization had also been founded of landowners capable of protecting the interests of those who had to give up land to the Karelians (not more than 25 hectares), in which again National Coalition Party supporters were prominent.[162]

Nonetheless, the spirit of the "agricultural front" was most clearly embodied in the Agrarian Union. While continuing to emphasize that this was a party of "smallholders"[163], the Union had created a composite set of policies that embraced a wide range of rural interests and between 1945 and 1955 its membership increased more than sevenfold.[164] In face of a phenomenon of this kind, the drive of the SKDL and the Finnish Communist Party to establish a legitimacy in the Finnish countryside meant the development of a class struggle there, taking land from the "haves" and giving to the "have-nots." The propensity of the Communist movement to attain its goals by strike action was condemned by the Agrarian leaders as "extra-parliamentary" and even "dictatorial."[165] Only in the poorest of rural districts did the Communists maintain a position.[166]

Instead, the main argumentation of the Agrarian movement—of standing up to urban interests and of exploiting them in the *national interest* of a home-grown food supply—seemed to have more to recommend it. The counter to this was not with the Communists but with the Social Democrats who demanded more food imports as a cheaper alternative to the subsidization of domestic agriculture. This deepened the cleavage between the Agrarians and the SDP, but the Communists and their allies in the SKDL were hardly to reap the wind.

The extra-parliamentary activities of the Communists (even alienating SKDL members like Reinhold Svento)[167] included strikes and town-square meetings and it had, by 1948, a negative impact on the Agrarians.[168] As the cooperation between the "Big Three" broke down and Paasikivi, with great

---

[162] ibid.,p.49

[163] Ahti Karjalainen, "Maalaisliiton viides vuosikymmen," & Johannes Virolainen "Maalaisliiton maatalouspolitiikka" in *Herääva maaseutu*,VI, Helsinki (Maalaisliitto r.y.) 1956, pp.262 &185.

[164] Karjalainen, ibid., p.240.

[165] ibid., p.253.

[166]Jaakko Nousiainen, *Kommunismi Kuopion läänissä,* Joensuu, privately printed,1956. This form of Communism was known as "backwoods Communism."

[167] By the spring of 1946, Svento was already worried about the pretensions of the Finnish Communists, even finding that they wished to go beyond anything the Russians might allow. He was wary of Leino as well as of the grass-roots in the SKP. Paasikivi,*Päiväkirjat I*,p.312 (entry of 20.5.1946).

[168] Johannes Virolainen, *Sanoi Paasikivi,* Helsinki (Otava), 1983, p.285. A statement of the Agrarian Union of 25.5.1948, in favour of the "lawful system," may also be found in Paasikivi, *Päiväkirjat*, I, p. 620 (entry of 26.5.1948)

regret, felt it necessary to sack the minister of the interior, Yrjö Leino[169]—a matter which incensed the Communists to take further strike action, the Agrarian Union felt a strengthening of its conservative roots and, in the 1948 summer election, received (by Finnish standards) a substantial victory, rising from 49 to 56 seats, while the SKDL slumped from 49 to 38. Significantly, an Agrarian election poster showed a farmer with his hand on a lawbook and a Bible.[170] But the mood of the moment had also been seized by the conservative National Coalition Party, a political force left out of all governments since November 1944. The sacking of Leino, at the instigation of the Right, was a reminder that, whatever the government of the day might be, there were other potential political combinations in the country.

The breakup of the "Big Three" coalition left a vacuum in Finnish politics. Several solutions were mooted and in the end a minority government of Social Democrats was formed. It was a critical period in Finnish politics and within several of the political parties. That went for the Agrarians, too. One of the most dynamic members of the Agrarian Union had temporarily to retreat from power. This was Urho Kekkonen, whom many members of the party felt was tainted by too close an aspiration to work with the SKDL, even though it had been this political grouping that had frustrated his attempts to form a government in 1946.[171] Kekkonen had then been marked out by Paasikivi as a powerful and capable political personality,[172] but the increasing rightward trend in the Agrarian Union, led by Juho Koivisto, had cut the ground temporarily from under Kekkonen's feet.[173] Kekkonen had still therefore to

---

[169] The *causa proxima* for this breakdown was the dismissal of Leino from his post as a result of a long-winded investigation by an official committee on the events of 1945 when Leino had expelled back to the Soviet Union Russian and former Russian citizens living in Finland (note 104 of this chapter). The committee found that Leino had behaved illegally, but he refused to resign and after a National Coalition Party motion of no-confidence went through Parliament. Paasikivi therefore felt compelled to dismiss him, and the resulting politics broke up Big Three cooperation,on which Paasikivi's own power leaned. Paasikivi believed that the National Coalition Party as a conservative party should have worked "to preserve society" and not engaged in a politics that broke up a government that *contained* the Communists: Paasikivi, *Päiväkirjat*, I, p.618 (entry of 24.5.1948).

[170] Virolainen, op.cit., p.287.

[171]On these tortuous negotiations of 1946, Polvinen, *Paasikivi*, 4, pp.266–69.

[172] In talking to Mannerheim (who had distrusted Kekkonen), Paasikivi had marked Kekkonen out as his possible successor as prime minister in 1946 (Pekkala or Kekkonen): Paasikivi, *Päiväkirjat I*, pp.46 & 214, (entries of 10.11. 1944 & 18.9.1945). By 1950 Paasikivi had come to regard Kekkonen "as the best man for the presidency when I leave the office":ibid., II,p.161 (entry of 3.12.1950)—in spite of the fact that Kekkonen had challenged him in the presidential election of that year.

[173] Juhani Suomi, *Vonkamies*, Helsinki (Otava),pp.374–385. Juho Koivisto had said he was convinced that Kekkonen would have brought the SKDL into a new government. Suomi finds

convince his party that being a supporter of friendship with the Soviet Union did not mean a sell-out to Finnish Communism. On the contrary, as it was to turn out, friendship with the Soviet Union was to be the best assurance against the creation of a Finnish Communist state.

The tables were now beginning to turn quite nicely—from the standpoint of Finnish legitimacy. Domestic Communism had previously been exploited by Paasikivi to fend off too intrusive an interference of the Soviet Union in Finnish affairs.[174] Henceforward a new security relationship with Russia was to serve to confine domestic Communism.

A Soviet Contract with Constitutionalism

It is a matter of dispute as to who was the initiator of the Finnish-Soviet security treaty, the Treaty of Friendship, Cooperation and Mutual Assistance, briefly known as the FCMA treaty. In short, did the proposal come from the Finnish or the Soviet side? The present author's original view was that in 1945 Marshal Mannerheim, when President of Finland in the period of turning against Germany, was inveigled by Zhdanov, the head of the Control Commission, into considering the prospect of a military treaty with the Soviet Union—when Mannerheim had simply wanted a narrower agreement by which Finland might be allowed to keep its high-calibre coastal artillery as a safeguard against German naval power after the break with Germany.[175] But Polvinen's recent studies have shown that Mannerheim soon expanded his own ideas into a project for the defence of the naval approaches, and then was even prepared to consider that there might be merit in cooperation on land, too.[176] This would have been a military agreement. Interestingly, Paasikivi and the Finnish military themselves backed him up. Paasikivi, while welcoming cooperation on the western sea approaches, encouraged Mannerheim

---

this a groundless assertion (p.383) and claims that Kekkonen was "kicked upstairs" to be speaker of Parliament as a means of keeping him away from government formation (p.376). Suomi recalls that in 1946 Koivisto would have favoured a Communist head of government to one led by Kekkonen (p.383), a statement that bears witness to the personal in-fighting characteristic of Finnish politics, then and now. In respect of Kekkonen's election to the speakership in 1948, Virolainen, op.cit., p.290, simply states that in this election the opposition to Kekkonen was split and hence the latter's election to the post.

[174] See note 27 of this chapter.

[175] Maude, *The Finnish Dilemma*, London (OUP & the Royal Institute of International Affairs), 1976, p.28.

[176] Polvinen, *Paasikivi*, 4, pp.34–36. Screen,op.cit., pp. 351–352, seems to have come to a similar conclusion.

nonetheless to go for the wider agreement.[177] Zhdanov had appeared to want such an agreement and Mannerheim had "risen to the occasion," but suddenly Zhdanov backtracked.[178] A Finnish acceptance of such a treaty is understandable in terms of cooperation between the West and the Soviet Union. Unfortunately, as time went by, the emerging Cold War made the Finnish leadership ever more cautious. The British-Soviet alliance of 1942 had lost its significance rather rapidly and Paasikivi changed his stance so as to avoid all Soviet attempts to draw the Finnish leadership into a political-military alliance. It might be tantamount to ganging-up with a Soviet bloc.

The armistice between Finland on the one side and Russia and Britain on the other was followed in 1947 by a peace treaty, signed in Paris. These peace treaties were made with all the ex-enemy states and Finnish hopes of receiving some form of alleviation (for example, a return of a piece of Karelia) were dashed. The Finnish delegation was not allowed to participate in any negotiations and was treated extremely rudely, being expelled even from the visitors' gallery. Limitations on the Finnish armed forces were laid down broadly in terms of the limitations imposed in the Armistice Agreement of 1944, the British, however, insisting that the Finns take part in mine-sweeping in the Baltic approaches to their country.[179] This was hardly an indication that the West had begun to regard Finland already as a client state of the Soviet Union, and wished to circumscribe it. In general, the British encouraged the Finns to get on well with the Russians.[180] The principal arms limitation the British required was the prohibition on motor torpedo boats, a matter derided by Molotov, but one arising from common features in the peace treaties with the ex-enemy states, all being done together in Paris.[181]

The next step was a Soviet proposal for a security treaty and it angered Paasikivi when he heard that Prime Minister Pekkala (of the SKDL), scenting what was coming, had discussed the treaty issue himself when on a visit to Moscow. But Pekkala had been less worried when Molotov reminded him that some time before (1945) Mannerheim and Paasikivi had broached the issue.[182] Times, however, had changed: the Western-Soviet alliance had now given way

---

[177] Paasikivi, *Päiväkirjat*, I, p.93 (entry of 24.1.1945), in which Paasikivi wrote "kehoitin Mannerheimia ajamaan suurta asiaa"—"I encouraged Mannerheim to drive for the big matter."

[178] ibid. For a current discussion of this whole problem, see Timo Soikkanen's article "The FCMA Treaty: Who Fathered It?" in *The Cold War and the Politics of History*, ed. Juhana Aunesluoma & Pauli Kettunen, Helsinki (Edita),2008: pp.291–306.

[179] Polvinen, *Jaltasta Pariisin rauhan*, Porvoo- Helsinki (Werner Söderström) 1981, pp. 276 & 238–239. Polvinen, *Paasikivi*, 4, p.340.

[180] Polvinen, *Paasikivi 4*, p.304.

[181] Polvinen, ibid., p.340.

[182] Heikkilä, op.cit., p.301. On this still contentious aspect, see note 173 above.

to the Cold War. If Pekkala thought that in this way he was pre-empting a cause that might serve the future of the SKDL, time was to prove him wrong. In the first instance, however, he had to suffer the wrath of his president, whose anger with the prime minister only concealed a presidential determination to summon up every source of strength at his disposal to make the best of a bad job. In the meantime, the wretched prime minister relapsed into the refuge of his alcoholism.[183] The president took refuge in his diary.[184]

For now began one of the cleverest pieces of negotiation in diplomatic history. What emerged could be called neither an *alliance de revers* nor "an unholy alliance": the very thing the Finns wanted to avoid was an alliance. Instead, a Treaty of Friendship, Cooperation and Mutual Assistance was signed with conditions that were even contradictory. This did not soothe the West, the Americans and the British being equally negative about Finland's future in the light of the treaty.[185]

According to a British commentator, Peter Lyon, writing a decade and a half after the signing of the treaty, the principal contradiction lay in the fact that while the preamble of the treaty stated "Finland's desire to remain outside the conflicting interests of the Great Powers," the first article in the body of the Treaty contradicted this by decreeing that "in the eventuality of Finland, *or the Soviet Union through Finnish territory*, becoming the object of an armed attack by Germany *or any state allied with the latter*" Finland would fight to repel the attack.[186] According to Paasikivi's radio talk of 9 April 1948 to the Finnish people, the Finns would do this anyway, treaty or otherwise.[187] From the Finnish side, his argumentation was an attempt to place the treaty in the context of a defence of neutrality, but the specifics of this scenario of defence added a tendentious element.

---

[183] ibid., pp. 304–308.

[184] Paasikivi, *Päiväkirjat*, I, p.562 (entry of 29.2.1948), where he stated that it would be better if no treaty had to be made, but that it was impossible not to go into negotiations with the Russians as Ståhlberg wished.

[185] Polvinen, *Paasikivi 4*, pp.463–466, (following to some extent Nevakivi and Lundestad) on the Western concern for Norway and the possibility that Finland might have been asked to join NATO. In the early 1970s, the author of this current work was asked sardonically by a "friend of Finland" in Britain as to whether there was a secret protocol attached to the treaty. On the latter, Polvinen, *Paasikivi*, 4, p.487, Minister Toivo Vilhula's belief that there *was*: in a crisis situation, the Finnish army might be integrated into the Soviet armed forces, he believed.

[186] Peter Lyon, *Neutralism*, Leicester, Leicester Univ.Press, 1963, pp.97–98 A bold teacher in the Univ. of Turku, Jouko Siipi, wrote a pamphlet-style book in the same period pointing out that the FCMA treaty made the Finnish army a possible vanguard of the Soviet army.

[187] Paasikivi,*Paasikiven linja. Puheita vuosilta 1944–1956*, Porvoo-Helsinki (Werner Söderström), 1962, pp.114-118.

Paasikivi had mentioned this commitment previously—in an attempt to avoid a treaty.[188] For the current treaty foresaw the possibility of a breakdown in international relations in which Finland would, declaredly, have to take a side, the Russian side. This was underlined in article 1 with a reference to Soviet aid "in case of necessity" should an attack occur. Though Lyon does not say this, the point was also underlined in article 2 which mentioned consultations between Finland and the Soviet Union where it was established "that the *threat* of an armed attack as described in article 1 is present." Presumably, such consultations could only occur before the attack, that is, in a crisis period, in short, when peace still endured. In making the treaty at this point, Molotov queried whether the Finns really wanted the word "threat" since the Finnish draft was now different from the original draft, but the exhausted Finnish negotiators nonetheless accepted it.[189]

In terms of the geographical scope of the treaty, the Finns succeeded in limiting its scope. It was not to apply to sea-areas[190] (Mannerheim's 1945 proposal would have been extended to the Baltic sea-areas adjacent to Finland). Nor was it to apply to land-areas outside Finland, a matter which at first Kekkonen and J.O. Söderhjelm opposed, imagining that military operations could not necessarily be restricted to operations within the Finnish frontier.[191] They may have been right, but the point was to prevent the sort of operations developing as were laid down, for example, in the Romanian-Soviet Treaty or that made between the Soviet Union and Czechoslovakia, both of which envisaged *immediate* Soviet aid, whereas in the Finnish treaty such aid was a matter for negotiation in terms of need[192] without an automatic assumption of general war-fighting. In short, the Finnish treaty was *sui generis*[193] and in the limitation of its provisions recalled, *mutatis mutandis,* the desire of the Finns in the Continuation War to have their own war regarded as distinct from the rest of the Second World War, as a sort of *co*-belligerency.

Thus, when the Warsaw Pact was formed in May 1955, the Finns were never slotted into it.

The Finnish-Soviet treaty was a defensive treaty in old-fashioned terms and nothing in it was said about a pre-emptive strike of Soviet forces across Finland to the Norwegian coast should the Soviet Union feel itself to be in a

---

[188] In an article published on 10. 2.1947. Maude, *The Finnish Dilemma*, p.28.

[189] Polvinen, *Paasikivi*, 4, pp.483–484.

[190] ibid., p.468.

[191] ibid., p.479.

[192] It was Paasikivi who insisted on the phrase "if necessary" (*tarpeen vaatiessa*) being inserted into the first paragraph of article 1 with respect to the *possibility* of Soviet military aid. Polvinen, ibid., p.475.

[193] ibid., p.457.

"crisis leading to war" situation,[194] apart from consultation in a period of threat as was laid down in article 2 of the Treaty. So worried was General Heinrichs about the position of Lapland in such an eventuality that he at first was prepared to think in terms of a Finnish Lapland placed at the disposal of Soviet troops.[195] He suppressed the thought, however, but a variation of his proposal was to surface later. For the moment, it will be enough to say that the Treaty bore witness to the limitations of its limitation.

This was apparent in another sense when General Heinrichs insisted that the first duty of defence of Finnish territory was the duty of Finland (and not an automatic function of Soviet aid) as Urho Kekkonen seemed to want to have it.[196] Whatever it might turn out be in reality, in the treaty Soviet aid was secondary, a back-up. This made the obligations laid down in the treaty patriotic, as if to integrate Finnish control of the situation.

There is another aspect of the treaty, however, that merits a lot of attention. As Polvinen points out, a sort of politics of national will floated out of the negotiations on the Finnish side. This was evident in the role played by the Finnish military in the person of General Heinrichs, who had three years earlier had to resign because of his entanglement with the arm-caching affair against a possible Soviet invasion!

But the politics of national will also brought in some tricky manipulations of party politics, too. The fears of the extreme Left (whose representatives were also in the negotiating team) that the SDP and the Right might sabotage the prospect of a treaty (and the grand old man of Finnish Liberalism, the former President Ståhlberg cautioned against signing)[197] were a possible factor in encouraging the Soviet side, when it listened to these SKDL fears, to move more cautiously in its own demands.[198]

The historian Jukka Nevakivi has added to this the rumours that, in the pre-NATO negotiations, Finland was at least considered as a possible member.[199] This was presumably another factor that inhibited the Soviet negotiators, in their turn, from pressing the Finns too hard.

In the complicated politics of making a treaty with the Soviet Union, one of the members of the SKDL, Reinhold Svento, urged Paasikivi nevertheless

---

[194] Maude, *The Finnish Dilemma*, pp.66–68.

[195] Polvinen, *Paasikivi*, 4, p.452.

[196] ibid.,pp.473–474.

[197] Ex-President Ståhlberg served as one of Paasikivi's confidants. His opposition to a treaty comes out in Paasikivi, *Päiväkirjat*, I, pp. 534, 546–548, & 562 (entries of 9.1.1948, 25–26.1.1948, & 29.2.1948).

[198] ibid., p.467 (entries of 7.7. & 8.7.1948).

[199] Jukka Nevakivi, *Zdanov Suomessa*, 1995, p.257.

not to let Parliament itself lead. Parliament, asserted Svento, had to be led.[200] This was true in the sense that, apart from the SKDL and the Swedish People's Party, the parliamentary groups wanted nothing to do with a "defence alliance"[201] and their deliberations in open debate might rapidly have offended the Soviet side.

Parliament was thus not openly consulted; apart from its foreign affairs committee, which was not given written material, but was "informed" of the negotiations.[202]

But Parliament served. Its basic opposition to a treaty being known to the Soviet authorities, it remained as a bastion of strength behind the qualifications the Finnish negotiators wanted to make in the face of Soviet demands. Paasikivi hoped that Parliament would not very willingly accept the treaty (so as to let the Soviet negotiators know the difficulty it had in making concessions).[203] But it had still to ratify it and Paasikivi worked on the parties to get it through.[204] In spite of its fears therefore, Parliament had to *serve*.[205] Otherwise Paasikivi would resign.[206]

The third executive, in Moscow, had thus influenced the first Finnish executive, the Finnish presidential government, which in its turn had given orders for *negotiating* a treaty to the second Finnish executive, the limpid and confused political executive of the Finnish parliamentary government, embodied in a delegation that included two rather powerful non-ministers, Åke Gartz and Urho Kekkonen. The third executive had got its treaty, but with many reservations built into it as far as issues of foreign-security policy were concerned. The treaty was not an automatic mechanism. In a critical period, it would, at least in theory, be operated by *conferring* as to whether a threat of an armed attack against the two parties to the treaty existed (article 2) or whether Soviet aid or Soviet military action with the Finns was needed (article 1). It is hardly surprising that in the deliberations of the confidential Parliamentary Defence Committee in 1970, Lieutenant-General Lauri Sutela,

---

[200] Polvinen, *Paasikivi*,4, p.479.

[201] ibid., p.476.

[202] ibid., p.459.

[203] ibid., p.490.

[204] Paasikivi, *Päiväkirjat I*, pp.593 & 596–597 (entries of 7.4., 13.4., and 14.4.1948). It received a two-thirds majority and not the five-sixths majority such a constitutional change might have been expected to demand. The author is grateful to Antero Jyränki for a discussion on this aspect.

[205] The Finnish National Coalition Party M.P. Arvi Ahmavaara could not but agree with Paasikivi that Parliament should not be given *carte blanche* to discuss the results of the negotiations but that these results should simply be *presented* to Parliament. Paasikivi, *Päiväkirjat I*, p.597 (entry of 14.4.1948).

[206] Polvinen, *Paasikivi*, 4, p.485.

found three stages in Finnish military defence under the treaty: doing it oneself, doing it with Soviet military aid, and doing it with the Soviet forces.[207] However, at this point in the narrative, it is worth recording that by this time the Finnish military had already worked out another—and quite contrary—set of operations.

The Triumph of Finnish Presidential Power

In his diary entry of 14 April 1948, J.K. Paasikivi wrote as follows in connection with the handling of the treaty with the Soviet Union:

"It has become clear to the Finnish nation and to the whole world that we would rather be without such a treaty if circumstances allowed it."[208]

Yet his action in continuing to negotiate the treaty (known as one of Friendship, Cooperation and Mutual Assistance—the FCMA) represented a triumph against his own doubts and those of the majority of the country's party political groupings and, additionally, their manipulation even when he, too, actually shared their doubts. Nor was this all. Presidential government not merely triumphed over Parliament, but also over parliamentary government. The prime minister was Mauno Pekkala of the SKDL, who, prompted by leading Finnish Communists, had, off his own bat and without instructions from Paasikivi, spoken of the need to enter into a defensive alliance with the Soviet Union in the autumn of 1947, and done so both in discussions in Finland and in the Soviet Union itself.[209] The concluding of a firm defensive alliance with the Soviet Union was held by the Finnish Communist leaders to be a move that would redound to the credit, in Soviet eyes, of the SKDL (Pekkala was a member of the SKDL) and of Communism in Finland. Discussions with Zhdanov of this kind had gone on already on 30 June 1947 and were to continue on 9 January 1948.[210] Pekkala continued to try to take "a party line" in private discussions with Molotov as late as 26 March 1948,[211] but by this time it was too late. The politically-diverse Finnish delegation that Pekkala claimed to fear had won the battle in the negotiations, irrespective of

---

[207] *Parlamentaarinen puolustuskomitea*, 1970, pp.1–2.

[208] Paasikivi, *Päiväkirjat*, I, p.597 (entry of 14.4.1948).

[209] Polvinen, *Paasikivi*, 4, pp.419–427.

[210] ibid., pp.418 & 437. Kimmo Rentola, *Niin kylmää että poltaa*, Keuruu 1997, p.26. Rentola stresses that this was meant to have a significance in electoral politics for the SKDL, but also in "state appointments."

[211] ibid., pp.471–472.It seems to have been a solo venture, unknown to the other SKDL negotiators.

the fact that most of them viewed the treaty with reluctance, and Pekkala and the Communists were apparently hot for it.

Pekkala's position was all the more complicated since on 28.10.1947 he had not told the government's foreign affairs committee that he had already discussed a military alliance with the Russians.[212] In spite of his timorousness, however, Pekkala had been following the Finnish line. A few months later, in the statement referred to above and recorded in his diary,[213] Paasikivi had lied, saying that it was the Soviet Union that had taken the initiative for the treaty: "the initiative has come from the Soviet Union." In fact, in the heady period of the fall of German power and in the first months of postwar Allied friendship, it had been the Finns who had seemed to take the initiative for a treaty with the Soviet Union to be called a "defence alliance," and had at least seized the opportunity provided by Zhdanov in response to Mannerheim's clumsy attempts to keep his coastal artillery. Those Finns included, as well as Mannerheim, Paasikivi and Heinrichs.[214]

What was even more significant was the fact that Paasikivi's confidant, ex-President K.J. Ståhlberg, had also supported such a "defence alliance"–and as late as 26 April 1946.[215] This had an enormous importance for Paasikivi since he claimed to believe that the ex-President "had never made a mistake."[216] This belief was a somewhat strange one since, in the 1920 Tartu discussions between Finland and Soviet Russia, Paasikivi was for more territorial concessions than the then President Ståhlberg would grant and in 1939 Ståhlberg was not for territorial concessions at all, while Paasikivi believed in the necessity for more territorial concessions than the Finnish government would grant. But now, the late 1940s, it did not take long for Ståhlberg to reverse to his traditional view, that of his old party, the Progressives. He urged that the "Soviet request" for a treaty be ignored in the increasing antagonism between the West and the Soviet Union.[217] Once again, Paasikivi ignored the advice of his confidant. But this may be said–that Ståhlberg embodied for Paasikivi what Paasikivi in 1947–1948 did not really want. However, by 1947-1948 times had changed. It was to take till 1992 before the country was to get rid of the burden.

---

[212] Polvinen, *Paasikivi* 4, p.421.

[213] Note 177, this chap.

[214] Polvinen, *Paasikivi* 4, pp.35–40.

[215] Paasikivi, *Päiväkirja*, I, p.299 (entry of 26.4.1946 -admittedly Ståhlberg then made the same reservations that were later to be incorporated in Paasikivi's treaty). Model, article 3 of the Molotov-Kuusinen treaty!

[216] J.O.Söderhjelm, *Kolme matkaa Moskovaan*, Helsinki, (Kirjayhtymä), p.113.

[217] Polvinen, *Paasikivi*,4, p.437.

What was characteristic of Paasikivi was nonetheless his capacity for holding conversations with the wise. He hand-picked his cronies and he hand-picked those who negotiated for Finland with the Soviet leaders in 1947-1948. Thus, he dropped Lennart Heljas from the negotiating machine and put Kekkonen in his place, though Heljas was the choice of the Agrarians [218]and Kekkonen was being kicked upstairs by this party to the "neutral" position of the speaker of Parliament. Kekkonen's role as a key negotiator with the Soviet leaders was a fateful choice, for the third executive was to serve him well.

But Paasikivi had tried to serve him well, too. In the internal political crisis of the spring of 1947, when the government looked as if it was breaking apart, Paasikivi offered him either the post of prime minister or minister of justice, though for the former post, Sakari Tuomioja of the Progressive Party was the first choice, and one promoted even by Kekkonen. Neither was yet to serve, however, as premier nor even as a minister and the weak SKDL prime minister Pekkala continued in office, though he had already given in his resignation.[219]

The Relation of Forces

In terms of history as a linkage between political personalities in leading positions, the role of Paasikivi as an indicator of a successor called Kekkonen must seem clear enough. But in 1947 Paasikivi was wrestling with representatives of several parliamentary parties to secure a working government. For a prime minister of that government, Paasikivi went from Tuomioja (Progressive), to Kekkonen (Agrarian), then to Fagerholm (SDP), and finally back to Pekkala (SKDL). The SKDL did not want Tuomioja, the Social Democrats did not want Kekkonen, they were split as to whether they could accept Fagerholm, and *faute de mieux* Paasikivi was back with Pekkala, whom the Social Democrats did not want.[220]

But the internal splitting of a party that occurred in the Social Democratic Party over Fagerholm also occurred in the Agrarian Union over Kekkonen. And this could also be connected with the relegation of Paasikivi's old party, the National Coalition Party. The cause was the same: the existence of the old forces that the war-guilt trials of the venerable leaders of yester-year had not succeeded in extirpating. The past, the recent past, had to be renounced—even Tuomioja was tainted by his association with the Brothers-in-Arms of the

[218] Söderhjelm, op.cit., p.116, says this was partly because Kekkonen was a jurist: this may have been Paasikivi's excuse.
[219] Juhani Suomi, *Vonkamies. Urho Kekkonen 1944–1950*, Helsinki (Otava), 1988, pp.295–299.
[220] ibid., pp.293–296.

wartime fighting men's coalition.[221] A pluralism existed in Finland, but it was not legitimate as far as relations with the Soviet Union were concerned.

The source of government was Parliament, but Parliament was in one sense crippled by the belief of so many of its members in the legitimacy of the old order. This was akin to the situation in Parliament in the 1920s, when, for example, the Swedish People's Party and the Social Democrats, followed for several years a self-denying ordinance of not going into government, though it might be offered. But since the Finnish constitution was flexible to the extent of allowing non-parliamentarians to be accepted into ministerial office, the question arises as to why the importance of parliamentary government should be observed. The question can be answered in two ways. Without parliamentary government, there might have been more extra-parliamentary activity than had already arisen (strikes and meetings in the town-square). From another point of view, it has to be said that parliamentary support for the postwar status quo was a vital matter for the Soviet Union, whose own aim was the direction of Finnish society towards a friendly approach to the Soviet state and society (the security treaty, after all, was one of "Friendship"). This policy *ultimately* compelled the Soviet Union towards a policy of acceptance of Finnish constitutionalism. But it took time: many decades of time.

The policy required restraint on the part of Parliament. A number of those who did not like the Friendship Treaty abstained from voting against it and were prevailed upon to watch their talk.[222]

In this way the presidential power attained for the passage of the treaty the majority of two-thirds of the parliamentary vote for the passage of more permanent legislation, while at the same time satisfying the Soviet agenda that national support for the treaty would be evident. A certain link began to be formed between Soviet needs and Finnish constitutionalism. But many of those who had voted for it in Parliament felt that they were faced with a *fait accompli.*[223] The chairman, of the National Coalition Party, Arvo Salminen, felt that a rejection of the treaty would open a breach between Parliament and Presidency.[224]

This link was fostered, too, by statements made directly to the citizenry by the Finnish leadership over the next few years. Immediately after the signing of the treaty, Paasikivi, in a radio speech of 9 April 1948, assured the nation

---

[221] ibid., p.296.

[222] Paasikivi, *Päiväkirjat,* I, pp.596 & 604, (entries of 14.4.1948 & 28.4.1948). The treaty was ratified by Parliament by 157 to 11 votes. Thirty-two M.P.s did not turn up on that day.

[223] For the Agrarian Party's line to this effect, note Paasikivi, *Päiväkirjat,* I,p.604, (entry of 28.4.1948).

[224] ibid., p.604,(entry of 28.4.1948).

that if an attack on the Soviet Union through Finland was to occur, then *in the first place* it was the Finns' duty to defend their own land: we do it anyway.

The treaty became "understood" as an adjunct to Finnish self-defence.[225] Kekkonen, in his turn, in an article in the Agrarian journal *Kyntäjä* ("The Ploughman") in 1952 urged its readers to think "in a Finnish way," which meant that it was to the Finns' advantage if the Soviet Union helped them to defend their own country.[226] The basic idea of these and other statements was to make the treaty "Finnish." They were direct appeals to the people that cut through reservations expressed in the press and the grudging acquiescence of a number of parliamentarians.

In spite of the adoption of the treaty, tension between Finland and the Soviet Union did not initially disappear in its entirety. The treaty was, in fact, being used by its would-be protagonists from the Finnish non-Communist camp as a buffer to fend off Soviet interference in the *internal* politics of Finland. This was quite legitimate in terms of the treaty itself since article 6 defined for the "High Contracting Parties" a policy of "non-interference in the internal affairs of the other state." The reverse of this was that in foreign-security matters there might be cooperation (articles 1 & 2) In this connection, it represented a message of reassurance to the Soviet Union that—if the crunch came between the West and the Soviet Union—the Finns would, should circumstance so require, not let the West in and even fight the West back. However! From the exigencies of their recent wars, the Finns had developed a talent for switching sides, though, as a later work was to point out, this might turn out to be a "double-edged sword."[227] Here was the rub.

While the treaty was only one instrument in Finnish-Soviet relations, having accepted Finnish constitutionalism, the Soviet Union had to pay the price. It became driven to take some kind of a stand towards the very *internal* politics it had committed itself to be aloof from. The Soviet government needed assurance that the successive Finnish governments would honour the treaty if the need arose *as an instrument of foreign-security policy.* Parliamentary politics in Finland had its own momentum, due partly to the fact that the electoral process did not produce a one-party majority—ever except in the low-poll year of 1916—hence all governments tended to be at best unsteady coalitions. In this scenario, deals were made and unmade and the

---

[225] Paasikivi, collection of speeches,*Paasikiven linja,* 1956, pp.114–118.

[226] The article is mentioned by Ahti Karjalainen in "Maalaisliiton viides vuosikymmen" in *Herăävä maaseutu,* VI,1956 p.251.

[227] Those already "in the know" about Finnish matters will realize that the reference here is the work by Pertti Joenniemi and Jaakko Blomberg, *Kaksiteräinen miekka* ("The Double-edged Sword."),Helsinki (Tammi), 1971.On pp.25 & 92, the authors expressed their reservations about using the treaty for a "defence of neutrality."

governments engendered by Parliament often led the ship of state on to rocky shoals. From this point of view, the Finns gave the Soviet Marxist concept of "the relation of forces" a tough time.

The question then arises as to why the Soviet Union should bother, since the presidential power would back the treaty in any case. The answer to this conundrum lies in the War Guilt trials, which continued to cast their shadow, though already held and the selected culprits imprisoned. But would the old gang and its sympathisers gradually come back?

In Jul 1948, a new government was formed by K.A. Fagerholm, a middle-of-the roader from the Social Democratic Party, and it was a minority government only, a matter that did not stand well with the Soviet commentators on Finnish affairs. A crisis began to develop in Finnish-Soviet relations. Looking back on this crisis in 1972, the Finnish peace researcher Raimo Väyrynen, postulated the idea that the Soviet commentators did not so much object to Fagerholm himself as to the other ministers of his government, several of whom had, in Soviet eyes, a shady past associated with their wartime views.[228] Nonetheless, Väyrynen himself showed that Fagerholm was dismissed negatively by the commentators as "Tanner's apprentice," too.[229] The irony of all this is that in the establishment of the Fagerholm government President Paasikivi offered the SKDL posts in the new government, but, considering their electoral losses, that party claimed a great deal, the ministry of the interior, a deputy foreign minister's post and yet a third ministry. At this point, the power of the Soviet Union, stridently expressed in the Soviet press, could not compensate for the electoral losses of the SKDL. The latter were now living and working in a milieu in which constitutionalism set the rules.

But Fagerholm's government *was* a minority government. At one point he tried to get over this by taking in the Agrarians, whose relations with the SKDL were worsening, but equally the Agrarian feeling that Fagerholm was disfavouring agriculture made them draw back, while a section of the Agrarian Union would still have preferred an alliance with the SKDL.[230] There was no way of reconstituting the Big Three (SKDL,SDP, and Agrarians), but yet Fagerholm's government hung on for twenty months. He received support from the national Coalition Party in his attempts to bridle the costs of agriculture, and from the SKDL when he sought to develop the ARAVA system of lending state funds at a cheaper credit rate for the building of flats

---

[228] Raimo Väyrynen, *Conflicts in Finnish-Soviet Relations:Three Comparative Case Studies,* Tampere(Acta Universitatis Tamperensis, ser.A. vol.47),1972, p.117.

[229] ibid., p.225.

[230] ibid., p.188.

for ownership in mainly urban centres.[231] These votes and operations belonged, too, to the workings of Finnish democracy called cross-voting.

Be that as it may, Finnish democracy throughout the 1950s was far from distinguishing itself by the workings of its democracy. The treaty with the Soviet Union that should have put its foreign and defence policy on a clear footing became rapidly entangled in the question of which political groups could be relied on to follow it. When Norway and Denmark joined NATO in 1949, this impacted negatively on the position of Finland from the point of view of Soviet commentators. In the end the important trade between Finland and the Soviet Union came to a standstill, and in consequence, after the re-election of Paasikivi to the presidency in 1950, Fagerholm found it impossible to go on and impossible to widen his minority government. In Soviet eyes, Finnish politics had become tainted by the threat of "the old gang" coming back in one form or another. This did not help the National Coalition Party to enter any government, nor did it make the position of the Social Democrats all that much easier since the more the party became unified (as attempted under the Fagerholm government) the greater the danger of Soviet suspicions arising about the secret power of the Tannerites. As for the SKDL, once the Soviet government had endorsed Finnish constitutionalism any direct intervention by some kind of main force from the Soviet side became a very improbable option.[232] This left only one big Finnish party still in the picture, namely the Agrarian Union. Even, the Agrarian Union was divided, however.

The older end of this party would not have been averse to seeing the Fagerholm government fall and in its place a new government of the non-Left parties established.[233] But such a government, *without* the National Coalition Party plus the smaller bourgeois parties, would not have had a majority; it would have been as weak as Fagerholm's government. But *with* the National Coalition Party, such a government would have run the risk of bringing "the old gang" back once more.

However, a new line was developing in the Agrarian Union. This became known as the "K-line" after the initials of three of its leading members: Arvo Korsimo, the unscrupulous Agrarian Union organizer, Urho Kekkonen, the unscrupulous front figure, and Ahti Karjalainen, Kekkonen's dogged supporter. Within its party, the K-line began to triumph and in its triumph

---

[231] Lehtinen,*Fagerholm*. pp.171–172 & p.176.

[232] Juhani Suomi, op.cit., p.386 tells how on returning from Moscow in November 1948 the chairman of the Finnish Communist Party, Aimo Aaltonen, recounted that the Soviet Union was not inclined to seek the overthrow of the Fagerholm government at that point of time, at any rate. Were they waiting for better?

[233] ibid., p.405.

made its mark upon Finland, a mark that the country has, in part, retained to this day.

Agraria

In an informative article published in the Agrarian Union's series entitled *Herääväa maaseutu* in 1956, Ahti Karjalainen pointed proudly to the quiet success of both his party and of Finnish agriculture. He mentioned that between 1945 and 1955, party membership had increased more than seven-fold to 253,000 in the latter year, while the conviction of the "extreme Left"(the SKDL) that *they* were to be "the new faces" in post-1944 Finnish politics had been set at naught.[234] However, the Agrarian Union, a party mainly of smallholders, had succeeded in renewing itself to seize the opportunities at hand. The party claimed to be intensely democratic and not inclined to engage in strikes and street violence as sections of the Left did.[235] But in its own way it was ruthless enough with an organizing secretary, in Arvo Korsimo, who has been described as a "strong-willed, intriguing, cunning countryman."[236]

But in these features Korsimo was matched by the man he supported as the future front-runner of the party, Dr.Urho Kekkonen (the doctorate was in law). But Kekkonen played his politics as a countryman, too.

At the turn of the forties and fifties, he was affirming that the "Agrarian Union is the only party that pushes for the countryside."[237] But this was not then true. For the Social Democratic Party, in the days of the hated crofter regime, had worked hard to get rid of it. And after the Second World War, the SDP had a smallholder wing led by two knowledgeable figures, Matti Lepistö and Hannes Tiainen. In certain respects their outlook, to be based on the potentiality of the smallholder, was not dissimilar to that of the Agrarians. But the shades of difference did have a significance, with the SDP gurus emphasizing a preference for dairying, the possibility of a growth in cheese exports, the production of fodder in the homeland, and a straight denial of the value of trying to cultivate corn up north (hardly a vote-wining proposition, rational though it was),the need for restraint in the payment of export bounties (hardly a vote-winning proposition either) and a closer

---

[234] Karjalainen, op.cit., p.241.

[235] ibid., p.252.

[236] Kalle Kaihari, *Ratkaiseva ääni*, Espoo (Weilin & Göös), 1981, p.58.

[237] Juhani Suomi, *Vonkamies*, p.440.

relationship to the wood industry.[238] The SKDL were also interested in the farming population's great number of smallholders, particularly in areas like Kainuu in the north-east of Finland, where the Agrarian Union clashed with the so-called "backwoods Communism" (*korpikommunismi*).

And it was this area that was Urho Kekkonen's electoral stamping ground. In short, Kekkonen, both as a local and a national figure, had to take on the Social Democratic Party and the SKDL. In his electoral campaigns therefore, he found a joint grievance by lumping these two parties together as barely-concealed proponents of land nationalization.[239] By the turn of the decade, the Communists and their allies had gone quiet on this and they expressed sympathy for many Agrarian attitudes.[240] The SDP, it is true, while in favour of sawmills and forest areas in common, was also a defender of the private ownership of forests, too.[241]

For election purposes, Kekkonen lumped the SDP and the SKDL together as the protagonists of land nationalization. Unfair to both parties, Kekkonen widened his call to speak for the maintenance of democracy, and opposition to both Social Democracy and People's Democracy.[242] However, this sterling pronouncement was only a beginning. For though it might seem that Kekkonen and K-line would in consequence find allies in the non-Socialist forces, an inherent danger in this solution lay in the too dominant position of the National Coalition Party and its traditions in any possible coalition with the Agrarians.[243] Further, the K-line was a reformist attempt within the Agrarian Union, in respect of which the Right-wing of the Union were sceptical. In the background of that party still lurked the figures of Tyko Reinikka and Anssi Kukkonen, who had now served their war-guilt sentences. Essentially therefore the K-line adherents had to indulge to a certain degree in eclectic politics, seeking allies whence it could. This was reciprocated. When Kekkonen and the other members of his party (Sukselainen and T.N.Vilhula, who were not K-line men) were negotiating in the summer of 1949 with the bourgeois parties, it did not escape the attention of the leading Communist, Hertta Kuusinen, that there was a *section* of the Agrarian Union, with whom

---

[238] Matti Lepistö,*Maataloutemme ajan puntarissa*, Helsinki, 1948, esp.pp.19,20,31 47–49, & 51-52.

[239] Juhani Suomi, *Vonkamies*, p.441.

[240] The SKDL did not like the Fagerholm government's reduction of the price of butter and milk in June 1949. ibid., p.411.

[241] ibid., pp.44 & 52.

[242] ibid., p.439.

[243] ibid., p.410.

cooperation might be possible. That section also showed some interest in cooperation with the SKDL.[244]

This farrago of attitudes and political potentialities was part of the Finnish postwar reconstruction. Who were to be the new faces? Who could make the switch from being German-friendly to Russian-friendly, without selling the Finnish system down? The pattern of government by coalition afforded manifold opportunities for a kaleidoscope of parties, providing the "old hands" were kept out. But in a coalition, one party is dominant until the break occurs. Since in the seven years between March 1950 and March 1956, there were seven governments in Finland, and five of them were headed by Urho Kekkonen, it is clear enough that the Agrarian Party, whatever its internal dissensions, was on the way to becoming the dominant party in Finnish coalition politics. Since 65% of the population in 1948 were living in the Finnish countryside,[245] these politics represented an economic conservatism, which the adherents of the National Coalition Party and many of those in the urban working-class resented as a loss of capital for more productive sectors of the economy, because a striking fact of Finnish agriculture was the extent of its subsidization. Since that part of the population living on or in connection with agriculture was high, and well organized, what was being represented appeared to be a national force. To the other 35% of the population, the sustaining force of Finnish agriculture, namely subsidization, was sold like this; it kept food prices low, which was a benefit to the urban worker as well as being an anti-inflationary policy. If it did not occur, then wage increases were inevitable, and tended to be escalatory.[246] If matters were to be argued out, at, say, the "grass-roots level," it could be that while the taxes that paid the subsidies were progressive, the food prices were not and thus benefited the middling tax-payers. The question was also one of how much the highest tax-payers actually paid per individual and how much the total amount of their taxation came to. There was another way of looking at things, too. It was the amount of labour employed in agriculture, then still a somewhat labour-intensive branch of the economy. But, equally, it may be argued that the more capital going into industry (at that time) the more workplaces there were created. And, above all, the argument was rarely put that food could more cheaply be imported from abroad than grown at home. When this argument *was* put, it was readily dismissed on grounds of national security.

---

[244] ibid., pp.407–408.

[245] Lepistö, op.cit., p.42

[246] Karjalainen, op.cit., p.259.

The Fagerholm government left office in March 1950. It had become the custom in Finland to reconstitute government after a presidential election and Paasikivi, in the same month, had been re-elected to the presidency. Fagerholm's administration had been beset by enemies—the Soviet press, the SKDL (particularly in the trade union movement where it controlled seven important unions)[247] and the Agrarian Union. In 1949, the extra-parliamentary activities (strikes) of the workers at Kemi resulted in clashes with the police that led to the deaths of two workers. Paasikivi was prepared to back a new government that would include the SKDL, in short, a return, if possible, to the Big Three, a government, he hoped, that would be favourably seen by the Soviet Union.[248]

He entrusted this task to the speaker of Parliament, Urho Kekkonen, whose star was now rising in his own party in consequence of the apparent neglect of agriculture by the previous government. But Kekkonen was unable to reconstitute the Big Three, largely because of the antagonism between the SDP and the SKDL, even though Fagerholm himself showed an initial inclination to join an Agrarian-led government.[249] In the end, President Paasikivi gave Kekkonen the mandate to form a government on different lines—which Kekkonen did. It was another minority government, this time of Agrarians, Progressives, and Swedish People's Party members, with one non-party minister, the foreign minister, Åke Gartz. The Soviet Union had now to put up with the antagonisms—and rapprochements—of the Finnish political parties. But in this party-political scenario, they had seemingly found an anchor-man in the new prime minister, Urho Kekkonen, for on his becoming premier, the Soviet press toned down its critique of Finland.[250] What is of equal importance in the scenario is the coalescing of interests in Finland, and the consequent formation of governments however temporary they were, that is, the workability of a system in spite of the intense vulnerability of those who took over power. As noted above, Fagerholm had received occasional support from the National Coalition Party in opposition, even sometimes from the Agrarians in opposition, and, most remarkably, from the SKDL. And in the wings, as the first Kekkonen government was to show, were those smaller parties, which came along to help out for their own price tag.

---

[247] Lauri Hyvämäki, "Valtioneuvosto toisen maailmansodan jälkeen vuoteen 1957" in *Valtioneuvoston historia 1917–1966*, II, Helsinki (Valtion painatuskeskus), 1977, p.344.

[248] ibid., p.347.

[249] ibid., p.463.

[250] Raimo Väyrynen, op.cit., p.210, believes that the advent of the Kekkonen government in March 1950 ended the 1948–1950 crisis in Finnish-Soviet relations. For a more cautious though positive view, Juhani Suomi, *Kuningastie*, Helsinki (Otava), 1990, p.39.

The Triumph of Agraria

Being prime minister five times in the 1950s, Urho Kekkonen then became president. This period has been named by Kekkonen's biographer and with reference to his hero, "the royal road," but the biographer himself shows that this term was used to describe also the progress of the *Agrarian Party's* road to power.[251] The latter was a quite distinctive phenomenon in European twentieth century political life, for it represented a triumph of the country over the town. Since Kekkonen emerged as one of the most striking personalities in Finnish politics, there has been a tendency to see his success in terms of the success of a ruthless politician, who nevertheless had great bargaining skills. Rarely was a politician so disliked in Finland and even more so when he became president.[252] Yet his capacity for staying the course in spite of the antagonism of opinion surrounding him was remarkable. It was easy to see Finnish politics in terms of "anything but Kekkonen," a negativity that hid an even greater negativity, however.

For his success was enabled by the twisted nature of the relation of forces in the country as a whole.

In Finland, by this time, a certain settling-down in politics after the signing of the security treaty with the Soviet Union had brought on—paradoxically—a great degree of confusion. *Within* many of the political forces, both inside and outside Parliament, opposition reared its head. Kekkonen himself has been described as essentially a politician of the opposition.[253] That meant being in opposition, too, to the traditional leadership of his own party, which, from 1943 onwards, disliked Kekkonen's—often solo—toying with peace projects, his growing stand-off from wartime party coalitions, and in the postwar period, backed by the organizational skills of Arvo Korsimo, his increasing control at the grass-roots level of the party. As in other parties, there existed in the traditional postwar leadership of the Agrarian Union a strong reflection of wartime patriotism that was difficult for many to relinquish—as they felt Kekkonen *was* relinquishing it by tacking to the former enemy who had come dangerously over the border. And there was something more, a partly-hidden, half-understood change in the nature of Agraria, manifest by

[251] Juhani Suomi, *Kuningastie* ("the royal road"). For the reference to the Agrarian Party, p. 274, where one of Kekkonen's principal enemies, Väinö Leskinen of the SDP, described "the royal road " as one of Kekkonen's "and the Agrarian Party."

[252] When the author of the present text arrived in Finland in 1958, he was confronted by negative remarks about Kekkonen along the lines of "we have always had presidents we could admire here—until Kekkonen came along" (fil.lis. Katri Oksanen, who summed up for many of certain political persuasions).

[253] Juhani Suomi, *Vonkamies,* 480.

the re-settlement of the Karelian evacuees in the rest of Finland, farmers who were essentially smallholders, a class whose future Kekkonen determined to champion in several ways not always congenial to those who farmed the larger units of land in Western Finland.

The re-settlement of the evacuees up and down Finland was an act of social justice, but it did not necessarily reflect the maximization of agricultural productive capacities. The question of alternatives rapidly resolved itself into the question of where the dispossessed Karelian smallholders were to get their new parcel of land—from existing cultivated or uncultivated lands of the larger estates or from forest land owned by big timber companies, the state, or the church, and hack out from the wilderness a tract of land as the pioneers so greatly admired by the nineteenth -century poet Runeberg had done.[254] The preference seems to have been for the former way.

In truth, before the involvement of Finland in the Second World War, an intelligent Conservative called Bruno Suviranta had produced, in the mid-1930s, a scheme for the economic development of Finland that would have linked urban expansion to a more dynamic agriculture than that of peasant farming. In his scenario, the feared-for flight from the countryside should not be feared but welcomed, for industry would then increase in the towns while the growing urban population would provide a wider market for Finnish agricultural produce, leading thereby to the creation of ever-larger agricultural units, which in turn would mean cheaper food. [255]But after the wars, a scenario of this kind had no chance of realization. The wars had hindered building work in the towns, the city of Viipuri had been lost, and a housing shortage prevailed in the larger urban areas, where compulsory tenants were foisted on those having any spare space in their flats or houses. In contrast, those who were resettled on the land were capable of building their own homes by cutting down the timber that always existed behind the Finnish farm.[256] The stage was set for a smallholders' democracy over vast tracts of Finland.

The legacy of war confirmed the destiny of the Agrarian Party to be a leading force in Finland. But the conviction of destiny, in the form in which it emerged, took its time to work through the party, for it did not directly arise from the party. An external force was working upon the party, in fact, two

---

[254] As in his poem *Saarijärven Paavo.*

[255] Johannes Virolainen in his article "Näkökohtia maanhankintalain toimeempanossa," *Kansantalousaikakauskirja,* 2/1946, p.150, gives a succinct account of Suviranta's plan, which he did not himself endorse, preferring the establishment of small factories in the countryside for the development of a market: ibid., p.147.

[256] ibid., p.169;Virolainen maintains that the smallholders could secure 40% of their own housing costs.

external forces. The first was the force of President Paasikivi, who, even when competing with Kekkonen in the 1950 presidential election, regarded him as his successor.[257] Was this but a trial -run for Kekkonen? In fact, the phenomenon called Kekkonen had become a creation of presidential power. Kekkonen was minister of justice in Paasikivi's first postwar government, and, as Hyvämäki emphasized, had supported Paasikivi's view of the necessity of the war-guilt trials and been a key figure in the negotiating process with the Soviet Union for a security treaty. The fact that Kekkonen was "kicked upstairs" to be speaker of Parliament from 1948–1950, partly as a result of the jealousy of his opponents within the Agrarian Union so as to get him off the party-political scene,[258] was hardly a matter that could diminish Paasikivi's evaluation of his merits, for Paasikivi, too, had been a figure reviled by his own party. Above all, Kekkonen shared Paasikivi's view of the necessity of working well with Russia. In short, the needs and power of two executives were functioning already in the Kekkonen case, the Finnish presidency and the perception of the Finnish presidency of what the Soviet executive expected of Finland. Lest at this point, the angered reader will cry "Finlandization," let the author of the present text immediately make an assertion later to be proved: that both countries in their relations influenced each other.

In any case, it is worth emphasizing that Kekkonen had formed his five governments in the early 1950s at the instigation of presidential power, according to the Finnish constitution's way of doing things. The problems of these governments were not caused by the Soviet government, but by the intransigent nature of the relation of forces within Finland.

It has been noted that the Agrarian Union itself was divided in its reactions to the legacy of wartime, epitomized not so much by defeat as by the imposition of war-guilt trials afterwards.

But the divisions within the Agrarian Union were even so less painful than those of the Left where officially for several years, three parties (the SKDL and SKP were in a sense, but not completely two-in-one) and the third, the SDP, was riven into two and more groups, while outside the parties the trade union movement, the SAK, played its own policy between them all. Yet the SKDL had been an attempt, on the Communist side, to form a united party of the Left (with an invitation originally to the Agrarians to join in). What its formation had, however, led to was the siphoning off from the Social Democratic Party of its more radical members so that the gulf deepened between the Communists and the Social Democrats. This was in party terms, while at the grass-roots in the trade unions at the workplace Communists and

---

[257] Lauri Hyvämäki, op.cit., p.350.

[258] Juhani Suomi, *Vonkamies*, pp.374–376. Kekkonen had wanted to be chairman of his party.

Social Democrats were driven to cooperate over labour-practices and wage demands. Such practical politics strengthened the power of the extra-parliamentary over-arching organization of the unions, the SAK, loosely structured as it nevertheless was. A Left-led government had difficulty in resisting the claims for attention projected by the SAK and it member-unions. Fagerholm as prime minister produced a 7.5 % wage increase for them and on leaving office in the spring of 1950 negotiated with the employers a further wage increase for the trade unionists,[259] the government of the day being a mere by-stander. But the government of the day was now the government of the Agrarian prime minister, Urho Kekkonen, whose party demanded in consequence compensation in the form of higher prices for milk and butter and protested at the low price they were paid for the corn they grew.[260] Though this first government of Kekkonen's contained an expert minister of Right-wing outlook (Åke Gartz) and members of the centrist parties as well as Agrarians, it did not contain a representative of the National Coalition Party, whose disbelief in the impossibility of the government's stabilization policy led that party to propose a vote of no-confidence. True to their growing urban outlook, the Social Democrats voted with the National Coalition Party against the government—which was saved, however, by the SKDL's voting in favour of the Kekkonen government.[261]This was a classic example of the division of the Left. A spiralling of prices continued and Kekkonen's second government (17.1.1951–20.9.1951) witnessed an attempted rapprochement with the Social Democratic position with leading Social Democrats as ministers. This government tried to work on a policy of reconciling, in part by extra-parliamentary negotiations with labour-market organizations and those of agriculture, the diverse interests of the country. Characteristically, though the SKDL vote had saved Kekkonen's previous government, they were not represented in his second government, nor were their great enemies, the National Coalition Party. Over the whole country, however, a fragile "peace of the castle" (*linnanrauha*, a kind of executive agreement sponsored by the government with the interest-group organizations) prevailed.[262] This paved the way for Kekkonen's third government (20.9.1951–9.7.1953), primarily based on Agrarians and Social Democrats (as the previous government) with a sprinkling of centrists. The government had the initial advantage of the short boom in the timber trade produced by the Korean War, but as the Korean War wound down by 1953 the demand for timber, especially in Britain,

---

[259] Juhani Suomi, *Kuningastie*, pp. 22 & 34.
[260] ibid., pp. 25 & 42–43.
[261] Hyvämäki, op.cit., p.361.
[262] ibid., pp.369–370.

slackened. To maintain exports, Kekkonen proposed in place of the devaluation wanted by industry, a stiff deflationary programme that would have involved not merely cuts in social security but also rather severe wage cuts. Neither the Social Democrats nor the National Coalition Party in opposition would endure this, the latter simply because it was in their opinion not workable, the former on grounds of the injustice of such a one-sided share-out policy of unequal sacrifices.[263] At root was the old conflict between town and country, between industry and agriculture. But, in fact, the two drafters of the K-plan, by which the deflationary policy was laid out, were not Agrarians. They were Teuvo Aura and Sakari Tuomioja, members of the Progressive Party, who had formerly served in Kekkonen governments, and it can only be assumed that their proposed wage cuts and cuts in the social security budget, industry taxation, and so forth, were easier to suggest than cuts in agriculture as well as having a more immediate application than a policy of tinkering with agriculture. But, in any case, the suspicious Kekkonen conceived that they had suggested a plan to get rid of himself.[264] As it turned out, neither the conservative National Coalition Party nor the Social Democrats, let alone the Communists, would join a new government. For the moment, Kekkonen, in his fourth government (9.7.–17.11. 1953), soldiered on with his own party, a handful of Centrists, and a professional or two, including Aura!

The triumph of agraria had thus brought Finland, by the mid-fifties, into a situation in which the practice of politics was becoming a set of bargainings with temporary adjustments and reversals, often in an atmosphere of betrayal. It is small wonder that Lauri Hyvämäki wrote, in connection with the additional budget for agriculture in Kekkonen's second government of "the doubling of the agricultural milliards,"[265] while in his third government—with the SDP—the latter, as times worsened, refused to accept the proposed policy of wage cuts and the government fell.[266] In this nerve-wracking period, Kekkonen himself was often ill, but he was nevertheless one of the few figures in politics who sought to divine a way out of the constant storm and stress of governing his nation.

An Alternative Economics

Kekkonen's ingenious character had, after warning the Agrarian interests of the threat of land nationalization from the Left, nonetheless come to the

---

[263] ibid., pp.393–394.
[264] Juhani Suomi, *Kuningastie*, pp.254–255.
[265] Hyvämäki, op.cit., p.368.
[266] ibid., pp.393–394.

conclusion that the nationalization of certain branches of the economy, the telephone services and the chemists' shops, had something to recommend it, on grounds of either efficiency or social justice. The latter of these plans would have been frustrated by the Right at the committee stage.

But, undaunted, Kekkonen did not abandon his belief that state-power could do far more for Finland's industrial development. Yet this was not to occur by nationalization of existing industry. Instead, Kekkonen produced a blue-print in 1952 for state industry that would be *supplementary* to existing industry and would arise only when private industry could not cope. It was, first of all, a matter of the old problem of capitalization; the state could, apparently, find the wherewithal more easily than private enterprise; it could tax, decree a compulsory loan from the citizenry, float its own companies on the share market, gather money by setting a cap on consumption for a couple of years (not cutting existing consumption but preventing a temporary growth in it—in short, wage restraint presumably), or, since reparations would be finally paid off in 1953 (Soteva payments) use the money saved for industrial expansion.[267]

But how was it that private industry was falling short? Kekkonen had to admit that (in 1952 when he published his book) exports were doing well (the Korean War), but this was only stimulating consumer demand and an extension of social security, while many voices were urging that there was too much investment in the country.[268] Kekkonen, on the contrary, felt that far more investment was needed, in part because consumer demand was stimulating the inflation that began at the end of 1944 when the Bank of Finland printed excess note issues to get by.[269] In the midst of the political wrangling of which he and his group were part consequence and part cause, Kekkonen looked to the creation of a more stable economic future for his country.

Industry, he believed, was in a "key position," but he also had to acknowledge that agriculture was the greatest source of livelihood in the country.[270] Neither he nor his party would ever want to imagine that a replacement of agriculture by industry was in mind—so that the potential conundrum between these two standpoints was strangled at birth by an explanation along the lines that industry and agriculture should draw more closely together. This meant the mechanization of agriculture justified by *more*

---

[267] Urho Kekkonen, *Onko maallamme malttia vaurastua?* Helsinki (Otava), 1952 (2nd.ed.), pp.13 & 121-124.
[268] ibid., pp.51-53 & 59-60.
[269] ibid., p.17.
[270] ibid., pp. 35 & 43.

fields for the smallholder—and *better* fields for the smallholder with field-drains instead of open ditches, and the boulders excavated or just blown away. Industry, however, was not simply a helping hand for the field work. It was itself to be placed among the fields and forests and by the waterside, for the schemes that Kekkonen wished to see realized were intended to be promoted in the north of the country, the two administrative provinces of Lapland and Oulu, being, according to Kekkonen, brimful of unexploited "natural resources." [271] First of all, this meant harnessing the great rivers of the north, Kemijoki and Oulujoki, for the creation of a sufficiency of hydro-electric power. This was the task of the state and after it had been accomplished private enterprise was welcome to move in, for the aim of this act of state power was the creation of energy for industry, agriculture, and populace and not the creation of an economic monopoly for the state itself.[272]

But monopoly was a heady word in Finnish politics, especially when Kekkonen and his phalanx were under assessment. For the attainment of the invigorating of the back-country was not going to be a straightforward act. It had a lot to do with political will and, under the conditions pertaining in the Finland of the 1950s, the office-holder who could best exercise that will was the president. The way to the presidency was not, after all, a royal road; it was a way fraught with pitfalls and many fractious forces waiting to subdue the progress of the hopeful. But Kekkonen wanted the exercise of the presidential power, which could come dangerously close to the power of a monopoly, once it began to be exercised over the relation of forces.

The Presidential Election of 1956

Even before the election occurred in March 1956, Kekkonen was able to manipulate the relation of forces. He had been five times prime minister and once, in the Törngren government of 5.5.-20.10.1954, he served in the important post of foreign minister. Paasikivi had more or less designated him as a successor in the presidency, though hardly being consistent in his attitude to Kekkonen.[273] The election took place in the electoral college of 300 electors chosen by the people and there were to be three ballots unless a candidate received a simple majority in the first ballot. Kekkonen received 88 votes (his own party) on the first ballot and thus proceeded to the second ballot, which was to choose the two candidates with the highest scores, Kekkonen receiving 102 but Fagerholm(SDP) receiving 114. This second ballot was a product of

[271] ibid., p.97.
[272] ibid., p.128.
[273] see note 275.

strategic voting, which knocked out the "dark horse" candidate Paasikivi who had received in this ballot 85 votes (Paasikivi was not in the first ballot and was introduced into the second ballot as a potential Condorcet winner).[274] Then, in the third ballot, more strategic voting (in which electors changed their previous voting pattern) Kekkonen won by 151 to Fagerholm's 149. In this decisive third ballot, the 88 Agrarian electors were joined by the 56 SKDL electors (thus making 144), while the Finnish National Party had already agreed with Kekkonen that 5 of their voters would vote for him (thus making 149) and Verner Korsbäck of the Swedish People's Party, an old acquaintance of Kekkonen's and Penna Tervo of the Social Democratic Party made up the final two third -ballot votes for Kekkonen (total 151). Thus Kekkonen became a winner as a result of strategic voting.

This tricky situation emerged through an exploitation of a complex balloting system in the course of which certain electors changed their ballot-stand in return for a promise of favours to be received: the Finnish National Party, led by Professor Kaitila, changed votes in the final ballot in exchange for a promise of two ministerial posts in the next government (they only got one, but two in the following government of the Agrarian V.J. Sukselainen), while Verner Korsbäck of the Swedish People's Party had to wait till 1962 for his post. Penna Tervo of the SDP seems to have urged the SDP electors to vote throughout for Fagerholm, while he himself on the final ballot switched to Kekkonen.[275]

The SKDL under Hertta Kuusinen played a devious power-game. The "dark horse" in the second ballot, the then president J.K.Paasikivi, seems to have believed that the 56 SKDL electors would vote for him along with the National Coalition Party [276]—curious, but this was Finnish politics. In the event, the SKDL did not vote for him, but split their votes between Kekkonen and Fagerholm in the second ballot and then in the third ballot voting for

[274] In a three-barrelled electoral system, each ballot produces a majority winner, but in the final ballot the "dark horse" introduced in the second ballot becomes the winner in the third ballot. On this, see the section on the Marquis de Condorcet in *The Cambridge Dictionary of Philosophy*, 2nd.ed.,Cambridge (C.U.P.), 1999, p.172.

[275] On the politics of Kaitila and Tervo in this election, see Tuomo Polvinen,*J.K.Paasikivi. Valtiomiehentyö,. 5, 1948–1956*, Helsinki (WSOY), 2003, pp.251–252. Tervo was killed in a car crash a week after the vote so the prospect of any *quid pro quo* he carried with him to his death, but Kaihari, op.cit., p.110, states that Tervo did not take a reward, but was motivated by a belief in the need to return to "Red-Earth" politics, i.e. a governmental coalition between the SDP and the Agrarian Union.

[276] Some of the National Coalition Party electors were, however, afraid that if they succeeded in voting Paasikivi back in, then Kekkonen would remain as prime minister—a clear statement of how they anti-Kekkonen forces were strongly motivated by considerations of internal policy. Rentola, *Niin kylmää että poltaa*, p.392.

Kekkonen in their entirety, to secure his election, as part of a policy considered fitfully over several years as Kekkonen seemed to be the leading politician from the non-Socialist camp least likely to give the Soviet Union trouble.[277] But this SKDL politics has yet another aspect. For the Soviet Union itself would have been prepared, initially, to see the 85-year old President Paasikivi re-elected as candidate drawing in a wide support across the political spectrum and having a firm conviction in the necessity of friendship between Finland and the Soviet Union. The aim was to prevent Tanner or a Tannerite from running. Presumably, it was the persuasive power of the SKDL (Hertta Kuusinen?) that helped to bring this change of attitude whereby the Soviet Union accepted the wisdom of the Finnish SKDL and decided to show Kekkonen their favour. On the other hand, the Communists did not make their final decision to vote for Kekkonen rather than Paasikivi until the evening before the election and after a worried Kustaa Vilkuna had told Viktor Vladimirov (KGB) of his concern that the SKDL might vote for Paasikivi.[278] No doubt, too, the influence of the KGB men on the ground in Helsinki helped this switch in the Soviet outlook and that of the Finnish Communists.[279] Above all, the influence of the new general-secretary of the Soviet Communist Party, Nikita Krushchev, was a key factor in the Soviet support for Kekkonen rather than Paasikivi, after which the Finnish Agrarian position, which had briefly warmed to Paasikivi as an all-party candidate, swung back to Kekkonen, too,[280] thus pulling the Communists with them.[281] Right to the end, the Communists alleged that they would have been prepared to run with the SDP a joint candidate of the Left, another "dark horse" such as Onni Peltonen or Penna Tervo of the SDP. All that happened was that this served as an exculpation for their voting for Kekkonen instead since the SDP wanted nothing to do with this scheme of things.[282]

A certain lability was in evidence even in the Soviet position, which, simply said, may be understood as to some degree arising from the complications of Finland's own many-sided party relationships and political antagonisms. The key to the Soviet fears lay in their obsession to prevent the return to political power of Väinö Tanner or a Tannerite such as Väinö Leskinen: the SDP candidate, K.A. Fagerholm, actually a middle-of-the roader, was equally distrusted as a front-man for the Tannerites. This was something

---

[277] Juhani Suomi, *Kuningastie,* p.89, tells how in November 1950, it was the SKDL votes who saved Kekkonen's first govermment on a vote of no-confidence.

[278] Rentola, *Niin kylmää että poltaa . .,* pp.405–406.

[279] ibid.,pp.395–397.

[280] ibid., pp.405–407.

[281] ibid., p.406.

[282] ibid., pp.500 & 588.

of a misconception, since Tanner himself might even have preferred Kekkonen as president rather than Fagerholm.[283] It was so difficult to know, as the post-election crisis in Finnish-Soviet relations was soon to reveal. However, the Soviet diplomats and KGB men in Helsinki did a fair amount of work in their endeavours to clarify the situation. They even, in the pre-election period, went to talk to the National Coalition Party on various aspects of Finnish affairs, including Finnish participation in the Nordic Council and the forthcoming presidential election in respect of which the National Coalition Party tried to make the point that their presidential candidate, Sakari Tuomioja, actually a Progressive, did not have views on relations with the Soviet Union that were different from the front-runners in the presidential campaign—to which the Russian guests replied that they knew *already* how Paasikivi and Kekkonen felt about the Russian connection, but Tuomioja. . .[284] The expression of these doubts and the preferences between which the Russian visitors indicated they might make *their* choice have been seen by Rentola as a sign of the impress of the 1948 security treaty between Finland and Russia.[285] But they might equally be seen, *nemine contradicente,* even more fundamentally as an expression of the wishes of the foreign executive that did not want an adverse change in the politics on its borders and was, in consequence, *carefully endeavouring to come to terms with a diverse set of political forces there.*

But in Finland, the ultimate triumph in the presidential election of Urho Kekkonen was regarded by many to have occurred by the operations of sleight of hand. To adapt the poet's line: *buying and selling we do use our powers.* The placemen were around and a collapse of dignity was occurring on many sides: the moralistic National Coalition M.P., Margit Borg-Sundman spat in the face of Verner Korsbäck, whom, it was believed, had sold his vote for a ministry.[286] The ins-and -outs of strategic voting as evinced in the deceptive result of the second ballot—which put Fagerholm in the lead—were not perhaps immediately grasped by the voters but were to be left to the sharper reflections of subsequent pundits.[287] For the straightforward in politics, another later statement may have more relevance: the loser Fagerholm's words as quoted by Kaihari, "I am glad that my election did not occur on bought votes." In honesty, it is, however, also necessary to quote a bit more of what he said

---

[283] Kaihari, op.cit., p.67.

[284] Rentola, *Niin kylmää että poltaa . .,* p.395.

[285] ibid., p.41.

[286] Juhani Suomi, *Kuningastie,* p.497.

[287] Hannu Nurmi,"On Rationality and Legitimacy of Voting Procedures" in *Rationality and Legitimacy Essays in Political Theory,* ed. Dag Anckar et al., Helsinki (The Finnish Political Science Association), 1992, esp. pp.143–144.

about the result: "I believe that it was the best from the point of view of the country."[288]

Consequences

But doubt about the result of the presidential election—and the way that result arose—was to persist. A feeling of dissatisfaction haunted many Finns as they thought of their state-power. The question of who switched votes or offered to do so became an obsessional question as the years went by. Kekkonen himself took part in the revelations and in 1974 admitted that the National Coalition elector, Niilo Kosola, (the son of the quondam leader of the Lapua movement),had let him see his ballot paper. It was marked "Kekkonen." Kosola denied that he had done so,[289] but in the third Fagerholm government (29.8.1958–13.1.1959) this not-too-well known politician became a minister. Rentola believes that only two or three of the Finnish National Party electors actually voted for Kekkonen (not 5, let alone 7).[290] One of the "suspects" actually denied it.[291] Juhani Suomi has thus regarded the question of the "vote-switchers" as a "weak theory,"[292] but at any rate there were several possible and Kekkonen could not have been elected without some of them.

As Suomi, *inter alia,* indicates, the key fact was that the Communists, in the second ballot, engaged in a strategic vote that knocked out the "dark horse" Paasikivi, so that in the third ballot only Fagerholm and Kekkonen were left—and the odd "vote switchers" did the rest. Yet, irony of ironies, even at the period just before the second ballot the Communists (SKDL) would have been prepared to vote, *with the SDP,* for a joint candidate[293]—presumably Fagerholm—who might then have won with 170 votes.[294] This was yet another example of the ineptitude of the Finnish Left, the Socialism of which had fallen away with the demise of a nationalization programme.

For the non-Socialist sector of the Finnish community (Agrarians apart), the Communist vote for Kekkonen was yet another sign of an unhappy transition in Finnish politics. But the SKDL was not taken into the government, following Kekkonen's narrow presidential success. Six governments were to pass before the fateful third government of Fagerholm

---

288 Quoted by Kaihari, p.95.

289 Juhani Suomi, *Kuningastie,* p.499

290 Rentola, *Niin kylmää että poltaa . .,* p.403.

291 Juhani Suomi, *Kuningastie,* p.499.

292 ibid., p.500.

293 ibid., p.500.

294 It is, of course, possible that even with a joint Left candidate some of SKDL and SDP electors might still have cast a vote for Kekkonen.

set up in August 1958, and though the SKDL ferociously joined in the labour disputes that started almost immediately upon the election of Kekkonen to the presidency, these disputes, particularly at the grass-roots in conjunction with SDP trade unionists, remained almost a thing apart from the Kekkonen presidency and the country's parliamentary government. As far as the latter's functioning was concerned, parliamentary government from the end of November 1957 to the end of August 1958 was in abeyance and the two governments formed were headed, respectively, by the head of the Bank of Finland and the head of the Supreme Administrative Court, all ministers in these governments being professional men. In consequence of the "share-out" of national resources between the urban and agricultural interests, the country had been thrown into an inflationary situation that professionals sought to handle by retrenchment. Politically, the Social Democratic Party began to buckle under the strain. A section of that party, representing the trade union interest and more favourable now to doing a deal with the Agrarians, entered the reconstructed government of V.J. Sukselainen in the autumn of 1957 though this government lasted only a little under three months.

What is interesting is that throughout this period of instability of government after the election of President Kekkonen, the Soviet government and the Soviet media did not exploit the Kekkonen presidency, though they had taken the step of backing him against Paasikivi in 1956 and Kekkonen had come to power by the help of the votes of the extreme Left. It was a fact, too, that the von Fieandt caretaker government, which lasted for almost five months in 1957–1958, was an extremely severe example of the Rightist retrenchment outlook. Alternatively, however, this government had been set up after the failure to establish a government composed of Agrarians, SDP oppositionists, and members from the SKDL[295] In short, the Soviet line may have been to wait patiently for the gradual introduction of the Communists into the government. But this Soviet quiescence came to an end on the formation of the third Fagerholm government on 29 August 1958.

Then the sins of the previous six governments (1956–1958) were suddenly remembered, though in all governments were Agrarians or professionals of Agrarian disposition, in short, Kekkonen's party. What were these sins? The country had been trading westwards, while trade with the Soviet Union was unbalanced—the Finns were not importing enough. The question was a wide one as the first attempts at Western European integration were now occurring.[296] Other points were raised, too, especially those connected with the

---

[295] Rentola, *Niin kylmää että poltaa*, . .,p.456.

[296] Raimo Väyrynen, *Conflicts in Finnish-Soviet Relations*, Tampere (Acta Universitatis Tamperensis:Ser.A, vol.47), 1972, pp.84–87.

expression of opinion—the publication in Finland of books that could be regarded as anti-Soviet or of a delicate nature[297] and the refusal to grant a visa to the grand old man of Finnish Communism, Otto Wille Kuusinen, now living in exile in the Soviet Union, but wishing once more to visit the old country. It was particularly unfair to throw this refusal at Fagerholm's head on the formation of his third government, since it had been the previous caretaker government Reino Kuuskoski (brought from the Supreme Administrative Court, to be prime minister for a while) which had taken the negative decision.[298] But the key factor in the crisis started by the Soviet Union was the nature of Fagerholm's third government.

There had been a general election in the summer of 1958 and the vote-winner was undoubtedly the SKDL, a party which won 50 seats out of 200. It was left out of Fagerholm's government coalition, which otherwise appeared to be something *in spe* of "a government of all the talents." This omission may not have been the cardinal sin, however, since the Soviet interest was now concentrated more and more upon the Agrarians as the reliable force in the Finnish system. They were certainly in the new government, but some of them were distinctly Rightist in outlook, especially the foreign minister, Johannes Virolainen, and Martti Miettunen, the minister of agriculture. The mortal sin was the appointment of two out of the four Social *Democrats*, Olavi Lindblom, the minister of communications and employment, and Väinö Leskinen, the minister of social affairs. These men were suspected of being Tannerites, and Leskinen had a distinct "Brothers-in-Arms" background.

The "night frost-crisis" in Finnish-Soviet relations began. The Soviet ambassador, Lebedev, was withdrawn and so, too, were Soviet credits for Finnish industry, while orders for shipping were suspended with the result that 4,000 workers from the Wärtsilä shipyard were laid off in December 1958.[299] The government had stuck it out for months, but in November the Agrarians began to break. On 14 November Martti Miettunen resigned and on 4 December the foreign minister Johannes Virolainen did likewise.[300] Miettunen, at first, had warned Kekkonen against having the Agrarians in the government, but had later gone in with Virolainen, for which he was to be

---

[297] This factor was mentioned by Urho Kekkonen in his broadcast of 10.12.1958. published in *Neutrality:the Finnish Position,* 1970, p.73. Kekkonen did not go into detail, but one of the works was Unto Parvilahti's *Beria's Gardens,*London (Hutchinson) 1959. Finnish edition: *Berijan tarhat,* Helsinki (Otava), 1957.

[298] Kimmo Rentola, *Niin kylmää että poltaa . .,* p.488.

[299] Raimo Väyrynen, op.cit., p.159.

[300] Krister Wahlbäck, *Mannerheimista Kekkoseen,* Porvoo-Helsinki (Werner Söderström), 1967, p. 272, & Rentola, *Niin kylmää että poltaa . .,* p.497.

blamed by Kekkonen and by the new prime minister V.J.Sukselainen.[301] Kekkonen was disturbed that the Agrarian Union as a whole was moving rightwards.[302] Was this, for the Soviet government, a portent of the future in which the Right would be strengthened by a gradually built up strengthening relationship between Tannerites, Agrarians (whom the Tannerites had previously been inclined to shun), and the National Coalition Party -now also in the government with four ministries? Kekkonen himself was aware of the fact that in the formation of the third Fagerholm government, Virolainen, the principal Agrarian participant in the government, and Päiviö Hetemäki of the National Coalition Party, had had their own discussions, behind his back.[303] In Soviet terms, Rightist forces were there in most of the major parties, and, unless balanced in a government by more moderate representation, they could easily transform the Finnish political scenario. It all went back to the war-guilt trials, and, as Krushchev was to put it crudely a little bit later, with reference to prime minister Fagerholm—behind whose "broad back . . . they saw Tanner and his supporters, Mr. Leskinen and others hostile to the Soviet Union."[304] Perhaps it was much more than that the Soviet commentators had in mind. For if the SKDL might be gradually introduced into a Finnish government, so also it was possible for other *gradual* changes to occur, such as a remoulding of the Agrarians by the anti-Kekkonen forces, within and without the Agrarian Union. The relation of forces was not to be understood merely in terms of one party's alignment with another, but in terms of a change in disposition, of a political mood that might run and spread through many parties, providing new opportunities. Apart from any other reasons, this was a natural feature in a politics that rested upon. temporary coalitions between the parties. In making the appropriate deals for a politics of this type, personalities, loyal to their parties, but expressing different shades of feeling and sympathies were of value, for the formation of the next coalition. But some parties had difficulty in handling operations of this kind. Soviet pressure after the defeat of Finland in 1944 had brought the Communists into parliamentary politics and thus had extended Finnish parliamentary democracy, but by 1958 it was beginning to look as if the Soviet Union could no longer harbour great expectations

[301] Juhani Suomi, *Kriisien aika. Urho Kekkonen 1956–1962,* Helsinki (Otava), 1992, pp.137, 152, & 161.

[302] ibid., p.138.

[303] ibid., pp. 143 & 152.

[304] N.S.Hrustsev, *Neuvostoliitto ja Pohjola,* Helsinki (Weilin & Göös), 1964, containing Krushchev's speech in honour of President Kekkonen given on the latter's visit to Leningrad on 23.1.1959. This reference was in stark contrast to the speech of welcome given to Fagerholm less than a year earlier on his visit to Moscow. ibid., pp.13–14.

from them. For they themselves had expected too much from the Finnish system, which then made the adequate shuffles to reject them.

Thus, the third, the foreign, executive had secured the dissolution of the second Finnish executive, the parliamentary government of a majority. It had not been enough to have a pro-Soviet figure in the Finnish first executive, the presidential power. President Kekkonen had not wanted the sort of government that had transpired (he said).[305] Yet the existence of this parliamentary-majority government was a felt need in a country that was badly divided over the Kekkonen presidency. For the Right bore with it a certain patriotic *cachet*. In extreme form, as the opposition-Social Democrat Emil Skog was later to say, "probably in all parties there were the brothers-in-arms, who looked[306] farther into the future." Reconciliation with this powerful undercurrent had not occurred and the current kept forcing its way to the surface.

The Kekkonen front had at its disposal other resources, however. In the latter part of 1958, the Soviet government behaved clumsily towards Finland, but contact points had been built up between the two states and, ultimately, between the three executives in this political scenario. One of the important links was to be played, as Kimmo Rentola has made clear, by the KGB.[307]

These frightening initials, for they were the initials of the Soviet secret service, had begun to constitute in Soviet-Finnish relations one of the more sophisticated arms of post-Stalin policy. As early at least as 1954, a number of KGB figures had begun to cultivate, wherever possible and profitable, members of a wide range of the parties making up the Finnish political spectrum. It has already been pointed out in this text that, in the run-up to the 1956 presidential election, S.T. Loginov, counsellor of the Soviet embassy, had listened to the views of National Coalition Party leaders about the election.[308] Loginov had also suggested at this time to his own deputy-foreign minister that the foreign ministers of Finland and the Soviet Union should consult regularly together.[309] Later, Mikhail Streltsov was talking to the young Kalevi Sorsa of the SDP, while the Agrarian Kustaa Vilkuna, at Vladimirov's say-so, performed the task of talking to Kalle Lehmus and Väinö Tanner, the latter being met in the National Museum.[310] Vladimirov, too, developed the idea of

---

305 Juhani Suomi, *Kriisien aika*, p.157. The chief organizer of the Agrarian Union, Arvo Korsimo, was even more upset, predicting dire foreign-policy consequences: Paavo Kähkölä et al., *Suomi k-limjalla*, Helsinki (Otava), 1974, p.127.

306 ibid., p.117.

307 Rentola, *Niin kylmää että poltaa . .*

308 note 284 of this chapter.

309 Rentola, *Niin kylmää että poltaa . .*, *p.395.*

310 ibid., pp.389–390.

consultation with the Finns over UN policy, particularly with respect to relations with China and problems of disarmament.[311]

The pursuit of such contacts and their ensuing discussions were also open to other states and both the United States and Britain were already engaging in them. But for the Soviet government this attempt to penetrate the minds of Finnish political leaders was much more of an attempt to create a system. Its clearest manifestation lay in the use of what came to be known as the *kotiryssä*, the Russian official whom you met in your home or in a restaurant and with whom, as a responsible person in your party or in the administration you talked politics.[312] It was a recognition on the Soviet side that their government had to come to terms with a *constitutional* state as gradually the Finnish Communists were learning to do. Since the political parties were being thus consulted, the second executive, the parliamentary government was being addressed–and not merely the presidential power of the first executive. A discursive process was going on in which the Soviet executive sought to persuade as well as bully. It was a piece of constitutionalism.

Alas, the Soviet leaders had not, as noted above, abandoned other tactics either. The losers in this interplay of the forceful and the convincing were the supporters of the Finnish Communist Party and the umbrella organization of the SKDL. They were gradually moving to the idea of coming to power by the strength of the parliamentary ballot-box and they had won, as noted, fifty seats in the 1958 parliamentary elections. In spite of this, and their support for Kekkonen at the last minute in the 1956 presidential election, they were not taken into the government either in 1956 or in 1958 or in January 1959 when the government was reconstituted in a way that satisfied both the dominant political force in Finland and the Soviet Union: a minority Agrarian government under V.J. Sukselainen was set up. It is certainly true that as the major party after the 1958 parliamentary election the SKDL had to be asked by Kekkonen to form a government. Eino Kilpi of the SKDL tried and failed: no other party wanted to serve with them. Hertta Kuusinen, a leading Communist in the SKDL, was angry that Kilpi had blown the chance: she had herself waited to be asked to do the job.[313] With Ville Pessi, she had less than a year previously told the Soviet ambassador Lebedev, in the government crisis of October 1957, that the Communists would soon be in the government and further a policy of industrialization when they got in.[314] Now, before the

[311] ibid., p.463.

[312] Juhani Paasivirta,defines this phenomenon well in the penultimate chapter of his *Suomi ja Eurooppa 1939–1956* Helsinki (Kirjayhtymä),1992, pp.459–460.

[313] Juhani Suomi, *Kriisien aika*, p.136.

[314] Rentola, *Niin kylmää että poltaa . .*, pp.451–452.

formation of the third Fagerholm government, the chief fixer of the Agrarian Union, Arvo Korsimo, had also promised Ambassador Lebedev that the SKDL was to be taken into the government and the ministry of labour might be given to one of their members.[315] Nothing happened and Lebedev did not appear to have pressed. Nor did Krushchev press in January 1959.

With the advent of the Sukselainen government at that point, the country was to endure minority government for the next seven years. The second executive, parliamentary government form, was damaged. The presidential governance was strengthening, but it could not rely on a majoritarian parliamentary government. It could more easily rely on the Soviet government and the Agrarians. The Finnish legislative organ was democratic in the sense that extremes of political opinion, whether of the extreme Left or the extreme Right, could be tolerated within its chamber and its committees. But it was powerless to form a government corresponding to its representation. The continuance of the Kekkonen presidency prevented this. Something had to be left out in the spectrum of the country's political forces. It happened to be the Communists. And, as is well known, constitutionalism can certainly endure without a democratic base, Communist or otherwise!

But constitutionalism is difficult nonetheless once your *representative system* is supposed to be an issuance of parliamentary democracy. The problems that arose were compounded of two factors. The political parties themselves had a hidden agenda, preventing their development as organs firm of purpose. In the Agrarian Union and in the Social Democratic Party a patriotic under-current kept flowing to the surface linking members of these two parties with the classical patriotism of the National Coalition Party. Since all majoritarian governments in Finland had to be coalitions, the under-current seemed to provide opportunities for further alignments that expressed, nonetheless, recently neglected tradition. The second factor was the disjunction between the first and second executives, that is, between presidential power and potential parliamentary government. The relationship did not work harmoniously and its corrosive edge lay in the matter of strategic voting for the presidential candidate. The Communists and the SKDL as a whole had switched their votes, left Paasikivi and gone for Kekkonen. But there was no reward for this at the governmental level, since Kekkonen was afraid of the non-constitutional elements in, and the non-constitutional element of, at least the Finnish Communist Party.[316] With respect to the relations between the

---

[315] ibid., p.612.

[316] ibid., p.463. Statements made by Frol Romanovich Kozlov,"the second man" in the Soviet system, concerning a Communist Party take-.over of Finland, were boldly revelatory and

presidency and a parliamentary government, Erik Lagerspetz has written of "the whole instability typical of post-war Finnish politics " as being due to the fact that "a coalition formed at one of the (political) dimensions could be broken by manipulating the other dimension."[317] It may, however, be that the situation has been worse than he has indicated. To reconstruct the embryo-theory, it could indeed be that the coalition at the top (presidential level) has sometimes prevented, *by its very existence,* the formation of government below.

Strategic voting had brought Kekkonen the presidency, but this voting pattern could not be reflected at the governmental level. In Parliament, the differences were fierce and here the un-genuineness of strategic voting, "preference misrepresentation," as it is sometimes correctly called,[318] came out all too clearly. Kekkonen had reneged on the pay-back for the SKDL vote, and thus cut himself off from 50 votes behind a formation of government, a self-denying ordinance, but had the Agrarian Union agreed and added 48 votes of their own to a government, then for a simple-majority based government a few votes of say the Swedish People's Party (they had won 14 in the 1958 election) would have been enough. But even if Kekkonen *had* agreed to start with the SKDL, the Agrarian Union would hardly have agreed to join such a government. Characteristic was the attitude of the new minority-government prime minister Sukselainen, who, relying on SKDL and TPSL[319] votes for the survival of his government, intrigued with the Right-wing of the SDP to form an alternative government.[320] Similarly, the former foreign minister, Johannes Virolainen, even spoke with the Soviet ambassador Zaharov about the possibility of a government between the Agrarians and the "third-line" SDP members (Social Democrats who stood between the Tannerites on the Right and the Skogists on the Left of that party), but Zaharov did not believe in the existence of an effective third line.[321] These people were afraid to act against Tanner and Leskinen, not wishing to see any further open divisions in their party. The essence of the situation was that the victory of Kekkonen in the presidential election had antagonized the Tanner-Leskinen faction to such a

---

contrasted clearly with Otto Wille Kuusinen's advice to the Finnish Communist Party to try to draw closer to the Social Democratic Party and not in haste: ibid, p.435.

On the other hand, the "penetration" politics of Marrti Malmberg of the Finnish Communist party seemed to be echoing the line taken by Kozlov: ibid., pp.453–454.

[317] Erik Lagerspetz, Essay on "The Theory of Social Choice," 2008, pp.13–14.

[318] Erik Lagerspetz, "Social Choice in the Real World," *Scandinavian Political Studies,* vol.16, no.1, 1993, p.14, uses this term. His essay is an informative analysis of the 1956 Finnish presidential election.

[319] The TPSL was a breakaway party from the SDP under the leadership of Emil Skog, claiming to represent the combined interests of trade unionists and smallholders.

[320] Juhani Suomi, *Kriisien aika,* pp.253–255.

[321] ibid., pp.256 & 266–268.

degree as to paralyse the workings of government formation, which was something to be talked about almost underhand. A consequence of strategic voting was an Agrarian president and Agrarian minority governments. Kekkonen himself, either from self-interest or sheer despair at the impossibility of change, refused to countenance the idea of holding new parliamentary elections.[322]

After the "night-frost crisis," in 1958, Kekkonen tried every so often to form majority governments from some of the existing political forces, basically from the National Coalition Party either with the Social Democrats, or else with the Agrarians or the smaller parties of the Centre.[323] No such back-up appeared possible for Kekkonen. And he had already ruled out, a government of the extreme Left.[324] Instead, the stage had to be set for the next presidential election.

The Second Round: the Consolidation of Presidential Power.

In spite of the difficulties Kekkonen was having with the parliamentary forces, he claimed that he wanted the support of Parliament throughout the period from 1959 to 1962,[325] though a majoritarian parliamentary government was not realized till 1962. What then did the presidential power want from Parliament, the backing of a Parliament that would give him no trouble or a parliamentary government strong enough to wrestle with him?

For many years both alternatives were impossible of fulfilment. An attempt was made in the late spring of 1960 to widen the Sukselainen government by a combination of National Coalition Party members on the Right, Swedish People's Party members and Finnish National Party members on the Centre, and TPSL members from the Left (a small party) as well as trade union members from outside Parliament. Such a government would have had a simple majority of 102 members, with the Agrarians, impossible for permanent legislation, which required a two-third majority, but certainly better than Sukselainen's minority Agrarian government. But the project crashed: the Swedish Party quarrelled with the number of ministries to be given to the TPSL. So Kekkonen's idea of a government composed of Right, Centre, and some part of the Left came to naught. In the previous year suggestions for governments on the basis of the SDP and Agrarian Union

---

322 ibid., p.259.

323 ibid., pp. 255, 300, 309, & 360. Neither the National Coalition Party nor the Swedish People's Party, let alone the SDP would treat these offers seriously.

324 For his view that he hoped for the decline of the TPSL, ibid., p.259.

325 ibid., pp.223, 300, & 360.

were frustrated, *inter alia*, by the fear of Viktor Vladimirov (the KGB man) that such governments would be dominated by the followers of Väinö Leskinen.[326] The SKDL were still out of the picture by Kekkonen's fiat, but any talk of a united Left government (a maximum of 98 votes) was also outlawed by the determination of most of the SDP to shun cooperation with the Communists. The first and the third executive consulted together, sharing the same disdain for the creation of a strong second executive, a parliamentary government.

The situation was compounded by the corruption of what parliamentary government there was. In the building of the Midwives' Training College (*kätilöopisto*) and the National Health Administration headquarters both the SDP and the Agrarian Union were engaged in shady practices. Prime minister Sukselainen and his whole government felt they had to resign in connection with the later issue even though the verdict was quashed on appeal.[327]

Yet it was in this period that one of the most momentous features in post-war Finnish external policy was launched, namely the entering of Finland into a working arrangement with the European Free Trade Agreement (EFTA). This was achieved, in 1961, by a special agreement known as FINEFTA, which safeguarded the peculiarities of Soviet-Finnish trade, while opening the markets of seven Western European countries to Finnish products when the seven began to reduce their tariffs between themselves. A result of hard Finnish bargaining both eastwards and westwards Finland took its first step into the developing European integrative process. From the Finnish side, the negotiating was done by Finnish diplomats, other officials and, above all, by the foreign minister—alternatively trade minister, Ahti Karjalainen, of the Sukselainen and Miettunen *minority* governments, *dominated* by the Agrarians. On 13 April 1962, Karjalainen, a key figure of the K-line, moved into the post of prime minister of a majority government, based on 112 seats in Parliament, of Agrarians, Swedish People's Party, National Coalition Party, and Finnish National Party.

Karjalainen's achievements were considerable. But he lived within the shadow of a greater political personality, the re-elected President Kekkonen. What this meant was that the presidency had now tamed Parliament, a long process that had begun in 1956. Kekkonen and the Agrarians had done this with the aid, whether begged for or just graciously received, from the third executive in Moscow, which, on 30 October 1961,had presented a note to the Finnish embassy there. Much time and energy has been spent on trying to find out whether or not Kekkonen himself or one of his henchmen, put in a

---

[326] ibid., pp. 256 & 266.

[327] Jaakko Hissa, "Ministeristöt ja hallituspolitiikka" in *Valtioneuvoston historia 1917–1966*, II, p.493.

request for such a note. Unless something turns up in the Soviet archives, there would seem to be little chance of getting any further with this question important though it is. Either way, the presentation of the note helped Kekkonen, for he was fighting for the presidency in the forthcoming 1962 election.

The note was something of an amalgam. Reading it, and the previous statements made in the name of Soviet and Finnish policy, there is adequate reason to assume that the case of Finland had become an excuse for a concern about an aspect of Soviet security. Since this matter took up a large part of the note, the problem arises as to how far the note to Finland was really intended to put Finnish issues to right. Kekkonen's avowed goal was to secure for Finland a firm recognition of Finnish neutrality. Such a policy hardly laid the grounds for statements about controversial aspects of world politics. But Soviet politicians and commentators were, on their side, exhibiting consternation about the revival of a *revanchist* Germany in the form of the Federal Republic of West Germany and its impingement on the Scandinavian and Baltic environment It is fair to say that, at least officially, Finnish politicians and pundits had not troubled themselves to give statements on this. What they had been doing was to try to get their country into a workable relationship with the European Free Trade Association, a negotiating task that consumed the energies of several leading Finns—not only Kekkonen—for a considerable period of time. What was actually contested from the Finnish side, in the tough negotiations with the Soviet side, was that by entering EFTA Finland was entering a trade bloc, which, in Soviet terms, could only be the precursor to joining a political bloc. In this sense, therefore, it was easy enough to infer that EFTA and the EEC (the European Economic Community) were, in effect, two sides of the same coin, and, *mutatis mutandis*, would fuse in future (which they did), and were a part of a wider Western resilience with a political content.

But looking into the crystal ball and telling what you saw was no help in the Finnish negotiations of the moment. Acceptance of a wider view had therefore to be on Soviet terms, and had to include a condemnation of the visit of the West German minister of defence, Franz-Josef Strauss, to Norway and the setting up of BALTAP, a joint command in the Baltic, by West Germany and Denmark.[328]

Preparations for BALTAP had, however, not disturbed Finnish decision-makers until the Soviet note of 30.10.1961. All this protestation could just about be squared with Finnish neutrality by using the argument that the hitherto stable environment of the North was being disturbed by West

---

[328] Urho Kekkonen, *Neutrality:the Finnish Position*, (speech of 19.11.1961), p.98.

German military pressure and that a policy of neutrality could prevent the North from further commitment to the Powers. Kekkonen's speeches at this time were interlaced with references to the traditional peaceableness of Northern Europe. In Krushchev's presence, he had described Finland as an unswerving "traditional Scandinavian democracy" and in the General Assembly of the UN referred to "our Scandinavian friends."[329]

It was left to the Soviet leadership to say what might happen to defend the peace of Scandinavia and the Baltic if the Scandinavian ethos failed and West German revanchism continued on its way, for in the final paragraph of the note there was a request for the opening of military consultations under the Finnish-Soviet Security Treaty. Now came Kekkonen's finest moment. Less than one month after the note was received, he travelled into the Soviet Union and half-way across Siberia to meet Krushchev and secured the *suspension* of military consultations. It was a brilliantly -devised solution by the one who devised it. For the solution contained a threat, not exactly *expressis verbis,* but the same kind of threat that is there in the suspended sentence of the courts.[330] On the other hand, the bulletin from Novosibirsk embodied Kekkonen's view that the starting of military consultations would worsen the atmosphere throughout Northern Europe.[331] Returning to Finland, the next day Kekkonen broadcast good news: "if the Soviet Union has no doubts about the Finnish attitude to foreign policy, it need not seek military assurances from Finland."[332]

Since, in the note, apparently in response to a request from the Finnish Communist Party, a piece was included criticizing the supporters of Kekkonen's principal opponent in the presidential election as a group "which put out unfriendly statements about the Soviet Union, in contradiction to the Peace Treaty and the Finnish-Soviet Security Treaty," then the Finnish voters could not do more than vote for Kekkonen if they wanted to avoid their country's falling into military consultations with the Soviet Union. The combination of forces behind the Chancellor of Justice Olavi Honka, the main alternative canddate for the presidency, simply collapsed after Novosibirsk. The SKDL candidate, chosen before the debacle, and certainly not a member of the Honka-group, still kept in the field, and a couple of Social Democrats, from either side of that broken party, but Kekkonen won

---

[329] ibid., speech of 4.9.1960 & speech of 19.10.1961, pp.84 & 95.

[330] Since there is no clear equivalent in Finnish to the verb "suspend" in this context, it is pertinent to point out that the Finnish verb "siirtää" as used in the Novosibirsk bulletin can also mean "postpone" or "transfer."

[331] A copy of this bulletin can be found in H.Peter Krosby's *Kekkosen linja,* Helsinki (Kirjayhtymä), 1978, pp.407–409.

[332] Kekkonen, *Neutrality: the Finnish Position,* Broadcast of 26.11.1961, p.103.

hands down. The attempt to breach the political deadlock between Parliament and President through a capture of the presidency by dissident parliamentarians had failed.

Rejection and Dejection

The forces that had latched together to form the Honka-front were at first sight a strange combination: Conservatives of the National Coalition Party, Social Democrats (who had invited Honka to run), Swedish People's Party members, Finnish National Party trimmers, and the break-away figure from the Agrarian Union, Veikko Vennamo. In Finnish terms, they were a mix from the bourgeois parties and those who still called themselves Socialists. This combination has previously been designated as a negative one, as simply being anti-Kekkonen, as if to say that the fault was with the man. And truly the speed with which Honka withdrew from the fight when Kekkonen hit back would seem to indicate a weakness at the high point of the oppositional construction in seeking to challenge an experienced politician with a chancellor of justice whose career had culminated in a series of practically-unchallengeable cautions.

However, the oppositional forces, with the exception of the Vennamo camp, did embody also deeply-felt aspirations for policy change. These aspirations might be expressed as industrial and urban, as opposed to agrarian and rural.

To rush immediately to the defence of Kekkonen, it must be said that by 1961 Finland's relationship to the European Free Trade Association had been resolved by Kekkonen and his negotiators. This, through the special FINEFTA agreement, kept the markets of Western Europe open to the principal Finnish exports those of the forest industries; timber, pulp, and paper. The FINEFTA achievement mounted by Kekkonen won several of the leaders of industry to his side, men who were, in general, even supporters of the National Coalition Party or of the Swedish People's Party. What the Honka-front had sought to project was a need for a wider industrialization of the country and not merely for the maintenance of the conditions by which the forest industries could go on exporting westwards. It was a question of the resources of the country and their utilization. With the exception once again of Vennamo, who had his own axe to grind, the Honka-front opposed the ethos upon which Kekkonen's agrarianism was built, namely that Finland could progress by peasant agriculture, a standpoint reaching back to Hannes Gebhard, a founding father of Agrarianism, and his belief that the smallholder would produce a larger yield per hectare than the estate owner, a standpoint containing a plenteous dose of the virtue of country life.[333]

The arguments of the anti-Agrarians derived from the conviction that rural life was dissipating the capital resources of Finland: the taxation of wage-labour in the towns and *ruukit*[334] was flowing in hand-outs (subsidies) to unprofitable farmers or to more profitable farmers who did not need them, with a resultant over-production of foodstuffs that had to be exported by the aid of export bounties.

Additional costs were to be found in the construction of roads to remote areas that had hitherto been off the beaten track, while roads to important commercial and industrial installations were being neglected.[335] Even worse, according to the critics, was the fact that as smallholding was becoming more and more uneconomic, the smaller units in agriculture became compensated for by chunks of forest land and the timber companies themselves were restricted from buying this land.[336] Loans were readily available for settlement in the countryside, while housing accommodation in the towns showed a shortfall.[337] The two housing programmes did not balance and migration to Sweden grew apace.[338] Yet the Agrarian programmes had been intended to populate the extensive tracts of Finland.

These economic realities did not always surface in the presidential election debates. But there was an even stronger passion flowing. Honka himself was considered to be a man of rigid integrity, whose task it had been to watch, as Chancellor of Justice, that mistakes in the etiquette of governmental politics were not being made. He had now become the head of a moral coalition, indeed of a moral majority in so far as the parliamentary forces behind him were added up.[339] Though Kekkonen claimed to be "president of all the Finns,"[340] in the summary of his sins, published a couple of years after the

---

[333] A hectarage of from 6–10 hectares was Gebhard's criterion. For a critique of this outlook, note the statements of the main organizer of the Honka-front, Ahti M.Salonen, *Linjat*, Helsinki (Tilgmann), 1972, p.138.

[334] These were industrial establishments in the countryside.

[335] Salonen, op.cit., p.177.

[336] ibid., pp.148 & 150.

[337] ibid., p.178.

[338] ibid., p.179.

[339] The author regrets that in his earlier work, *The Finnish Dilemma*, p.21, he made the mistake of assumimg that support for Honka was throughout insufficient to get him elected. The mistake was first pointed out to him by the Senior Librarian of the University of Turku, Ilmo Impivaara.

[340] Juhani Suomi, *Kriisien aika*, p.518,quots from Kekkonen an explanation that the president's active role for the nation comes forth when exceptional internal difficulties exist or when the country's foreign-political situation is endangered. In "normal times" when Parliament and

1962 election, he was accused of having favoured in the early years of his presidency the interests of his own party.[341] Actually, during these years, he quarrelled with a large section of his party, as was recounted a quarter of a century later, by a leading figure in the Agrarian Union and its successor, the Centre Party.

These quarrels revolved around the opposition within the Agrarian Union to the K-line, the policy of which, described in the words of the Agrarian Union organizer Arvo Korsimo, was "so far Left as to be frightening." But Korsimo was ready to be frightened and to see governments with the breakway Left of the SDP, the Skogists, even if the SKDL were to be ruled out. He began to list those members of the Agrarian Union who would support Kekkonen and made his own contact with Moscow. He even dreamt of putting the National Coalition Party into such a government—as long as the Tannerites of the SDP were kept out of it. His politics began to appear impossibly fanciful, his outlook curiously twisted and antagonistic to the grass-roots outlook in many parts of the country, and his personal behaviour unpleasant The party in many areas wanted Korsimo to go.[342]

To close ranks, Kekkonen began to rule through presidential government. It meant minority governments or governments of officials. Either way, the governments were mainly staffed by Agrarians. Majority government seemed impossible, for no other group went in willingly with the SKDL, and just to leave them out would have been considered by the Soviet side as discrimination of democratic forces and thereby contrary to the terms of the peace Treaty.[343] By showing his strength as a president, Kekkonen pulled his party together and satisfied the third executive, which then lambasted the Honka-front as secret Tannerites—and it broke up in the feeling that the country would be endangered if it came to power. Meanwhile, by his trips to Austria, another neutral state, and to the Nato lands of Norway, Britain, Canada, and the USA, Kekkonen showed his other face.

---

government were doing their job, the presidential power was only representative. Representative of what, it might be asked. A certain impossibility lies therein.

[341] Tuure Junnila, *Suomen taistelu turvallisuudestaaan ja puolueettomuudestaan*, Porvoo-Helsinki (WSOY), 1964, pp.116 & 121.

[342] Johannes Virolainen, *Vallankäyttö Kekkosen kaudella*, Helsinki (1986),pp.59,62, 71-72, & 113. It is worth bearing in mind nevertheless that in 1958 before the formation of the Fagerholm government, the Soviet ambassador had suggested the setting up of a government of all parties—including the National Coalition Party and the SKDL—but leaving out the Tannerites: ibid, p.111. In January 1959, Kekkonen wanted to put the SKDL and the Skogists in the government under Sukselainen:ibid., p.101.

[343] ibid., p.107.

The reader will recall that Fagerholm in losing the presidential election in 1956 was happy that he had not been elected on bought votes, while admitting that from the standpoint of the country the election of Kekkonen was a better choice.[344] Now, in 1962, it could even more clearly be seen that the struggle between morality and power had been won again by power.

That power was Soviet power, but the utilization of this power was also Finnish. A play between the balance of forces was evident on both the Soviet and the Finnish side. On the Soviet side, Krushchev had been, in 1957, victorious in his fight against the Molotov-Shepilov group of hard-liners[345], but the Soviet military represented a hard line of their own in insisting—till Novosibirsk—that consultations with Finland under article 2 of the Finnish-Soviet security treaty were necessary.

The suspension of such consultations in 1961 was a triumph of the Krushchev line. In itself, this would seem to have reinforced the *political* relationship between the two countries, as Kekkonen had argued, in his own personal explanation of what happened. But then, too, he followed this up by stressing that it was the primary task of the Finnish leadership, after Novosibirsk, to watch out for any deterioration in the Northern European and Baltic milieu that might require a resort to consultations under the treaty with the Soviet Union, a standpoint the Soviet authorities were later to call into question as an arrogation from the Finnish side.[346] In any case, the watchdog role was a military one!

As it turned out, Kekkonen was already in a bit of a fix with the military in his own country. He did not have the reputation of getting on well with the leadership of the armed forces, but he did have a positive relationship with the old warrior Wolf Halsti, who had urged him in the mid-fifties to strengthen the defences of northern Finland against a possible NATO thrust through Finnish Lapland towards Russia.[347] Rentola points out that Halsti followed the treaty, not assuming that the Soviet forces would invade Norway through Finland. A few years later Halsti was one of those who claimed to have indicated to Kekkonen that had the Finnish armed forces had better equipment, the Soviet generalship might have been unable to make such a stringent case for consultations in 1961.[348]

---

[344] note 288, this chapter.

[345] Virolainen, *Vallankäyttö Kekkosen kaudella*, p.77.

[346] Kekkonen,"Broadcast of 26.11.1961" in *Neutrality: the Finnish Position*, p.105. Max Jakobson, *Finnish Neutrality*, London (Hugh Evelyn), 1968, p.79. This view was contested by P.Krymov & K.Golovanov,"Finland's Foreign Policy," *International Affairs* (Moscow),October 1969.

[347] Rentola, *Niin kylmää että poltaa* . . pp.337–338.

[348] Discussion with Halsti at the Turku Historical Society meeting in the Turku Officers' Club some 25 years after the Note Crisis.

Halsti interpreted the 1948 security treaty straightforwardly as an obligation upon Finland in the terms in which it was written. Other military men were interpreting the scenario in a more complex fashion. In a work published in 1995, Ermei Kanninen, the former head of the general staff (1978-1982), quietly presented the idea that "our soldiers were of the opinion that our country should be defended in all directions."[349] His statement was made in connection with the Note Crisis. Kanninen had worked under General Kalle Heiskanen in the operative section. In Robert Brantberg's biography of Heiskanen, published in 2000, there are similar indications of previous defence plans against the East.[350]

Kekkonen himself sensed a certain confusion among the military. In 1961 the military leadership felt that they could not frustrate the Soviet request for consultations. The air defences of Finland were weak: if war came, NATO planes might attack the Soviet Union through Finnish air-space, which might lead in turn to a Soviet demand to strike through Finland into northern Norway.[351] Kekkonen did not want to let the army chiefs be carried away. He informed General Sakari Simelius, the commander of the defence forces, that the mood in many army circles was anti-Soviet.[352] The implication of this presidential caveat was that a closer relationship with the Soviet armed forces might be counter-productive. Kekkonen wanted, instead, to balance things out by confirming the treaty's *political* import and arguing with the Russians the need to lower tension in Northern Europe. In this, he sized up the international situation more adequately than his generals.

Tension on the military relationship with Russia was, however, to continue throughout the next two decades. Referring to the relationship in the early 1970s, Lauri Sutela, in a biography of himself published a few years ago, seems to have felt that the Soviet Union doubted whether the treaty would be honoured if it came to the crunch.[353] It is certainly true that throughout the sixties attempts had been made to improve the equipment deficiencies in the Finnish armed forces and this had included a successful endeavour to bridge the *lacunae* between the obligations imposed by the Finnish-Soviet security treaty and the limitations imposed by the peace treaty, a source of somewhat delicate negotiations to overcome British hesitations.[354]

---

[349] Ermei Kanninen, *Vuodet myrskyn varjossa*, Helsinki (Otava), 1995, p.139.

[350] Robert Brantberg, *Kylmä-Kalle*, Jyväskylä (Gummerus), 2000, p.203.

[351] Juhani Suomi, *Kriisien aika*, pp.480–481.

[352] ibid., p.510.

[353] Matti Lukkari, *Lauri Sutela. Puolustusvoimain komentaja*, Helsinki (Otava), 2003, p.150.

[354] The main military problem has been defined by Risto E.J. Penttilä, *Puolustuslinjat*, Helsinki (Otava), 1988, p.147, as a lack of adequate air support from the Finnish side, which, after the

All this notwithstanding, the Finnish position was to refuse to use the treaty to build up additional *institutional* structures with the Russians and to resist Soviet efforts to develop such structures.[355] This was, of course, the most delicate aspect of the relation of forces, the point at which the power of the last resort was to be employed

The Kekkonen policy therefore constituted a rejection of the would-be operations of the third executive, but in such a way that Kekkonen fenced with it in political terms. Before the 1961 Note, the Finnish military leadership, in August, had come to the conclusion that it would be impossible to resist a Soviet demand for military consultations under article 2 of the treaty.[356] Sutela has contested the idea that "the generals openly wanted consultations."[357] Perhaps not. But when feeling that they had no choice but to go along with the Soviet wishes, Kekkonen showed them that there was a choice. But he had to make it. He did make it, risking, however, the development of further weaknesses in the Finnish defences. He would not have the protocol that Stepanov wanted for a detailed application of the treaty.[358] Kekkonen was certainly inclined to give way on the proposal for joint staff talks later in the 1970s, but the then head of the armed forces, General Lauri Sutela, persuaded him to forget the idea.[359] So that by this time, the Finnish armed forces had recovered their panache, fortified, as Sutela admitted, by the increase of war material from the Soviet Union.

The third executive had failed in its aspirations to control a very deeply-felt element of the Finnish being, the name of which was, at best, "neutrality,"

Note Crisis, was to some extent resolved by the buying of MiG-21s from the Soviet Union, p.154. In this connection a political problem arose because the missile weaponry used in the MiGs was forbidden by article 6 of the 1947 peace treaty. The British took time to give way on this, p.156. In the English version of Penttilä's text, *Finland's Search for Security through Defence, 1944–1989,* London (Macmillan), 1991, note esp. pages 105–106.

[355] A decade after the Note Crisis, the Russsians were again expressing their dissatisfaction with Finnish air defence. Initially, this was a question of the absence of ground-to-air missiles to defend against NATO planes coming through Finnish air space to the Soviet Union: later Admiral V.A. Andrushkevitch offered forces for the defence of Lapland,while pointing out weaknesses in Finnish maritime defence.ibid.Kekkonen had to agree about air-defence missiles:ibid., Lukkari, op.cit., pp.151–155. The Soviet ambassador to Finland, Vladimir Stepanov, worked from 1974 onwards throughout the 1970s to try to get the Finns committed to more detailed discussions on the application of the treaty. He wanted a specific protocol drawn up on this. It did not occur, but in 1978 and onwards the defence minister Dmitri Ustinov raised the matter of joint manoeuvres between the forces of the two countries:,ibid., pp.169–186.

[356] Juhani Suomi, *Kriisien aika,* p4.81.

[357] Lukkari,op.cit., p.159.

[358] ibid., p.170

[359] ibid., pp.181–182.

for these military reservations were a form of politics. But there was a price to pay. Kekkonen had been incensed in the 1960s when he heard that defence courses were being taught in which the scenario was the repulsion of attacks on Lapland whether from the NATO or the Soviet side.[360] This might be termed "neutrality," too, or, as the author once dubbed it, the Finnish dilemma.

Consolidation

What was significant, however, about the attitude of Finnish and Russian decision-makers was that a sort of double-level understanding had emerged as a result of the pre-Note Crisis period. The Finnish military leaders had felt that they had to go along with a Soviet demand for consultations[361]

One national military arm understood the concerns of another national military arm. Similarly, Kekkonen and Krushschev had an understanding about avoiding further military measures. This as at the level of a civil understanding. One of Kekkonen's most important tasks was to maintain this kind of relationship with the Soviet government. He was to run into difficulties, particularly when Brezhnev came to power and the Russian military were able to renew their demands. On the other hand, within Finland a shift in the relation of forces had now occurred. The re-election of Kekkonen to the presidency in 1962 was a significant part of that shift. Consensual politics began in Finland. A mood developed before most Finns had a word to explain it.[362]

What was happening was that after the Note Crisis Kekkonen was able to close the gap between presidency and Parliament. After his presidential victory, in which the opposition had all but collapsed, he used his presidential power to pick and choose governments as he had done before, but now secure in the knowledge that the backing of a majority-based government need no

---

[360] Sakari Simelius, *Puolustusvoimien puolesta,* Porvoo-Helsinki (WSOY), 1983, p.251.

[361] Lukkari,op.cit., refers to the later opinion of Sutela according to which the Finnish generals did not really want consultations (see note 353). But in the Finnish outlook there is a phrase "pakon edessä" "circumstances compel" and this much may explain the Finnish generals'attitude.

[362] The concept came into more general use some ten years later at the time of the CSCE negotiations and conference in Finland. The term "laaja suostumus" "wide consent" was then concocted, but the Finnicization of the international word ("consensus") soon thereafter took over.

longer be a declared aspiration.[363] He was possessed of enough power to survey the whole system and take his time to make and unmake governments.

Fate was a great help. The principal source of opposition, the ageing Väinö Tanner of the old wing of the Social Democratic Party, retired from Parliament in 1962, the *summum malum* taking him in 1966. In the same year, a younger leader of the same stream, the "brother-in-arms" Socialist Väinö Leskinen, made his trip to Canossa (Moscow) in the same year. Apart from Vennamo, the only political force that had not accommodated to the new regime was the National Coalition Party—and even they supplied members to the 1962–1963 government of Ahti Karjalainen, though contesting the 1968 presidential election of 1968 as Vennamo did (separate candidatures). Significant, too, was the waning power of the great Agrarian fixer, Arvo Korsimo, who lost his secretaryship of the Agrarian Union in 1960, some 16-odd months before the Note Crisis, was compensated by a leading position in the new Neste Oil company and by a ministerial position (for two months)in the Sukselainen government (to the evident dislike of Sukselainen).[364] His relegation from active politics weakened the influence of the K-line in Agrarian Union politics. The name change of the party in 1964 to Centre Party was meant to widen the appeal of this political organization so as to be something more than a representative organ of smallholders, the outlook which the K-line had embodied.[365]

Kekkonen himself was engaged, as one might say, in seeking new friends, a successful endeavour that tended to diminish the need for his older K-line cronies. The steadfast support he had gained from his former colleague Ahti Karjalainen, who did a great deal of the negotiating for the FINEFTA agreement, which had kept open to Finnish exports many Western European lands, was a factor Kekkonen did not greatly bear in mind. Truly, Karjalainen headed a government from 1970–1971, but Kekkonen poured scorn on Karjalainen's well-known wish to be considered the heir apparent for the presidential office, and, in 1967, had preferred to appoint Mauno Koivisto[366] to the post of Head of the Bank of Finland. Koivisto was a Social Democrat.

From the point of view of the academic qualifications for this high office, there was not a great difference between these two men. Koivisto's doctorate

---

[363] Johannes Virolainen, *Vallankäyttö Kekkosen kaudella*, Helsinki (Otava), 1986, discounted the idea that in the period between the "night frost crisis" and the Note Crisis Kekkonen genuinely sought to work with majority governments as he claimed.

[364] ibid., p.140.

[365] The author remembers discussing the proposed name-change in the early 1960s with the veteran Agrarian Tyko Reinikka, who then tried to cast doubt on the whole idea, though he was not a member of the K-line faction.

[366] Virolainen, *Vallankäyttö Kekkosen kaudella*, p.236.

was in sociology, while Karjalainen's doctorate, though in economics, was not particularly distinguished. But Kekkonen was seeking new friends and a wider ambience. The K-line had claimed to be radical, even Left, though its origins were rooted in respect for the sterling qualities of the countryman with a hectare and a cow or two.

But by 1966 another Left had finally shown its head to lead a government—a Social Democratic Party that had received 55 seats in the general parliamentary election and which, with the SKDL (41 seats), was prepared to form a government with the Centre Party (49 seats). Leskinen had been to Canossa, but he was not taken into this government. Since in 1968, the Left parties did not field their own presidential candidate(s) but supported Kekkonen, this became a factor in Kekkonen's own closer identification with at any rate the Social Democrats than with his own party.[367] There was, indeed, a certain social reformist outlook in Kekkonen. And it might certainly come into play when the mildest of Socialist prime ministers (as the SDP's Rafael Paasio was) became prime minister from 1966–1968, and was followed by another cautious case, Mauno Koivisto, of the SDP, from 1968–1970.

In this period, the most striking change in the cultural atmosphere was the attempt to bring self-government to the universities, which originally, in the mode conceived by Hannu Tapani Klami of the Faculty of Law of the University of Turku, meant student rule. This was not realized in that form, but student representation throughout the organs of the university was introduced in Turku. In the University of Helsinki, reform was defeated by a caucus of professors. The President did nothing. Quite a lot of serious discussion took place about democracy at the workplace, but nothing serious occurred.

Yet Kekkonen did use his power. The power he used over the parliamentary government was the power he had to dissolve Parliament and the parliamentary government and call elections. Thus the almost three-year long government of the SDP prime minister Kalevi Sorsa, a coalition with a firm majority based on SDP and Centre Party cooperation, was dismissed in 1975 at the height of the successful hosting of the third stage of the CSCE conference in Finland.[368] It was followed by a five-month long non-party government—not much of a testimony to Finnish parliamentary democracy, but to the certainty of presidential power. The Centre Party popped up again in two brief governments led, not by the increasingly alcoholised Karjalainen,

---

[367] Virolainen, *Vallankäyttö Kekkosen kaudella*, pp. 270 &.301.

[368] ibid., pp.365–367.

but by the quietly-walking Martti Miettunen, the ex-governor of Lapland, and an old-time Agrarian: the big stick was in the hands of Kekkonen.

Kekkonen's power was drawn from the relationship he had developed with the Soviet state. The core of his power was in this. It was the Soviet state that formed the cement binding together Finnish political society which had hitherto been disjointed.[369] But Kekkonen was no lackey of the Soviet system. He tried to build upon the surety of the Soviet connection by linking his country up with the rest of the world and, in so doing, give comfort even to the troubled monolith itself.

Other Friends and Acquaintances

Since Kekkonen himself had become a substitute for military consultations (in spite of the insistent attempts of the Soviet military under the Brezhnev regime to engage in closer military cooperation with Finland), the question of the kind of Finnish parliamentary government he had to live with mattered less and less to him: majority, minority, or caretaker government. He could get the service he wanted from most sides and if he did not get it, then he could sack the government and get another.

For his trip to North America in 1961, had afforded him the chance to try for a policy that had the widest dimension; he was becoming a "Statesman for Peace."[370]On 19 October 1961, Kekkonen addressed the UN General Assembly on "Finland's Attitude to Problems of World Politics." In it, he defined the position of the Finns in the world as being that of "physicians rather than judges; it is not for us to pass judgement nor to condemn, it is rather to diagnose and to try to cure."[371] It was to take a bit of time for Kekkonen and his men to have the opportunity to practise their medicinal arts, but it should be noted straightway that Kekkonen's grandiose vision slotted neatly into an earlier Finnish statement, that of their UN ambassador Ralph Enckell, given on 12 December 1957, according to which for the Finns "East" and "West" could simply be regarded as geographical expressions. At this point, though the Finns were being prompted by the Russians to take a

---

[369] ibid., p.243 Virolainen makes two points:that Kekkonen was the guarantor of confidence in Finnish-Soviet relations and that without his complete support Finnish government formation would not have been possible. The present author puts these two points together.

[370] A book of essays with this title was ultimately published in 1975.*Urho Kekkonen. A Statesman for Peace*, ed. Keijo Korhonen, Helsinki (Otava), 1975

[371] Urho Kekkonen, *Neutrality*, p.94.

stand on Cold War politics, they were not going to do so.[372] Nor were they going to play anti-Soviet politics either. They were neutral.

The danger with neutrality and the policy pursued in its name lay in its escalatory spin-off. This was a curious phenomenon, particularly for Finland, whose new projects, drafted in the name of neutrality, aimed at de-escalation.[373] But what was de-escalation for Finland might turn out to be a hindrance to its neighbours' employment of would-be escalatory policies. The theory of Northern or Nordic Balance rested primarily upon the fact that Norway, Sweden, Denmark and Finland did not have nuclear weaponry on their soil, whereas, say, Soviet pressure on Finland, might result in Norwegian re-think about this, as the prime minister of Norway told Kekkonen before the Note Crisis. Prime Minister Einar Gerhardsen seemed even glad that changes in nuclear-weapon technology favoured Norway in this respect [374] When Kekkonen, in 1963, began to urge these neighbouring states to enter into a Nordic nuclear-free zone, he was, in the Norwegian view, upsetting this chance of ever threatening an aggressive turn in Soviet policy in the north by a response that pointed out that in these circumstances the Norwegian non-nuclear option might be abandoned. Such a Norwegian threat might even safeguard Finland from Soviet pressure. That's how the balance was said to work.[375]

Bearing all this in mind, another proposal of Kekkonen's, a couple of years later, ran into the same difficulties. He suggested to the Norwegians an agreement safeguarding the Finnish-Norwegian frontier from military action, a kind of neutralization of that frontier, which would prevent the building up of forces and equipment on either side of that frontier. This was aimed at reducing the need for military consultations with the Soviet Union in time of crisis. It may be connected with Kekkonen's concern about the NATO project of a Multi-Lateral Nuclear Force that would include West Germany, a change, indeed, in nuclear dispositions, that bore witness to the standpoint expressed by Gerhardsen to Kekkonen four years earlier. Once again, the Finnish approach was aiming at de-escalation, but in terms of neutrality an escalation seemed to be occurring that was putting Finland into an anti-NATO position,

---

[372] Maude, *The Finnish Dilemma*,p.138.

[373] ibid., p.70.

[374] Juhani Suomi, *Kriisien aika*, p.370.

[375] It is fair to say that the Northern or Nordic Balance analysis was not concretized by Arne Brundtland till the mid-1960s. *Cooperation and Conflict*, 2, 1966. This is not to deny the practical working of such a phenomenon before this.It is equally fair to say that another Norwegian, J.J.Holst,felt in 1963 that the Kekkonen scheme might prevent the siting of Soviet nukes on Finnish soil: Risto E.J.Penttilä, op.cit., English edition, p.113.

particularly as Kekkonen's criticism of the NATO MLN-Force was contained in a speech he gave at the Finnish Embassy in Moscow.[376] But this was the Finnish security problem. The country lay in-between.

Thus, in 1969, the Finnish military expert, Wolf Halsti, recommended that Finland should consider, if suitable circumstances arose, abandoning that part of Lapland adjacent to the Norwegian frontier for territorial compensation elsewhere,[377] presumably for part of the Karelian Isthmus, which Kekkonen himself longed to take back. Be that as it may, Kekkonen did not abandon his plans for seeking to circumvent, as it were, the tense conditions that might arise were Finland to find itself faced with an international military crisis. In 1978, he produced yet another version of his scheme for a Northern European nuclear-weapon -free zone.[378]

But by now he had tried to produce quite a lot more. Relaxing his relationship with what was left of the K-line men, Kekkonen had surrounded himself by a much wider fraternity, individuals who knew more of international politics than was contained in talks with Soviet officials. Max Jakobson, a newspaperman who had accompanied Kekkonen on his trip to the United States in 1961 before the Note Crisis, and Risto Hyvärinen, a former naval officer, who had spent a year at Princeton before taking his Ph.D in Finland, were truly men of international stature. It was the latter who put the former before Kekkonen's eyes in 1971 as a possible candidate for the post of UN Secretary-General once U Thant withdrew.

Hyvärinen turned out to be a clever theoretician, who moved in practical waters from a naval to a diplomatic career; *une carrière ouverte aux talents.* Acknowledging an intellectual debt to Harold Sprout and Richard Snyder, his teachers at Princeton, Hyvärinen became an advocate of the pluralistic view of international relations.[379] Unfortunately, in the case of the Jakobson

---

[376] Kekkonen's statements can be found in *Neutrality*, pp.175–190.

[377] Wolf Halsti, *Me,Venäjä, ja muut*, Helsinki (Otava), 1969, p.73. Later, in the newspaper *Uusi Suomi* of 21.5.1983, Halsti upraided the present author for having made the suggestion that Lapland could not be defended. For further on this, see Maude, *The Finnish-Norwegian Tangle*,Turku,(Univ. of Turku: Dept.of Sociology & Pol.Science,Studies on Pol.Science,no.9), 1987, p.116.

[378] The speech of 8.5.1978 is in *Ulkopoliittisia lausuntoja ja asiakirjoja 1978*, Helsinki, 1979, pp.20–26.His point was that the cruise-missiles of the Powers might fight a war in Scandinavian air-space.

[379] Risto Hyvärinen, *Monistic and Pluralistic Interpretations in the Study of International Politics*, Helsinki (the Finnish Academy of Sciences), 1958.In his defence of pluralistic interpretations, he came to the *assumption* of the plurality of causes, a tautologous position, or to the practical view that because the theoreticians themselves differed in their conceptualisation of basic laws, it was safer to adopt a pluralistic view that would take everything in: pp.130–131.

candidature, the practice of politics needed more knowledge than he, or Kekkonen, or Jakobson had. It was hardly conceivable that the Finnish movers in this case would be unable to count on the support of the United States *and* the Soviet Union for the powerful Finnish candidate. Both Powers, in the event, preferred a former officer in the *Wehrmacht*, the Austrian Kurt Waldheim, to a man of Jewish ancestry who had served his country when Finland was fighting with the support of the *Wehrmacht* in the Continuation War! The Powers were agreed on a weaker candidate.

The contempt for the United Nations exhibited by the United States is a well-known matter and the choice of Waldheim thus followed. The attitude of the Soviet Union was an issue of far greater complexity. Ostensibly regretting Jakobson's Jewish background (Jakobson called this background in a TV interview his "shadow"),the Soviet Union did not want to lose bonus points from the Arab and other Islamic nations by supporting him.[380] But this besmirching of a man of superior intelligence and capability may have been a clumsy pretext. In this period, Kekkonen was working hard to achieve from the Soviet side a firmer recognition of Finnish neutrality. Finnish-Soviet relations were outwardly good, but inwardly a tension existed between them.[381] The happy meetings round the forest bonfire of Kekkonen and Brezhnev were a warming-up of personal relations that lasted only till the morning dawned. Then, another reality took over, one founded upon the manipulation of state power by men of the ilk of Andrei Gromyko and Mikhail Suslov. They were not going to let Finland risk breaching this power by finding an instrument in the United Nations. Finland was endeavouring to rise beyond the status of a friendly country bordering on the Soviet Union. Had Jakobson won, it would not have been possible to tie this man of integrity down.[382]

The CSCE

But then came to fruition, nevertheless, a very successful endeavour from the Finnish side. It was the furtherance of the Conference on Security and Cooperation in Europe (the CSCE), the first and third sessions of which were actually held in Helsinki. This was, as matter of fact, in origin a Soviet-sponsored attempt to stabilize the frontiers of Europe and thereby the Soviet

---

[380] Maude, *The Finnish Dilemma*, p.142

[381] Some years ago, with reference to the early 1970s, Professor Juhani Mylly told the present author that "we thought relations with the Soviet Union were good, but in fact they were not in those years." Kekkonen wanted a Soviet acknowledgement of Finnish neutrality.

[382] Sakari Määttänen, *Tapaus Jakobson*, Helsinki (Weilin & Göös), 1973, p.223, suggested that with Jakobson as UN Secretary-General Finnish neutrality might have gained a greater defender.

hold upon the states of eastern Europe, after the trouble they had got from Czechoslovakia in 1968, when the Czechs and Slovaks wanted to go their own way with Socialism.

To the Finns, however, the whole CSCE process was an aspect of détente and the principles laid down in the" First Basket" such as "refraining from the threat or use of force," "the inviolability of frontiers," and "the territorial integrity of states" were as honey to their ears. The Balts [383]and no doubt some of the Czechoslovaks might be aware of a certain hypocrisy in all this, but Finnish neutrality was now apprised of détente—to which the West, by coming to the European Security Conference, was formally acknowledging. So, because of this rapprochement between East and West, the neutrality of Finland was less at the risk of a dangerous escalation arising from taking sides. Indeed, in the early days of the CSCE euphoria, the Finnish government reversed its hitherto cautious stand on the two Germanies (no diplomatic representation in either state, but only at the consular level) and now went for diplomatic representation in both Germanies. This venture at challenging the West German Hallstein doctrine—by which West Germany would not have diplomatic representation in any state that recognized East Germany—was upstaged by Willy Brandt's own Ost-Politik of a West German recognition of East Germany. With the accompanying demand of the Finns for compensation from both Germanies for the harm done by the retreating German forces in Finnish Lapland in 1944, their so-called "German package-deal" in all its elements now appeared, nonetheless, as rather a clumsy anti-climax.

In truth, it may be said that Kekkonen and the Finnish politicians working for him were once again operating to reduce the impact of articles 1 and 2 of the 1948 Finnish-Soviet security treaty, in which a country called "Germany" was named as the potential enemy. And, in any case, the final document of the CSCE process did have it use-value—a recognition of neutrality as an option for a state, which was secured by Swiss initiative. And there was also the notification of troop manoeuvres in advance of their holding. These were specific results of European détente. But there was to be another result, the creation of an atmosphere for change in Europe, something about a détente that should last and spread, even to countries it was meant "to stabilize."[384]

---

[383] The Finnish Conservative newspaper *Uusi Suomi* of 25.4.1971 published an article, however, on "The Baltic Question in the Present-Day World."

[384] For a previous discussion of the CSCE process, see Maude, *The Finnish Dilemma*, pp.77–93.

Immediately, however, there was apparent a consequence of détente of special significance for Finland. This was the hosting in 1972 of the first (and only completed part) of the Strategic Arms Limitation Talks (the SALT talks and agreement of that year). In several ways the holding of these talks in the Finnish capital redounded to the credit of the host country. Both Powers, on this occasion at least, seemed to trust aspects of Finnish neutrality; so that Finland would ensure the security of their representatives and the privacy of their deliberations. This hosting cannot be divorced either from the splendid work Kekkonen and his men engaged in to spread the knowledge of Finland as a neutral state. In a way, this was a compensation for Kekkonen's failure to gain previously an *explicit* Soviet recognition of Finnish neutrality.

The SALT talks were independent of the CSCE process as such. But since the Finns continued in the latter talks to be haunted by the idea of a Nordic nuclear-weapon free zone, all these nicer points were left in the lap of the gods. In a period of détente, this meant de-escalation in a carefully-balanced *global* form and it was all done over the heads of the smaller states, whose only duty was to serve the gods. What was undoubtedly left out, in this particular disagreement between small states (Nordic option for nukes if necessary versus Finnish NWFZ), was the specific interest of a small state, its identity, its protest against the world in which it had a right to participate and a right to be left alone.

The Audience

Kekkonen and his men were thus trying to speak to the world. But how did they speak to themselves? Most commentators are agreed that Ahti Karjalainen, who did so much to widen his country's contacts with both West and East, was a victim of Kekkonen's spite, particularly in the period of Karjalainen's second government (July 1970 to October 1971).[385] Kekkonen felt no firm inclination to retire and he secured a free-trade agreement with the European Economic Community in 1973 by a deal with the Soviet side by which his re-election by special law to the Finnish presidency was guaranteed through a parliamentary act.[386] Karjalainen, who had believed himself to be

[385] Viktor Vladimirov, *Näin se oli . . .*, Helsinki (Otava), 1993, p.192, & Virolainen, *Vallankäyttö Kekkosen kaudella*, p.361 & 366–367. On the sacking of Sorsa's majority government in 1975 shortly before Finland was to host the CSCE process again, ibid., pp.363–367.

[386] Note that the election of a Finnish president by act of Parliament or by a vote of Parliament is not a rarity.

the successor of Kekkonen, stricken by what his wife once called "a longing to be president" (*presidentti kipeys*), gradually sank into an alcohol addiction.[387]

What is clear is that Kekkonen treated his governments in a cavalier fashion. With the exception of Vennamo's party, Kekkonen could range over the whole political spectrum to get a government or even make one up without bothering about Parliament. He had unified the state system–and without radically changing the economy, though where necessary he would even exert a measure of control over the latter.

The key to Kekkonen's power in relations with Russia lay in the Soviet doctrine of peaceful co-existence. Far from being a glib piece of propaganda, the concept of peaceful co-existence safeguarded a traditional Finland. As defined by the KGB agent Viktor Vladimirov, peaceful co-existence meant that the Finnish system was not to be *changed* but *maintained*.[388] This, at first sight, was strange since Finland had the same kind of special relationship with Moscow that the so-deemed Socialist countries of Eastern Europe had: relations between the Soviet Union and these states often went through the Communist Parties of the respective states.[389] But the Finnish Communist Party was not in power, and its annex, the SKDL, was increasingly considered in the Soviet Union as being liable to break off into a completely independent party.[390] In addition, the Finnish Communist Party was by 1970 clearly divided, the minority, the *taistolaiset*,[391] were by 1970 committed to strike action to bring down the system. It was this group that won the sympathy of the International Department of the Central Committee of the Soviet Communist Party and when, in 1970, the second man in the International Department, Alexei Belyakov, became ambassador to Finland, he at once struck up close relations with the *taistolaiset*. It was his undoing. The strikes that occurred were a factor in upsetting the Karjalainen government, in March 1971 the internally-divided Communists left that government, and Kekkonen

---

[387] Vladimirov (the kindly KGB man)was of the opinion that Karjalainen, whom he respected, did not consume a great amount of alcohol, but simply had a physiological system that could not easily take alcohol: op.cit., p.365.

[388] ibid., p.138.

[389] ibid., p. 207 & 212.

[390] ibid., p.355–361.

[391] Sometimes rather erroneously called Stalinists: their leader was called Taisto Sinisalo, whose first name meant "battle" as in the phrase in the Internationale *viimeinen taisto*, "the last battle" It is fair to say that Taisto Sinisalo has stated that he was by no means the key figure people think he was; Rentola,*Vallankumouksen aave*, Helsinki (Otava), 2000, p.14. The fact that Mikhail Suslov thought that the alcoholised Väino Leskinen could be a leader showed how out of touch this section of the Soviet apparatus had now become:ibid., p.413.

took to solving labour disputes and complaining about his position to his own Soviet cronies.[392]

Belyakov was a professed believer in revolution in the West.[393] But he had to go home from Finland. Kekkonen did not want him. A decade before the Soviet Union had written Kekkonen a Note to get him elected in his second presidential election.[394] He was their anchor-man. The role of the Communists, in various shades of meaning, was to furnish information to Moscow. That they did, according to Vladimirov, with varying degrees of one-sidedness, for example, that the Agrarian Union represented "big capital."[395]

This was partly right. There was an Agrarian economic establishment as Vladimirov himself maintained.[396] And they were in the trade with the Soviet Union. So, too, were more powerful Finnish economic fixtures, like the Wärtsilä combination of metal industries, including shipbuilding, as well as textiles. In 1973 this combination employed over 16,000 workers and its leader, Tankmar Horn, was a member, from 1972 onwards, of the Finnish-Soviet chamber of commerce and from 1980 was deputy chairman of the Commission for Finnish-Soviet Economic Cooperation. Vladimirov said he was often in Tankmar Horn's office.[397] And for years one of the KGB man's closest associate among the Finns was the half-businessman, half-politician Päiviö Hetemäki, whose relations with Kekkonen were at times close. Leaving aside for a moment these personal touches, it is clear that by the 1970s the channels through which the Soviet leaders kept in touch with Finland ran not merely into the Communist International Department, nor into the KGB headquarters, but into the Soviet foreign ministry, too, as well as into that country's ministry of foreign trade.[398]

Particularly through the growth of Finnish-Soviet trade, which, by the 1980s, had risen over the 25% limit suggested as a maximum by the late President Paasikivi, there arose a spillover of contacts between the Soviet representatives in Helsinki and the Finns who were significant in the business world, many of whom were also close to the Finnish political scene. Moscow might not view the results of these contacts in quite the same light, as its representatives in Helsinki did. For when evidence emerged of Kekkonen's

---

[392] Vladimirov, op.cit., pp.172–184.
[393] ibid., p.170
[394] ibid., pp.129–132. Vladimirov credits V.V.Zhenikov with dreaming up this gesture, which had, of course, a wider scope in challenging a militarily-revived West Germany.
[395] ibid., p.232.
[396] ibid., p.374.
[397] ibid.,p. 373.
[398] ibid.,p.312

struggle with mortality and he had to quit his twenty-five years presidency,[399] opinions differed between Helsinki and Moscow and not only between Finns and Russians. Moscow, in some confusion, tried to see a successor in Ahti Karjalainen, backed as he was by the young aspirant Paavo Väyrynen. But among the confabbings of the elite in the Soviet embassy in Helsinki, the name of Harri Holkeri of the National Coalition Party was not found to be all that displeasing, better any way than that of Mauno Koivisto, the current prime minister and therefore acting president in Kekkonen's illness! Nor was this all. Ambassador Sobelov travelled to Moscow along with Vladimirov, where the latter said that neither Virolainen (on the Right of the Centre Party) nor Holkeri, a real Conservative, would upset Finnish-Soviet relations if elected. And not even Koivisto would go so far as to do that.[400]

The wheel had come full circle. Kekkonen and the K-line had convinced nearly everyone of the virtuous necessity of engaging in relations with Russia by following a set of defined limitations. That being the case, the pursuit of favourites in the Finnish political system by the Soviet leadership had moved from the Communist Left to the Agrarian Centre and now almost any political party would fill the bill. The least desirable was the Social Democrat Koivisto, but it was he who was elected president. A form of constitutionalism had triumphed.

This form of constitutionalism also had its triumph in international relations. It was triumphing through the European Conference mechanism. Many of the ideas therein expressed, such as the reunion of families, were fostered in conjunction with neutrality and ceased to be simply the propaganda outpouring of an aggressive West. Care had to be taken with the Soviet delegates.

Jaakko Blomberg, now an official of the Finnish foreign ministry, wrote of the necessity to stand by the FCMA treaty (the security treaty) with the Soviet Union.[401] Yet all the time, the neutrality of Finland, from a sceptical start, strengthened.[402] Meanwhile the "human dimension" (specifically the "Third

---

[399] For an account of the breakdown in Kekkonen's health, see Pentti Sainio, *Mitä tapahtui Urho Kekkoselle?*, Porvoo-Helsinki (WSOY), 1982.

[400] Vladimirov, op.cit., pp.351–354 & 379–381.

[401] As mentioned in Markku Reimaa's book, *Helsinki Catch*, Helsinki (Edita), 2008, p.41, Blomberg wrote in the journal *Ulkopolitiikka* (April 1973) that the Finnish-Soviet security treaty came before neutrality.

[402] Reimaa suggests in his summing-up, ibid., p.309, that a conflict had emerged in the Soviet Union between the "military-industrial complex," on the one hand, and the Kremlin and. foreign office on the other, the former being antagonistic to the CSCE. Blomberg encouraged caution about neutrality, but a process was occurring and it was to be Gorbachev, who, in 1989, as Reimaa said, spoke for "a clearly Nordic, *neutral* Finland."

Basket" issues) began to feed into what became the Gorbachev policy in the Soviet Union and where governments faltered the citizenry might take courage and form "Helsinki Rights" groups to egg them on. In the end, even the international relations of the European states changed: what had started as an attempt to solidify frontiers, helped to bring the restoration of states that Yalta had rubbed out.

As to Finland, for decades, it had lived with the imputation of being "Finlandized," that is, of trimming their system to that of the decisive requirements of the Soviet Union. Now, through the CSCE, and its offshoots, the Soviet state became penetrated by a battery of ideas the Soviet state had not itself engendered. All this—and more-contributed to the breakdown of the Soviet experiment.

CHAPTER 5
THE POWER OF DISEQUILIBRIUM ECONOMICS

Independence Day, 6 December 1981, was not a particularly inspiring occasion, especially because of the illness and incapacity of the president, while the acting president, the prime minister Mauno Koivisto, decided to perform presidential duties without a lot of comment, perhaps because he was to be a prominent contender in the forthcoming election for the presidency—which he was to win. The great presidential ball was not held on Independence Day 1981, but a subdued reception of 1,700 M.P.s, Cabinet members, civil servants, foreign and domestic diplomats, cultural dignitaries and sportsmen assembled in the recently-built Finlandia Hall The "shower" of medals, normally a prominent feature of the news of the day, did not occur.[1]

However, military parades took place all over Finland and the one designated to be the "national parade" was held in the small town of Joensuu in south-eastern Finland. But a snowstorm prevented the fly-past of the Mig-fighter planes These Soviet planes, with the accompanying Fouga-Magister fighters bought from Sweden, were the pride of the Finnish defence forces, the former, at least, being equipped with air-to-air missiles in accordance with the hard-won alleviation of the terms of the 1947 Finnish peace treaty.[2] The Joensuu parade thus showed the more conventional artillery and anti-aircraft guns of the land forces, but demonstrators there reached the peak of modernity by distributing leaflets advocating the establishment of a Nordic nuclear-weapon-free zone.[3] Ironically, this latter was still a pet-project of Kekkonen's, who, late in life, had begun to believe that working for peace was a more patriotic endeavour for youth than the ideal of "the soldier boy."[4]

Kekkonen had worked hard for his country, inspired by the premise that a continual reiteration of the need for good relations with Russia was the key to the survival of post-Second World War Finland. That meant not merely the

---

[1] *Suomenmaa*, 5.12 & 8.12.1981.

[2] This alleviation was a result not merely of new weapon technology but of the Finnish military's view of the Note Crisis, which, in their opinion, might not have occurred if the Finnish military forces had been better prepared to fill their obligations under the 1948 treaty. It was the British who went slow on granting this alleviation of article 17 of the Peace Treaty, which forbade the use of guided missiles.

[3] *Helsingin Sanomat*, 8.12.1981.

[4] Juhani Suomi, *Presidentti*, Helsinki (Otava), 1994, p.262.

hope of avoiding the military clauses of the security treaty: it also meant that, under the cover of good relations with Russia, the opening and strengthening of trading relations would occur. Above all, the cement of good relations with the Soviet Union, now acknowledged by nearly every political party in Finland, provided a clamp of political unity (or official conformity) through a presidential power that had become used to the fractious shifts and turns of the parliamentary parties.

But the use of this sort of presidential power was, in fact, being challenged by the bold even before Kekkonen left office. The reception of his final text—called *Tamminiemi* after the name of the presidential residence,[5] was critical in some quarters, or with respect to some aspects of the work. Among others, Krister Ståhlberg of the Åbo Akademi (the Swedish-speakers'university in Åbo/Turku) produced a leading article about the necessity of being honest with regard to Soviet affairs. Especially did Ståhlberg point to the contradiction inherent in a situation in which it had become unpatriotic to question the leader's (read: president's) view about good relations with the Soviet Union, while the essential content of that view was hidden away from discussion. What political responsibility could the citizen in Finnish democracy have therefore for his country's foreign policy? He had to accept in silence what he could not know, because he was not told.[6]

Krister Ståhlberg was referring, in particular, to Kekkonen's defence of secret diplomacy, which undoubtedly covered the president's personal style of diplomatic approach, but which was hardly characteristic of Kekkonen alone.[7]

But the title of Ståhlberg's introductory piece referred to the ban in Finland on criticizing the Soviet Union as a society and the whole issue of the journal had plenty to say about the defects of this society—and in a reasoned manner at that.[8] What had built up over the years, however, in Finnish-Soviet relations was a flow of praiseworthiness about Soviet society, something that came to be known as a liturgy. Even when, as Kristian Gerner said, criticism was being ostensibly encouraged, the end-product was "dressed up and adjusted to suit."[9] Nearly thirty years later, the former ambassador to the Soviet Union, Heikki Talvitie, addressed the problem of the liturgy by asserting its inevitability—the Finnish liturgy, he affirmed, could not be

---

[5] Urho Kekkonen, *Tamminiemi*, Espoo (Weilin & Göös), 1980.

[6] Krister Ståhlberg, "Rätten och behövet av att i Finland diskutera Sovjet Unionen," *Finsk tidskrift*, H.6-7, 1980, pp.267-271.

[7] For Kekkonen's defence, see *Tamminiemi*, pp.164-168.

[8] E.g.,the article of Kristian Gerner "Från antisovjetism till sämhällskritik" related the previous lack of critique within Soviet society to the basic economic problems of the Soviet state.

[9] ibid., "friserat och tillrättalagt," p.285.

expected to cover all the relations between the great Power and the small state.[10] In a subsequent article in the next day's *Turun Sanomat,* Ambasador Talvitie saw fit to praise President Mauno Koivisto for allowing time to do its work, that is, keeping on with the treaty from his inception in office in 1982 until in 1992,with a collapsing Soviet Union, the treaty lost its validity and was set at naught.[11]

System-change

If the abrogation of the treaty was anything to go by, disengagement from the Kekkonen era was slow. The Kekkonen rule had been a powerful system with a hard core that reflected an external force. But the presidential election of 1982 was proof enough of the popular feeling for change, for its tenour was different. In the 1978 presidential election, Kekkonen had been the only major candidate and had even had the backing of the National Coalition Party, which had fiercely contested the 1968 election in the person of Matti Virkkunen. In between, in 1974, Kekkonen had been voted in by Parliament so as to secure Soviet support for a free-trade agreement with the EEC.

In the 1978 election, there had, indeed, been other candidates from the lesser parties, most notably Vennamo, the populist, but these had received rough treatment from the television media.

Now, in 1982, eight candidates sat before the TV camera in a semi-oval, smiling and even waving, most of them leading figures in their parties.[12] What was interesting about the election was that the candidate most favoured previously by Moscow, Ahti Karjalainen, had been pushed out of place the year before by Kekkonen when sponsoring Paavo Väyrynen to be chairman of the Centre Party, but, in contrast, the party faithful themselves had preferred Johannes Virolainen, a more Right-wing Centre Party man, to be their choice for the presidential office.[13] In any case, Väyrynen, a K-line man, had, according to Vladimirov, made a tactical mistake in waiting for Kekkonen to resign before seeking his party's candidacy.[14] A presidential candidate from the radical Left had no chance of becoming elected by the Finns, but, funnily enough, the candidature of Kalevi Kivistö, a teacher and researcher, was

---

[10] Heikki Talvitie,"Neuvostoliiton katoaminen ja YYA-sopimuksen loppu," in the seminar on the 60th year anniversary of the FCMA treaty held by the Political History Dept. of the Univ.of Turku, 3.4.2008.

[11] Heikki Talvitie, "YYA-sopimus solmittin 60 vuotta sitten," *Turun Sanomat,* 4.4.2008.

[12] This picture is reproduced in *Suomi vuosi 1982,* Malmö (K.G.Bertmark), p.16

[13] Timo Vihavainen, "Hyvinvointi Suomi" in *Suomen historian pikku jättiläinen,* Porvoo-Helsinki, (Werner Söderström), 1987, pp.901–902.

[14] Vladimirov, op.cit., p.369.

regretted by the Soviet side because he was from the SKDL and not the Finnish Communist Party, while, according to one Soviet commentator, this reflective figure " lived in a different dimension."[15]

Within the electoral debate, some play was made about Mauno Koivisto's Socialism. In a side-swipe, Johannes Virolainen, the Centre Party candidate, said that he himself, at any rate, was not going to divide the nation, while a leading industrialist, Stig Hästö, made the negative point (for him) that a Socialist president might be expected to lead the country towards Socialism.[16] But those who knew about Koivisto's Socialism knew that his Socialism was of the tepid kind favoured by Bernstein, in which, far from the end justifying the means, there appeared to no end in sight at all. Since Koivisto was acting president already, he chose to conduct a very quiet campaign so as not to pre-empt power. One newspaper called him faceless, but, when he did move out on a limb and suggest that Finnish-Soviet trade should be reconstructed from its existing basis as a clearing trade into a trade based on foreign exchange, the same newspaper in the same leading column accused him of failing to realise that this change would stimulate unemployment in Finland.[17]

These allegations were not exactly the minutiae of politics, but they underestimated the nature of the change that had been occurring in Finland for some time. *What* was occurring was a shift in focus that Koivisto, among others, was trying to sum up. Dividing the course of current history along a line that had to be—for Finland—a mainly reactive one, he told the public the mistakes that their democracy was making and which could be seen in the very reactions their political forces were entangled with. Like Kekkonen, Koivisto had become sceptical of governments and political parties. But whereas Kekkonen wanted a viable and compliant government, Koivisto wanted a government that would do the right thing.

The Dour Reformer

Inclined to pessimism as he was, Koivisto had already published, a few years before the change of power as a result of Kekkonen's incapacity, a collection of his writings and personal reflections entitled "Wrong Policy."[18] It was a

[15] ibid., pp,359–361.

[16] *Suomenmaa*, 5.12.1981 & 9.12.1981 respectively.

[17] ibid., 10.12.1981.

[18] Mauno Koivisto, *Väärää politiikkaa*, Helsinki (Kirjayhtymä), 1978. His pessimism comes out on p.8:"the fact is that economic policy is always wrong, the question being only from whose standpoint and what standpoint." In short, scarce means. and the accompanying problem of selectivity.

critique of governments, political parties, and labour-market organizations. A lot of them were doing the wrong thing. Though a long-serving member of the Finnish Social Democratic Party, Koivisto, in his stance, did not bother much with Bernstein, let alone Marx, and nationalization projects were not set out in his pages either. Though he had written a doctorate in sociology, Koivisto had later turned himself into an economist and had done a long stint as head of the Bank of Finland from 1968–1982, with time off to be prime minister from 1968–1970 and from 1979 to 1982. It is important therefore to survey his pre-presidential career.

Koivisto gave two principal examples of necessitarian reactionism. The one was from political history in 1944 in the cessation of hostilities between Finland and the Soviet Union, which produced, in Koivisto's view, the friendship with the Soviet Union that gave rise to what he regarded as the positive policy of Finlandization. The other was from economic history and derived from the United States' policy in 1971 of ceasing to back the dollar by gold reserves, an operation that led to a fall in the value of the Finnish mark. His book dealt mainly with the latter problem, but a triumphant acceptance of Finlandization is also there in it.[19] Koivisto wanted no problems with Russia, but, as the *Suomenmaa* had noted in its issue of 10.12.1981, he was not satisfied with the current form of Finnish-Soviet trade and did not believe that a simple increase in this trade was the solution to Finland's economic problems.[20] And it was these latter problems that loomed large for him so that he sought to turn away from the obsessive concern of his country with the political-military security relationship with the Soviet Union.

Conversely, in his economic concerns, he did not get carried away either by the policies of the United States, a country that had suddenly tried to solve its trade imbalance by devaluing the world currency. Koivisto did not like devaluation in spite of the traditional adherence of the Finnish forest industries upon a once-a-decade devaluation of the Finnish mark to cheapen their exports. While devaluation, as Koivisto saw it, did have the advantage of producing capital for Finnish industry, it had the greater disadvantage of engendering inflation throughout society by stimulating price-rises, demands for wage increases by the unions and for compensatory measures from the state to counter subsequent unemployment as domestic industry suffered.[21] The short-term advantages of devaluation for a certain sector of industry were thus producing longer-term disadvantages for the whole of society. Koivisto's views received much support from the positive reception to his ideas from the

[19] ibid., on Finlandization, pp.286–287, and on the 1971 dollar crisis, pp.121–122.
[20] ibid., p.100: Koivisto seemed to think that part of the problem lay with the Finns.
[21] ibid., p.88 & 94.

Korpilampi discussions in 1974 and, three years later, from the admittedly more restrained interest of the industrialists.[22] What he was basically advocating as a solution to inflation was revaluation,[23] a policy that led him later in the 1980s to sponsor the maintenance of a high mark. In practice, this was devaluation by other means, not indeed of the currency unit, but of the cost of the product by a combined policy of raising the base lending-rate so as to control the state's own investment ("limit"), expressing a reluctance to go in for regional policy, and attempting to curb the thirst for subsidies and imports of an increasingly over-burdened agriculture, while holding a scepticism towards the famed income-policy of wage negotiations.[24] All were endeavours to cut domestic consumption. As to that maddening problem of unemployment, his own sense of irritation drove him to a characteristic over-valuation of export industries' growth as a better source of solution for the workless than government-backed projects.[25] *Summa summarum.*

Well, not quite, for Koivisto's difficulties in devising—and even more in pursuing—what he felt to be "the right policy" pinpointed certain defects in the Finnish system of political management, behind which was a major impediment in Finnish parliamentary democracy. That impediment had ceased to be the failure to produce a united Left. Though Koivisto had taken the SKDL into his government in 1968–1970, he was not interested in having the Social Democratic Party compete for their votes in an election and he regarded their absence from the government after 1971 as a condition for the passage of a free-trade agreement with the European Economic Community,[26] and this in spite of the fact that a set of "protection laws" (for a permanent system of counter-cyclical funds, for price control powers, for a law against market distortion, and for an investment fund)[27] were drafted in the early 1970s to quieten the more vociferous opponents of the EEC-agreement in the trade union movement.

All this notwithstanding, Koivisto seemed to be becoming indispensable. When Kalevi Sorsa, a Social Democrat, led a government between 1977 and

---

[22] ibid., pp.213 et.seq.

[23] ibid., pp.11–12 & p.185, though in 1975 he settled for a flotation of the mark that certainly raised its value.

[24] ibid., pp.11–13 & p.90 for his criticism of the SAK, pp.22–23 & p.135 for his criticism of what he called "agricultural payments," and p.93 for his general disbelief in state investment in public projects.

[25] ibid., p.202 & pp.292–295, the section entitled "Jälkipuhe" ("Afterword") where Koivisto moderated his pessimism so as to see an expansion of world trade as the source of employment and redistribution (even) of income.

[26] ibid., pp.253 & 114.

[27] ibid., pp. 101 & 109.

1979, it was found impossible within that government of several parties to agree on the percentage of devaluation then felt necessary. The percentage was left to be decided by Koivisto at the Bank of Finland.[28] In 1979, he became prime minister, performing presidential functions as Kekkonen fell ill, and being elected president in Kekkonen' place in 1982.

Westward Ho?

Koivisto's long history has mirrored much of the fate of Finland, almost as much as that of Paasikivi's and that of Kekkonen. It is thus necessary to go therefore even further back into Koivisto's endeavours so as to note a certain counter-trend (and even parallelism) to Kekkonen's own line. (the influence of Paasikivi will be seen later).

A certain hesitancy was always typical of the Koivisto line, a reflection of the underlying hesitancy throughout the whole country. Koivisto had learned to be cautious about the Soviet Union and realized full well that there was an aspect of stability in its existence and that, economically, it might have more potentialities than the majority of Finns were prepared to believe–without FINEFTA Koivisto felt that Finnish-Soviet trade might have expanded even more.[29] These views Koivisto had shared with Kekkonen, but unlike Kekkonen Koivisto had a grasp of the Russian language.

Notwithstanding all this, having developed as a practical economist, and flushed with the uncertainties of Bernstein revisionism, Koivisto saw Finland's own future in an expansion of trade (not the clearing trade) and thus wanted to bring his country more closely into the world of its traditional Western trading partners. He had thus worked much with the idea of a Scandinavian economic unit, a protected customs area of its own, which, became concretized in 1968 as Nordek, a free trade unit of over 20 million people, consisting of Finland, Denmark, Norway, and Sweden. The question was, right from the start, of whether the unit was an end in itself or a half-way house towards entry into the European Economic Community. Koivisto himself, in a statement made at the Oslo meeting of 19.10.1968, spoke of the idea that a Nordek, once created, might be "a more favourable starting-point for whatever kind of market area might in future be in question."[30] Later, he backed down on this stating that the Nordek project was not a means for

---

[28] ibid., p.209.

[29] ibid., p.100. Koivisto may have been right, but it is worth noting that under FINEFTA the volume of Finnish trade had more than doubled in the years 1962–1972. Maude, *The Finnish Dilemma*, p.98.

[30] ibid., p.37.

getting Finland into the EEC.[31] The Norwegian representative, Per Borten, rather saw Nordek clearly as an *alternative* to the EEC, but stated that the Norwegian political parties were not themselves committed.[32] The basic situation was that it had become difficult for any of the Nordic states to go through with the project, partly for internal differences in points of view. In Denmark, the pressure soon arose for membership in the EEC, because it was felt that Britain, Denmark's most important trading partner was going into the EEC, membership in which would also open the agricultural markets of Central Europe to the Danes.[33] This, as Kirby has noted, later enabled Koivisto to lay the blame on the Danes for sabotaging the Nordek proposal.[34] It was nicely done, instead of laying the blame, as far as Finland was involved, on the Russians, who were grimly opposed to the whole idea. Kekkonen, whose indifference from the beginning was evident about Nordek, preferred Finnish spokesmen to blame its failure rather on "those who preferred the EEC *before Finland did*" (my italics) than to lay the blame on the Russians.[35]

So it was in economics as in security policy between these Northern states. In security policy, in spite of the Norwegian Arne Brundtland's clever concoction of a Nordic or Northern balance, two Northern states had gone with NATO and two chosen neutrality of somewhat differing kinds. In the politics of economics, the fate of the Nordek project showed that Denmark wanted to be in the EEC for fear of being left out of Europe; that, as time would show, the majority in Norway preferred a degree of economic isolation from the great trading bloc of the EEC, a view expressing a fear of Europe; that Finland feared that Russia would, if Nordek went ahead, isolate Finland from Europe; only Sweden under Olof Palme was ready to plunge into Nordek and failed to understand why Kekkonen felt he could not do so.[36] Yet the quotation above, cited from Seppinen, showed that Kekkonen, too, had the conviction that in some form or another Finland had to improve its relationship with the main integrative stream of Western Europe. It was Koivisto who lost out, while Ahti Karjalainen did Kekkonen's dirty work for him, as Seppinen says.[37]

---

[31] ibid., p.49.
[32] ibid., p.50.
[33] ibid., p.38.
[34] David Kirby, op.cit.,p.263.
[35] Jukka Seppinen, *Ahti Karjalainen. Poliittinen elämä,* Helsinki (Otava), 1997, pp.362 & 364-365.
[36] ibid., pp.363-364.
[37] ibid., p.367.

Where There's A Will

The failure of Nordek could not be put down to the inevitable quarrel between the Social Democrats and the Centre/Agrarian forces (behind which was the fight to maintain the privileged position of agriculture in Finland). Nor could it be put down to the internal collapse of Nordic cooperation, due to the confusion of national and interest-group goals. As far as Finland was concerned, the project collapse because the Soviet leaders saw in it an extension of the EEC. Subsequent history has proved these leaders guessed right. But there *was* a problem of Finland's foreign trade and so the Kekkonen line was to start negotiations directly with the EEC, narrowing down any agreement strictly to trade, while–*quid pro quo*–Kekkonen's continuation in the presidential office should be guaranteed, a sign of the unchanging security relationship between Finland and the Soviet Union. These negotiations between Finland and the Soviet Union were supposed to be occurring in secrecy and the fact that they were revealed to the Finnish (and Swedish public) resulted in a political upset in Finland in which some people lost their jobs. The transmission of the information about the Zavidovo talks, held in Brezhnev's hunting lodge, in 1972, became a *cause célèbre* in Finland, but one might ask what all the fuss was about since the Soviet Communist Party was quick enough to tell the Finnish Communists what was going on.[38]

Yet the political flurry had its significance. Apart from the Swedish journalist, Tor Högnäs, who revealed the matter to the Swedish and Finnish public and who refused to mention his sources, a group of Left-wing figures in Finland suffered frustration in their attempt to raise the awareness of the Finnish public about the encroaching power of the European Economic Community. Kekkonen ruled. The Soviet Union had bent to *his* will. The Soviet leaders simply did not care about the incipient Left resistance to the EEC in Finland. This Soviet reaction does not say much for those who found Finland to be Finlandized. Nordek had been, in Soviet eyes, an economic bloc or a means to full entry into a wider economic bloc, the Western European integrative system, and, in Soviet eyes, both would serve as a basis for an extended Western European *security* system. History seems to have more or less confirmed this Soviet reaction. And more. Even the free-trade agreement of the Finns pointed ultimately the same way. The issue, as an aspect of Soviet politics, might be summed up like this: the Soviet system in respect of this border state worked on the existing presidential fulcrum of the Finnish system. The Soviet system could live with this. The Finnish forces were in balance.

---

[38] Matts Dumell, *Vuoto*, Helsinki (Tammi), 1973 p. 27.

Capital formation?

Or so it seemed. But the task of keeping that balance was way beyond the resources of the Finnish-Soviet nexus. For already in 1971, the United States had floated the dollar away from gold. This was the root cause of the devaluation of the Finnish mark in the same year. Following on were the two devaluations of 1977 and a third in 1978[39] In the meantime, however, something else had happened. In 1975, Finland received a substantial loan from the International Monetary Fund. In fact, there were two loans on offer: an open letter of credit of 500 million dollars, using the special drawing rights of the IMF, but, as a precondition, the use of a so-called "oil loan "from the IMF of just over 71 million dollars[40] in the light of the 1973 hike in oil prices (part of an offer open to IMF member-countries–including Britain).[41] In the outcome, the open letter of credit was not taken up since Finland managed to get other private sources of funding, while Koivisto, then head of the Bank of Finland, had distinct political reasons for not using the IMF's special drawing rights.[42]

The root cause lay nevertheless in the workings of the Finnish economy. In the early months of 1975 the foreign exchange reserves of Finland became rapidly depleted even though temporary remission was obtained by the payment of rouble credits from the Finnish-Soviet trade.[43] To stiffen the economy, Finland had introduced a system of import deposits and, in conjunction with the minister of finance, Johannes Virolainen, Koivisto wanted to postpone investments of a non-essential nature.[44] A system of import deposits was contrary, however, to the OECD rules, Finland having been a member state since 1969.[45] There was thus something in Koivisto's policy that conflicted with Finland's other international obligations of a trading nature. Fulfilling as best Finland could, the requirements of the IMF loan (including the exercise of restraint with regard to the use of the special drawing rights) should have impressed organizations like the OECD, EFTA, and GATT, but, on the other hand, restrictions imposed by Finland to hinder import raised howls of complaint from an EFTA member such as Sweden.[46]

[39] Kari Nars, "Suomalaisten yritysten valuuttastrategia," *Kansantaloudellinen aikakauskirja*, 1979:4, p.341.
[40] Koivisto, *Väärää Politiikkaa*, pp.167–168 & 172.
[41] ibid., p.179.
[42] ibid., p.181 & 167–168.
[43] ibid., p.166–167
[44] ibid., p.169.
[45] ibid., p.168.
[46] ibid., pp.173 & 175.

But, it was not merely, the international milieu that was tricky for Koivisto. There were a lot of problems, too, on the home front. His reluctance to take up the open latter of credit had partly sprung from a fear that the public would panic at the knowledge of this use of "the last reserves": the alternative was to badger the government to take measures to restrict excessive consumption, but such a line was wearisome, nerve-wracking.[47]

The criticism of Koivisto went on. The Centre Party governor of Lapland, Martti Miettunen felt that some of the IMF oil-money should have gone to support governmental building and other projects so as to alleviate unemployment.[48] In the summer of 1977, in the columns of the radical journal *Ydin*, he was accused by Antero Jyränki (who was later to become his supporter), of a breach of constitutional practice in making the agreement with the IMF: it was an infringement of the budget rights of Parliament and, in any case, would have needed the endorsement of Parliament to come into force.[49]

Since Jyränki was well on the way to becoming a constitutionalist–law expert, this was, in one sense, a challenge based on different premises to the sort of premises Koivisto was working from.

In another sense, Jyränki, however, was speaking less for expertise than for parliamentary democracy. In other words, Jyränki was speaking for open debate. This is a hazardous position that must lead, particularly in a Finnish type political system, to compromise, claims for special interest, to demands to follow the rules even when time is short, and yet all this leading to an aspiration to paint the whole picture.

But from his side, Koivisto had already painted the whole picture. It was a picture of his society in a dangerously fragile situation. Yet it was painted against a background of something that had become very natural to Finland. The country had, for some time, been framing itself, almost unconsciously, in a manner that no longer rested on the old forthright doctrine of self-subsistence. The international milieu was not only dangerous. It also provided opportunity. Some Finns were ready for this. They had been saving for years.

Behind protective tariff walls, and deeply entrenched in the Finnish political system, the more prosperous part of the agrarian interest had linked itself together through a network of local savings banks.[50] This interest was in

---

[47] ibid., pp.167–168 & 181.
[48] ibid., pp. 165,181, & 205.
[49] ibid., p.165.
[50] A striking example of the strength of this connection was evidenced pre-war in the career of President Kyösti Kallio, a farmer who became head of the district's savings bank and ultimately received a seat on the board of the Bank of Finland on the way to the presidency. According to

receipt of subsidies from the state and the localities were further developed in pre-war Finland by the introduction of primary schools, people's colleges, and agricultural colleges, as well as by the improvement in transport communications. On top of this, a further development of the hinterland was produced by the operations of Finland's great export industry of sawn timber, pulp and paper,[51] now increasingly intertwined with agriculture and no longer antagonistic to it. The forest industries, backed by two important urban commercial banks, were capital-creating and in the hinterland often sponsored workers' housing projects, which were meant to foster a satisfied, skilled, and modestly prospering labour force.[52]

The economic historians Riitta Hjerppe, Matti Peltonen, and Erkki Pihlaja have found that the three key sources of capital formation in Finland have been savings, the depreciation allowance, and—increasingly from the 1960s—foreign debt, the burden of which was eased by inflation.[53] Perhaps to this list of sources should be added (it being Finland) a special category for taxation. True enough Keynes said that taxation is only saving by other means, but it may be worth distinguishing this compulsory saving from voluntary saving through the banks—and for two reasons. In the first place much Finnish industry has been financed historically by governmental grants-in-aid,[54] and agriculture by subsidies and by investment in communications, with funds derived from taxation. In the second place, the state has been the national lender of last resort, channelling back-up funding, whether from taxation or more recently from foreign loans, into a private sector which runs into difficulties. In the third place, therefore, the state as an agent of compulsory saving enables the private sector to experiment with risk-capital to a degree far-

---

Hjerppe, even in the 1950s a considerable part of Finland's capital formation took place in agriculture, p.47. See below.

[51] By 1935 the export of paper exceeded that of the less sophisticated product of sawn timber. Ritva Hjerppe et al., "Investment in Finland, 1860–1979," *Scandinavian Economic History Review*,no.32, 1984, p.46. With independence, the large-scale forest companies gradually ceased to buy up forest land from the peasantry and wood-growing became more and more an adjunct to agriculture.

[52] As at Myllykoski in connection with the United Paperworks factory in that village, on which see B. Seebohm Rowntree & G.R.Lavers, *English Life and Leisure (appendix)*, London (Longmans, Green & Co.),1952, p.457.

Before the Second World War,the company was regarded as anti-union.

[53] Hjerppe et al., p.53, recount that in 1979 the foreign debt of Finland constituted 15% of the GDP. It is worth stressing that the more negative effects of foreign debt did not appear till the 1990s. The authors' article was published in 1984, and they seem to rely much on the basic stability given by a savings rate which "has been permanently high in Finland," p.52.

[54] It is worth pointing out that Hjerppe et al., p.45, contest this. Yet they supply historical evidence to the contrary!

exceeding the definitions of the narrow use of that term. These roles of the state, in an allegedly free enterprise system, are a reflection of its traditional conservatism as the bulwark of security for society.

Was society going to be changed?

Koivisto, in his time, had maintained that the presidential election of 1982 was "not going to change our social and economic system"[55] His statement had undoubtedly reference to the charges made by the Right and by the Centre Party according to which (as noted) he was said to be bringing in Socialism. But, in spite of the fact that he had headed as prime minister, two governments with Communist ministers in them, there was no fear of much of a variant of the Left with him. The question is whether or not he changed the system in the other direction.

He was certainly prepared to castigate the leaders of Finnish industry, shortly after his election as president he told the Finnish Club in Helsinki that the attitude of too much of industry could be summed up in the words of the Finnish proverb, "miksi ottaa lainaksi kun saa ainaksi?" Crudely translated, "why take a loan when you can get a handout?" In short, as Koivisto reminded his elite audience, "don't always expect that the taxation will be used in your favour." *He* recommended the taking of a loan, a policy he had, after all, supported himself when head of the Bank of Finland in 1975 in taking an IMF "oil loan" in the difficult days of the early 1970s.

But in the 1980s, during the Koivisto presidency, the role of the Bank of Finland, underwent a considerable transformation. As a result, the private banking system expanded, too, being freed from the controlling power of the central bank;[56] from 1980, private banks could borrow freely from foreign money markets to cover foreign currency exposure for commercial customers, interest rate deregulation started in 1983, capital movements were liberalized in 1986 and 1987, and then bank CDs became freed from the cash reserve requirement.[57] These changes occurred in the light of a growing conviction among the experts that the Finnish private banking system was sound, being

[55] Mauno Koivisto, *Kaksi kautta*, Helsinki (Kirjayhtymä), 1994, p.38.

[56] ibid., p.102

[57] Peter Nyberg & Vesa Vihriälä, *The Finnish Banking Crisis and Its Handling*, Helsinki (Bank of Finland), Bank of Finland Discussion Papers, 8/93, pp.10–11. Certificates of deposit, e.g. with a local bank, are meant to be a low-risk deposit for the investor over a fixed period of time and with a higher rate of interest than a regular savings account. According to Rolf Kullberg, head of the Bank of Finland from 1983 to 1992, these changes were gradual over a period of 11 years from 1980 to 1991; they are mapped out in his ... *ja niin päättyi kulutusjuhla*, Porvoo-Helsinki (WSOY), 1996, pp.14- et seq.

based as it was on a high rate of saving among the citizenry.[58] The fact was, however, that the changes put the system at risk; previously, when there had not been interest-rate competition, banks competed within the country by placing their branches in strategic positions with the hope of serving a profitable catchment area, but now the banks were to compete by providing better terms for their depositors. As early as 1962, when already a member of the board of the Bank of Finland, Koivsto himself had argued for a more flexible interest-rate policy for the private banks.[59] Now, when this was occurring, not enough concern was shown by some banks in checking out the collateral for loans.[60] Since, initially, these banks kept open their numerous branches, their operating costs were high.[61] This was part of a larger picture, however. A domestic credit market was being created in which the private banking system submitted itself to ruthless competition for business. The Bank of Finland had relaxed control only to stimulate the emergence of a consumer market, which had links to the money markets abroad as loans were taken in foreign currency with the usual exchange risk.[62] Those who pioneered the taking of loans from private sources of capital abroad had thought rather of the expansion of Finnish exports thereby and not consumption in the domestic market.[63] Koivisto's downgrading of taxation as a source of capital ignored the use of taxation as a tool for restraining credit excess on the domestic market. Koivisto's call "to defend a low tax rate"[64] continued to be given priority. Equity capital, curiously, was taxed more heavily than debt and banks found encouragement to lend by taking in savings in the form of interest-free low-yielding deposits.[65]

Savings banks, in particular, became over-ambitious and went in for industrial development. The SKOP bank took over Tampella, an industrial complex in Tampere, and had, in consequence to be taken over itself as a result by the Bank of Finland.[66] A separate association of savings banks had aggressively expanded its market shares, but by 1992 was in trouble, and, on

---

[58] ibid., p.8. Also note 55.
[59] Mauno Koivisto,*Kansantaloudellinen aikakauskirja*, 1962.
[60] Nyberg & Vihriälä, p.12
[61] ibid., p.8.
[62] Nyberg & Vihriälä, op.cit., p.15
[63] Koivisto, *Väärää politiikkaa*, p.197. Statement made as early as 30.10.1975.
[64] Koivisto, *Kaksi kautta*, p.24. Nyberg & Vihriälä, op.cit.,p.13.
[65] Nyberg & Vihriälä, op.cit., pp. 11–12. speak of a "subsidy" given to the banks by a permissive government.
[66] Nyberg & Vihriälä,*The Finnish Banking Crisis and Its Handling*, Helsinki (Bank of Finland), Bank of Finland Discussion Papers, 7/94, p.35.

the advice of the Government Guarantee Fund, had to merge with a larger and still successful commercial bank.[67]

The Collapse of the Soviet Market

The expansion of the domestic credit market in Finland occurred in the wake of the successful growth of exports of the years 1986–1989 when the terms of trade were very favourable to Finland and in 1988 bank lending as a whole swelled 30%.[68] But in 1991 the Soviet Union collapsed and with it the Finnish export to that country: the shock to Finland was of the order of 2.5% of the GDP.[69] Because of the peculiar nature of the Russian trade, these exports from Finland could not be requited by seeking markets elsewhere. Suddenly, the power of Russia, so constant a factor in Finnish reckonings, had slumped away. For the collapse of Russia was not merely economic, but was also a security-political event of the greatest magnitude by the side of which the Finnish bank crisis was, by far, a phenomenon more easily containable. Yet in both cases, Russia and Finland, lurking factors of system-change were quite influential. They both relate to the stimulus of consumer demand. But the parallel has a contrastive side to it. In Russia, the stimulus was to be a feature of a general overhaul of the economic system in which the consumer was often a somewhat reluctant participant,[70] whereas in Finland the consumer was carried away by the lure of excessive opportunity, which proved in many cases to be deceptive. In both cases, nevertheless, the outcome was hardly the one intended by the decision-makers, whether administrative, political, or of the citizenry.

Both systems were in the grip of reform, though the word was not used in connection with the Finnish system. The latter system was felt to be merely spreading downwards by virtue of extended offers of credit (local savings banks, for example) and the accompanying absence of a controlling organ, a function the Bank of Finland had previously exercised. Characteristically, the consumer boom in Finland affected not merely the buying of homes and summer cottages, but also the buying of second homes or second or third cars.

---

[67] ibid., pp.39–40.

[68] Nyberg & Vihriälä, *The Finnish Banking Crisis and Its Handling*, Helsinki (Bank of Finland), Bank of Finland Discussion Papers, 8/93, pp.12–13.

[69] ibid., p.17.

[70] Some reformers felt that the consumer "had to be compelled to be free" while, in 1989 & 1990, others rioted against the hike in prices that the attempt to produce equilibrium prices for consumer goods caused. These less affluent folk preferred the old régime's subsidized prices, esp. for foodstuffs. Pekka Sutela, *Economic Thought and Economic Reform in the Soviet Union*, Cambridge (CUP, Cambridge Soviet Paperbacks, no.5), 1991, pp.142 & 166.

In the greatest of contrasts, in the Soviet Union the attempt was made, in the beginning of the Gorbachev period, to develop consumer prosperity by encouraging the citizenry to start growing their own food on an allotment of land![71] More sophisticated projects were, indeed, later engendered.[72]

In truth, it has to be acknowledged that the Soviet system was—on the broadest of fronts (and not merely in regard to consumer needs)—challenged from within by would-be reformers at least from the early 1960s.[73] But the struggle against Soviet tradition (yes) was overwhelming. An over-investment in heavy industry and misplaced forms of investment in agriculture (more land-use instead of a more intensified cultivation) continued.[74] While the reformer Abel Albakin saw that the rate of savings in the 1960s showed a hidden consumption demand,[75] a combination of growth acceleration at a time when the Gorbachev reforms were supposed to be underway furthered disequilibrium. Attempts to find equilibrium prices as against the cumbersome Soviet system of pricing everything in the ministry (some 24 million prices),[76] brought inflation that broke Ryzhkov's government as prices rose.

And this brought along, too, a growing inequality. Something burst out into the open that had been half-hidden for years. The old Soviet Union had not been all that monolithic. It had rather become, as perceptive Russian economists had observed, a kind of a bargaining system, inefficient, and perhaps waiting for the creation of a clearer monetary domestic economy.[77] In social terms, however, the researcher who came nearest to expressing the underlying system *within the system* wrote as early as the Andropov period (in 1983) about the Soviet Union as a forum for antagonistic groups competing for resources and position. This researcher was Tatiana Zaslavskaya and what she was doing was to apply to her own society that elegant tool of Soviet thinking, "the relation of forces,"[78] formerly in use to judge other societies.

The Soviet Union had not yet stopped itself, but it had not produced the paradise of Communism, which Krushchev declared it would do in 1961. When it did stop itself in 1993, it did so in terms of failure, in terms of failure in the light of its own ideal. At the time this occurred, Finland was in the

---

[71] Dev Murarka, *Gorbatsov*, Finnish edition, Porvoo-Helsinki (WSOY), 1987, p.150.

[72] Such as Gavriil Popov's plan to sell the citizenry security certificates in the automobile industry so as to receive a car at a later date. Sutela, op.cit., p. 125.

[73]ibid., p.32.

[74] ibid, pp.51 & 71. Sutela speaks of the law of diminishing returns in this connection.

[75] ibid., p.104.

[76] Murarka, op.cit., p.198–199. Sutela, pp.105 & 166.

[77] Sutela,ibid., p.140 refers to S.Shatalin for this perception.

[78] Murarka does not use this term to describe her thinking; op.cit, p.109.

thick of its own march towards inequality. What has been noted hitherto is that the failure of a *perestroika* (reconstruction) under Communism and the difficulties under which the Finnish banking system struggled shared at least a partial similarity in respect of the handling of consumer interests. Into this limted parallelism, however, must now be placed the impact of the failure of the existing Soviet-Finnish trading system. This failure was as much a cause of the developing Finnish recession as the weaknesses of Finland's own private banking system. In a sense, the failure of the Soviet trade was the failure of a piece of Sovietism within the Finnish system. This particular failure helped to drive Finland along the road to an ever more ruthless form of capitalism.

The basic characteristic of Soviet-Finnish trade was that it was a clearing trade. This was essentially a bartering of goods between the two countries, in which both countries were supposed to balance over a five-year period, an amount of goods of equal value. An economic commission, with two chairmen, Russian and Finnish, would supervise this trade and a protocol would be drawn up at the end of each period by the respective central banks of both countries. Payment would be made in the currency of the exporting country.

In September 1988, Vladimir Kamentsev, the Russian chairman of the economic commission, stated that trade between the two countries had, thanks to the *clearing system*, increased forty-fold in forty years.[79] By the end of he eighties, nonetheless, the trade was under threat. It was even revealed that during the years 1981–1986, Soviet exports to Finland had fallen in volume 29% [80]—whatever Kamentsev might be saying. And things were not getting any better, largely because the Soviet Union was exporting raw materials, above all, oil, the price of which followed the Rotterdam prices, which were broadly falling throughout the decade.[81] The result of this was that the trade could not be balanced; Finland had a vast surplus of exports that could not be requited within the system.

Some ingenuity was applied to find a way out. The essential advantage for the Finns of operating a clearing system was that, as barter trade, it saved Finland's foreign currency reserves for the trade westwards. Now it was suggested that the Soviet Union should pay by convertible currency, but, in this case, the Soviet officials found that they had themselves better use for this currency by trading westwards themselves.[82] Since the Finns had formerly played a leading role in the creation of the great Kostamus industrial project

[79] *Helsingin Sanomat*, 8.9.1988.

[80] *Turun Sanomat, 27.4.89.*

[81] *Helsingin Sanomat*, 15.7.1987 & 4.8.1988; *Turun Sanomat, 18.7.1987.*

[82] *Turun Sanomat*, 5.9.1988.

just over the Soviet border[83] (which was outside the clearing trade), it was suggested that similar projects should be started that could be incorporated *within* the clearing trade, but then quarrels began over such schemes for the Kola Peninsula, and Pekka Sutela,[84] of the Soviet trade branch of the Bank of Finland, warned of the underlying uncertainty involved. The most extreme idea mooted came from the lips of a member of the small Liberal Party, Kyösti Lallukka, who suggested that the Soviet Union should pay its debts by giving back some of the Finnish lands lost in 1944. The suggestion was immediately repudiated by the National Coalition Party M.P., Liisa Hilpelä.[85] This was at a period when every major political party in Finland was preaching the necessity of keeping good relations with the Soviet Union and of avoiding any imputation of *revanchisme*. Lallukka's proposal was to surface quite soon again, however.

Perhaps the most relevant comments on the breakdown of the Finnish-Soviet clearing trade came from the former Finnish minister of foreign trade and head of the customs department, Jermu Laine. In July 1988, he implied, in the light of Soviet criticisms about Finnish shortcomings, that the basic situation was one in which economic reform in the Soviet Union was getting in the way of solving the problems of Soviet-Finnish trade. It was difficult to know with whom to deal.[86]

By June 1988, the debt from the Soviet side of the clearing trade was 6 billion marks.[87] At the presidential level in Finland, Mauno Koivisto, re-elected for a second time in 1988, kept cool about the problems of Soviet-Finnish trade and stuck to the liturgy about security policy.[88]

The great project to pipe natural gas from Russia through to Finland and Sweden, probably the worthiest of all the proposals to solve the problems of Soviet-Finnish trade, was let slip. With three national economies involved, an uncertainty as to both the source of capitalization and the point at which a fulcrum of negotiability could be found, the project lingered on unfulfilled.

---

[83] The Kostamus project had fascinated the Finns—the playwright Esa Kirkkopelto was to write a ballad about it. The project gave much work to Finnish craftsmen and boosted the economy of north-eastern Finland.

[84] *Helsingin Sanomat*, 27.7.1988.

[85] *Turun Sanomat*, 26.7.1988.

[86] *Helsingin Sanomat*, 24.7.1988. For a slighlty more conventional view of Laine's outlook, *Helsingin Sanomat*, 30.7.1988. For Soviet criticisms of the Finns, note Vladimir Pugin's remarks;*Turun Sanomat,16.8.1988.*

[87] As stated by Tauno Matomäki, the head of the Rauma- Repola company,*Turun Sanomat*, 21.6.1988. In September, the Finns were mooting the idea of a loan of 1.5–2. billion marks to tide the Soviet side over its repayment problems;*Turun Sanomat*,3.9.1988.

[88] *Helsingin Sanomat*, 8.4.1988. Also the letter of Pentti Saarenheimo,*Turun Sanomat*, 27.1.1988.

Twenty years later, the Baltic lands, including Finland, struggle to reconcile themselves to the construction of a pipeline on the bed of the Baltic Sea, a scheme of things not without environmental dangers from a maritime floor littered in parts with the débris of the Second World War.[89] In the background lie other negative features: the higher costs of natural gas (stated quite early by the Danes)[90] as well as the reliability of a Russian supply in the light of Russian manipulation of supplies for the Ukraine and Georgia[91] in addition to the simple fact that if Russian supplies run short for their own needs these domestic needs might take preference over exports westwards. The consequence in Finland of an increasing resignation to use nuclear power seems a pity when the emissions from a natural gas system are comparatively low.

In this tale, the course of recent Finnish-Russian history produced again an irony of its own. By the mid-eighties, the citizenry of Finland, had two Soviet-built nuclear power stations thrust upon it partly in response to the general problem that Russians had in requiting their side of the clearing trade. Others were being planned for Finland, but the 1986 Chernobyl nuclear disaster put paid to these Soviet nuclear projects for Finland. Thereafter, the prospects for the clearing trade had sunk even lower.[92] Energy meant the pipeline, but when this project lingered on and on, a desperate resort to nuclear energy was again made by the Finns—but this time to the West. A supplementary alternative—bringing electricity by cable from the Russian nuclear works at Sosnoviye Bor on the other side of the Gulf of Finland—was regretted by the Finnish president.[93] And the clearing trade has gone, too. Yet the fact of the matter is that almost half of Finland's energy is imported from Russia[94]—and a large part of this is electricity produced by Soviet nuclear reactors, some of them refurbished.

[89] *Helsingin Sanomat*, 9.3.2008.The Nordstream Corporation planning this pipeline is essentially a German- Russian venture backed by Angela Merkel and Putin (Medvedev) with German, Dutch, and Russian capital behind it, the latter 51% (Gazprom). Poland, Sweden and Estonia have expressed opposition to the scheme. The Lithuanian chargé d'affaires in Helsinki also expressed reservations to the author of this work. How far Finland may benefit is still an open question.

[90] *Helsingin Sanomat*, 23.3.90.

[91] In January 2006, the president of Georgia,Mikhail Shakashvili, appealed to the Finns not to trust the Russian government in this question; *Helsingin Sanomat 21.1.2006* A moderate statement of the Ukrainian situation was expressed by Juha-Pekka Raeste in the *Helsingin Sanomat of 17.1.2006.*

[92] Unto Hämäläinen & Terho, *Lännyttymisen lyhyt historia*, Porvoo-Helsinki (WSOY), 1998, p.18.

[93] *Helsingin Sanomat*, 6.9.2006.

[94] Finnish TV1 20.30 news, 26.6.2008.

The breakdown of the Soviet-Finnish clearing trade and its partial replacement by "normal" trading relations between Russia and Finland has most certainly contributed to the emergence of a significant economic transition in Finland. The clearing trade was a prop that actually protected some branches of the Finnish economy from the ruthlessness of international competition.[95] It was, in fact, a form of protection. The loss of the clearing trade compelled the Finns to take capitalism more seriously, whether in its current Russian form of aggravated semi-political stances or in its pristine form projected, *inter alia*, by the Western world.

Modern economics

On 6 September 1984, Finland's most powerful newspaper, the *Helsingin Sanomat*, had held a one-day stand in the new Finlandia Centre. It was in honour of a triumph in economics, but was modestly called a "seminar on the business cycle." A picture of a smiling group of businessmen and half a businesswoman's face appeared in the next day's paper. Things were going well with business, and one of Finland's leading money-makers, Professor Pentti J.K. Kouri, proclaimed that Finland would long continue to be the "Japan of Northern Europe"

The day was a field-day for the bankers. Jaakko Lassila, the head of the Kansallis-Osake Pankki, said that Finland was returning to "civilized conditions" and was breaking free from "a contractual economy" into a more resourceful outlook. More advice came from the deputy-director of the world's leading bank, the Citibank. His name was Thomas Theobald and he was a confidant of the recently-retired banking guru, Walter Wriston. Inspired by Wriston, Theobald urged Finnish banks to borrow: the old norm of borrowing no more than 15% of the value of the country's exports was not necessarily enough-you might borrow more, as Japan was doing. The managing director of the First Boston Corporation, Yves-André Istel, said that Finnish firms should think of borrowing inter-nationally. They were soon to do so.

There *were* politicians present, too. One of them, Harri Holkeri, of the National Coalition Party, was shortly to become prime minister, and already sat on the board of the Bank of Finland, which gave him a good jumping-off ground to lecture the audience. He urged his hearers to get rid of fixed currency-exchange rates and fixed interest rates. The current prime minister, the Social Democrat Kalevi Sorsa, put in a word of caution, however. Though

[95] And even protected certain Finnish agricultural exports (eggs,e.g.) from Russian competition, a situation which changed when *perestroika* initially led to an increase in investment in agricultural production in Russia; *Turun Sanomat*, 13.1.1988.

the leader of a coalition government, he did not seem to think that decisions made through consensus were inevitably the best possible. His finance minister, the Centre Party Ahti Pekkala, was inclined to agree and felt that next year's budget, then being drafted, was not going to be tight enough.

So there you had the ingredients: the Finnish private sector should take money from abroad ("debts spoke of growth" ran the headline) and the Finnish public sector's guardians should be cautious and even verge towards parsimony.[96]

Less than three years after the Finlandia Centre euphoria, Harri Holkeri, in April 1987, became prime minister. The backbone of his government was the "blue-red" alliance of the National Coalition Party and the Social Democrats. This alliance may strike a foreigner as strange, but under Finnish circumstances it was natural enough, since the Social Democrats had lost their Socialism, and both parties were Western-oriented. So was the Centre Party, but a bit less. With its Agrarian base and hinterland outlook, the Centre Party were more defiantly nationalistic at the grass-roots, wary of a more comprehensive association with European integration, and wary, too, of Finland's own commercial-industrial urbanism as expressed by one of the National Coalition Party's leading thinkers, Martti Tiuri.[97] In addition, the powerful figure of Paavo Väyrynen in the Centre Party still hoped for a resurgence in the Russian trade. His party had not joined Holkeri's government.

However, being now in office, Holkeri himself, by the end of 1988, was less ebullient about prospects in international trade. The country had run into an imbalance on current account. It was consuming more than it should. Holkeri began to speak of stabilization and restraint, even when voices from the moderate Social Democratic Left had said that "in its entirety," 1988 had been a successful year.[98]

But the year 1988 also saw the explicit emergence, *from within the Conservative side,* of a critic who took a new look at what had become known as " the casino economy." The term had arisen as a result of the operations of those who had taken loans for purposes of speculation, that is to say, loans which were not directly used for the expansion of production. Arguing in the

---

[96] *Helsingin Sanomat,* 7.9.1984.

[97] Tiuri was the classic Westernizer. An electronics specialist, his book *Tulevaisuus alkaa nyt* (*"The Future Begins Now"*), Helsinki (Otava), 1984 was part of the above-mentioned euphoria of its year of publication. In it, he suggested that dynamic Finland fell primarily along the line Helsinki-Turku, and regretted the continuance of agriculture even in southern Finland, let alone in Lapland, where he said, three-quarters of the costs were in the form of subsidy; pp.194–200.

[98] *Turun Sanomat,* 31.12.1988: statements from Holkeri's New Year's greetings and independent comments from the SDP columnist, Aimo Massinen, in the same issue.

columns of the *Helsingin Sanomat* that the terms "casino economy" or "consumers' feast" were misplaced, Raimo Ilaskivi, the burgomaster of Helsinki, castigated bank managers for granting loans almost unquestionably without thought for the purpose of the expenditure, then, too, the Bank of Finland for its loss of control, but more importantly Ilaskivi found that the Finnish economy was not the competitive economy it claimed to be. It was full of cartels and price-fixing in a wide variety of fields from constructional work to foodstuff production. The consumer did not live in a bonanza of ever-cheaper goods. He paid dearly for his goods because of quiet monopolies which were the true cause of the high cost of Finnish products—whether the question was of the internal market or the export-import market. He pointed out, with a swipe at the protectionism of Finnish agriculture, that meat could be bought more cheaply from abroad.

Ilaskivi was answered a day later by Ilkka Suominen, the minister of trade and industry, and himself a member of the same party (the National Coalition Party) as Ilaskivi. In answer to the latter's plea for stricter regulations on loan granting and business practices in general, Suominen argued that this might lead to the regulation of the economy. That was undoubtedly the case, but what Suominen missed was that Ilaskivi was arguing against another kind of regulation, that involving a collusion between certain market forces *to control competition and keep prices high* with, among other things, the acquiescence of a state-backed licensing board viewing foreign competition as particularly negative. He reminded the readers of the *Helsingin Sanomat* that the European Community was waiting in the wings.[99] What was, of course, at stake was the conflict between two forms of conservatism: between the old protectionism and the new liberalistic form of doing business, guided nonetheless by law. The latter was a very big project, even in spite of the US example, which Ilaskivi admired so much.

And there was a spectre haunting the scene Ilaskivi had set out. It was like this. The spectre indicated it could not be done. The prophets of yesteryear had foretold that the power of business development was so great that it would defeat all control until a *politics* emerged to do the job and take over the monopoly that free enterprise would bring. But that was all long-term, stretching into a future that was not then nor has been now realized.

For the time being, Ilaskivi and the likes of Suominen could take each other to task by engaging in a public dialogue *from within the system* about the quintessence of capitalism. It was small wonder that as the Holkeri government described its own policy as "controlled structural change" (*hallittu*

---

[99] *Helsingin Sanomat*, 13.11.1988 & 14.11.1988. Also Pertti Paloheimo's article in the *Turun Sanomat*, 31.12.1988.

rakennemuutos") the wags began to refer to a "Finnish *perestroika*."[100] Since Ilaskivi and Suominen were arguing about a price-mechanism, and since the Soviet Union, as noted, was in economic turmoil over precisely this question, a certain similarity between the two countries was again apparent. In both countries, it took time to get even close to a solution. And in Finland, harsher terms were used than *perestroika*. References began to be made to "controlled bankruptcy" or to "chaotic structural change."[101] A swift anti-cartelization policy, as a cost-reduction policy, seemed beyond the power of Finnish governments, whether Holkeri's or its successor. They were trying to rely on a new form of currency politics.

Since the ending of the Second World War, governments in Finland had tended to operate by *devaluing* the currency when costs had become too high for the export trade, especially with respect to the export of timber, pulp and paper. The Koivisto era (1982–1994) witnessed an attempted reversal of this policy: it was called *revaluation*.

Even before becoming president, Koivisto had backed revaluation in 1979 and 1980. Should revaluation be used, the young economist Seppo Leppänen wanted a more modest version of it.[102]

Divinations of the Illuminati

As devaluation had produced cheaper exports and made imports dearer, revaluation made exports dearer and imports cheaper. There is something strange, at first glance, in the quiet support among the pundits that revaluation began to gain in the 1980s. In 1988, Pentti Vartia, argued that "Finland is structurally a country that has a balance of payments problem."[103] This problem was that of the excess of imports over exports, but a simple boosting of exports, let alone devaluation as such did not appear possible. Instead, Varttia concluded that foreign capital should continue to be imported and a longer-term goal should be set as a corrective for the imbalance: this goal

---

[100] Or even worse, in the words of the dissident trade union leader, Risto Kuisma, to maintain that *perestroika* had not yet arrived in the former Russian province of North-West Russia (Finland, that is). Therefore, let Finland join the European Community, where conditions were better, Kuisma said: *Turun Sanomat*, 14.10.1989.

[101] Juhani Pekkala in the *Helsingin Sanomat*, 2.11.1989. Also the leading article in *Iltalehti*,2.11.1989.

[102] Seppo Leppänen, "Valuuttakurssipolitiikkaa," *Talouselämä*, 35, 1982, p.36. See also note 110 below.

[103] *Turun Sanomat*, 28.6.1988.

was the establishment of conditions for a stable mark.[104] Herein, however, lay a problem: was a stable currency to be found in a mark that would have a fixed rate of exchange, or was this dangerously simple—too rigid a solution to cope with the reactive position of the Finnish economy, an economy compelled to keep abreast of changes in the massive world outside Finland?

Those who had painstakingly been arguing for revaluation some years before were a cautious group, who had been dissatisfied with the shock given to the Finnish economy by the decennial series of devaluations. They were not arguing for swingeing changes in the reverse direction. Indeed, they thought first not so much of a change in the value of the Finnish mark but rather in terms of an adjustment of Finnish export prices to cope with fluctuations in pricing in the international market.[105] These Finnish changes were to be slight so as not to lose the market by disturbing the terms of trade, let alone produce the inflation that devaluation brought. A sophisticated version of this policy would be practised by forming a basket of certain export and imported goods and moulding the exchange-level of the Finnish mark accordingly; alternatively, the relevant comparison would be based on the differences between the inflation rate in the various currency areas.[106]

Nevertheless, as Seppo Leppänen,ultimately a member of the economic bureaucracy,[107] had always been quick to point out, by increasing the price of exports, revaluation could damage competitiveness on the international market and had for this reason to be balanced by cuts in costs. Since revaluation made imports cheaper, there was all the more justification to cut costs on the home market so as to avoid an inflationary situation there.[108] Eero Tuomainen, the then secretary of the Economic Council, was, a few years later, to remind his hearers that revaluation leading to a strong mark might be a boon to exports by providing access to the import of cheaper and more effective investment technology.[109] In fact, the risk of stirring up inflation was always present: after the 1989 revaluation (of 4%). [110]

---

[104] Pentti Vartia, "Vaihtotaseongelma kärjistyy" in *Kansantaloudellinen aikakauskirja*, 4/1988, p.366.

[105] Kustaa Hulkko & Jorma Pöysä, *Vakaa Markka*, Juva (Atena kustannus), 1998, pp.93-94, on the pioneer work of Hannu Halttunen & Sixten Korkman. Also Hannu Halttunen's, *Maailmantalouden asettamat ehdot Suomen talouspolitiikalle*, Helsinki (Bank of Finland Research Papers), no.10,1982, esp.pp.17-21.

[106] ibid., pp.99-100: note 26.

[107] In 1996, Leppänen became chief secretary of the Cabinet Office: ibid, p.476.

[108] Hulkko & Pöysä, p.100.

[109] ibid., p.183.

[110] *Vuosi 1989*, p. 69.

The Finnish banks' import of foreign credits rose from 30% to 55% in a year.[111] By the crucial year of 1992, the foreign debt of Finland had risen to 140 billion marks, of which the share of Finnish industry was 100 billion.[112] But by now the currency policy hitherto favoured had been reversed. For there *had been* a massive *devaluation* in November1991 (14%).[113] This was an act of policy the minister concerned, Iiro Viinanen, had said was not going to occur.[114] A believer in the stable mark, Viinanen had let it float the day before and then, in panic, devalued it, as foreign exchange left the country. [115] But, nothing daunted, less than a year later on 8 September 1992, Viinanen let the mark float again. This could hardly be called a prelude to revaluation either since the mark immediately fell 15–17 %. But it was not to be called devaluation; the mark had just been "floated, " a term that brought down the wrath of the European Economic Community upon Finland.[116]

The fact that "flotation" might mean either revaluation or devaluation was destroying the integrity of the country's currency, which had even tried, in 1991, to peg itself to the ecu (the European Currency Unit), hence the anger of Henning Christopherson, the deputy chairman of the European Commission. Finland's politics were now definitely tied to helping Finnish industry out, but to what extent was industry itself responsible for the mess the country was falling into? At least one half of the debts, as noted above, were caused by industry's own enthusiasm to import and invest. It is true that by 1992 a so-called "double deficit" had appeared, a deficit in the government's own income of 72 billion marks, partly caused by subsidies to the private banking world but partly also to support for industry.[117] In spite of the fact that government support for the private banking sector was in part

---

[111] Hulkko & Pöysiö, op.cit., p.232.

[112] ibid., p.383 (based on the researches of Jaakko Kiander & Pentti Vartia).

[113] *Vuosi 1991*, p. 274. The collaborators of this work actually put the external debt of Finland at 180 billion marks.

[114] Jaakko Kiander in his essay "1930-luvun pulakausi ja 1990-luvun talouskriisi" in *Lamakirja*, ed.Blomberg, Hannikainen & Kettunen, Turku (Kirja-Aurora), 2002, p.69, points out that Viinanen spoke out publicly against the proponents of devaluation on 4.9.1992. Devaluation ("flotation") occurred on 8.9.1992.

[115] *Vuosi 1991*, p.274.

[116] *Vuosi 1992*, pp.206–207. This meant the end of a mark adjusted to a basket of foreign currency.

[117] Hulkko & Pöysiö, op.cit., pp.403 & 426 (note 68).

due to the "consumers' feast,"[118] there is substance in what Leppänen had seen in 1982, namely that the key player in a tense situation was industry.[119]

To sum up, the concern for revaluation rather than devaluation was fostered by Mauno Koivisto even when, in the late 1970s, he was prime minister. The core of this idea was that by dismantling other constraints on economic activity a degree of control could be exerted by government and/or Bank of Finland through establishing a more or less stable currency primarily to be attained by carefully-made adjustments. Such a policy, devised before the slump of the 1990s,was shrouded in a certain kind of secrecy. Its aim was to stop an inflationary spiral by fixing a currency point after the breakdown of the Bretton Woods agreement in 1971.

After the failure of the Sorsa government in the spring of 1979 to devise a revaluation policy, the Bank of Finland, once Mauno Koivisto, its former head became prime minister, revalued the mark 1% on its own initiative on 13.8.1979. Koivisto, as prime minister, revalued it another 2% on 21.9.1979.[120] The political forces, especially the SDP, grew worried at the Bank of Finland's power, but the Communists and the SKDL would have wanted even a larger revaluation of from 5–7%. The Centre Party were converted to it, but the forestry industry felt it would damage exports.[121]

None of this was discussed in an election and it is difficult to imagine how it could have been, since the essence of such a policy was a cautious sleight of hand. This was emphasized all the more in the following year when, on 25.3.1980, the acting head of the Bank of Finland, Ahti Karjalainen, a politician not noted for his communicability, revalued the mark 2% off his own bat. Both industry and private banks were against it.[122] Things went a bit more smoothly in 1984 when a 1% increase in the value of the mark went hand-in-hand with a preceding modest wage settlement.[123] The disastrous consequences of the 1989 revaluation are mentioned above.

---

[118] Rolf Kullberg, head of the Bank of Finland from 1983–1992, wrote his memoirs under the title ." . . And so tthe consumers' feast ends" ("... ja niin päättyi kulutusjuhla," Helsinki (WSOY), 1995.)

[119] Seppo Leppänen, *Talouselämä*, no.35,1982, p.36. His incisive article is referred to in notes 104 & 110 of this chapter.

[120] *Vuosi 1979*, pp.204 & 229.

[121] ibid., p.229.

[122] *Vuosi 1980*, p.87.

[123] Hulkko & Pöysä, p.107.

The Solution

The solution, after all, was devaluation—in the guise of flotation. It was Viinanen's back-tracking in September 1992 that certainly helped the recovery. From this point onwards, Finnish exports increased by 10% a year.[124] But it was Viinanen's previous back-tracking in November 1991 that had helped, too, for in the early part of 1992 Finnish exports had already increased one-fifth.[125] In general, the terms of trade improved for Finland, though a campaign to boost exports also helped.[126]

Unfortunately, devaluation did not end with the currency. There occurred also a very many-sided—and is occurring still—a socio-economic devaluation. The breakdown of the private banking system, whose small banks had too readily and favourably granted loans, particularly for housing, led to closures of many branches and considerable loss of jobs. The failure of large sectors of small-to-medium industry, serving the domestic market, threw many into unemployment. This swelled the social budget as a result of the vastly increased number of people claiming unemployment benefit and brought cuts in other social benefits. The author well remembers an almost tearful TV presentation by the economist Pentti Vartia who stated that the citizenry were unaware of the fact that the social budget was growing, presumably because they were so depressed by individual changes in it, and were overlooking the cost of 600,000 unemployed and those on temporary lay-off in the year 1991.[127]

For apart from the invisible hand, there was also a visible hand at work. This was the hand of the government and its advisers. They paid out unemployment insurance, but they also bailed out banks and industry by increasing the sales tax and the citizens' social security payments.[128] The people did not like the cuts in their income.[129] Income tax lost the automatic index-adjustment and so, too, did pensions.[130] But it was a complex situation. In 1991, for example, an increase in family allowance had occurred, but in 1994 tax concessions for families with children were either abolished or reduced—

[124] Kiander in Blomberg et al., p.59.

[125] *Helsingin Sanomat,* 11.5.1992.

[126] Hulkko & Pöysä, op.cit., pp.437–438.

[127] A statement made by the *Turun Sanomat,*9.7.1992, with reference to the number of unemployed and laid-off.

[128] *Helsingin Sanomat,* 11.5.1991.

[129] Olli Kangas, "Muutos ja pysyvyys" in *Lamakirja,* ed. Blomberg et al., p.253.

[130] *Ilta-Sanomat,* 26.8.1991

and this outweighed the 1991 increase in family allowances.[131] In 1996, for example, the citizen's basic right to the national pension was reduced or abolished in so far as he had a reasonable pension from his work[132]–and this, in spite of the fact that the Nordic world prides itself on the maintenance of "rights once achieved."

On the whole, nevertheless, the commentators seem to be of the opinion that the Nordic welfare system has survived in Finland in its broad lines.[133] But there were reservations, too. Jorma Kalela put the point that a new and permanent under-class of unemployed may be emerging It is worth mentioning that there were still, approximately, 200,000 unemployed in Finland in 2002.[134] When the author of the current work came to Finland in 1958 there were 100,000 unemployed, a matter that gave cause for concern, for there was then no general unemployment insurance: it was expected that the worker would belong to an unemployment fund and many did not.[135] The new climate of opinion seems to give acceptance to unemployment for those locked in it. Olli Kangas has already given us to understand that the weight of a public opinion that would *protest-not just grouse* against social circumstance was not great and might well be side-tracked.[136]

In the spring of 1992, a historian of left-wing persuasion refereed to a transfer of income from the workers to capitalism.[137] Subsequent events have confirmed this trend.

It remains now to note a powerful (if also, in part, contradictory) analysis of the failure of the Finnish economy in the early 1990s. The analysis lays the blame squarely upon industry and its inability to make effective use of capital.[138] In 1996, a work by the economist Matti Pohjola refuted the idea of an economy primarily destroyed by a "consumers' feast."[139] Pohjola's initial stance was that Finland was not under-capitalized. Between 1960–1990, he argued, Finland had a higher investment and savings rate of 138 OECD countries, while out of 16 countries Finland had the cheapest–obtainable

---

[131] Heikki Hiilamo, "Säästöt ja perhepolitiikka" in *Laman pitkä varjo*, ed.Jaakko Kajander, Helsinki (Government Institute for Economic Research), 2000, p.117.

[132] Olli Kangas, op.cit., p.237.

[133] Even Hiilamo, op.cit., p.118 & his editor Jaakko Kiander, ibid., p.7.

[134] Jorma Kalela, "Syntyikö Suomeen 1990-luvulla uusi alaluokka?" in *Lamakirja*, ed. Blomberg, p. 381.

[135] *Helsingin Sanomat*, 5.4.1992.

[136] Olli Kangas, op.cit., p.253.

[137] Juhani Siltala in the *Helsingin Sanomat*,5.4.1992.

[138] See also note 117 of this text with its reference to figures given by Hulkko & Pöysä.

[139] Matti Pohjola, *Tehoton pääoma*, Helsinki (WSOY),1996, p.40.

capital.[140] Its income policy[141] ensured wage restraint, a significant part of the institutional structure of a firm society, which used social security as a compensatory alternative to higher wages. But, according to Pohjola, it was the wage-earner who paid, in this deal, for the savings and investments in society.[142]

Two sympathetic commentators have seen that the problem of Finnish capital was a high financial return on its investment in Finland and a low productivity nonetheless in terms of input/output ratio. In such a tight national economy, capital did not flow to the point of highest return. In general, these commentators have argued that the importance of capital may be in some degree of decline in the face of the management of a multi-factor based productivity.[143]

Equally, Pohjola has himself taken seriously the interpretation of Matti Vanhala according to which the excessive devaluations of the early 1990s (the devaluation of 1991 was 14%: the Bank of Finland would have been satisfied with 10%)[144] helped to destroy the home market, Vanhala argung that every Finnish mark gained by devaluation was paid for by a corresponding loss of the mark no longer imported into the real income of the country.[145]

Pohjola was, nevertheless, in his book, an exporters' protagonist. He could not desist from championing the forest industries for their technological prowess in spite of the fact that it was this industry that basically inflicted the decennial devaluations upon the Finnish economy.[146] More than a decade after he wrote, this model does not look too good.

The key to his vision is a certain internationalization of production in which process Finnish industry rather than "Finland" as an economic unit is an active, not to say even aggressive participant, and no longer simply a reactive one. Certain aspects of a *national* outlook are thus viewed with

---

140 ibid., pp.36–37 & 38.

141 The concept and practice of an incomes policy developed in Finland in the 1960s. The state conducted negotiations with the interest-groups (trade unions & agricultural organizations) for broad national lines on wages, salaries, and agricultural payments. The negotiations included consideration of taxation and the value of money. In the form of stabilization policies, incomes policy was meant to be an anti-inflationary instrument. According to *Uutispäivä Demari* of 25.3.2008, the first official deal was made on 27.3.1968.

142 Pohjola, op.cit., p.48.

143 Pirkko Aulin Ahmavaara & Jukka Jalava, "Capital and Its Productivity in Finland 1975–2001," *Scandinavian Economic History Review*, vo.51, no.3, 2003, pp.62–78.

144 *Vuosi 1991*,p.274. Kullberg, op.cit., pp.184–201, sees this high devaluation percentage as very much a triumph of the Agrarianism of the Aho government over the Bank of Finland.

145 Pohjola, op.cit., p.131.

146 ibid., pp.145–146.

scepticism such as a *regional* policy that requires a large input of capital.[147] Into this category might fall that darling scheme of Urho Kekkonen, the pulp mill at Kemijärvi in the north of the country, closed in the spring of 2008, a closure in which the concerns of the Swedish-Finnish company that owned it were not to be upset by the action of the Finnish government,[148] though the Centre Party (the former Agrarians) were a key element in the coalition government. Correspondingly, Finnish companies establish eucalyptus plantations in Uruguay and Brazil.[149] It is not that simple, however. Existing Finnish paper and pulp production has relied much on the import of timber from Russia, now increasingly set at risk by the threatening imposition of export tariffs from the Russian side (building up their own paper and pulp industry).[150] To maintain the Finnish industry, the current government will provide tax concessions for Finnish wood growers to sell their timbe. As for the electronics industry, whose standard bearer is the famed Nokia, the contention of Pohjola that these types of manufacturing would go to the technically-advanced countries of an integrative Europe[151], well, the story takes an almost macabre twist. Building up a large complex at Bochum in Germany, employing 8,000 people, Nokia shifted to Romania—lock, stock, and barrel. The point is not that Romania has hitherto been a country rather undistinguished for its technical expertise: we can all learn. The point is the current cheapness of its labour force. In the old economics it was known as "comparative advantage."

---

[147] ibid., p.116.

[148] Characteristically, according to press reports (*Turun Sanomat,* 24.5.2008), the company concerned, Stora Enso, is said to be planning to open a huge pulp and fine- paper complex in Russia in 2011. *Turun Sanomat,* 11.9.2008, announced 2,000 job losses as well in the whole of the Finnish paper industry. On 20 August 2009, the great paper producer Stora Enso announced thousands of job losses in Finland and the shift of production abroad:*Helsingin Sanomat,*20.8.2009.

[149] Such Finnish enterprise has produced ecological protests from the Argentinian side of the Rive Plate and disturbances from peasant farmers in Brazil as well as Finnish involvement in local politics there.

[150] Docent Arto Luukkanen of the Renvall Institute, Helsinki, has suspected the operations of a Russian private monoply and its international partner behind all this, in complete contrast to Russia's alleged desire to enter the WTO:*Helsingin Sanomat,* 5.5.2008.

[151] Pohjola, op.cit., pp.139–141.

Lurching westwards

Before lurching eastwards to Romania, the Finnish economy[152] seems to have had, at some point, a felt need to finalize itself *politically* by lurching westwards into what became the European Union. A sort of established cover would then be given to Finnish economics. Firms have to operate from somewhere, at least initially be given a character, or, at best, be given a bit of a background. Then, a German EU-commissioner called Günther Verheugen, could oblige by taking in a colonializable state like Romania. In terms of political history, these operations might be seen as a sort of hidden hand of destiny, spreading a technologically-advanced capitalism into a distant part of Europe, by the operations of a firm that had been clearly strong enough to develop behind the political barriers of the Finnish state and subsequently to go on developing by breaking through the barriers of a multitude of states; a classic Pohjola-type case. However, if economics is ultimately required to break into states having first made use of them, it is also apparent that politics, in its turn, makes sauce of a lot of economics. There *is* a citizenry.

The shift from Bochum to Romania produced outrage among the German citizenry, in which the German prime minister, Angela Merkel, shared. Compensation had to be given to the employees and some consumers boycotted Nokia wares.[153] Without an outbreak of violence Nokia was able to clear off to Romania, nonetheless. But here at least, in Germany, was a protest that Professor Kangas had felt he would not see in Finland. It constituted a thrust of nationality into economics.

And there have been other thrusts of this awkward constituent of grass-roots politics into the decision-making of the professional guru-clan: the two no-votes of France and the Netherlands on the projected European constitution, and the defeat of the European non-constitution by the constitutional processes of the Republic of Ireland. Whether with Nokia or with the EU which Nokia has favoured, a citizenry protests.

Why did Finland join the EU?

In accordance with what may be called Finnish manifest destiny, it was a culmination of a string of successful developments, starting with the FINEFTA

---

[152] With its vast international capitalization, it is a debatable point as to whether Nokia can be considered any longer a Finnish company, a development that Pohjola in his time did not foresee.

[153] Rumours circulated (*Helsingin Sanomat*, 28.4.2008) that Nokia has negotiated with the government of Nordrhein-Westphalen to pay the province 30,000,000 euros in compensation.

agreement of 1962 that got Finland a place in EFTA and Russia a place in Finland, followed by a Free Trade Agreement in 1973 that got Finland into the EU market (from outside) and got Russia (from inside) a Finnish president on whom they could rely. It looks as if the Finns were set on a trend that would ensure their markets in a paradoxical situation in which *blocs* had been created in Western Europe to *free* trade. A country was in danger of being left out as far as the wider aspects of integration were involve (trade apart). But from 1984 onwards work began to draw up a scheme for a European Economic Space, essentially between the (then-styled) European Community and EFTA,[154] and in 1991 this issued in the proposal for a European Economic Area, between the EC countries and those EFTA countries wishing to join in what was basically an extension of the Single European Market, that is to say, a trading area without obstacles on the movement of capital, labour, goods, and services. This was, in terms of a general principle, for agriculture was the great exception to these freedoms. No wonder that on 27 October 1992, the law was passed by the Finnish Parliament by 154 votes (the required two-thirds) with only twelve against, though 32 were absent. Had agriculture been included a wider battle would have been fought.[155] For with the preservation of the protection of agriculture, the hinterland of Finland appeared to be safeguarded. Otherwise you can believe in free trade.

All this notwithstanding, in a very short period of time the whole of the Finnish community, including agriculture, was faced with the prospect of its government committing itself to full membership in what was now becoming, after Maastricht (1993), the European Union. Was it that by lurching westwards you had to put agriculture in the lurch?

Not quite. In contrast to the Norwegians, who witnessed a successful campaign to thwart EU-membership—in particular, for the protection of their *fisheries,*[156] the Finns decided, on the time honoured principle "if you can't beat 'em, join 'em," to negotiate the best deal possible for the protection of their *agriculture.*[157] But this jump from the European Economic Space to the EU meant the inclusion not merely of agriculture but also of the forthcoming Maastricht Treaty, the provisions of which affected the Finnish constitution.

---

154 Hulkko & Pöysä, op.cit., p.266.

155 *Vuosi 1992* p.244.

156 *Vuosi 1994*, p.269.

157 Ilkka Hakalehto, in his book *EU-Kaappaus,* Hankasalmi (Havusalmen kirjapaino), 1995, pp.58–59, bemoans the fact that the Centre Party in Finland did not follow the Norwegian example. For one thing, the Centre Party in Norway was in the opposition: for another, there was a considerable difference between the economic value of the Norwegian fisheries and Finnish agriculture.

In any case, it looked as if the main political problem was to get the farming interest on your side. There were, indeed, in all parties in Finland people who opposed entry into the EU.[158] But when it came down to it, the question was one of the old Agrarian Party, which had become the Centre Party. In actuality, the question seemed to hang for many months upon the stance taken by the MTK, the Agricultural Producers' and Forest Owners' Association, the organization that aimed to speak specifically for the detailed demands of the classes whose income was drawn, in whole or part, from ownership of the soil. The MTK had hitherto taken the line that joining the European Community (soon to be with the Maastricht Treaty, the European Union) would be a detrimental step for Finnish agriculture and they were led by a powerful chairman, Heikki Haavisto, who had been in that position since 1975.

In April 1993, however, the volatile Centre Party foreign minister, Paavo Väyrynen, resigned, claiming that the government had abandoned confidence in him. The way was now open for the Centre Party to do a deal with Heikki Haavisto to become foreign minister in Väyrynen's place.[159]

Haavisto changed his tune and, at least in quiet conversation, took the line that the overriding concern in joining an integrated Europe was the security of Finland.[160] But the interests of the farming classes were by no means forgotten, for Haavisto's own successor at the MTK, Esa Härmälä, took a more conciliatory line towards the EU by indicating that the MTK stance would be redefined when the extent of the subsidies from the EU were known *as well as the amount of subsidy the EU would allow to be raised, additionally, from Finnish funding.*[161] The Swedes, in respect of their agriculture, did not ask for this privilege of being able to award themselves a national subsidy.

In Finland, there were also out-and-out opponents of the EU. Keijo Korhonen, a former Finnish ambassador to the United States and onetime deputy-chairman of the Paasikivi Society, a bright fellow from the Kekkonen era, and in the early 1990s editor of the Kainuun Sanomat (the organ of the less affluent north-east), fought in the presidential election of 1994 as an anti-EU candidate. He,too, came from the Centre Party, but was not their official candidate in the election, heading a National Independence Front of his

[158] With the probable exception of the National Coalition Party. Even in the Swedish People's Party, an M.P. (Håkan Malm, a farmer) voted against entry, ibid. pp.40–42.

[159] *Vuosi 1993*, p.86. Esko Aho, op.cit.,p.102, who was the then prime minister,has not recognized this as a deal.

[160] Private information.

[161] Vuosi 1994, p.79.

own.[162] He polled only 5.8% of the votes.[163] Shortly afterwards, he abandoned his fight and went for a professorship in international relations to Arizona.[164]

The official candidate of the Centre Party was Paavo Väyrynen, the ex-foreign minister, who, as noted, had resigned in April 1993 to fight in the presidential election. He received 19.5% of the vote—came third. His tactics in Parliament were, in the last resort, of the strangest, wanting to delay the Finnish popular referendum until the result of he Swedish referendum were published. By filibustering tactics, he and his followers succeeded in delaying the Finnish vote until after the Swedes had voted.[165] But both countries voted "yes" to entry. The irony did not end there. After the popular referendum of 16 October 1994, the parliamentary vote occurred. In this vote, Väyrynen voted against entry. But then, on the Centre Party ticket, he became elected to the EU-Parliament, being one of the two among the 16 Members-of-the-European Parliament from the Finnish Centre Party who had opposed the membership of their country in the EU.

The convolutions of the Centre Party did not end, however. The government of the day was now primarily built on a National Coalition Party-Centre Party alliance. The former were wedded to industry, but the Centre Party prime minister, Esko Aho, was also close to the industrial and commercial interest. This was, after all, a Centre Party, had been since 1965, and that "centre" meant "urban," even though the bulk of the vote still came from the hinterland or their urbanized children. Magnanimous in leadership after the parliamentary vote of 18 November (152–45), Aho gave a kind of centrist blessing for the future, hoping that henceforward there would be neither "no" nor "yes" parties but only one "Finland-party" that would get the best it could out of the EU.[166]

Aho's statement has its importance, but perhaps it is worth noting that in the popular referendum the differences were much greater than in the parliamentary vote, for the referendum produced a pro-EU decision but only by a vote of 56.9 % to 43.1%. A statement made by the new president, Martti Ahtisaari, caught the mood of popular politics a little more closely: "we should get down to work instead of lamenting that the country is divided."[167]

But what about the preceding president, Mauno Koivisto, president for two terms from 1982 to 1994? He had hesitated as to whether or not to go for

---

[162] *Vuosi 1993,p.28.*

[163] *Vuosi 1994*,p.16.

[164] For a sympathetic account of Korhonen's stand, see Hakalehto, *EU-Kaappaus*, pp.126–130.

[165] *Vuosi 1994*, p.265.

[166] *ibid, p.243 & 265.*

[167] Quoted in Hakalehto, *EU-kaappaus*, p.39.

a third term, but then decided not "to be a Kekkonen" after all. The retiring, cautious aspect of his character had become uppermost for some time—and not only in economic questions. It could be argued that as president he had wanted to let Parliament and the government of the day decide and had not wanted to follow his own party (the SDP) as they began to come out for *full* EU-membership and not just for the compromise originally offered by Brussels of participation in a "European space" in which Finland could share the free flow of capital, labour, goods and services. Being president, Koivisto was, naturally enough, "president of *all* the Finns." But what does a president do? What he did not do was to give a lead. A shrewd observer has pointed out that the Social Democrat foreign minister, Pertti Paasio, when leaving the office and saying goodbye to the president, did not tell him that the *very next day* he was going to speak for full membership of the European Union. The same observer has spoken of the lack of public debate in the early1990s as the parties debated *within.*[168]

The Politics of Constitutional Deviance

The division in the country was mainly between town and countryside. So much was this so that *geographically*-speaking, though not in terms of *population* most of Finland could be classified as being against EU-entry. One commentator has even gone so far as to lay the responsibility for this upon Väyrynen by suggesting that had he remained as chairman of his party, that party would have been united in opposition against EU-membership.[169] Be that as it may, the fact that the elite of the Centre Party took diverse positions vis-à-vis entry undoubtedly confused the rank-and-file supporters. Further, in the parliamentary vote, 31 Centre Party M.P.s voted for entry and 24 against entry. Hakalehto is right in saying that had the Party been united against membership, it would have been sufficient to block it.[170]

Now the story worsens. For, in reality, the supporters of EU-membership had long dreaded that they would *lose* the vote since, according to the Finnish constitution, a two-thirds majority to change any part of it is possible *provided*

---

[168] Olavi Sunnari, *Suomen EY-Liityntä poliittisena prosessina,* Turku (Univ. of Turku, Dept. of Pol. Science,) Research Study no. 11. 1993, pp.21,32, & 35.

[169] Unto Hämäläinen,*Lännettymisen lyhyt historia,* Porvoo-Helsinki (Söderström),1998, p.106. Väyrynen, surprisingly announced his intention of resigning the chairmanship of the Centre Party in March 1990. In June 1990 Esko Aho was elected in his place. *Vuosi 1990,* pp.71 & 134. In the following year,Aho became prime minister. Aho believes that Väyrynen made two mistakes, resigning the chairmanship of the Party in 1990 and the post of foreign minister in 1993: Esko Aho, *Pääministeri,*Helsinki (Otava),1998,p.20.

[170] Hakalehto,*EU-kaappaus,*p.40.

there is no re-election of Parliament only when a five-sixth majority have first declared the matter urgent. These steps did not occur and the Parliament elected in 1991 was allowed to vote on a constitutional change–going into the EU–by an illegal two-thirds majority (and that was a close shave: 152 out of 200 possible members).[171] To complete the irony, the popular referendum that persuaded M.P.s to vote for entry to the EU was only, as all constitutional referenda are in Finland, *advisory*. Small wonder was it that Hakalehto entitled his book, "The EU-Coup."

The coup was of such a kind that the European Union has continued to remain rather undefined in the Finnish constitution. Admittedly, the problem is one of great complexity, consisting to a considerable degree of an *adaptation* of existing Finnish norms to those of the EU.Anna Hyvärinen has found that, whether through EU-legislation or EU-court rulings, the majority of Finnish parliamentary and legal issues are touched.[172] The constitutional problem grows because of the inchoate nature of the EU itself. The deeper integration goes, however, the more difficult this problem of acquiescence to a developing EU becomes, Finland, for example, being unable to accept the rigidity of the traditions of the Catholic countries.[173]

The impact of the European Union on Finland, has, in another spectacular way, gone right to the heart of that country's constitutional system. It has led to a further downgrading of presidential power. After the heady days of the Kekkonen presidency, Koivisto's tenure of the office–a long one, from 1982 to 1994–was a period in which parliamentary government was given its head and consequently Koivisto became the object of admiration of leading constitutionalists like Antero Jyränki. As noted, after pondering for some time as to whether he should run for a third term, Koivisto decided to do the right thing and told the political community he would not run. This opened the door to a new development in Finnish presidential politics. It was decided to abolish the old form of a presidential election, which was through an electoral

---

[171] ibid., p.27.

[172] Anna Hyvärinen, "Kan Finland fortfarande betraktas som en suverän stat?" in *Wrtings in the Sociology of Law and Criminology,"* ed. Ahti Laitinen, Turku (Univ. of Turku. Faculty of Law), 2006, esp.pp.85–87. She comes to a conclusion of 76%. Matti Wiberg, in a study published in the same year, but on presumably narrower criteria, finds a high point in 2002 when 16.5% of Finnish laws showed a direct linkage with the EU: *Politiikka Suomessa*, Helsinki (WSOY), 2006, p.297.

[173] A Finnish Green Party Member of the European Parliament, Heidi Hautala, in a debate on mobility in an integrated Europe held in Turku on 1.9.2008, made all too clear the present stalemate in the search for common norms on issues such as abortion, divorce, and marriages between the same sex.

college of 301 electors—previously elected by the people, and instead devise a system whereby the people voted directly for the candidate of their choice. If a candidate secured a simple majority on the first ballot, he or she won the place: if not, a run-off was then arranged between the two candidates with the most votes.

It sounded as democratic as you could wish, avoiding any disgraceful horse-trading in an electoral college, as had occurred in the first Kekkonen presidential election.[174] The person elected president in 1994, Martti Ahtisaari, was not a strong party figure, though a member of the Social Democratic Party. A principal promoter of his candidature tried to compare him to Koivisto, who "was also chosen from outside the party machinery."[175] According to the independent journalist Pentti Sainio, his background was meant to indicate that Ahtisaari was "a candidate outside the boundaries of the political parties."[176] In other words, he was "the people's choice." But he was really the candidate of a caucus, whom the financial speculator Pentti Kouri has revealed was backed by Aatos Erkko, the owner of the leading newspaper in Finland, the *Helsingin Sanomat.*[177]

Mauno Koivisto, the outgoing president backed Ahtisaari, too, but though both figures had, in their time, operated outside the political-Party machinery, there was a difference in reputation. Ahtisaari had had several commissions from the United Nations, but was hardly well known in Finland, while Koivisto had been prime minister and head of the Bank of Finland before getting presidential office, and had, as noted in the beginning of this chapter, been acting president at the time of Kekkonen's final period of disability in the presidential office.[178]

In any case, Ahtisaari himself was being presented as a presidential candidate for whom citizens of all parties could cast their vote. But so, too, was the candidacy of his main rival, Elisabeth Rehn, a member of the small Swedish People's Party, which had only 12 members in Parliament. She did quite well, in the second round, receiving 46.3% of the vote to Ahtisaari's 53.9%.[179] It was the mood of the moment, a loosening of party ties, and both candidates were for entry into the European Union.

---

[174] Chapter IV, esp.with respect to the 1956 presidential election, pp.225–229.

[175] The statement was made by Lasse Lehtinen and was quoted, somewhat ironically, by Pentti Sainio,*Operaatio Ahtisaari,*Jyväskylä (Arthouse), 1993, p.7.

[176] ibid., p.82.

[177] Pentti Kouri,*Suomen omistaja,* Helsinki (1996), p.85.

[178] On the latter phase in Koivisto's career, see Pentti Sainio's other work,*Mitä tapahtui Urho Kekkoselle,* Porvoo-Helsinki,1982, chap.10.

[179] *Vuosi 1994,* p.36.

But in the Council of the European Union, the representative of each Member State was the head of state in his own country. In short, it was, with the exception of France, the prime minister, the French exception of both president and prime minister being allowed because it was France and because in France the president also had a role in the internal politics. But Finland, too, had both a president and a prime minister. The Tiitinen committee, which considered this representational problem, came to the conclusion that if the Finnish president were to sit in the Council, he (she) needed strengthened powers—otherwise, it would be natural for the prime minister to represent the country there. In any case, this committee argued that a strengthening of presidential powers would be against the present constitutional trend in Finland.[180] The underlying point was that membership of the EU, once it occurred, was not strictly a matter of foreign policy, and the president of Finland should only be present in the EU-Council *exceptionally* when matters of foreign or security policy were being dealt with there.[181]

The matter came up once Parliament had voted for entry to the Union. An M.P. from the diminutive Liberal Party, Tuulikki Ukkola, felt she was witnessing a return of parliamentary powers. Others were a bit less sanguine and did not want to see a quarrel develop between president and Parliament.[182] In this, they were to be disappointed. Ahtisaari wanted his seat at the EU-Council, and the wrangling went on while Ahtisaari sought to find a role. In the end, it was left to a new prime minister, Paavo Lipponen, to suggest, in his offhand way, a policy of laying the table "with a new plate."[183]

The Return of Security Policy

The problem did not vanish with the ending of the Ahtisaari presidency in 2000 and the entry into office of the less agitated Tarja Halonen, also a Social Democrat.[184] The hostilities between Georgia and Russia in the summer of 2008 confronted Finland with the fact that its own relations with Russia were not simply to be considered economic and environmental, but that, even in a

---

[180] The Tiitinen Committee sat from 1992 to 1994. Its report, *Euroopan Unionin vaikutukset Suomen valtiosääntöön*, Helsinki (Painatuskeskus), 1994: 4, dealt with the above-mentioned problem particularly on pages 358–362.

[181] ibid., p.361.

[182] *Valtiopäivät 1994,Pöytäkirjat 6*, 29.11.- 21.12 1994, esp. pp.6040–6049.

[183] Shortly after Paavo Lippponen'election victoriy in April 1995, Martti Ahtisaari was present at the first European Union meeting Finland attended. It was said, in a report on this, that he also represented Finland. *Vuosi 1995*, p.139.

[184] President Halonen has widened the question beyond representation at international conferences into a question of the reserve powers of the president.

general sort of way, Russia's borderland problem had to be thought over once more from the Finnish side.

"Thought over," yes. For in one sense, the Finnish position had greatly improved since the early 1990's vis-à-vis Russia. The trade had slumped, but the FCMA treaty had been abrogated by mutual agreement in January 1991. It had been replaced by a much milder political agreement without the possibility (or threat) of mutual aid, that is to say, with no longer a military content. And the new agreement was done in the spirit of international law (article 1), but article 2 did require mutual discussion even on regional questions. Interestingly enough, both parties were in agreement about safeguarding the Finnic peoples in Russsia(article 10) "and correspondingly those from Russia in Finland."

But what now about Georgia? It is an admitted fact that when in the early 1990s the Baltic states of Estonia, Latvia, and Lithuania won back their independence, the Finnish political establishment was on the whole quite cool, feeling perhaps this might disturb their own settled status with Russia.[185]

Constitutional Divergence

Now, as it turned out, thinking about the unthinkable in Finland, as a result of the Georgia "incident," when war began between Russia and Georgia on 7.9.2008, produced a speculation as to whether "one extra plate" would be enough to cover the diversity of Finnish official and media opinion about Russian policy! The leading press organ in Finland suggested three plates.[186]

One plate would be for the cautious president, Tarja Halonen, whose caution was said to derive from a combination of wanting to let the EU make its own decisions and from the need to let "the other two plates" in Finland formulate in peace *their* views. It is known in Finland that Halonen's caution derives in part from her adherence to the old Paasikivi line of not rocking the boat with Russia.[187]

A second plate would be for the Centre Party prime minister, Matti Vanhanen, who would be the official representative of Finland in the European Council. His views, stated clearly in Peking at the time of the Olympics, were to condemn Russian aggression in Georgia. A third plate might be there for the new Finnish foreign minister (of the National Coalition Party), Alexander Stubb, wh had already stated on 25.8.08 that Finland should

---

[185] *Helsingin Sanomat,* 2.8.2009 (article by Aki Petteri Lehtinen).

[186] Jussi Konttinen writing in the *Helsingin Sanomat,* 31.8. 2008.

[187] As pointed out by Eero Vuohula, an adviser to the Finnnish Institute for International Affairs, Halonen is wary about Finland's joining NATO:*Helsingin Sanomat,* 16.1.2009.

join NATO. A leading organ of the Centre Party later chimed in to complain that Halonen, in going to Brussels for the EU-meeting, would have to keep switching chairs (plates?) with Stubb and that it was the fault of the Finnish constitution that the president was director of Finnish foreign policy.[188] The solution, according to one press organ of a Centre Party persuasion, was for Finland in the EU to be represented only by the prime minister and foreign minister (two plates only).[189] But the *Uutispäivä Demari,* the SDP organ, found the correct way to be, when Halonen and Vanhanen were together in Brussels, that Stubb should get up and leave the table.[190] These trivia indicate deeper concerns.

In proclaiming his conviction that joining the EU strengthened the role of the Finnish Parliament, Esko Aho, a former prime minister and enthusiast for the EU, emphasized that Parliament could no longer be dissolved without the agreement of the prime minister and that the influence of the EU on Finnish politics had speeded this change up.[191]

This may be so, on the one hand, but, on the other, the complexity in the representation in the European Council of the Finnish executive organs points in the direction of a wobbly executive.

It also points to the thrust of party-political difference. President Halonen came from Social Democracy, prime minister Vanhanen from the Centre Party, and foreign minister Stubb is a National Coalition Party Conservative. In the vital question of Finland's relations with Russia the three have different views. These might be resolved within the Finnish political system, but can they be resolved within the EU political system?

For in the case of Georgia, and its border areas of Abkhazia and South Ossetia occupied by Russian troops, the European Union also turned out to have three separate opinions. Britain, Poland, and the Baltic States held back on their demand for sanctions, but wanted stalling on the proposed new agreement on trade, energy, and human rights: Germany grew concerned about its energy supplies and took a more accommodating line, along with Italy, while France took an intermediate position. Finland followed the Berlusconi line.[192] Once again, the response was clouded still further by the opinion of NATO, whose Secretary-General, Jaap de Hoop Scheffer, avowed

---

188 The legal historian Antero Jyränki has emphasized that the presidenial role in foreign-policy making has varied considerably over the years: *Presidentti*, Helsinki (the Finnnish Lawyers' Association), 1978, esp. pp.221–223. Also "Foreign Affairs as the Last Stronghold of the Presidency,"*European Constitutionnal Law Review*,no.3, 1907, pp.285–306.

189 *Suomenmaa*, 3.9.08.

190 *Uutispäivä Demari*,3.9.08.

191 Esko Aho,*Pääministeri*,p.248.

192 *The Times*, 1.9.2008 & 2.9.2008: the *New York Times* in *Le Monde*, 20.9.2008.

in the middle of September that if the Russians did not soon withdraw from the two territories "it would not be easy to restore the NATO-Russia Council."[193]

In all this, a potential threat for Finland arose much more from an intensified Western anti-Russian policy than from a Russian concern about its frontiers. An escalation of Western hostility to Russia in which Finland was seen by Russia as a *Western because an EU-country* could damage Finnish-Russian trade and, in particular, Finland's energy-imports from Russia. Such a threat was hardly seen when Finland entered the EU in 1995.At the moment, the Russian ambassador to NATO, Dmitri Rogozhin, has contented himself by saying that Finland and Russia are good neighbours "who have a splendid relationship," but that "Finland should not be trapped by NATO provocation." He was not enthusiastic about a NATO- membership for Finland.[194]

In the past few years, the path of Finnish-Russian relations has been prickly. Trade between the two countries has been substantial. But as far as road traffic is concerned, Finland has endured for years -long queues of lorries on the Finnish side sometimes stretching over thirty kilometres, due to tedious frontier inspections, insufficient points of entry into Russia, or sheer indifference to a problem that also concerns their own Russian lorry-drivers.[195] The imposition of a Russian external tariff upon Russian timber exported to Finland threatens the price of timber for Finland and has been a factor in the closing of many pulp and paper factories there. Since Russia is intending to develop its own pulp and paper industries, Swedish and Finnish complaints about these external customs duties were dismissed by the German commissioner Günther Verheugen as remarks that would be more appropriate if "made to a Third World country."[196] And though the EU's trade commissioner, Mandelson, even made a trip to Russia to seek an alleviation of these duties, well, it was to no avail.[197]

Those who reproached Verheugen were the fourteen Members of the European Parliament from Finland. What they told José Manuel Barroso, the chairman of the European Commission, was that the EU should speak with

---

[193] *Financial Times*, 16.9.08.

[194] *Helsingin Sanomat*, 18.9.2008.

[195] Owing to the global economic crisis affecting Russia, too, this trade has now dried up and the Finnish southern ports are full of unwanted cars: *Helsingin Sanomat*, 23.10.2008

[196] *Helsingin Sanomat*,28.5.2008.

[197] Mandelson. The Finnish government made tax cuts for Finnish timber growers to engage in timber-felling, but to little avail as far as the paper and pulp industry has been concerned: *Helsingin Sanomat*, 29.8.2008. Both sellers and buyers are dissatisfied:*Helsingin Sanomat*, 14.11-2008.

one voice. But there's the rub. It can't. A German *Drang nach Osten* does not necessarily please the British, the Swedes, and the Finns. Nor do British, Swedish,[198] and Baltic States' threats of sanction in connection with Russia's behaviour in Georgia necessarily please the Finns.[199]

These diverse reactions hardly testify to a determined political clout on the part of the EU-countries, at least not as far as the wider reaches of international politics might be concerned.

Has membership in the EU nonetheless strengthened the Finnish economy?

In a book published in 1992, Max Jakobson argues a number of powerful points with respect to Finland's position. Three years before the entry of Finland into the EU, he maintained that membership would strengthen Finland in a crisis situation, but that crises are increasingly likely to be economic crises which in turn threaten the political system.[200] As to the security obtained by membership in the EU in a crisis situation of international security dimensions, it not easy to be as definite as Jakobson assumes, particularly in the current calls from the Right for an additional membership in NATO. Since crises are, in Jakobson's opinion, likely to be economic at base, it is reasonable to assume that an organization calling itself for years the European *Economic* Community, might have come up with something.

It struggled to do so. Throughout the 1970s and 1980s, various attempts were made, most strikingly by Pierre Werner of Luxemburg, in 1970, to create a European currency rate mechanism that would end ultimately in a monetary union. These attempts failed, but in the late 1980s Jacques Delors and others revived the idea, realized in 1993 in the Maastricht Treaty of a two-stage rate adjustment system, a third stage of which would be the creation of a common currency in European Monetary Union, the euro.[201]As mentioned, the Finnish government had tried to bind the mark to the écu(a unit of measurement, not coinage) but had had to float it (devalue, in practice)–to the

[198] To be fair to Carl Bildt, the Swedish foreign minister, he has used harsh words about Russia, while claiming that the EU is speaking with one voice–a difficult line to take in the opinion of the present author. For Bildt's view, see *Helsingin Sanomat*,20.9.2008.

[199] For prime minister Vanhanen'rejection of sanctions, *Helsingin Sanomat*, 29.8.2008.

[200] Max Jakobson, *Vallanvaihto*, Helsinki (Otava), pp.381-383.

[201] Erik Jones, *The Politics of Economic and Monetary Union*, Oxford (Rowman & Littlefield), 2002, p.140: note the current irony of Erik Jones's statement, made in 2002, of the necessity of some kind of coordinate structure between euro and dollar.

anger of commissioner Henning Christopherson–in 1992. In short, the Finns wished for a currency stability they had felt unable to attain on their own and in consequence, having entered the EU in 1995, they embarked on the path of the first two stages of the European Monetary Union in 1996. What they accepted was the European Central Bank and, ultimately, in 2002, the euro. The latter was raised somewhat higher than expected, when it was to be exchanged for the old mark, even at the risk of a certain level of inflation, as a boon to industry and commerce; a kind of seigniorage for private enterprise.

The European Central Bank (in Germany) is independent and has, therefore, with the EMU, been described as "apolitical."[202] The very same author, however, almost immediately goes on to aver that: "the role of an independent central bank in producing favourable outcomes is dependent on other institutional conditions such as fiscal or wage-bargaining regimes," the core of a "culture of price stability."[203] It is certainly true that the ECB's function is to curb inflation and that, unlike the central banks of he United States and Canada, it does not itself have the explicit task of stimulating growth. But when the system of which it is a part was being built up, a Stability and Growth Pact was engendered (Amsterdam 1997) having "a set of norms and procedures for maintaining fiscal discipline."[204] Now we arrive at the final point made by Max Jakobson, the unravelling of the sins of the politicians who made an over-indebted state,[205] "an instrument of politics which can be used to invoke fear."[206]

To use a favourite word of Jones's, all these are "potentials." But some of them have become realities. The fall e.g., in the external value of the euro which was set too high in the beginning of its existence so that the domestic market paid the price and the exporters got a boost. Then, there is the increasing use of the euro as a foreign trading instrument, particularly with China. And there is the constant endeavour of national governments in the euro-zone to trim their budget and export their jobs. A lot is falling outside the democracy.

Democracy and Democratic Deficits

Finland had entered the third stage of the European Monetary Union on 1 January 2002 when the euro became not merely electronic money (as it had

[202] ibid., p.59.
[203] ibid., p.60.
[204] ibid., p.127.
[205] Jakobson, *Vallanvaihto*,p.384
[206] Jones, op.cit., p.180.

been since 1999), but coinage and a note issue. The European Central Bank, down in Germany, was already a reality and the Bank of Finland a branch of it, with its funds under ECB control, though private information reported that some funds had been leached away for national use. The essence of the situation was nonetheless that the ECB was independent and not under constitutional control. Since in Finland, the powers of the parliamentary representation in the national central bank had already been whittled away, this change was acceptable.

For in return the hope was that Finland would at last be freed from the torments of the search for a stable unit of currency. Curiously, because the euro had been pitched too high in relation to the dollar in 1999, it had fallen in value by 2002. This was swallowed because it helped Finnish exports for the moment. With the bank crisis of the early 1990s behind, books began to appear in Finland stressing the country's essential "vitality."[207] Without the interference of the third executive (Russia) and with a reduced burden upon the second executive (presidential power), governments, though still coalition governments, were lasting longer (a full four years), and became a play between two out of three (Social Democrats, Centre Party and National Coalition Party).And Pesonen and Riihinen wrote a good chunk about "regional policy and development"[208], along the lines of an EU-model state.

Then the current global economic crisis hit the country. At first, it has nevertheless to be said that the spirit reigning in Finland at least in banking circles was more confident than elsewhere,[209] partly due perhaps to the feeling that the domestic banking crisis of the early 1990s, which resulted in a trimming down of the country's banking system by a series of effective mergers brought into being a more solidly-based banking system. But the previous banking crises in Northern Europe had, *inter alia,*a strong, partially local cause, whether in Finland (the failure to counter the collapse of the Soviet market next door) or in Norway (the failure to cope with the price-expectations fall for the country's oil exports)[210] It might, indeed, be added that in the current Finnish crisis. an important additional factor is also partially local, namely the failure of the traditional forest industries to adjust its costs of production in

---

[207] Pesonen, Pertti, & Riihinen, Olavi, *Dynamic Finland,* Helsinki (Finnish Literature Society), 2002, esp. the final chapter.

[208] ibid.,pp.230–238.

[209] *Helsingin Sanomat,* 3.9.2008, quoting a certain cautious optimism from forecasts emanating from the Nordea Bank. "Better prepared than in the early 1990s," stated another economist about his country's citizens:*Helsingin Sanomat,* 10.11.2008.

[210] Koskenkylä, Heikki & Pensala, Johanna, "Pohjoismaiden pankkikriisi ja viranomaisten tukitoimenpiteet," *Kansantaloudellinen aikakauskirja,* 4,1992,pp.431.

Finland. Among other factors, the forest owners themselves have woken up too late to the need to adjust *their* prices.[211]

As to the economics of the EU, with its miniscule representation of Finnish members in its Parliament, it seems clear enough that Finnish adherence to the freedoms of its internal market has benefited the country. Whether the final Finnish adoption of the euro in 2002 was altogether a good thing is a more complex question. The Swedes kept their own currency, the crown, and at the moment are able to undercut Finnish prices for pulp and paper. It is doubtful how a Finnish delegation could ever influence the monetary politics of the ECB (the European Central Bank), down there in Germany, which has specifically been constructed as an institution to remain outside political influence.

Above all, the irony of the EU, which *in ultimo* was an issuance of Jean Monnet's and Robert Schuman's *energy* policy, is patent enough to see in its inability still to provide Europe with a planned policy in this sector.

Dealing with economics democratically in a constitutional state is a question that has preoccupied certain savants in Finland since the previous decade. Anu Kantola has blamed the development of a managerially-controlled society as a root cause of the matter, summing up the manager-type as a person divorced from both the values of politics and from its interest-groups.[212] As such, she has defined the economists among them as people of a certain training, conscious of having a kind of neutral, superior intelligence able to cope *pragmatically* with the shifting problems that are arising in a complex environment.[213] Since all governments in Finland are nowadays coalition governments that can sit for years in a combination of say, Social Democrat and National Coalition Party, or, as now, of National Coalition Party and Centre Party, there may be some backing in *this* development for the emergence of a Weber-style phenomenon. But it does not appear *in itself* to be a solution that says much for democracy whose eternal vigilance is needful. *Quis custodiet ipsos custodes?*

---

[211] Forest ownership is not necessarily identical with the ownership of pulp and paper production.According to Erno Järvinen, a spokesman from this sector, the average hectarage of forest owners in only 24 and fusion would improve the economics of cutting:*Helsingin Sanomat*,31.7.2009.

[212] Anu Kantola, *Markkinakuri ja managerivalta*, Helsinki (Univ. of Helsinki: Pallas-Sarja), 2002, p.253.

[213] ibid.,e,g., p.236.

The Two Colossi

The present economic world-crisis started in the United States of America. Drawing it out crudely, the failure of the American mortgage system, not to speak of more general bank failures, has meant unemployment in Finland. Debates in the two branches of the American legislature by the followers of McCain towards the end of the second Bush Administration showed little understanding of the use of social policy as a tool to maintain consumption. The current vogue of *cheapness* in production is all of a piece with this. It is the other side of the coin.

The vagaries of capitalism are still with us as the Communist replacement miscarried so miserably. Its fallen monument over the Finnish border is still an exercise in uncritically-exercised state power, with at least five human rights activists done to death since 2006, three of them in recent weeks, while a president and a prime minister do not seem to care and—even more importantly—neither does the Duma.

By the by, this year on 6 December the Finnish conscripts will be marching again. Who is the enemy?

Like the Taleban, the Finnish armed forces (in Finland) have their foot-mines, though Finnish peace-keepers in northern Afghanistan appear to be exemplary in their behaviour without them. As to the problems of little, old Europe, whether economic (Finland's economic crisis is deepening) or political, they are not resolvable by military measures.

The economics of energy with a Russian-German deal (note) called Nord Stream (the Baltic pipeline) have begun to recall the zaniest aspects of international relations, with piracy off the Swedish coast (Olli Kivinen, Helsingin Sanomat 25.8.2009) and projects to blow up the pipeline (Finnish TV news on 27.8.2009).

BIBLIOGRAPHY

This bibliography contains books and articles from learned journals. In it, the variations from the usual Latin alphabet in the Finnish and Swedish languages, that is, the letters å, ä, and ö are treated for purposes of enumeration as a and o.

The fusion in modern Finnish and Swedish between v and w is not maintained, but these are classified as separate letters of the alphabet as in the English language.

Ahmavaara, Pirkko Aulin, et al., "Capital and Its Productivity in Finland 1957–2001," *Scandinavian Economic History Review*, vol.51, no.3, 2003.

Aho, Esko, *Pääministeri*, Helsinki (Otava), 1998.

Äikiä, Armas, *Kolmas tie*, Helsinki (Kansankulttuuri), 1948.

Alanen, Aulis J., *Santeri Alkio*, Helsinki (Werner Söderström), 1976.

Alexander, Bevin, *How Hitler Could Have Won World War II*, New York (Crown Publishers), 2000.

Andreen, Per G., *Finland i Brännpunkten mars 1940- juni 1941*, Stockholm (Lindfors), 1980.

Apunen, Osmo, & Wolff, Corinne, *Pettureita ja patriootteja*, Helsinki (SKS), 2009.

Arnstad, Henrik, *Spelaren Christian Günther*, Stockholm (Wahlström & Widstrand), 2006.

Auer, Väinö, et al., *Finnlands Lebensraum*, Berlin (Alfred Metzner Verlag), 1941.

Barysnikov, Nikolai & Vladimir, *Terijoen hallitus*, Helsinki-Pietari (Johan-Beckman Institute), 2001.

Berry, R. Michael, *American Foreign Policy and the Finnish Exception*, Helsinki (SHS), 1987.

Björne, Lars, *Syihin ja lakiin eikä mielivaltaan*, Helsinki (Suomalainen Lakimiesyhdistys julkaisuja),1977.

Blomstedt, Yrjö, *K. J. Ståhlberg. Valtiomieselämäkerta*, Helsinki (Otava), 1969.

von Bonsdorff, Göran, & Jernström, Frank, *Från Självständighet till Lappo. Svenska folkpartiet, II*, Ekenäs (Svenska folkpartiet), 1984.

Brantberg, Robert, *Kylmä-Kalle*, Jyväskylä (Gummerus), 2000.

Bullen, John Roderick, "The Royal Navy in the Baltic 1918-1920," London Univ. Ph.D thesis, 1983.

Cambridge Dictionary of Philosophy, 2nd ed., Cambridge (C.U.P.), 1999 (on the Condorcet-winner).

Charmley, John, *Churchill, The End of Glory*, London (Hodder & Stoughton), 1993.

Churchill, Stacy, *Itä-Karjalan kohtalo*, Porvoo-Helsinki (Söderström), 1970.

Clerc, Louis, *La Finlande dans la diplomaties française*, I & II, doctroral dissertation (Strasbourg), 2007.

Cooperation and Conflict, no. 2. 1966, (On Brundtland's Nordic Balance theory).

Dallek, Robert, *Franklin Roosevelt and American Foreign Policy 1932-1945*, New York (OUP), 1979.

Deutscher, Isaac, *Stalin*, Porvoo-Helsinki (WSOY), 1979.

Djilas, Milovan, *Conversations with Stalin*, London (Penguin Books), 1962.

Documents on British Foreign Policy, Third Series, vols. VI & VII.

Dumell, Matts, *Vuoto*, Helsinki (Tammi), 1973.

Enckell. Carl, *Poliittiset muistelmani*, I, Helsinki (Werner Söderström), 1956.

Foreign Relations of the United States (FRUS), vol. III, 1944.

Gerner, Kristian, "Från anti-sovjetism till sämhallskritik," *Finsk tidskrift*, H-6-7, 1980.

Haanpää, Pentti, *Kenttä ja kasarmi*, Helsinki (Otava), 1976 (written in 1928).

Haapala, Pertti, *Kun yhteiskunta hajosi*, Helsinki (Kleio), 1995.

Haataja, Lauri, et. al., *Suomen työväenliikkeen historia*, Helsinki (Työväen Sivistysliitto), 1976.

Häikiö, Martti, *Maaliskuusta maaliskuuhun. Suomi Englannin politiikassa 1939-1940*, Helsinki (Söderström), 1976.

Hakalehto, Ilkka, *EU-Kaappaus*, Hankasalmi (Hankasalmen kirjapaino), 1995

——*Väinö Tanner. Taipumaton tie*, Helsinki (Kirjayhtymä), 1973.

Halsti, Wolf, *Me, Venäjä ja muut*, Helsinki (Otava), 1969.

Halttunen, Hannu, *Maailmantalouden asettamat ehdot Suomen talouspolitiikalle*, Helsinki (Bank of Finland Research Papers, no.10, 1982).

Hämäläinen, Unto ja Terho, *Lännettymisen lyhyt historia*, Porvoo-Helsinki (WSOY), 1998.

Heikinheimo, Ilmari, *Suomen elämäkerrasto*, Helsinki (Söderström). 1955.

Heräävä maaseutu, vols. II, III, and V (Maalaisliitto).

Hietanen, Silvo, "Voiton ja tappion saralla" in *Paasikiven hirmuiset vuodet*, Helsinki (Tammi), 1986.

Hiilamo, Heikki, "Säästöt ja perhepolitiikka" in *Laman pitkä varjo*, ed. Jaakko Kiander, Helsinki (Govt, Institute for Economic Research), 2000.

Hinkkanen-Lievonen, Merja-Liisa, *British Trade and Enterprise in the Baltic States 1919-1925*, Helsinki (SHS), 1984.

Hissa, Jaakko,"Ministerit ja hallituspolitiikka,"*Valtioneuvoston historia 1917-1966," II*. Helsinki (Valtion painatuskeskus), 1977.

Hjerppe, Riitta, *Suomen talous 1860-1985*, Helsinki (Suomen pankki), 1988.

——et al., "Investment in Finland 1860-1979," *Scandinavian Economic History Review*,

Hokkanen, Kari, *Kyösti Kallio 1873-1929*, I, Porvoo-Helsinki (Söderström), 1986.

Holodkovski, Viktor, *Suomen ja Neuvosto-Venäjän työväen vallankumous 1918-1920*, Helsinki (Tammi), 1978.

von Horthy, Nikolaus, *Muistelmat*, Helsinki (Otava), 1959.

Hovi, Kalervo, *Intressensphären im Baltikum. Finnland im Rahmen des Ostpolitik Polens 1919-1922*, Helsinki (SHS),1984.

Hrutsev, N. S., (Krushchev), *Neuvostoliitto ja Pohjola*, Helsinki (Weilin and Göös), 1964.

Hulkko, Kustaa & Pöysä, Jorma, *Vakaa markka*, Juva (Arena Kustannus), 1998.

Hyvämäki, Lauri, "Valtioneuvosto 2. maailman sodan jälkeen vuoteen 1957," *Valtioneuvoston historia 1917-1968*, II, Helsinki (Valtionpainatuskeskus), 1977.

Hyvärinen, Anna, "Kan Finland fortfarande betraktas som en suverän stat?" *Writings in the Sociology of Law and Criminology*, ed. Ahti Laitinen, Turku (Univ. of Turku, Faculty of Law), 2006.

Hyvärinen, Risto, *Monistic and Pluralistic Interpretations in the Study of International Politics*, Helsinki (the Finnish Academy of Sciences), 1958.

Itä-Karjala, Helsinki (Akateeminen Karjala-Seura), 1934.

Jääskeläinen, Mauno, *Valtioneuvoston historia*, I,

Jägerskiöld, Stig, *Gustaf Mannerheim 1918*, Helsingfors (Schildt), 1967.

——*Mannerheim rauhan vuosina*, Helsinki, (Otava), 1973.

Jakobson, Max, *The Diplomacy of the Winter War*, Cambridge (Mass.), 1961.

——*Finnish Neutrality*, London (Hugh Evelyn), 1968.
——*Vallanvaihto*, Helsinki (Otava), 1992.
Jalanti, Heikki, *Suomi puristuksessa 1940-1941*, Helsinki (Tammi), 1966.
Joenniemi. Pertti & Blomberg, Jaakko, *Kaksiteräinen miekka*, Helsinki (Tammi), 1971.
Jokipii, Mauno, *Jatkosodan synty*, Helsinki (Otava). 1987.
Jokisipilä, Markku, *Aseveljiä vai liittolaisia?*, Helsinki (SKS), 2004.
Jones, Erik, *The Politics of Economic and Monetary Union*, Oxford (Rowan and Littlefield), 2002.
Junnila, Tuure, *Suomen taistelu turvallisuudestaan ja puolueettomuudestaan*, Porvoo-Helsinki (WSOY), 1964.
Jussila, Osmo, *Suomen tie 1940-1948*, Porvoo-Helsink (WSOY)., 1990.
Jutikkala, Eino, A *History of Finland*, London (Thames & Hudson), 1962.
Juva, Einar, *P.E. Svinhufvud*, II, Porvoo-Helsinki (Werner Söderström), 1961.
——*Rudolf Walden*, II,
Jyränki, Antero, Presidentti, 1981, *Lakien laki*, Helsinki (Lakimiesliiton Kustannus). 1989.
——"Foreign Affairs as the Last Stronghold of the Presidency," European Constitutional Law Review, no.3, 2007.
Kähkölä, Paavo, et al., *Suomi K-linjalla*, Helsinki (Otava), 1974.
Kaihari, Kalle, *Ratkaiseva ääni*, Espoo (Weilin & Göös), 1981.
Kalela, Jorma, *Pulapolitiikka*, (Työväen taloudellinen tutkimuslaitos), 1987.
—— "Syntyikö Suomeen 1990-luvulla uusi alaluokka?" in *Lamakirja*, ed. Helena Blomberg, Turku (Kirja-Aurora), 2002.
Kalleinen, Kristiina, *Isänmaani onni on kuulua Venäjälle*, Helsinki (SKS), 2001.
Kangas, Olli, "Muutos ja pysyvyys," in *Lamakirja*, ed. Helena Blomberg, 2002
Kanninen, Ermei., *Vuodet myrskyn varjossa*, Helsinki (Otava), 1995.
Kantola, Anu, *Markkinakuri ja managerivalta*, Helsinki (Univ. of Helsinki: Pallas-Sarja), 2000.
Kautsky, Karl, *Der Erfurter Program in seinem grundsätzlichen Theil*, Stuttgart (J.H.Dietz), 1899.
——*Yhteiskunnallinen vallankumous*, Pori (Osuuskunta kehitys), 1906.
——*Köyhälistön diktatuuri*, Helsinki (Kansanvalta), 1918 & 1919.
——*Köyhälistön vallankumous ja sen ohjelma*, Helsinki (Kustannusosakeyhtiö Kansanvalta), 1919 & 1925.
Kekkonen, Urho, *Onko maallamme malttia vaurastua?* Helsinki (Otava), 1952.
——*Puheita ja kirjoituksia*, II, ed. Tuomas Vilkuna, Helsinki (Weilin & Göös), 1969.
——*Neutrality: The Finnish Position*, London (Heinemann), 1973.
——*Urho Kekkonen*. A *Statesman for Peace*, ed. Keijo Korhonen, Helsinki (Otava), 1975.
——*Tamminiemi*, Espoo, (Weilin & Göös), 1980.
Kemppainen, Jouni T. & Elomaa, Pekka, "Paha maisema," *Helsingin Sanomien Kuukausiliite*, March, 2002.
Ketola, Eino, *Kansalliseen kansanvaltaan*, Helsinki (Tammi), 1982.
Kiander, Jaakko, "1930-luvun pulakausi ja 1990-luvun talouskriisi" in *Lamakirja*, ed.Helena Blomberg, 2002.
King, Mervyn, "Risto Ryti ja Englannin keskuspankki, *Kanava*, no. 6, 2006.
Kivimäki,T. M. *Suomalaisen poliitikon muistelmat*, Porvoo-Helsinki (Werner Söderström), 1965.
Knaplund, Paul, *British Views on Norwegian-Swedish Problems 1880-1885*, *Oslo* (Norsk historisk kjeldeskrift institut), 1952.
Koivisto, Mauno. *Väärää politiikkaa*, Helsinki (Kirjayhtymä) 1978.
Komiteanmietintö 412, 1950 (on the nationalisation of chemists' shops)

Korhonen, Arvo. *Barbarossa suunnitelma ja Suomi.* Porvopo-Helsinki (Werner Söderström), 1961.

Korhonen, Keijo. *Naapurit vastaan tahtoaan.* Helsinki (Tammi), 1966.

Koskenkylä, Heikki & Pensala, Johanna, "Pohjoismaiden pankkikriisi ja viranomaisten tukitoimenpiteet," *Kansantaloudellinen aikakauskirja*, no. 4, 1992.

Kosonen, Pekka, et al., *Suomalainen kapitalismi*, Helsinki (Love), 1979.

Kostiainen, Arvo, *Santeri Nuorteva. Kansanvälinen suomalainen*, Helsinki (SHS), 1983.

Kouri, Pentti, *Suomen omistaja*, Helsinki, 1996.

Krosby, Hans-Peter, *Finland, Germany and the Soviet Union 1940-1941. The Petsamo Dispute*, Madison & London (Univ. of Wisconsin Press), 1966.

——*Suomen valinta, 1967.*

——*Kekkosen linja*, Helsinki (Kirjayhtymä), 1978.

Krymov, P. & Golovanov, K, "Finland's Foreign Policy," *International Affairs*, Moscow, October 1969.

Kuisma, Markku, *Metsäteollisuuden maa*, Helsinki (SHS),1993.

Kullberg,Rolf,. "*ja niin päättyi kulutusjuhla*," Porvoo-Helsinki (WSOY), 1996.

Kuusinen, Aino, *Jumala syöksee enkelinsä. Muistelmat vuosilta 1919-1965*, Helsinki (Otava), 1972.

Kuusinen, O.W., *The Finnish Revolution: A Self-Criticism*, London (The Workers' Socialist Federation), 1919.

——*Suomi ilman naamiota*, Moscow (Karjalais-Suomalaisen SNT:n valtion kustannusliike), 1944.

Lackman, Matti, *Heikki Repo-punainen jääkäri*, Oulu (Scripta historica offprint XI), 1987.

——"Pulaliike" in *Itsenäisen Suomen historia, 2*, 1991.

Lagerspetz, Erik, "Social Change in the Real World," *Scandinavian Political Studies*, vol. 16, no.1, 1993.

Lappalainen, Jussi T., *Punakaartin sota*, I, Helsinki (Valtion painatuskeskus), 1981.

Lappalainen, Matti, *Hannes Ignatius. Mannerheimin harmaa eminenssi*, Helsinki (Werner Söderström), 1966.

Lehmus, Kalle, *Kolme kriisiä*, Helsinki (Weilin & Göös), 1971.

Lehtinen, Lasse, *Fagerholm. Kekkosen tasavallan kakkonen*, Helsinki (Werner Söderström), 1981.

——*Aatosta jaloa ja alhaista mieltä*, Helsinki (Werner Söderström), 2002.

Lenin, V. I., *Lenin Suomesta*, Moscow (Kustannusliike Progress), 1983.

Leppänen, Seppo, "Valuuttakurssi politiikka," *Talouselämä*, no.35,1982.

Lindman, Sven, *Parlamentarismens tillämpning i Finland 1919-1926*, Åbo (Åbo Akademi), 1937.

Liukkonen, Väinö, *Sosialitoimiskomitean mietintö*, 1947.

Locke, John, "*An Essay on the True Original Extent and End of Civil Government," 1690, in* Sir Ernest Barker, *Social Contract Essays by Locke, Hume and Rousseau*, London & New York (OUP), 1960,

Lukkari, Matti, *Asekätkentä*, Helsinki (Otava), 1984.

——*Lauri Sutela. Puolustusvoimain komentaja*, Helsinki (Otava), 2003.

Lundin, C. Leonard, *Finland in the Second World War*, Bloomington (Indiana Univ., Press.) 1957.

Luntinen, Pertti, *Sotilasmiljoonat*, Helsinki (SHS), 1984.

——*F. A. Seyn*, Helsinki (SHS), 1985,

Lyon, Peter, *Neutralism*, Leicester (Leicester Univ.Press), 1963.

Lyytinen, Eino, *Finland in British Policy in World War I and Its Aftermath*, Oxford (D.Phil. Dissertation), 1973.

Määttänen, Sakari, *Tapaus Jakobson*, Helsinki (Weilin & Göös), 1973.

Majamaa, Raija, ed., *Enteitä ja uhmaa*, Helsinki (SKS), 1987.

Mäkelä, Jaakko, "The Radical Left and the Communist Party in Finnish Politics" in *Political Parties in Finland,* ed. Juhani Mylly & R. Michael Berry, Turku, (Univ. of Turku, Pol.History Dept)., 1984.

Mannerheim, Gustaf, *Muistelmat,* I, Helsinki (Otava), 1951.

Manninen, Ohto, "Saksa tyrmää Ruotsi-Suomen unionin," *Historiallinen aikakauskirja,* 1975.

——*Toteutumaton valtioliitto,* Helsinki (Kirjayhtymä), 1977.

——"Suomi toisessa maailmansodassa," *Itsenäisen Suomen historia,*3, Vantaa (Weilin & Göös), 1992.

Maude, George, "Finland and Britain 1854-1914," unpublished Ph.D. thesis, Univ. of London, 1970.

——*The Finnish Dilemma,* London (Royal Institute of International Affairs & OUP), 1976.

——*Historical Dictionary of Finland,* (Scarecrow Press), Lanham & London, 1st ed. 1995, 2nd. ed., 2007

Merikoski, Veli, *Suomen julkisoikeus pääpiirteittään,* Porvoo-Helsinki (Werner Söderstöm) 1974.

Moorehead, Alan, *The Russian Revolution,* London (Collins), 1958.

Murarka, Dev, *Gorbatsov,* Porvoo-Helsink (WSOY), 1987.

Myllyniemi, Seppo, *Baltian kriisi 1938-1941,* Keuruu, 1977.

Nars, Kari, "Suomalaisten yritysten valuuttastrategia," *Kansantaloudellinen aikakauskirja,* 1979.

Nousiainen, Jaakko, *Kommunismi Kuopion läänissä,* Joensuu (privately printed), 1956.

Nurmi, Hannu, "On the Rationality and Legitimacy of Voting Procedures," in *Rationality and Legitimacy. Essays on Political Theory,* ed. Dag Anckar et al., (Finnish Political Science Association), 1992.

Nyberg, Peter, & Vihriälä, Vesa, *The Finnish Banking Crisis and Its Handling,* Helsinki (Bank of Finland Discussion Papers, 8, 1993, and ibid.,7, 1994).

Nykopp, Johanna, *Paasikiven mukana Moskovaan,* Helsinki (Kirjayhtymä), 1975.

Paasikivi, J.K., *J. K. Paasikivis Dagböcker 1941-1944. Samtal i Ond Tid,* trans. Frank Jernström, Borgå (Söderström), 1991.

——*Päiväkirjat 1944-1956,* I & II, Porvoo-Helsinki (Werner Söderström), 1985-1986.

——*Paasikiven linja. Puheita vuosilta 1944-1956,* Porvoo-Helsinki (Werner Söderström), 1962.

Paasivirta, Juhani, *Suomen itsenäisyyskysymys,* I & II, Porvoo-Helsinki (Söderström), 1947.

——*Suomi vuonna 1918,* Porvoo-Helsinki, (Söderström), 1957.

——*Suomi ja Euroopa 1939-1956,* Helsinki (Kirjayhtymä), 1992.

Paavolainen, Jaakko, *Poliittiset väkivaltaisuudet Suomessa 1918: Punainen terrori,* Helsinki (Tammi), 1966, & *Valkoinen terrori,* Helsinki (Tammi), 1967.

Parlamentaarinen puolustuskomitean mietintö 1970 (defence report), Helsinki (Valtion painatuskeskus).

Parvilahti, Unto, *Berijan tarhat,* Helsinki (Otava), 1957. English version, *Beria's Gardens,* London (Hutchinson), 1959.

Penttilä, Risto E. J., *Puolustuslinjat,* Helsinki (Otava), 1988.

——*Finland's Search for Security through Defence 1949-1989,* London (Macmillan), 1991 (an expanded version of *Puolustuslinjat). Historian roolipeli,* Helsinki (Otava), 2006.

Pesonen, Pertti & Riihinen, Olavi, *Dynamic Finland,* Helsinki (Finnish Literature Society), 2002.

Pietiäinen, Jukka-Pekka, "Katse tulevaisuuteen" in *Itsenäistymisen vuodet, 3,* Helsinki, 1992.

Pihkala, K. U., "Siirtoväen ja rintamamiesten asuttaminen" in *Itsenäisen Suomen taloushistoria 1919-1950,* ed. Jutikkala, Eino, 1950

Plekhanov, G.V., *The Role of the Individual in History,* London, (Lawrence & Wishart), 1950.

Pohjola, Kyllikki, *Kuljen tietäni*, Helsinki (WSOY), 1966.
Pohjola, Matti, *Tehoton pääoma*, Helsinki (WSOY), 1996.
Polvinen, Tuomo, *Venäjän vallankumous ja Suomi*, I, Porvoo-Helsinki (Söderström), 1967.
——*Barbarossasta Teheraniin*, Porvoo-Helsinki (Söderström), 1979.
——*Between East and West*, Porvoo-Helsinki (WSOY),1986.
—— *J. K. Paasikivi. Valtiomiehen elämäntyö*, 1, 2, 3, 4, Porvoo-Helsinki (Werner Söderström), 1989-1995.
Prazmowska, Anita, *Britain, Poland and the Eastern Front 1939*, London (Cambridge Univ. Press), 1987.
Rasilainen, Ari, *Oikeudellinen argumentointi politiikassa*, Helsinki (Suomalainen lakimiesyhdistys), 2004.
Rautkallio, Hannu, *Kaupanteko Suomen Itsenäisyydellä*. Helsinki (Werner Söderström), 1977.
——*Suomen suunta 1945-1948*, Helsinki (Weilin & Göös), 1979.
Red Constitution, (Kapinan aikana painetut Suomen Asetuskokoelman numerot 10-33), Helsinki (Suomen Senaatin kirjapaino), 1918.
Reimaa, Markku, *Helsinki Catch*, Helsinki (Edita), 2008.
Relander, Lauri Kristian, *Presidentin päiväkirja, I & II*, ed. Jutikkala, Eino, Helsinki (Weilin & Göös), 1967-1968.
Rentola, Kimmo, *Niin kylmää että polttaa . .* Keuruu, 1997.
——"Stalin, Mannerheim ja Suomen rauhanehdot 1944," *Historiallinen aikakaus-kirja*, no.1, 2000.
——*Vallankumouksen aave*, Helsinki (Otava), 2005.
Riker, William, *The Theory of Coalition Politics*, New Haven (Yale Univ. Press), 1967.
Rinta-Tassi, Osmo, *Kansanvaltuuskunta punaisen Suomen hallituksena*, Helsinki (Valtion painatuskeskus), 1986.
Rintala, Marvin. *Four Finns*, Berkeley & Los Angeles (Univ. of California Press), 1969.
——*The Extreme Right-Wing in Finnish Politics*, Bloomington (Indiana Univ. Press), 1962.
Risto Rytin Puolustus, ed. Kyösti Lallukka, Helsinki, Tietokaleva ky, 1989.
Roiko- Jokela, Heikki, *Ihanteita ja Reaalipolitiikka*, Jyväskylä (Jyväskylän yliopiston studia historica), no. 52, 1995.
Roselius, Aapo, *Amatöörien sota*, Helsinki (Valtioneuvoston julkaisusarja). 2006
Rowntree, Seebohm R. & Lavers G. R., *English Life and Leisure. A Social Study, with an Appendix on Finland*, London (Longmans Green), 1951.
Ruge, Otto, *Krigens Dagbok. Annan Verdenskrig*, I, Oslo (Halvorsen & Larsen Forlag), 1946.
Rumpunen, Kauko & Manninen, Ohto, *Faktillisesti tämä tarkoittaa antautumista*, Helsinki (Edita), 2009.
Runeberg, Johan Ludvig, *Saarijärven Paavo* (poem *Bonden Paavo, 1830)*.
Saalas, Uunio, *Muistelmia lapsuuteen ja nuoruuteen*, Helsinki (Werner Söderström), 1963.
Saarikoski, Vesa, *Keskustajääkäri Aarne Sihvo*, Helsinki (SHS), 1997.
Sainio, Pentti, *Mitä tapahtui Urho Kekkoselle?* Porvoo-Helsinki (WSOY), 1982.
——*Operaatio Ahtisaari*, Jyväskylä (Arthouse), 1993.
Salkola, Marja-Leena, *Työväen kaartien synty ja kehitys punakaarteiksi*, I, Helsinki (Valtion painatuskeskus), 1985.
——"Työväen kaartit ja suojeluskunnat" in *Itsenäisen Suomen historia, I*, ed. Osmo Apunen, Jyväskylä (Weilin & Göös), 1991.
Salmi, Väinö, *Olin punikki*, Helsinki (Akateeminen kustannusliike), 1967.

Salmon, Patrick, "The Bank of Finland and England during the inter-war period," in "*Muille maille vierahille. . .*" *Kalervo Hovi ja yleinen historia*, Turku (Turun historiallinen yhdistys), 2002.

Salonen, Ahti M., *Linjat*, Helsinki (Tilgman), 1972.

Screen, J.E.O., *Mannerheim*, Helsinki (Otava), 2001,

Selen, Kari, "Tasavalta hakee suuntaa" in *Itsenäisen Suomen historia, vol. 2*, Helsinki (Weilin & Göös), 1991

——*Genevestä Tukholmaan*, Helsinki (Otava), 1974.

Seppälä, Helge, *Suomi hyökkääjänä 1941*, Porvoo-Helsinki (WSOY), 1984.

Seppinen, Jukka, *Ahti Karjalainen. Poliittinen elämä*, Helsinki (Otava), 1997

Sillanpää, Frans Emil, *Hurskas kurjuus*, Helsinki (Otava), 1955 (originally published in 1919).

Siltala, Juha, *Lapuanliike ja kyyditykset*, Helsinki (Otava), 1985.

Söderhjelm, S. O., *Kolme matkaa Moskovaan*, Helsinki (Kirjayhtymä), 1970.

Soikkanen, Hannu, *Kohti kansanvaltaa*, Helsinki (Suomen sosialidemokraattinen puolue), 1975.

Soikkanen, Timo, "The FCMA Treaty: Who Fathered It?" in *The Cold War and the Politics of History*, ed. Juhan Aunesluoma & Pauli Kettunen, Helsinki (Edita), 2008.

Ståhlberg, K. J., *Puheita 1818-1918*, Helsinki (Otava), 1951.

Ståhlberg, Krister, "Rätten och behövet av att Finland diskutera med Sovjet Unionen," *Finsk tidskrift*, H.6-7, 1980.

Steenson, Gary P., *Karl Kautsky., Marxism in the Classical Years 1851-1938*, Pittsburgh (Univ. of Pittsburgh Press), 1991.

Suksi, Markku, *Bringing in the People. A Comparison of Constitutional Forms and Practices*, Dordrecht (Martinus Nijhoff. Kluwer), 1993

Sundbäck, Esa, *Finland in British Baltic Policy*, Helsinki (Finnish Academy of Sciences and Letters), 2002.

Sunnari, Olavi, *EY-Liityntä poliittisena prosessina*, Turku (Univ. of Turku, Dept. of Pol.Science), no.11, 1993.

Suomi, Juhani, *Myrrysmies, Vonkamies, Kuningastie, Kriisien aika, Presidentti*: Helsinki (Otava), 1986, 1988, 1990, 1992, 1994.

Sutela, Pekka, *Economic Thought and Economic Reform in the Soviet Union*, Cambridge (CUP), 1991.

Suviranta, B., "Sotakorvaus 1944-1952 ja sen vaikutukset" in *Itsenäisen Suomen taloushistoria 1919-1950*, ed. Eino Jutikkala.

de Swaan, Abram, *Coalition Theories and Cabinet Formation*, Amsterdam (Elsevier), 1975.

Tanner, Väinö, *Kahden maailmansodan välissä*, Helsinki (Tammi), 1966.

Tarkka, Jukka, *13. Artikla*, Porvoo-Helsinki (Werner Söderström), 1977.

Tarrant, V.F., *The Red Orchestra*, London (Cassell), 1995.

Tietosanakirja, vol. 5, Helsinki (Weilin & Göös), 1994.

Tiitinen komitea, *Euroopan Unionin vaikutukset Suomen valtiosääntöön*, Helsinki (Valtion painatuskeskus), no.4, 1994.

Tiuri, Matti, *Tulevaisuus alkaa nyt*, Helsinki (Otava), 1984

Toivola, Urho, *Amerikka varoitti*, Helsinki (Oy Suomen Kirja), 1946.

Tokoi, Oskari, *Piirteitä maatalouskysymyksestämme*, Pori (Osuuskunta kehitys), 1911.

——*Maanpakolaisen muistelmia*, Helsinki (Tammi), 1959.

Turtola, Martti, *Risto Ryti. Elämä isänmaan puolesta*, Helsinki (Otava), 1994.

Turunen, Mirja, *Veripellot*, Jyväskylä (Atena), 2005.

Ulkopoliittisia lausuntoja ja asiakirjoja 1972, Helsinki (Finnish Institute of Interantional Affairs), 1973

ibid., 1978, published 1979 (on Kekkonen's nuclear-weapon-free zone plan for the North)

Upton, Anthony F., *Välirauha*, Helsinki (Kirjayhtymä), 1964

——"The Winter War" in *History of the Second World War*, London (Purnell), 1966.

——*Kommunismi Suomessa*, Helsinki (Kirjayhtymä), 1970.

——*The Finnish Revolution 1917-1918*, Minneapolis (Univ. of Minnesota Press), 1980.

Valtiopäivät, 1945, I, *Annexes. (Parliamentary Papers)*

ibid., 1946, I

ibid., 1994 (Pöytäkirjat)

Varjonen, Unto, *Todellinen demokratia*, Porvoo-Helsinki (WSOY), 1945.

——*Sosialistinen aikakauskirja*, 3, 1946.

Vartia, Pentti, "Vaihtotase ongelma kärjistyy," *Kansantaloudellinen aikakauskirja*, no 4, 1988.

Väyrynen, Raimo, *Conflicts in Finnish-Soviet Relations. Three Comparative Studies.* Tampere (Acta Universitatis Tameprensis), 1972.

Vihavainen, Timo, "Hyvinvointi Suomi," in *Suomen historian pikkujättiläinen*, Porvoo-Helsinki

Virkkunen, Sakari, *Relander. Hymyilevä presidentti*, Helsinki, 1979. (Werner Söderström), 1987.

Virolainen, Johannes, "Näkökohtia maanhankintalain toimeenpanossa," *Kansantaloudellinen aikakauskirja*, no.2, 1946.

——"Maalaisliiton maatalouspolitiikka," *Herääva Maaseutu*, Helsinki (Maalaisliitto ry.), 1956.

——*Sanoi Paasikivi*, Helsinki (Otava), 1983.

——*Vallankäyttö Kekkosen kaudella*, Helsinki, 1986.

Virrankoski, Pentti, *Suomen taloushistoria*, Helsinki (Otava), 1975.

Vladimir, Viktor, "*Näin se oli.* " Helsinki(Otava), 1993.

Wahlbäck, Krister, *Mannerheimista Kekkoseen*, Porvoo-Helsinki (Werner Söderström), 1968.

——*Veljeys veitsenterällä*, Porvoo-Helsinki (Werner Söderström), 1964.

Waris, Heikki, *Suomalaisen yhteiskunnan sosialipolitiikka*, Porvoo-Helsinki, 1961.

Wiberg, Matti, *Politiikka Suomessa*, Helsinki (WSOY), 2006.

Wohl, Robert, *The Spectacle of Flight*, New Haven & London (Yale Univ.Press), 2005.

Ylärakkola, Arvo, *Edvard Gylling*, Helsinki (Otava), 1976

Ylikangas, Heikki, *Tie Tampereelle*, Helsinki (WSOY), 1993.

Zetterberg, Seppo, *Viron historia*, Helsinki (SKS), 2nd. ed., 2007.

Ziemke, Earl, *The German Northern Theater of Operations 1940-1944*, Washington (Dept. of the Army Pamphlet, no. 20-271), 1959.

Studies in Modern European History

The monographs in this series focus upon aspects of the political, social, economic, cultural, and religious history of Europe from the Renaissance to the present. Emphasis is placed on the states of Western Europe, especially Great Britain, France, Italy, and Germany. While some of the volumes treat internal developments, others deal with movements such as liberalism, socialism, and industrialization, which transcend a particular country.

The series editor is:

Frank J. Coppa
Director, Doctor of Arts Program
in Modern World History
Department of History
St. John's University
Jamaica, New York 11439

To order other books in this series, please contact our Customer Service Department:

Kolibri 360 GmbH
Ferdinand-Jühlke-Straße 7
99095 Erfurt, Deutschland
produktsicherheit@kolibri360.de